CRIMINAL VIOLENCE

CRIMINAL VIOLENCE

Philip J. Cook
David P. Farrington
William F. Gabrielli, Jr.
Richard J. Gelles
Peter W. Greenwood
Deidre Klassen
Sarnoff A. Mednick
Edwin I. Megargee
John Monahan
Vicki Pollock
Jan Volavka

EDITED BY
MARVIN E. WOLFGANG
NEIL ALAN WEINER

SAGE PUBLICATIONS
Beverly Hills / London / New Delhi

For information address:

SAGE Publications, Inc.
275 South Beverly Drive
Beverly Hills, California 90212

SAGE Publications India Pvt. Ltd.
C-236 Defence Colony
New Delhi 110 024, India

SAGE Publications Ltd
28 Banner Street
London ECIY 8QE, England

Printed in the United States of America

Library of Congress Cataloging in Publication Data

Wolfgang, Marvin E., 1924-
    Criminal violence.

    Includes bibliographical references.
    1. Crime and criminals—Research—United States—Addresses, essays,
lectures. 2. Violence—United States—Addresses, essays, lectures. 3. Violence research—
United States—Addresses, essays, lectures. I. Weiner, Neil Alan. II. Title.
HV6789.W64   364.3'0973   81-23314
ISBN 0-8039-1800-3   AACR2
ISBN 0-8039-1801-1 (pbk.)

FIRST PRINTING

Contents

Acknowledgments

The present volume was prepared under grant number 79-NI-AX-0127 from the Center for the Study of Crime Correlates and Criminal Behavior of the National Institute of Justice of the U.S. Department of Justice. The editors wish to thank Dr. Helen Erskine, the former grant monitor of this project, and Mrs. Winifred Reed, the current grant monitor, for their assistance in organizing and administering the workshop on criminal violence, for which these chapters were prepared, and for their assistance at later stages of this work.

Our appreciation is acknowledged to Rhoda Piltch, administrative officer of the Center for Studies in Criminology and Criminal Law, and Esther Lafair and Elizabeth Jane McCartney, of the Center secretariat, for their able assistance throughout the preparation of this volume.

Our thanks are also extended to Selma Pastor, the librarian at the Center for Studies in Criminology and Criminal Law, for helping to coordinate the technical work required for preparing this volume.

Finally, we express our appreciation to Erica Ginsburg for her graphics work on the figures in this volume.

Introduction

Marvin E. Wolfgang
Neil Alan Weiner

In the decade since the National Commission on the Causes and Prevention of Violence presented its extensive review of the state of our knowledge about violence in America and its recommendations, criminal violence has climbed to an unacceptably high level. Now, as then,

> the time is upon us for a reordering of national priorities and for a greater investment of resources in the fulfillment of two basic purposes of our Constitution . . . to "establish justice" and to "insure domestic tranquility" [National Commission on the Causes and Prevention of Violence, 1969: xxv].

Policies formulated to reduce criminal violence require a solid theoretical and research foundation. Since the report by the National Commission, much new work has been done on the topic of criminal violence, but with few efforts to synthesize it. The desire for syntheses, particularly in newly emerging theoretical and substantive areas, prompted the organization of a workshop on criminal violence which was held on 30-31 January 1981 at the Center for Studies in Criminology and Criminal Law at the University of Pennsylvania. The workshop was sponsored by a grant from the Center for the Study of Crime Correlates and Criminal Behavior of the National Institute of Justice. The grant, which is part of a five-year Research Agreements Program, established the Center for the Interdisciplinary Study of Criminal Violence.

One of the concerns of the Center for the Interdisciplinary Study of Criminal Violence is to integrate the state of our knowledge about criminal violence as a way to provide an informed point of departure for future research in the area.

Realizing this objective involves selecting for comprehensive review important substantive areas and major perspectives that incorporate an interdisciplinary orientation into theoretical formulations. These concerns led us to commission reviews of various subject areas which together form the rich blend of studies presented in this volume.

As a complement to the literature reviews, a set of abstracted bibliographies on selected topics in criminal violence was prepared in collaboration with the National Criminal Justice Reference Service, several of which pertain to the subject areas covered in this volume. These bibliographies are:

- Criminal Violence: Biological Correlates and Determinants
- Criminal Violence: Psychological Correlates and Determinants
- Domestic Criminal Violence
- Criminal Violence and Race
- The Violent Offender in the Criminal Justice System

The bibliographies will soon be available from the National Criminal Justice Reference Service as part of their document loan program.

In "Biology and Violence" by Sarnoff Mednick et al., extensive material on the relationships among biology and aggression, violence, antisocial behavior, and criminal violence is reviewed. Only those biological factors are selected for discussion that involve nonsocial and nonbehavioral measures of the human constitution and functioning. Based on this criterion, material falling into the following categories have been included: genetic studies (for instance, on the XYY chromosomal abnormality and on adoptees), studies on sex differences (mainly based on testosterone level), works on autonomic nervous system functioning (measured primarily by skin conductance), investigations in neuropsychology (for instance, localized brain lesions), studies in neurophysiology (explored primarily through visual and, less often, quantitative electroencephalographic procedures), and works in biochemistry and psychopharmacology (including pieces on alcohol, amphetamines, phencyclidine, marijuana, opiates, testosterone, and glucose). Excluded from analysis are studies on intelligence, because it is only partially of biological origin and behaviorally measured.

Perhaps the major point of Chapter 1 is that the combined weight of the evidence in the various topic areas argues for the existence of a general relationship between biological factors and violence, but that extreme caution must be used when interpreting any particular finding. Considerably more work is needed to identify the mechanisms by which specific biological factors influence the various forms and degrees of violence, aggression, antisocial behavior, and criminal violence.

The authors outline a psychophysiological theory of rule-violative behavior that relates (1) the lack of emotional anticipation of punishment and (2) slow skin conductance recovery to the inability to learn behavioral inhibition. The theory argues that without the anticipation of punishment and the anxiety that accompanies it, there is low motivation—meaning anxiety reduction—for inhibiting behavior that is expected to produce punishment, such as violent behavior. The theory further proposes that the reduction in anxiety occasioned by the inhibition of punishment-producing behavior is reinforcing, thus implying that there will be little reinforcement of behavioral inhibition in the absence of a substantial reduction in anxiety as measured by slow skin conductance recovery. Research on violent offenders tends to confirm that both learning processes are operative.

"Psychological Correlates and Determinants of Criminal Violence," by Edwin I. Megargee, summarizes a wide range of theoretical and empirical literature on the psychology of aggression, violence, and criminal violence. The definitions of these terms are presented along with several problems raised by them, such as whether intentionality *(mens rea)* need accompany the behavior, whether injury must occur to the victim and to what degree, whether psychological damage qualifies as a form of injury, and whether aggression can involve acts of omission. Excluded as major foci are ethological, psychoanalytic, social learning, and psychophysiological theories because they have been covered elsewhere.

Selected for discussion are the following forms of criminal violence: murder, assault (and general violence), familial violence, forcible rape, kidnapping and hostage-taking, violence against property, terrorism, bombing, arson, and robbery. Each is examined by surveying the prominent typologies that have been formulated. Each typology implies that subtypes differ in developmental and personality dynamics. Although different in their specifics, some conceptual similarity exists across the several typologies. Formulations typically encountered are that criminal violence can be a normal response to provocation, that it can be a response that is consistent with norms supporting its use, that it can be an instrument useful in obtaining some end (instrumental aggression), that it can be intrinsically rewarding behavior (angry aggression), or that it can involve the acting out of some psychopathology.

The chapter points out that the efforts at constructing typologies have not been matched by work on their being operationalized or validated. Future research might concentrate on these issues by specifying measurable psychological factors associated with different offender types and by determining their relative contribution to specific kinds of offense behavior.

Megargee proceeds to develop a general formulation of the psychological dynamics of aggression, or what he calls the "algebra of aggression," which involves five major components: instigation to aggression, which might be defined as the sum of all factors motivating aggression; habit strength, which might be defined as behavioral preference based on past rewards; inhibition against aggression, which may be defined as behavioral devaluations based on past rewards and punishments; stimulus factors, which may be defined as situational variables functioning either to promote or to inhibit behavior; and response competition, which may be defined as viable response patterns alternative to some standard pattern. The main argument is that aggression is directly related to the instigation to aggression, to the strength of aggressive habits, and to stimulus factors facilitating aggression, and is indirectly related to inhibitions against aggression. Under these conditions, aggression is possible, given that a stronger competing response does not exist. The conceptual model just presented is then discussed in detail, with variables and relationships falling within each of the five components carefully reviewed.

David Farrington's chapter, "Longitudinal Analyses of Criminal Violence," surveys findings from the major longitudinal studies conducted worldwide on criminal violence. Included for review are only those studies taking repeated measures on the same subjects or on samples drawn at different times from a single subject population. The strengths of the longitudinal design, the relative advantages of different longitudinal designs, and the reasons for mixing longitudinal and cross-sectional designs are detailed.

Particular attention is paid to the way the longitudinal design can provide insight into the prevalence and evolution of violent juvenile and adult criminal careers and into their extended relationship with aggression and deviance, including alcoholism, mental illness, sexual promiscuity, and vagrancy. Although career generality appears to be the norm—meaning that offenders typically mix violent and nonviolent offenses over the span of their careers—more refined studies focusing on violent offenders are nevertheless suggested because they may yield unique results. For instance, there is much more to be learned about the relationship between age at onset and career seriousness and persistence, and about age-specific, age-interval-specific and offense-rank-specific probabilities of specialization and career seriousness. Several studies have found relationships between criminal violence, various kinds of deviance, early juvenile aggression, intergenerational criminality, and certain important and usually disruptive life events. Additional work is required to establish these results more firmly.

Farrington argues that we also need longitudinal studies that focus on predicting criminal violence—specifically, studies that use alternative operational and statistical definitions of prediction and alternative operational definitions of violence. For example, prediction can be operationally defined in terms of rearrest or reconviction, and statistically defined as either a correlation or the false-positive rate; and violence can be measured alternatively using official or self-report data, in each case defined either by statute or by the presence of injury to the victim.

Especially useful for formulating policy, longitudinal analyses can identify offender types and their peak offending ages. When linked to offense prediction and offender discrimination, penal applications become apparent, for example, in developing an optimum incapacitative intervention strategy.

The chapter on "Domestic Criminal Violence" by Richard Gelles points out that domestic violence and its more delimited form, domestic criminal violence, have emerged within the last decade as an important lay, professional, and research concern. Despite the increased concern and the growing recognition that more research is needed in the area, several obstacles to such research have been encountered. First, there are definitional problems. Domestic assaults identical to ones that would be treated as criminal if they occurred outside the family have often been definitionally grouped with other nonharmful or noncriminal acts. Definitional imprecision has led researchers to aggregate very different kinds of behaviors, with the general result that domestic criminal violence and other related forms of domestic violence have not been investigated separately.

Second, problems have arisen about the availability of data. The traditional official response to domestic violence has been to treat it, even in its most aggravated forms, as a personal or interpersonal problem, that is, as a social welfare concern, rather than as a public issue legitimately falling within the purview of the criminal law. Therefore, except for homicide, because it is so serious, domestic assaults typically have not been recorded as criminal assaults but rather have been labeled as domestic disturbances. As a consequence, either very little or very ambiguous official data exist, creating very serious research problems.

Gelles observes that since 1970 both the problem of domestic criminal violence and the obstacles to research posed by it have received increasing attention, and has led to several large-scale research efforts, such as a national survey of family violence and a national study of child abuse and neglect. He also notes that portions of the National Crime Survey are related to the problem of domestic criminal violence. These projects, together with numerous others of a more modest scale, have linked domestic criminal violence with several factors, although the precise strength of the relationships is still undetermined: gender, developmental experiences, social and economic status, race, stress, social isolation, and certain patterns of substance abuse. Gelles cautions, however, against outright acceptance of these findings, because they are often based on studies using small or nonrepresentative samples or because they are flawed methodologically in other ways. Research is needed that includes cross-sectional analyses and alternative and more refined measures of violence.

The author also reviews prominent theories of intrafamilial violence falling at the psychiatric, social-psychological, and sociocultural analytical levels.

Philip Cook's chapter, "The Role of Firearms in Violent Crime," discusses several issues relating to firearms, particularly handguns and violent crime. Recent trends in gun availability are examined and linked to patterns of acquisition and criminally violent use. Three of the most common measures are analyzed: gun-ownership density, effective price, and the propensity to bear arms.

A theoretical framework relating weapons use and violent crime is developed, the core concepts of which are intent (or "task definition"), weapon type, and event outcome. Most crucial to the theoretical framework is the proposition that a weapon provides a technological advantage to its user in obtaining a desired goal. According to Cook's formulation, the type of weapon selected depends on its perceived effectiveness in achieving some end relative to a particular target. In the case of violent crime, the less vulnerable and more attractive the target, the greater is the likelihood that a weapon will be used, with the most sophisticated and powerful weapons reserved for use against the least vulnerable and most attractive targets. Well-protected commercial establishments holding articles of considerable value are therefore especially likely to be victimized by offenders wielding firearms.

In general, considering the vulnerability thesis, firearms are most likely to be used by the weak against the strong—for instance, by women against men, by the old against the young, and by a single offender against a group. Victim vulnerability is, then, a key variable in weapon selection, and, reciprocally, weapon selection and acquisition are key variables in offense capability, opportunity, and choice of target. The chapter examines these and similar relationships by tracing patterns of gun use across three types of violent crimes—murder, assault, and robbery—paying attention in each case to salient attributes of the offender, the victim, and the specific situation.

Starting from the target-vulnerability thesis, several research hypotheses are derived which suggest that firearm availability has different impacts on homicide, assault, and robbery. Increased gun availability simultaneously increases the proportion of young male homicide victims and the proportion of robberies committed against commercial and other well-defended targets. The hypotheses further suggest that within each of these violent-crime categories, firearm availability differentially affects the character and seriousness of the violence.

Cook concludes with a discussion of three recently implemented gun-control laws. Selected evaluative research focusing on these laws is critically reviewed. He notes that the effectiveness of the laws has not been firmly demonstrated, partly because of methodological weaknesses in the evaluation studies.

The chapter by John Monahan and Deidre Klassen, "Situational Approaches to Understanding and Predicting Individual Violent Behavior," begins by noting that situational approaches to studying criminal violence have recently emerged as an important analytical orientation in criminology. Integrating materials drawn from psychology, environmental and social psychology, ethnography, and social ecology, situational analysis examines the way in which personal and contextual factors interact to produce criminal violence. The expected practical benefits of the approach are twofold: the more situational factors can be identified as linked to criminal violence, the more improved will be prediction; and the more these situational factors can be changed, the more effective will be prevention of criminal violence.

Several situations have been related to criminal violence: family, peer group, and job. Within the family, actual or encouraged use of violence by parents often leads to its later use by children who have been exposed to it. Also associated with domestic violence are high residential mobility, a higher-than-average number of children in the household, disruption of routine status relationships between husband and wife, and unemployment, income, and financial stress.

Peer groups also play a role in criminal violence, for example, in providing normative support for the use of violence. Research has shown that victims and offenders are often friends or acquaintances. Peer groups, therefore, not only encourage violence but suffer as victims of it.

Work has increasingly been related to criminal violence. Those parolees who secure jobs easily, who remain on the job, and who are the most satisfied with their jobs have a higher probability of parole success. Moreover, work can indirectly produce violence within nonwork situations like the family, for domestic violence is directly related to employment problems and reduced family income.

Situational analyses can be used to predict individual violence as part of a two-step procedure: first, situations in which an individual behaves violently are identified; second, an assessment is made of the kinds of situations the individual is likely to encounter in the future. If future situational involvements are projected to be similar to ones in which violence has previously occurred, violence is predicted to be highly likely.

Besides the different kinds of situations that have been related to criminal violence, such as the three discussed above, internal dimensions of these situations have similarly been related to it, notably the presence of alcohol and a firearm.

Monahan and Klassen point out that an organizing concept useful in situational analyses is that of stress, which may be defined as the internal condition induced by an imbalance between environmental demands and the ability of the individual to modulate them. An important response to stress is aggression and its behavioral manifestation as violence.

"The Violent Offender in the Criminal Justice System," by Peter Greenwood, begins with a discussion of the three major ways that the criminal justice system can reduce the violent-crime rates: by deterrence through penal sanctions, by rehabilitation through correctional treatment, and by incapacitation through physical detention. To date, there is little evidence that deterrence or rehabilitation works. What studies have been done in these two areas are methodologically flawed or find no discernible effects. When a deterrence effect is found, it is most strongly associated with the probabilities of arrest, conviction, and incarceration and most weakly with sentence length. Of the three crime-reduction strategies, incapacitation appears to be the most likely to be effective, but this strategy depends on the validity of the assumption that an incarcerated offender would continue offending without incarceration.

Greenwood proceeds to identify the major processing stages constituting the criminal justice system, pointing out the impact that each stage is expected to have on the violent-crime rate and whether evidence exists to confirm the presence of the expected effects. Because so few studies find a rehabilitative effect, incapacitation emerges as the priority objective, with deterrence a potential by-product. These objectives depend crucially, however, on the ability of the criminal justice system to apprehend, convict, and incarcerate the violent offender.

The processing stages from arrest onward are diagrammatically presented and discussed by using selective data on homicide, forcible rape, robbery, and assault. Branching ratios are displayed from arrest to sentencing, with accompanying comments about the often-observed discrepancy between initial arrest charge and final conviction charge. Plea negotiation is noted to bear strongly on this entire process.

Because the effectiveness of incapacitation mainly depends on the probabilities of conviction and incarceration, factors strongly related to them are selected for review, most important among which are (1) whether the victim and offender knew one another, with offenses involving strangers having higher conviction rates, and (2) the strength of the prosecutor's case, with the number of witnesses a key variable.

When convicted of violent crime, most offenders are incarcerated, but no recent study has examined the consequences in detail. The probability of incarceration has been related to several factors, including length of prior record, whether the victim and offender knew one another, the presence of a firearm, and the offender's age.

Greenwood suggests that incapacitation is the most likely consequence of incarceration. Its effectiveness depends on the probability of arrest and conviction, the kinds of offenses an incarcerated offender would commit without incarceration, the rate at which these offenses would be committed, and the offender's expected career length. The effectiveness of a selective incapacitation strategy directed at violent offenders can be maximized by first determining their high-intensity offending periods and then administering long prison terms to offenders convicted during these periods. Research indicates that such a policy would involve identifying relatively few high-rate offenders. Several factors have been found related to high-rate offending and, consequently, might be used to identify such offenders: prior conviction (but not prior incarceration), age at first arrest, seriousness of juvenile offense career, drug use, and age of instant offense.

Together, these chapters constitute a careful survey of much theoretical and research literature on criminal violence. Yet, comprehensive as this set of studies may be, more work remains to be done. We believe, however, that this volume provides firm analytical bases for future hypotheses to be tested by social scientists concerned with the major issues of criminal violence.

REFERENCE

National Commission on the Causes and Prevention of Violence. *To Establish Justice and to Ensure Domestic Tranquility.* Washington, DC: Government Printing Office, 1969.

1

Biology and Violence

Sarnoff A. Mednick
Vicki Pollock
Jan Volavka
William F. Gabrielli, Jr.

Violent behavior is infrequent. In a Danish cohort, for example, only 1-2 percent of the individuals were convicted for violent acts. For one-third to one-half of violent offenders, the violent act is their first offense. The remainder of violent offenders (50-75 percent) also tend to be recidivist property offenders (Wolfgang and Ferracuti, 1967). McClintock (1963) reports that among violent offenders, 40 percent had five or more previous convictions. In a large (N = 31,436) Danish male birth cohort (Witkin et al., 1977), we have found that the first violent offense for a cohort member tends to occur on an individual's eighth (median) offense. More than half of the victims of assault are familially related or friends of the perpetrator. The other victims of violence are strangers, usually attacked in connection with crimes for gain.

These gross epidemiological statements have implications for biological research. Apparently some major proportion of individuals who commit violence do so as part of a pattern of crime for gain. To the extent that biological factors are distinctive for individuals who commit property crimes, these same biological factors might also characterize this type of violent offender. There may, in addition, be factors that differentiate this type from the type who expresses violence against family members and friends. We must be alert to the

Authors' Note: Significant portions of this chapter originally appeared in "Biology and Crime," by S. A. Mednick and J. Volavka, pp. 85-158 in *Crime and Justice: An Annual Review of Research,* Volume II, N. Morris and M. Tonry, eds. Reprinted by permission of The University of Chicago Press, © 1980 by The University of Chicago. The writing of this chapter has been aided by the following research grants and contracts by the Center for Studies of Crime and Delinquency, NIMH, and the National Institute of Justice: MH 24872, MH 19225, MH 25311, MH 31353, 79-NI-AX-0087.

possibility that these two types of violent offenders have differing biological characteristics. Such a possibility should guide the design of our research and data analyses.

There are a number of factors that have been shown to have strong relations with violent crime: sex (Wolfgang, 1978), age (Mulvihill et al., 1969), education (Strasburg, 1978), occupation (Wolfgang and Ferracuti, 1967), availability of handguns (Block, 1977), geographic location (Newman, 1979), crowding in cities (Gunn, 1973), cultural factors, and socioeconomic status (Wolfgang, 1978). While some of these factors may have biological implications (e.g., sex and age), the majority are social variables. It is our position that if biological factors are related to violence, they will not replace social variables as explanatory constructs. Rather, the biological factors may explain violence in those cases not explained by social variables. It is even more likely that biological factors may interact with social agents in determining the likelihood of violent acts.

Definition of Biological Factors. By the term "biological factors" we will refer to nonsocial, nonbehavioral measures of man's constitution and functioning. In this essay we will discuss genetic, autonomic-nervous-system, central-nervous-system, and biochemical factors as correlates of or influences on criminal behavior. We will exclude behaviorally defined characteristics (such as intelligence) which may have a partial biological origin.

The Plan of This Essay. If genetic factors play any role in the etiology of antisocial behavior, then this relationship *must* be mediated by biological factors. For this reason we begin with a review of the literature linking heredity with crime and violence. This literature demonstrates that genetic factors do play an etiological role in antisocial behavior; the role of genetics in violent behavior specifically has not been clearly demonstrated. We then summarize criminological research literature in selected areas of biological investigation.

GENETIC STUDIES

Sex-Chromosomal Abnormalities

The XYY chromosome affair may have been one of the most publicized criminological events of this century. Men usually have 46 chromosomes; two of these are the sex chromosomes, one X and one Y. The usual notation for this chromosomal configuration is XY. That there are XYY men who have two Y chromosomes was first announced by Sandberg et al. (1961). The historic XYY man they discovered was *not* a criminal. Some surveys began to suggest, however, that XYY men are disproportionately represented in maximum security hospitals. The descriptions presented of the crimes perpetrated by these

XYY men would supply material for a series of horror films. A media image quickly developed of the huge, dangerous hulk of a "supermale" with superaggressiveness spurred on by his extra male chromosome. Other hospital studies contradicted these findings. However, if the XYY-aggression relation was reliably established, the legal implications for establishing criminal responsibility would be of some importance (Georgetown Law Journal, 1969.)

Sophisticated observers soon realized that the inconsistent findings resulted from the arbitrary, small-size samples being investigated (Kessler and Moos, 1970). Other observers were politically opposed to the possibility of any "internal causality" in "the causes of crime," referring to the XYY research as "demonism revisited" (Sarbin and Miller, 1970). Sarbin and Miller called for a study that would "eliminate the sampling bias by obtaining XYY subjects from the general noninstitutionalized population. . . . This in itself would be an overwhelming project, requiring the chromosomal typing of possibly thousands of potential subjects."

Precisely such a study was undertaken by Witkin et al. (1977) at the Psykologisk Institut, Kommunehospitalet, in Copenhagen, Denmark. A total cohort was identified consisting of all the 31,436 men born in the municipality of Copenhagen in 1944, 1945, 1946, and 1947. All those men who were 184 centimeters or more in height (N = 4,139) were visited in their homes. Blood samples were taken and karyotypes (systematically arranged photographs of their chromosomes) prepared. This process yielded 12 XYY men. The XYYs and their controls were checked in the official Danish criminality records. There was little or no recorded evidence of violent behavior by the XYY men. They did, however, evidence significantly more criminality than did XY men of their age, height, intelligence, and social class. Their low intelligence did not account for this excess criminality. An ongoing extensive examination of their electrical brain activity indicates that, in comparison to a control group, the XYY subjects evidence remarkably slow alpha and excessive theta activity (Volavka et al., 1977c). Their EEG response to visual stimulation is inadequate (Volavka et al., 1979). They also show very low skin conductance responsiveness and a slow rate of recovery. (These physiological variables are defined below.)

Note that this study selected all of the XYYs from among a total birth cohort of tall Danish men. The results are reliable (despite the small yield of XYYs) and generalizable to the population represented by the cohort. Careful genetic investigation (also from other laboratories) helped explode a disagreeable myth and tended to relieve a class of men (albeit a small group) of a nasty label and perhaps of other unpleasant consequences.

But the XYY man is an exceedingly infrequent fellow. The critical question is whether more commonly observed criminality and psychopathy are influenced by genetic factors.

Family and Twin Studies

It has long been observed that antisocial parents raise an excessive number of children who become antisocial. In the classic study by Robins (1966), father's criminality was one of the best predictors of antisocial behavior in a child. In terms of genetics, very little can be concluded from such family data, as it is difficult to disentangle hereditary and environmental influences. The criminogenic effects of social and economic adversity mask the possible influence of genetic factors.

A review of twin studies (Mednick and Volavka, 1980) suggests that identical twins evidence greater concordance for criminal behavior than do fraternal twins. In the first eight twin studies we were able to find in the literature, identical (monozygotic, hereafter referred to as MZ) twins evidence about 60 percent concordance and fraternal (dizygotic, DZ) twins about 30 percent concordance for criminality. These eight studies are summarized in Table 1.1.

These eight twin studies suffer from haphazard sampling methods. Many were carried out in Germany or Japan during a politically unfortunate period which may, in some cases, have biased the method of interpretation. They report too high a proportion of MZ twins. Concordant MZ pairs are more likely to be brought to the attention of the investigator, because identical twins are usually easier to detect, especially if they end up in the same prison. All of these factors tend to inflate identical-twin-pair concordance rates in nonsystematic studies. The recent and continuing study initiated by the late Karl O. Christiansen, and being continued by Mednick, Gottesman and Hutchings in Copenhagen minimized these sampling problems. In a major pilot study, Christiansen (1977b) studied *all* twins (3,586 twin pairs) born in a well-defined area of Denmark between 1881 and 1910. He used a complete national criminality register. Christiansen (1977b: 93) notes that "there are several important characteristics of the Danish law enforcement process that relate to its statutory uniformity regarding treatment of the offender and sentencing by the court. . . . An elaborate court appeals system is aimed at achieving national uniformity of sentencing. The social status of a Danish police officer is comparatively high; he is regarded as being incorruptible."

In this, the largest and best designed of the twin studies of criminality, Christiansen (1977b) reports 35 percent concordance for male MZ pairs and 13 percent concordance for the male DZ pairs. In this unselected twin population, the MZ concordance rate is lower than in previous studies. More cases are discordant than concordant. Nevertheless, the MZ rate is 2.7 times the DZ rate. This result suggests that MZ twins show some genetically controlled biological characteristic (or set of characteristics) which in some unknown way increases their common risk of being registered for criminal behavior.

This is not some mysterious force, as is implied by the title of the first twin study, "Crime as Destiny" (Lange, 1931). For example, if alcohol addiction

TABLE 1.1 Twin Studies of Psychopathy and Criminality MZ and Same-Sexed DZ Twins Only

Study	Location	Monozygotic			Dizygotic		
		Total Pairs	Pairs Concordant	Percentage Concordant	Total Pairs	Pairs Concordant	Percentage Concordant
Lange, 1931	Bavaria	13	10	77	17	2	12
Legras, 1932	Holland	4	4	100	5	1	20
Rosanoff, 1934	U.S.	37	25	68	28	5	18
Stumpfl, 1936	Germany	18	11	61	19	7	37
Kranz, 1936	Prussia	32	21	66	43	23	54
Borgström, 1939	Finland	4	3	75	5	2	40
Slater, 1934-1945 (psychopathy)	England	2	1	50	10	3	30
Yoshimasu, 1961	Japan	28	17	61	18	2	11
Total		138	92	67.2	145	45	31.0

increased the probability of antisocial behavior, and alcohol addiction had some partial genetically based predisposition, the twin research might yield positive genetic findings; or positive genetic findings may be observed if the child's learning of law abidance is facilitated by some neurophysiological characteristic, the functioning of which is influenced by genetic factors.

A recent study of a group of 139 Norwegian male twins reports 25.8 percent MZ concordance and 14.9 percent DZ concordance (Dalgaard and Kringlen, 1976). Though the MZ-DZ differences are smaller than in previously reported studies, they are in the same direction. Dalgaard and Kringlen explain the difference as due to the fact that "MZ pairs are usually brought up more similarly than DZ." This is a problem also discussed by Christiansen (1977: 221). This group of twins seems to have been drawn disproportionately from the lower classes; they have a "less-than-normal degree of education; they are to a lesser degree married; and frequency of alcoholism seems higher in this group than in the general population." In Christiansen's larger Danish twin investigation, MZ-DZ concordance differences were considerably lower in subgroups characterized by these sorts of variables. It would seem prudent for Dalgaard and Kringlen to sample additional segments of the Norwegian twin register (which contains 33,000 twin pairs) in order to attempt to overcome this social deviance skew.

Mednick, Gottesman, and Hutchings are attempting to expand Christiansen's study to include approximately 14,000 twin pairs. This number should be sufficient for a more detailed analysis (e.g., by type of crime) than has been possible before. Despite the limitations of the twin method, the results of these studies are compatible with the hypothesis that genetic factors account for some of the variance associated with antisocial behavior.

What is of interest in the present context is the extent to which a propensity for violent behavior might be transmitted genetically. These twin studies were not designed especially for this purpose. As pointed out above, violent crimes are infrequent. Even the Christiansen study (1977b) with 3,586 twin pairs does not have a sufficient number of violent cases in its extensive data file to permit conclusions to be drawn regarding violence. Christiansen (1977b) has reviewed each of these twin studies in great detail. Violence is rarely mentioned. Regrettably, we cannot draw conclusions regarding violence from these studies.

Adoption Studies

One great weakness of these twin studies is that in most of the cases, genetic and environmental factors are not easily separated. A design that does a better job in this regard studies individuals adopted at birth. A register of all nonfamilial adoptions in Denmark in the years 1924-1947 has been established in Copenhagen at the Psykologisk Institut by a group of American and Danish investigators (see Kety et al., 1968). The register records 14,427 adoptions and includes information on the adoptee and his biological and adoptive parents. Thus, the register contains information on approximately 72,000 persons. (Only about 80 percent of the biological fathers are definitely identified.)

This adoption register may help us determine whether genetic factors influence human characteristics. For example, if male criminal fathers have disproportionately high numbers of criminal biological adoptees (given appropriate controls), this would suggest a genetic factor in criminality. This is especially true since in almost all instances the adoptee has never seen the biological father and does not know who he is; the adoptee may not even realize he has been adopted. Another research possibility is to study adoptees whose biological parents are criminal and who were placed with noncriminal adoptive parents; or we can take adoptees whose biological parents are not criminal and who were placed with criminal adoptive parents. This design is called the "cross-fostering" model and is useful for comparison of the effectiveness of genetic and certain environmental criminogenic forces. The adoptive method permits reasonable separation of environmental and hereditary influences.

We will report two completed investigations studying the subpopulation of adoptees born in Copenhagen. From 5,483 Copenhagen adoptees, Schulsinger (1977) identified 57 psychopaths from psychiatric registers and police files. (Rates of criminal behavior are high among psychopaths.) He also selected 57 nonpsychopath control adoptees matched for sex, age, social class, neighborhood of rearing, and age of transfer to the adoptive family. The numbers are small, but among the relatives, the biological relatives of the psychopathic adoptees manifest the most psychopathy. Since the postnatal contact between the adoptee and the relative (especially male relative) was in most cases nonexistent, environmental factors probably did not play a very important role in this relationship. The existence of some heritable factor seems the most reasonable interpretation.

Using the same adoptee register, Hutchings and Mednick (1977) studied the arrest records of a pilot sample of the 1,145 male adoptees born in Copenhagen between 1927 and 1941. Of 1,145 male adoptees, 185 had been convicted of a violation of the Danish Penal Code. Of these 185 criminal adoptees, we were able to identify 143 for whom we were certain of the biological father's identity. To each of these 143 criminal adoptees we matched a noncriminal adoptive son for age of child and social class of adoptive father. For the criminal and noncriminal groups, the age of parents and the age of child at adoption proved to be about the same. In most cases, there was no contact between the adoptee and the biological father. Table 1.2 indicates that the heaviest weight of the registered criminality in the fathers is in the cell of the biological fathers of the criminal adoptees. Again, we have evidence that genetic factors play some role in the etiology of registered criminality.

TABLE 1.2   Registered Criminality in Biological and Adoptive Relatives of
Criminal Adoptees

	Biological Father	*Adoptee Father*
Criminal Adoptive Sons (N = 143)	70	33
Control Adoptive Sons (N = 143)	40	14

TABLE 1.3   "Cross-Fostering" Analysis

		Is Biological Father Criminal?	
		Yes	*No*
Is Adoptive	Yes	$\dfrac{21}{58} = 36.2\%$	$\dfrac{6}{52} = 11.5\%$
Father Criminal?	No	$\dfrac{46}{214} = 21.5\%$	$\dfrac{35}{333} = 10.5\%$

NOTE: Tabled values are percentage of adoptive sons who are registered criminals.

Table 1.3 presents this information in a different form, analogous to the cross-fostering paradigm. In this table minor offenses are omitted. As can be seen in the lower righthand cell, if neither the biological nor the adoptive fathers are criminal, 10.5 percent of their sons are criminal. If the biological father is not criminal but the adoptive father is, this figure rises to only 11.5 percent. In the lower lefthand corner of Table 1.3 note that 21.5 percent of the sons are criminal if the adoptive father is not criminal and the biological father is criminal. The 21.5 percent and the 11.5 percent figures are not quite significantly different (.05 level). Note that in this table the influence of the adoptive father's criminality is statistically significant only in those sons whose biological fathers were also criminal (36.2 percent versus 21.5 percent). We have, however, expanded the adoptee population to 14,427 by registering all adoptions for the Kingdom of Denmark for this period. Results on the total population confirm the role of genetic factors in criminal behavior.

We examined the transmission of *violent* behavior in a subset of a cohort of 14,427 adoptions. Figure 1.1 depicts violence and property crimes committed by biological sons of convicted criminals, who had been reared by noncriminal parents. There is a slight tendency for violence in the adoptees to be greater if the biological parents have been convicted. This tendency is not statistically significant. At this stage of the analysis we must conclude that the evidence does not support a role for genetic factors in the etiology of violence. This conclusion is tentative. It is possible that there may be some intrusion due to psychiatric factors in these relationships. That is, some proportion of the violent acts may be cleared before the involvement of the court because of psychiatric factors. We are currently coding all admissions to psychiatric hospitals in

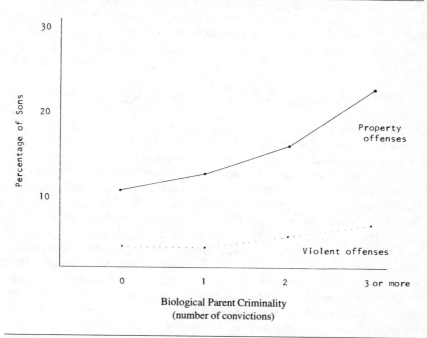

FIGURE 1.1   Percentage of Male Adoptee Property Offenders and Violent
Offenders by Biological Parent Criminality (cases in which adoptive
parents are noncriminal)

Denmark for this entire cohort in order to attempt to account for any possible
influence of this factor. But at this point in the analysis, evidence for the
influence of genetic factors in violent behavior is not convincing.

Thus, the comparison analogous to a cross-fostering experiment seems to
support a partial genetic-etiology hypothesis. We must caution, however, that
simply knowing that the adoptive father has been a criminal does not tell us how
criminogenic the adoptee's environment has been. On the other hand, at con-
ception, the genetic influence of the father is already complete. Thus, as we
have arranged the cross-fostering table it is not a fair comparison between
environmental and genetic influences. But the genetic effect does seem to exist.

A third adoptee project has been completed by Crowe (1975) in Iowa. This
investigation finds evidence of a relationship between criminality in an adopted
child and its biological mother.

Cadoret (1978) reports on 246 children adopted at birth. He indicates that
antisocial behavior in the adoptees is significantly related to antisocial behavior
in the biological parents. His data were gathered by telephone interview with

the adoptive parents and adoptee. It is difficult to judge how this method influenced the reported results. Bohman (1978), in a study of Swedish adoptees, first reported no significant relationship between criminality in the biological parents and the adoptees. When he takes recidivism into account, however, a genetic effect becomes apparent (Bohman, personal communication, 1978).

SEX DIFFERENCES IN AGGRESSION

Despite recent changes in sex role behavior in many areas of human functioning, violence safely remains a male-dominated activity. This dominance may be due to social learning or biologically related sex differences. To the extent that social-learning factors could be ruled out, interesting sex hormone and brain difference hypotheses could be productively entertained. There are developmental studies (cited by Maccoby and Jacklin, 1980) indicating that children's imitation of behavior of like-sexed adults does not begin before the age of six. For this reason Maccoby and Jacklin explore the literature on peer-directed aggression to determine whether sex differences appear before the age of six. In a review of 32 studies (on children under six years), they find no instance of girls manifesting greater aggression than boys. Boys are significantly more aggressive in 75 percent of the studies. They also note that "boys' aggression is most often displayed in the presence of male partners." Further, the effect seems to be due to a small group of very highly aggressive boys. Males are more active in general, but this variable does not explain the sex difference in aggression. The evidence from cross-cultural studies (including study of the free-ranging chimpanzees) is in the same direction. Rates of punishment or reinforcement for aggression between male and female children are not different.

These data suggest strongly that greater male aggressiveness is present in children before social learning can explain it. It is a likely hypothesis that greater aggressiveness in males is related to their higher levels of male sex hormones.

Olweus has completed two reports that may aid in the interpretation of these data. First, he finds in a sample of 16-year-old Swedish males that plasma testosterone levels are significantly related to self-reports of physical and verbal aggression (Olweus, forthcoming). In an older study by Hawke (1950), levels of aggressive destructiveness were increased following testosterone administration in a sample of imprisoned, castrated sexual offenders. The second report by Olweus (1975) indicates that levels of aggression evidenced in nursery school are excellent predictors of aggressive behavior throughout childhood and into adolescence. Aggression before age six, then, may have implications for later assaultiveness.

If male sex hormones are involved in adult aggressive behavior, they may be effective in either or both of two ways: (1) The blood level of testosterone may immediately influence aggressive behavior in adults; (2) the level of circulating male hormones influences the organization of the fetal brain in ways that may determine later violence propensities. The evidence is not conclusive but may be interpreted as slightly favoring the importance of these influences on the developing brain.

AUTONOMIC-NERVOUS-SYSTEM STUDIES (SKIN CONDUCTANCE)

The psychopath is described by Hare (1978a) as among the most aggressive, dangerous and recidivistic clients of a prison. While there is low agreement about the diagnosis, most clinicians describe the psychopath as unsocialized and callous; he feels no guilt, remorse, or shame, lacks emotion, and is incapable of love. He does not alter his behavior as a result of punishment and fails to learn from punishing experiences. He is unable to control impulses and cannot anticipate consequences (American Psychiatric Association, 1968; Craft, 1965; Cleckley, 1976; Buss, 1966). Many of these symptoms describe a lack of emotional expression (no guilt, no emotionality, incapable of love, callous). Other symptoms relate to emotion-mediated learning (failure to learn from punishment, inability to anticipate negative consequences or to be socialized).

Psychophysiologists have techniques appropriate to systematic study of emotions and emotional learning. Inevitably, some psychophysiologists became curious to determine whether this clinically described psychopathic lack of emotion was expressed in lower levels of objectively measured physiological indices of emotional expression such as heart rate, blood pressure, respiration, skin conductance. This section reviews physiological research with antisocial individuals relating to three of these clinical characteristics: lacking emotionality or emotional responsiveness, or callousness; lacking ability to anticipate negative consequences; and failure to learn from punishment, or unsocialized.

The discipline of psychophysiology is most concerned with studying peripheral signs of autonomic-nervous-system (ANS) activity. The ANS mediates physiological activity associated with emotions; hence its importance to the study of psychopathy. Examples of peripheral manifestations of ANS activity include changes in heart rate, blood pressure, respiration, muscle tension, pupillary size, and electrical activity of the skin.

The measurement of electrical properties of the skin—called galvanic skin response (GSR), or skin conductance—is the most commonly used peripheral indicant of ANS activity both in psychophysiology and in criminology. There are several reasons for this. Technically, it is relatively simple to obtain reliable skin conductance recordings. There is a sizable methodological literature for procedural guidance. The responses are typically recorded as waves that have a relatively slow rate of change and are consequently readily amenable to hand scoring or computer scoring. If we administer a stimulus, we typically observe a discrete response that can be readily and immediately identified.

The skin conductance response as it is usually measured is most heavily dependent on the activity of the sweat glands of the palms. Individuals who are often emotionally aroused, anxious, and fearful tend to have clammy, wet handshakes because their emotional responsiveness is reflected in the overactive sweat glands of their palms. Such emotional individuals usually exhibit high skin conductance even when they are not stimulated. Very calm, unemotional types typically have very low skin conductance. (This "emotional" perspiration is also abundant in the soles of the feet but is typically less evident, since people we encounter are usually wearing shoes. The soles and palms are called volar areas.)

When frightened or otherwise emotionally aroused, normally calm individuals will evidence episodes of volar sweating. This sweating moistens the skin with a salt solution that increases its electrical conductivity. (More detailed information can be found in Venables and Christie, 1975.) If a weak current (generated by a battery) is leaked through the fingers we can monitor the electrical resistance (or its inverse, conductance) of the skin to the passage of this current. If we stimulate the individual to become emotionally aroused (e.g., shoot off a gun behind his back) his ANS will activate his volar sweat glands. The skin will be suffused with perspiration, which will increase its conductance; if we are monitoring this conductance on a polygraph we will see an excursion of the pen that (all other things being equal) will be proportionate to the extent of ANS arousal experienced by our subject. Subjects who are relatively unaroused by stimulation will produce little or no pen excursion. Individuals who are highly aroused by the gunshot will evidence a substantial pen excursion. The extent of pen excursion can be calibrated so that it can be expressed in electrical units of conductance. This process yields an objective score that reflects, at least to some substantial extent, the subject's degree of emotional arousal and ANS activation. There is a considerable body of methodological literature describing application of this technique; despite some complaints on details in the literature, there is good standardization of technique, which makes it possible, with due caution, to compare results from different laboratories.

Skin conductance is the most frequently measured psychophysiological characteristic of antisocial individuals. The pattern of results reported regarding certain conductance characteristics of antisocial persons has been relatively consistent across many laboratories, nations, experimental procedures and definitions of antisocial behavior. For these reasons, this review is restricted, in the main, to a discussion of skin conductance.

Much of the reported work involved prisoners as subjects. The prisoners are typically divided and compared on the basis of assessed psychopathy level, seriousness of criminality, recidivism, or some combination. Nonprisoner controls are rarely assessed. In only a handful of studies are groups of violent individuals so identified. In view of the fact that so large a proportion of violent offenders are also property offenders, we will first describe offenders and then, with this background, delineate the specific differentiating skin conductance functioning of the violent offender.

Studies on the skin conductance of prisoners or nonincarcerated criminals must be interpreted with considerable caution. The criminal life and the prison experience very likely affect a person's emotional response patterns (D'Artri, 1978). Thus, skin conductance deviance in antisocial individuals may be the result of their criminal careers or incarceration. Etiological interpretations of such data must be very cautiously proffered. However, some tiny beginnings of prospective research have been undertaken in which young people are assessed and the results related to their delinquency years later. Assessments of prisoners have also been related to their subsequent recidivism. These few prospective studies will be emphasized in this review.

Emotionality and Emotional Responsiveness

The descriptions of the callous, remorseless, unfeeling psychopath present a challenge to the psychophysiologist to produce an objective measure that might make it possible to subject this clinical description to analytic study. The psychophysiologist has responded to this challenge rather productively by investigating the psychopath's customary (relatively unprovoked) or *basal level* of emotionality, and his emotional *responsiveness* when provoked by a variety of challenging stimuli.

Basal-Level Emotionality

To measure basal level emotionality, the subject is brought into the laboratory and appropriate electrodes are applied; his skin conductance level is then continuously recorded under conditions of no special stimulation. The psychopathic prisoner tends to evidence a slightly lower level of skin conductance than the nonpsychopathic prisoner. For some studies this difference is statistically significant (Blankenstein, 1969; Dengerink and Bertilson, 1975; Hare, 1965, 1968; Mathis, 1970; Schalling et al., 1973). In other studies the difference, while not statistically significant (perhaps in part because of the low reliability of the diagnosis), is usually in the direction of a lower skin conductance for the psychopath (Hare, 1972, 1975; Hare and Craigen, 1974; Fox and Lippert, 1963; Hare and Quinn, 1971; Hare et al., 1978, forthcoming; Borkovec, 1970; Schalling et al., 1973; Schmauk, 1970; Parker et al., 1975; Lippert and Senter, 1966; Sutker, 1970). Hare, noting this consistent but weak tendency, combined the results from eight independent studies in his laboratory. In most of these studies statistically significant basal-level skin conductance was *not* observed, although in each study, psychopaths had lower skin conductance. The combined results are statistically significant (Hare, 1978b).

Loeb and Mednick (1977) report on a ten-year follow-up and delinquency ascertainment of a group of 104 normal Danish adolescents. In 1962, these adolescents had been subjected to a skin conductance examination; in 1972, their officially recorded delinquency was ascertained from the Danish National Police Register, which has been described by Wolfgang (1977) as "probably the most thorough, comprehensive and accurate in the Western world. . . . The reliability and validity of the Danish recordkeeping system are almost beyond criticism." At a ten-year follow-up, seven males of the 104 adolescents had been registered for mildly delinquent acts. Seven of the other boys were matched to these mild delinquents for social factors and age. The predelinquency basal skin conductance level of six of the seven delinquents was below that of all the controls. (T tests between the delinquents and nondelinquents were not significant.) Note that in this study mild registered delinquency, not psychopathy, defined the groups.

Spontaneous Skin Conductance Responses

After a subject is attached to the skin conductance recording device, he is usually permitted a 5- to 10-minute rest. During this time, continuous recording of skin conductance takes place. Although no stimulation is being systematically provided by the experimenter, the subject will almost always exhibit episodic increases in skin conductance that produce pen excursions. These are called spontaneous responses. They may be instigated by thoughts, images, sounds outside the laboratory, or unknown factors. Subjects who are more aroused and anxious tend to exhibit more spontaneous responses (Szpiler and Epstein, 1976).

As in the case of basal level, the results of several experiments are inconclusive but suggest that psychopaths have fewer spontaneous responses during a pre- or postexperimental rest period. (Hare, 1968; Hare and Quinn, 1971; Schalling et al., 1973). Fox and Lippert (1963) observed that antisocial psychopaths exhibit less spontaneous activity than do inadequate psychopaths. Lippert and Senter (1966) did not find significant differences between psychopaths and controls. Hemming (1977) found no differences between prisoners and students. Siddle et al. (1973) report no spontaneous response differences between groups varying in degree of delinquency. Hare (1978b) combined the results of several studies from his laboratory in which the psychopath tended to evidence fewer spontaneous responses but still did not obtain statistically significant differences.

If this review had found consistent evidence of a lower skin conductance basal level and fewer spontaneous reponses for the psychopath, this would have suggested that he continuously experiences an underaroused, unemotional state of being. The picture, unfortunately, is inconsistent. The cumulative impression of the studies suggests that if indeed the basal skin conductance of the psychopathic prisoner *is* relatively low, the differences from the nonpsychopathic prisoner are not very great or consistent. Inspection of the reported variances in some studies suggests that the psychopathic group may have a greater range of basal levels and number of spontaneous responses. This may reflect the possibility that a subgroup of the psychopaths consistently lowers the groups means.

It is a pity that these studies do not include nonprisoner comparison groups. This would give us a frame of reference for evaluation of the results. The differences within prisoner populations may be totally dwarfed by the differences between prisoners and noncriminal populations. Evidence for such a difference has been mentioned by Hare (1978b).

The assumption underlying both the basal level and the spontaneous response studies is that the observed skin conductance behavior is unstimulated. Actually, as each experimenter fully realizes, the subject is rather heavily stimulated by being introduced and attached to the apparatus. These skin conductance measures may be heavily influenced by these situational characteristics.

Skin Conductance Responses to Stimulation

Cleckley (1976) has described the psychopath as evidencing a general poverty of emotional reactiveness. Psychophysiologists have attempted to confirm this description by use of physiological recordings of psychopaths' skin conductance responses to stimuli, such as simple tones, loud noises, electric shock, insertion of a hypodermic needle, and slides of horrible facial injuries. The results of most of these studies are rather consonant: The psychopath, the prisoner, the criminal and the delinquent are decidedly emotionally hyporeactive to stimulation (Blankenstein, 1969; Hare, 1972; Mathis, 1970; Sutker, 1970; Aniskiewicz, 1973; Hare and Craigen, 1974; Schalling, 1975; Borkovec, 1970; Siddle et al., 1973; Hinton and O'Neill, 1978; Hare, 1975; Hare and Quinn, 1971; Hodgins-Milner, 1976; Hemming, 1977).

Hare et al. (forthcoming) report that in their studies psychopaths evidence only diminished responsiveness to exceptionally loud noise (120 decibels). Their research is carried out in a prison. Subjects were selected by inviting 250 prisoners to participate in the research. Of these, 87 volunteered and 64 were finally tested. The investigators are aware of the difficulty of generalizing from such a selected population. In addition it should be emphasized that all of these subjects (both psychopaths and controls) were recidivistic criminals. Perhaps this is the reason differences between psychopaths and nonpsychopaths were apparent only under extreme stimulus conditions. In another study using similar subject selection methods, Hare (1975) reports no differences between psychopaths and nonpsychopaths. Lippert and Senter (1966) also report no differentiation of psychopaths by skin conductance amplitude (size of response).

In the one published *prospective* study described above (Loeb and Mednick, 1977) skin conductance amplitude was measured on a group of 104 Danish adolescents some ten years before delinquency was ascertained. Predelinquent skin conductance amplitude of the seven delinquents was markedly (and statistically significantly) lower than that of controls. In 1962, the nondelinquent controls evidenced a mean response amplitude that was 5 to 10 times as great as that of the boys who eventually evidenced delinquency. The transgressions involved were mild.

Cleckley's clinical description is consistent with the physiologically assessed emotional responsiveness of not only the psychopath but also the criminal and the delinquent. The finding is substantially consistent across a considerable variety of national settings, laboratory procedures, levels, and definitions of antisocial behavior. The single prospective study has a pitifully small group (7) of mild delinquents but the results do not contradict the hypotheses and are bolstered considerably by the other cited literature.

The robustness of the cross-sectional findings encourages the inclusion of skin conductance responsiveness among the reliable characteristics of individuals who are officially noted as having transgressed. The single prospective finding suggests that ANS responsiveness should not be excluded from the group of variables showing potential etiological significance in the *development* of antisocial behavior.

Anticipation of Negative Experiences

The psychopath is marked by his inability to foresee the negative consequences of his acts. This includes negative consequences for himself and for his victims. Psychophysiologists have attempted to create laboratory situations in which foreseeable negative consequences (e.g., electric shock, very loud noises) would result from designated conduct. Skin conductance responses are then monitored to test whether antisocial individuals evidence normal emotional (skin conductance) apprehension in anticipation of the shock or noise.

In 1957, Lykken reported that psychopaths evidence relatively small skin conductance responses in anticipation of electric shock. Hare (1965a) presented prisoners with numbers (1-12) in serial order and warned them that they would experience an electric shock at the number 8. The nonpsychopathic prisoners evidenced strong electrodermal responses early in the number sequence preceding number 8. The psychopaths evidenced little or no anticipation until just before 8. The nonpsychopaths also demonstrated greater responsiveness immediately before the electric shock. In a more recent study (Hare et al., 1978), prisoners were warned that they would experience a very loud (120 decibels) aversive "blast" of noise after a 12-second countdown. The psychopathic prisoners did not begin to show anticipatory skin conductance response until just before the blast and even then their responses were rather weak. The nonpsychopathic prisoners were evidencing substantial skin conductance anticipation after 3 seconds. The highest level of skin conductance anticipation reached by the psychopathic subgroup just before the blast, 12 seconds, was at the level reached by the nonpsychopaths after just over 6 seconds.

This lack of emotional anticipation by psychopaths of (to-be-experienced) pain or aversive stimulation is well documented (Hare and Craigen, 1974; Lippert and Senter, 1966; Schalling and Levander, 1967; Hodgins-Milner, 1976; Schalling et al., 1975). Tharp et al. (1978) repeatedly presented trials consisting of a countdown followed by a very loud noise (95 decibels). After a few countdown-noise trials, the psychopaths showed no skin conductance response whatever in anticipation of the aversive loud noise. The controls (nonprisoners in this study) continued to evidence skin conductance anticipation of the impending noise.

There are other ways to measure ANS functioning in anticipation of stress that do not deal with skin conductance. Lidberg et al. (forthcoming) observed catecholamine levels in the blood of Swedish men just before they were to appear in criminal court to be tried. Catecholamine levels in normals are highly elevated during ANS excitation such as states of anxiety or fear; it would be expected that men just before such a court trial would have elevated levels. The pretrial men were divided into groups high and low in psychopathy. The more psychopathic men evidenced no heightening of their catecholamine levels just prior to the trial. The less psychopathic men had strongly elevated levels. The anticipation of the court trial evoked no physiological inkling of anxiety or fear from the psychopaths.

In some studies the subjects have the opportunity to anticipate that others are about to be shocked or blasted with noise. Sutker (1970) studied noninstitutionalized psychopaths and controls while they observed an individual experiencing an electric shock when a countdown from "one" reached "four." The psychopaths displayed no or minimal skin conductance response in anticipation of the other's pain. This result has been replicated by House and Milligan (1976) in a study on prisoners. Similar results have been obtained by Aniskiewicz (1973) and Hare and Craigen (1974).

Psychopaths, prisoners, and delinquents evidence minimal or no physiological signs that they are apprehensive about a forthcoming painful or aversive stimulus to themselves or to others. Nonpsychopathic (or less psychopathic) prisoners, and individuals not officially registered as delinquent, do evidence physiological anticipation of such events. The intended analogy of these laboratory confrontations to the development of "real-life" acts of lawlessness is clear.

Of course, most elements of criminal acts in the "field" are only remotely modeled by this laboratory paradigm. Yet the relatively consistent confirmation of the hypotheses that instigated these studies cannot be ignored. These studies give no reason to reject the hypothesis that lack, or diminution, of a "normal" ANS fear reaction anticipating negative or painful consequences may be partly responsible for the relative ease with which certain individuals commit deviant acts.

As pointed out above, the evidence in support of this hypothesis is all correlative. A more rigorous examination of the role of this variable in the etiology of antisocial behavior can only be carried out in the context of a prospective, *experimental-manipulative* project (primary or secondary prevention). Training techniques could be tested which improve the young person's ability emotionally to foresee the aversive consequences of his acts. The more effective the training techniques (taking into consideration social factors and initial level of emotional anticipation), the greater should be the reduction of delinquency. Given use of an adequate control group in such a study, this experimental-manipulative approach (as opposed to the traditional weak correlative approach) would improve our capacity to test this hypothesis.

Failure to Learn from Punishment: A Biosocial Theory of Antisocial Behavior

The clinical characteristic of the psychopath which is perhaps most critical to understanding the origins of his condition is his reputed inability to learn from punishment. This failing certainly relates to his hectic recidivism; even more important, it suggests a mechanism that would make the young psychopath-to-be relatively unresponsive to one of society's important moral training forces, namely, family and peer punishment for transgressive acts.

This section presents a minitheory of the bases and consequences of some individuals' inability to learn from punishment. Viewed inversely, the theory is an explanation of the development and learning of morality and law abidance. The theory postulates the interaction of specific social factors and specific ANS aptitudes. After presenting the theory, we present skin conductance evidence relating to the theory and to the examination of the antisocial individuals' abilities to learn from punishment in laboratory situations.

We will begin with a discussion of how we define morality. An early publication on this topic was chipped in stone and brought down from Mount Sinai. The major thrust of that message was negative: "Thou shalt *not*. . . ." While subsequent moral authorities have added *some* positive acts as prescriptions of moral behavior (e.g., "Love thy neighbor"), they have retained the original, basic inhibitory definitions of moral acts. Very few will denounce you if you do not love your neighbor; but if you seduce your neighbor's wife, steal from him, or kill him, you may be certain that your behavior will be classified as immoral. Statements of moral behavior which are critical for everyday activities are essentially negative and inhibitory. That these strictures were enumerated and then carved onto stone tablets suggests that, at some point, there must have been a strong need for insistence on these inhibitions.

How are these inhibitions taught to children? Simple instruction suffices for some; for others the instructions must be reinforced. There seem to be three learning mechanisms that could help parents teach children civilized behavior: modeling, positive and negative reinforcements, and punishment. Positive acts such as loving neighbors, helping old ladies across the street, and cleaning the snow and ice from the front walk can be learned by modeling. But for the more inhibitory moral commands, modeling appears impracticable. Artificial arrangements can be imagined in which modeling is used to teach children not to be adulterous or aggressive, but if our civilization had to depend solely on modeling, it is likely that things would be even more chaotic than they are today. It is also possible to use positive reinforcement (rewards) to teach inhibition of forbidden behavior; but again, reinforcing a child twenty-four hours a day while he is *not* stealing seems both inefficient and unfocused.

Following the excellent exposition of Gordon Trasler (1972), we would suggest that the avoidance of transgression (that is, the practice of law-abiding behavior) demanded by the moral commandments is probably learned through punishments administered by society, family, and peers. The critical inhibitory, morality-training forces in childhood likely to be important are (1) the punishment of antisocial responses by family, society, and friends, and (2) the child's individual capacity *to learn to inhibit* antisocial responses.

Here is one explanation of how children learn to inhibit aggressive impulses. When child A is aggressive to child B, child A is often punished by a peer or a parent. Eventually, after enough punishment, just the thought of aggression should produce a bit of anticipatory fear in child A. If the fear response is large enough, the raised arm will drop and the aggressive response will be successfully inhibited.

This theory suggests that what happens in this child after he has successfully inhibited such an antisocial response is critical for his learning of civilized behavior. Let us consider the situation again in more detail.

(1) Child A contemplates aggressive action.
(2) Because of previous punishment or the threat of punishment he suffers fear.
(3) Because of fear he inhibits the aggressive response.
(4) *Because he no longer entertains the aggressive impulse, the fear will begin to dissipate, to be reduced.*

Fear reduction is the most powerful, naturally occurring reinforcement that psychologists have discovered. The reduction of fear (which immediately follows the inhibition of the aggression) can act as a reinforcement for this *inhibition* and will result in learning inhibition of aggression. The powerful reinforcement associated with fear reduction increases the probability that the inhibition of the aggression will occur in the future. After many such experiences, the normal child will learn to inhibit aggressive impulses. Each time such an impulse arises and is inhibited, the inhibition will be strengthened by reinforcement, since the fear elicited by the impulse will be reduced following successful inhibition.

What does a child need in order to learn social norms effectively?

(1) a censuring agent (typically family or peers)
(2) an adequate fear response
(3) the ability to learn the fear response in anticipation of an antisocial act
(4) fast dissipation of fear to provide a natural reinforcement for the inhibitory response.

We have already summarized evidence in this essay that suggests that the antisocial individual exhibits an abnormally diminished ANS response to frightening (or neutral) stimuli (point 2 above) and is relatively unable emotionally (ANS) to anticipate negative events (point 3). Below we will discuss point 4, the antisocial individual's ability to experience a normally fast dissipation of an (ANS) fear response and to be reinforced for inhibiting the antisocial response.

The speed, size, and quality of a reinforcement determines its effectiveness (Mednick, 1973). An effective reinforcement is one which is delivered immediately after the relevant response. The faster the reduction of fear, the faster the delivery of the reinforcement. The fear response is, to a large extent, controlled by the ANS. ANS activity can be estimated by use of peripheral indicants such as skin conductance.

A child who has an ANS that characteristically recovers very quickly from fear will receive a quick and large reinforcement for inhibiting the aggression response and will learn inhibition quickly. If he has an ANS that recovers very slowly, he will receive a delayed, small reinforcement and will learn to inhibit aggression slowly, if at all. This perspective would predict that (holding constant family training, critical variables such as social status, criminal associations, poverty level, and similar factors), many of those who commit antisocial acts should be characterized by slow autonomic recovery. The slower the recovery, the less the learned inhibition and the more serious and repetitive the antisocial behavior predicted.

Skin Conductance Recovery

There was little precedent for measuring skin conductance recovery when in 1962 we began examining its functioning characteristics (Mednick and

Schulsinger, 1964). It was a critical element in a theory of inhibition learning in schizophrenia (Mednick, 1962, 1974). We examined 104 normal adolescents (controls for children at high risk for schizophrenia) with a variety of assessment devices including skin conductance. The seven adolescents (of the 104) who later were registered for mild delinquent acts had a distinctly and significantly slower rate of skin conductance recovery than their controls.

Siddle et al. (1973) examined skin conductance responsiveness of 67 English Borstal inmates, divided into high, medium, and low antisocial groups. When Siddle learned of the recovery hypothesis, described above, he rescored his data for skin conductance recovery; speed and rate of recovery varied inversely as a function of antisocial behavior levels. Recovery measured on a single trial was surprisingly effective in differentiating the three groups (Siddle et al., 1977). Bader-Bartfai and Schalling (1974) also reanalyzed skin conductance data from a previous investigation of criminals, finding that criminals who tended to be more "delinquent" on a personality measure tended to have a slower recovery. Hare (1975) reports slow recovery (for a novel tone) for psychopaths among prison inmates. There have been other supportive findings reported (Hemming, 1977; Hinton et al., 1977; Eisenburg, 1976; Plovnick, 1976; Waid, 1976). Hare, Cox, and Frazelle (forthcoming) and Hare, Frazelle, and Cox (1978) found that prison psychopaths evidence slow recovery both in anticipation of a loud noise (120 decibels) and to the noise itself. Lidberg et al. (1977) and Bader-Bartfai and Schalling (1974) report slow skin conductance recovery in psychopathic criminals and delinquents.

Hare's studies find that the psychopaths from prison populations evidence slow ANS recovery under extreme stimulus conditions. In one study he compared prisoners with college students. There are serious difficulties of interpretation in such comparisons but it is nevertheless interesting that the students' average recovery speed was more than twice that of the prisoners.

> Thus, while it may be possible to differentiate between psychopathic and nonpsychopathic inmates in terms of electrodermal recovery to intense stimuli, it may be easier to differentiate between criminals and noncriminals or between groups who show marked differences in asocial behavior [Hare, 1978a: 128].

In 1964, Hare examined skin conductance in prisoners (all in a maximum security prison). Ten years later he checked to see how seriously recidivistic the prisoners subsequently became. Skin conductance recovery in 1964 was used to predict the degree of recidivism. As might be expected, the extent of the relationship between skin conductance and recidivism within this group composed exclusively of serious offenders is not great ($r = .24$, $p < .05$, one-tailed test). Interestingly enough, a small group of the slowest recoverers was almost entirely composed of individuals repeatedly convicted of fraud (Hare, 1978a).

This attempt to link specific antecedents with specific types of offender characteristics is a research mode worth emulating.

The theory assumes that skin conductance recovery is mediated by central ANS processes. Bundy (1977) has argued that recovery is *not* mediated by central ANS processes. He suggests that recovery reflects peripheral sweat-gland activity. In a recent report, Levander et al. (1980) present evidence relevant to this point; their results suggest that recovery is, in large part, mediated by central processes of the ANS.

The relationship between slow recovery and antisocial behavior seems rather robust across national boundaries, experimental procedures, and definitions of "antisocial." There are small prospective studies (which gain some credence from the cross-sectional findings) that do not contradict the hypothesis.

Siddle (1977: 206-207), in a recent review, states:

> The results concerning skin conductance recovery and antisocial behavior appear to be quite consistent. Subjects who display antisocial behavior (psychopaths, adult criminals and adolescent delinquents) also display significantly slower SCR recovery than do matched controls.

Some semicontradictory evidence has come from Hare's experiments. Hare finds reliable differences only between his psychopathic, serious criminals and nonpsychopathic serious criminals under specific (usually, in some way, extreme) stimulus conditions. As he himself suggests, the minitheory described above relates only to moral training and subsequent law abidance. The theory is not confounded by the discovery that it is difficult to observe recovery differences between two groups that have exhibited behavior reflecting somewhat negatively on the adequacy of their moral training. In addition, Hare has only reported on recovery. Within such prisoner groups it would be wise also to examine ANS responsiveness (another critical aspect of the theory).

Quite a number of studies have tested the hypothesis that antisocial behavior is associated with slow ANS recovery. Not one study unequivocally refutes this hypothesis. There are tentative indications from two *prospective* studies that slow ANS recovery precedes the onset of recorded delinquency and predicts recidivism. Consequently, slow ANS recovery must be included among the factors that may be etiologically related to antisocial behavior.

Conditioning Studies Using Punishment

The classic research in the field of ANS factors in antisocial behavior is the 1957 study by Lykken. In the Lykken task, one type of maze error caused a red light to flash, thus indicating to the subject that he had made a mistake; another type of maze error subjected the subject to an unpleasant electric shock. Antisocial individuals as well as controls learned to negotiate the push button maze to avoid the red light. The controls quickly learned to avoid the buttons, which resulted in shock. The antisocial individuals showed little evidence of learning to avoid the shock button.

Schachter and Latané (1964) and Schmauk (1970) replicated the Lykken findings. Schmauk's study demonstrated that the psychopath has normal ability to learn with positive reinforcement (rewards). When shock or social censure (i.e., punishment) was involved, the psychopath evidenced relatively poor skin conductance conditioning. In other words the psychopath's deficiency is most apparent where an ANS response is needed to mediate learning. This result has been observed by several investigators (Hare, 1970; Hare and Quinn, 1971; Rosen and Schalling, 1971; Schoenherr, 1964). The Loeb and Mednick (1977) *prospective* study also found that those boys who later became delinquent evidenced poor skin conductance conditioning to noxious stimuli.

Several explanations for the psychopath's deficit in ANS-mediated learning have been mentioned in the literature. It is known, for example, that conditioning of skin conductance response is facilitated if the subject is consciously aware that the conditioned stimulus tone will be followed by an electric shock. (Dawson, 1973; Dawson and Faredy, 1976.) It has been argued that the psychopath is simply not able to verbalize this contingency. Studies by Syndulko et al. (1975) and Ziskind et al. (1978), however, indicate that even when the psychopaths were clearly aware of the contingencies and could verbalize them, they still evidenced a deficit in skin conductance conditioning.

It has also been suggested that the psychopaths are at such a low level of arousal that they are unable to condition. It is not clear why this low arousal level does not affect learning involving positive reinforcement. In support of this interpretation, Schachter (1971) has demonstrated that imprisoned psychopaths who evidence poor skin conductance conditioning will show normal conditioning under the influence of an injection of adrenaline. The adrenaline will of course increase the subject's state of ANS arousal. Hare (1973) has offered some cogent criticisms of the basis of this study. Chesno and Kilman (1975) noted that psychopaths who evidence poor ANS conditioning under low-background-noise stimulation will learn normally under high-background-noise stimulation. Background noise increases level of ANS arousal. Allen et al. (1976) reasoned that if the delinquent's problem is low ANS arousal, perhaps recidivism would be decreased by administration of a drug that would increase arousal. They report that a pilot trial with subjects seemed exceptionally promising.

The antisocial individual evidences relatively poor skin conductance conditioning. This finding is reliable and not contradicted. In discussions of this literature there has been a tendency to imply that the psychopath simply cannot learn an ANS-conditioned response. Perhaps it would be more accurate to say that at a given level of aversive stimulation (noise or electric shock), the antisocial individual evidences a deficit in ANS conditioning. This deficit has generated hypotheses regarding the etiology of a failure in moral learning. It also suggests that if rehabilitation or prevention programs are contemplated, consideration should be given to arousal manipulations to improve emotional learning.

Skin Conductance and Violence

Most investigators who have published research on skin conductance and antisocial behavior have not been overly concerned with subtypes of offenders (such as the violent offender). As mentioned above, an exception is Robert Hare. He has consistently seriously attempted to devise procedures for distinguishing the Cleckley-type psychopaths from the remainder of the prison population studies. The psychopath he identifies he classes among the most recidivistic and violent of the prison population. His skin conductance reports (Hare et al., 1980, 1978) describe the psychopath as having reduced skin conductance responsiveness. This is especially true in the case of spontaneous fluctuations. They also evidence slow recovery of their response to a noxious stimulus. Fox and Lippert (1963) also report fewer spontaneous fluctuations for violent criminals than for nonviolent criminals. Kotses et al. (1977) also report that the violent criminal was less autonomically responsive than nonviolent criminals. Both groups were less responsive than the prison guards. Aniskiewicz (1973) found that "criminal sexual psychopaths evidenced reduced skin conductance responsiveness in a conditioning paradigm compared to 'secondary psychopaths'" or normal controls.

There is one prospective study that is relevant but that studied another peripheral indicant of ANS activity, pulse rate. The study concerned the delinquents in a "sample of 5,362 single-born, legitimate, live births drawn from all 13,687 births occurring between March 3 and 9 in England, Wales and Scotland" in 1946 (Wadsworth, 1976). This classic longitudinal birth cohort study was begun by Douglas (Douglas and Blomfield, 1958). Wadsworth (1975) described the cumulative officially recorded delinquency in this birth cohort at 21 years of age, and then examined the relationship of this delinquency to a predelinquency measure of ANS response to anticipation of stress. The survey members were subjected to a school medical examination at age 11. The period during which they waited for this examination was designed to be somewhat stressful. Their pulse rates were measured to assess the effects of this anticipation. Delinquents were defined as those who "either made a court appearance or were formally cautioned by the police between the ages of 8 and 21 years" (1975: 249). Those who were *later* registered as delinquents had a lower anticipatory pulse rate. The delinquent-nondelinquent differences were significant for those committing indictable offenses and sexual and violent offenses.

The Wadsworth study is important because it is based on a large, national birth cohort and the results must be seen as representative. The data on pulse rate were gathered by hundreds of different physicians in different schools using rather primitive methods. Not all of these measurements were equally accurately taken. About ten years intervened between the recording of the pulse rates and the ascertainment of the sexual and violent offenses. The hypothesized results emerged despite these conditions—which in most research do not tend to inflate positive findings. The violent individuals evidenced a low level of emotional, ANS, physiologically measured anticipation of an aversive experience. Those who did not suffer anticipatory "fear" before the examination were those boys who later were more likely to become delinquent. Perhaps this anticipatory fear was also lacking before they committed the act (or acts) that placed them in the delinquent group.

One other feature of the Wadsworth study warrants emphasis. The low anticipatory pulse rate was observed ten years before the delinquency was assessed. It is unlikely that the delinquency experience produced the low pulse rate. The prospective nature of the study establishes low pulse rate in anticipation of stress as a variable worthy of consideration as a potential etiological factor in delinquency.

How salient a predictive factor is pulse rate? Not very. In the Wadsworth study it predicts delinquency about as well as the "broken home" variable. It is naive to expect that any variable alone (whether biological or social) will explain large amounts of delinquency variance. Delinquency is likely to be as complex in its causation as it is in its manifestation.

At the beginning of this chapter we presented some information on the epidemiology of violence. The data suggested the existence of two types of offenders. One type tends to commit offenses against strangers in the context of crimes for gain. The other type commits violence against family and friends. Interestingly enough, a team of English investigators found that a group of violent criminals (patients in a maximum-security hospital) divided themselves nicely into these two categories. "A 'high public risk' group was chosen on the following combined criteria: (a) at least one offense against strangers, (b) five or more different types of crime, and (c) at least one crime of acquisition. A 'low risk' group was selected on the following criteria: (a) offense only against a person well known to the offender, (b) no more than two types of crime recorded, and (c) no crimes of acquisition." Those judged to be in the high public risk group evidenced a markedly low skin conductance recovery and few spontaneous fluctuations (Hinton et al., 1980).

This study has small numbers of subjects but is an independent replication of an earlier study (Hinton and O'Neill, 1978). The method of dividing the violent offenders into subgroups follows nicely from research on the epidemiology of violent behavior. The offender who commits violent offenses in the context of crime for gain resembles (autonomically) the recidivistic property offender. These individuals commit the bulk of the violent offenses; hence they represent an important threat to organized civilized existence. Hinton et al. (1980) present evidence to suggest that many of the family-violence individuals Wadsworth studied may be suffering from serious mental illness in contrast to the crime-for-gain type of violent offenders.

NEUROPHYSIOLOGICAL STUDIES

A variety of assessment strategies have been used to examine central-nervous-system functioning in violent individuals. Many of these studies are based on electroencephalographic (EEG) evaluation of central-nervous-system functioning. This aspect of brain activity has generated considerable research as related to violence. In addition to providing a relatively simple method for evaluation of intact central-nervous-system activity, the EEG provides reliable and culture-free assessment of function.

Electroencephalographic Features

Since some of the research reviewed in this report relies on electroencephalographic findings, a brief presentation of facts concerning the EEG is in order. Electrochemical processes in the living brain produce periodic voltage oscillations that can be detected by recording from the scalp in humans. The detected brain activity is described in terms of its amplitude (size) and its frequency (rhythmicity). EEG amplitudes are generally 20-100 microvolts (1/1000 of a volt). Frequency of EEG activity usually discussed in current literature ranges between .5 and 40 Hz (cycles per second). For descriptive convenience, the frequency range is, by convention, classified according to the following scheme: delta, .5-3 Hz; theta, 4-7 Hz; alpha, 8-12 Hz; beta, 13-40 Hz (Kooi et al., 1978).

The occurrence and amplitudes of activity within these frequency ranges are known to be dependent on characteristics of the subject (such as age and sex) as well as behavioral state (asleep or awake). Clinically, EEG evaluation has proven most useful in the diagnosis of epilepsy (Kooi et al., 1978). Much current research is directed toward elucidating associations between EEGs, subject characteristics, and behavioral states. Current research is also under way to discover the specific relationship between EEG and neuronal activity.

EEG records can be evaluated in two ways. First, they can be inspected visually by an electroencephalographer and rated according to some classification scheme. Usually, such ratings result in EEG records being classified as normal, abnormal, or "borderline." Second, EEGs can be quantitatively analyzed, typically by computers. Such a procedure results in a set of parameters with numeric descriptors that can be used for direct comparison of EEGs. These two methods of analyses are complementary.

Quantitative computer analysis is not as effective as the human eye in detection of aberrant wave complexes (as are found in epilepsy). Estimates generated by quantitative computer analysis of EEG parameters (e.g., of wave frequency and amplitude) are more precise than is possible by qualitative evaluation.

Prevalence of EEG Abnormality Among Violent Individuals

Research has been conducted to establish prevalence of EEG abnormalities in violent individuals. For this purpose, visual ratings have been widely used for EEG evaluations; quantitative computer EEG analyses have rarely been reported.

The earliest reports are based on studies of murderers (Hill and Pond, 1952), and subsequent studies provide estimates of EEG abnormalities in violent prisoners (Okasha et al., 1975; Sayed et al., 1969; Winkler and Kove, 1962). Hill and Pond (1952) report about half of 105 murderers had EEG abnormalities. Sayed et al. (1969) examined 32 murderers and reported that 65 percent of their EEGs were abnormal. Winkler and Kove (1962) studied 55 persons convicted of manslaughter or murder and reported 24 percent had EEG abnormalities.

More recent reports have not limited the scope of study to murderers. Williams (1969) studied 333 persons incarcerated for crimes of violence and reports that about half exhibited EEG abnormalities. Bach-y-Rita et al. (1971) also report that approximately half of 79 outpatients who were having difficulty controlling their violent tendencies were characterized by EEG abnormalities. Mark and Ervin (1970) reviewed EEGs of over 400 violent adult prisoners and reported approximately one-third were abnormal. These results suggest that the prevalence of EEG abnormalities in violent individuals ranges from 25 to 50 percent. Qualitative evaluation of EEG abnormalities among normal populations ranges from 5 to 20 percent (Kooi et al., 1978).

Two studies have reported much lower incidences of EEG abnormalities among violent individuals. Riley (1979) found 6.7 percent EEG abnormalities among a group of 212 violent individuals referred for outpatient treatment for violent behavior and episodes of rage. Riley's low percentage may be related to the fact that he screened out subjects with any neurological history. Knott et al. (1975) report that only 4 percent of 73 persons accused of murder evidenced EEG abnormality. It is not clear why Knott et al. (1975) report discrepant results.

Specific EEG Features

Subgroups of violent individuals can be based on degree of violence or according to frequency of past aggressive behaviors. Early results (Levy and Kennard, 1953; Arthurs and Cahoon, 1964) did not suggest estimates of EEG abnormalities differ for more as compared to less violent individuals. However, when subgroups of violent individuals are formed on the basis of frequency of aggressive activity, a slightly different picture emerges. In these studies, recidivist aggressors are compared to persons who have committed only one or two violent acts. Williams (1969) reports that EEG abnormalities are four times as great in habitual aggressors. Neziroglu (1979) found that rates of EEG abnormalities were twice as high in a habitual aggressive group. Monroe et al. (1977) cite evidence that 88 percent of recidivist adolescent aggressors exhibit EEG abnormalities.

Findings that recidivist aggressors have higher rates of EEG abnormalities suggest underlying organic dysfunction. Two specific types of EEG abnormalities have been identified. The EEG may be characterized by an excess of slow activity (usually in the theta range) or an excess of fast activity (in the beta range).

Hill (1952) noted that approximately half of the psychopaths who persistently commit aggressive acts have increased theta in their EEGs. Williams (1969) also reported that 80 percent of 333 violent prisoners exhibited excess slow activity in the theta band. Hill (1952) as well as others (Monroe, 1970; Williams, 1969) have interpreted this EEG slowing to reflect a maturational lag in cerebral development. Hare (1978b) has offered an alternative to the maturational lag hypothesis in accounting for increased theta activity. Hare suggests increased EEG theta may reflect a low level of cortical excitability and tendency to drowsiness during rather dull experimental settings.

Blackburn (1975) provides evidence relevant to these hypotheses. Quantitative EEG analysis was used to compare theta and alpha activity of 80 subjects divided into two groups based on frequency of assaultive behavior. There were no statistically significant differences in amounts of theta or alpha activity that distinguished more from less habitual aggressors. However, when exposed to a painful stimulus, habitual aggressors manifested greater reductions in alpha activity, indicating a *greater* arousal.

It is certainly conceivable that subgroups of violent individuals may be characterized by different EEG features. Lorimer (1972) studied violent individuals and identified two subgroups. One subgroup was characterized by excess slow activity (6-8 Hz); the second subgroup was characterized by excess fast activity (beta, 30-40 Hz). Earlier reports do not comment on EEG beta (Blackburn, 1975; Hill, 1952; Monroe, 1978). It is difficult, therefore, to assess the likelihood that slow (theta) and fast (beta) activity characterize distinct subgroups of violent individuals. The possible association of specific EEG features to subgroups of violent individuals deserves more rigorous attention, particularly by quantitative EEG assessment.

Two additional EEG patterns have frequently been associated with violent behavior. These syndromes are 14-and-6 spikes and temporal lobe epilepsy.

The 14-and-6 EEG Pattern

An EEG wave form characterized by a fast spike followed by a slow wave is termed a 14-6 pattern. Perhaps early reports of this EEG pattern in bizarre murderers (Schwade and Geiger, 1960) promoted association of the 14-6 pattern and violence. Schwade and Geiger reviewed findings in over 1,000 children and adolescents, and report that the majority of those who behaved violently also display the 14-6 pattern. However, in view of the high prevalence of this pattern in normal children (20 percent; Gibbs and Gibbs, 1964), it seems unlikely that the 14-6 pattern is specifically related to violence.

Temporal-Lobe Epilepsy

Probably the EEG syndrome most extensively investigated with regard to violence is temporal-lobe epilepsy (also known as psychomotor seizures). Probably the earliest link to violence appeared in a description of an individual case: a male who had committed an unmotivated murder had paroxysmal EEG features (Hill and Sargant, 1943). Since that time, much evidence has been collected toward clarifying the association between psychomotor seizures and violence.

Some reports examine the prevalence of temporal-lobe epilepsy in violent individuals. For example, Mark and Ervin (1970) report that temporal-lobe epilepsy is ten times higher in a sample of 400 violent adult prisoners than would be expected in the general population. Hill and Pond (1952) estimate that between 17 and 26 percent of their murderers were epileptic. Lewis (1976) reported that 72 percent of 78 violent juveniles experienced symptoms indicating psychomotor seizures. Bender (1959) reported 10 percent of juvenile murderers subsequently developed epilepsy. However, none of Sayed et al.'s (1969) 32 murderers was epileptic. Gunn and Bonn (1971) compared epileptic with nonepileptic prisoners and failed to obtain differences on the basis of their violent behaviors.

These findings are not entirely inconsistent with the notion that violence and temporal-lobe epilepsy are associated. The results suggest that perhaps this relationship could be clarified by examining the prevalence of violent behavior among temporal-lobe epileptics. However, this evidence is also equivocal in outcome. Falconer et al. (1958) report that 38 percent of temporal-lobe epileptics exhibit "pathological aggressiveness." Currie et al. (1971) report that 29 percent of the temporal-lobe epileptics they studied behaved aggressively. Among 100 children studied by Ounsted (1969), none of the 36 that demonstrated outbursts of rage received a diagnosis of temporal-lobe epilepsy. Rodin (1972) reviewed over 700 psychomotor-seizure patient's histories and identified only 5 percent who had committed aggressive acts.

No definitive conclusions for the association of temporal-lobe epilepsy to violence are possible, since the results of these studies are quite contradictory. There are two important methodological considerations that hamper investigation of this association. Diagnosis of temporal-lobe epilepsy (or psychomotor seizures) on the basis of EEG is complicated by the fact that paroxysmal discharge occurrences in the temporal region are not always accurately reflected in the scalp-recorded EEG record (Bach-y-Rita et al., 1970). Further complications arise because visual EEG assessments are not perfectly reliable (Sayed et al., 1969). At this point the relationship of temporal-lobe epilepsy to violence remains unresolved. The evidence has been interpreted both in support of the association (Pincus, 1980) and against it (Goldstein, 1974).

Activation Techniques

In order to increase the sensitivity of EEG as a measure of underlying brain dysfunction, activation techniques to trigger EEG abnormalities can be used. Typical procedures designed to elicit abnormalities include administration of drugs, exposing subjects to flashing lights, and asking subjects to breathe deeply or go to sleep.

EEG recordings subsequent to specific drug administration have been evaluated in violent individuals. Kido (1973) studied 186 male juvenile delinquents. The subjects were classified into groups on the basis of criteria such as the number of times they had been detained and whether they had committed murder or physical assault that resulted in death. Pentamethylenetetrazol (PMT) or diphenehydramine (Diph) were administered intravenously to trigger possible EEG abnormalities. Individuals in the group of subjects with the most recidivistic tendencies and the group of subjects who had committed murder exhibited the most vulnerability to these drugs. None of the subjects in the group that had committed physical violence resulting in death manifested sensitivity to these drugs. These results provide support for the notion that quite different subgroups of violent individuals may be identified.

Monroe (1970) reviews evidence that another pharmacological agent, alpha chloralose, induces EEG abnormalities in many epileptics and in patients with histories of neurologic disease or head trauma. Alpha chloralose is considered an experimental drug by the FDA, which may explain the paucity of research with this drug. The most obvious side effects are certain types of seizures.

Monroe (1978) administered alpha chloralose to 93 male prisoners. Most were convicted of aggressive crimes at least six times. Each subject underwent EEG testing twice. Between 40 and 49 percent abnormal EEGs were obtained on the basis of routine EEG assessments, which included sleep and hyperventilation as activators. However, when alpha chloralose was administered, detection of EEG abnormalities increased to approximately 82-88 percent. This result demonstrates the potential utility of alpha chloralose as a routine activator, especially in assessment of potentially violent behavior. It should be noted that approximately 15 percent of normal individuals demonstrate EEG abnormalities after alpha chloralose (Monroe, 1978).

Kido's (1973) report indicates that PMT and Diph are effective activators in juvenile males, especially those with violent and recidivistic tendencies. Monroe's (1978) results demonstrate the potential utility of including alpha chloralose activation in EEG assessment of violent male offenders. The use of these activators in the study of the EEG of violent offenders seems promising.

We shall defer consideration of the implications of these neurophysiological findings. We shall first discuss the results of the neuropsychological examination of violent individuals.

Prospective EEG Research

Prospective studies that examine features of brain functioning as potential predictors of criminality are few. To our knowledge, only two such studies have been conducted. The incidence of violent behavior is low in both reports.

Subjects examined in the first study were drawn from a Danish birth cohort. The cohort consists of all children born between 1 September 1959 and 31 December 1961 at Rigshospitalet in Copenhagen, Denmark (Mednick et al., 1981). During 1971-1972, a prospective study of delinquency was initiated, and EEG measures on 265 Danish children (aged 11-13 years) were obtained. By 1978, many of these 265 children had been arrested for a variety of offenses. (The Danish Police Register maintains official records of individuals apprehended for criminal behavior.) In this way, the EEG measures obtained in 1971-1972 could be examined in relation to a child's delinquency status in 1978.

Each subject was classified into one of three groups: noncriminal (no official contacts with police), one-time offender, or multiple offender. Only males were included (N = 129). These three groups were then compared on the basis of EEG measures in the delta, theta, alpha, and beta frequency bands.

Statistical analyses revealed that future multiple offenders (especially thieves) exhibited slower alpha frequencies (8.0-10.0 Hz) than either noncriminals or one-time offenders (Mednick et al., 1981). Of the 129 boys examined, 72 were selected because they had psychiatrically disturbed parents and thus an elevated risk of delinquent behavior. In order to "remove" the influence of the parents' psychiatric condition, statistical analyses were undertaken separately for the 57 normal male controls included in this investigation. The results of these analyses indicate that slow alpha affords greater predictability of delinquent behavior among normals than among boys with psychiatric involvement. Delinquent offenses committed by psychiatrically deviant boys may tend to be an expression of their psychiatric problems rather than an indicant of persistent antisocial tendencies.

Our finding that slow alpha characteristics may predict criminal behavior was replicated by a similar analysis on an independent sample in Sweden

(Petersen et al., in progress). In 1967, EEG measures on 571 healthy Swedes (aged 1-21 years) were obtained. In 1980, 22 recidivistic criminal offenders were identified by access to the Swedish National Police Register. The registered offenses for which these 22 persons had been apprehended consisted chiefly of thievery. EEG characteristics of the 22 multiple offenders were compared to age-matched controls. In 1967, average alpha frequency was lower among multiple offenders (9.07 Hz) than among noncriminals (9.25 Hz). Certain EEG abnormalities (e.g., paroxysms during sleep) were also more prevalent among multiple offenders. These results indicate that deviance, such as slow alpha, characterizes persons *before* they begin criminal behaviors. Some subgroup of violent offenders comprises recidivistic property offenders; this fact suggests that EEG evaluations may be useful measures in prospective studies of violent offenders.

NEUROPSYCHOLOGICAL EVIDENCE

Neuropsychological test results allow inferences relevant to localization and lateralization of brain dysfunction. The reliability and validity of various neuropsychological test batteries have been demonstrated in the identification of specific types of organic brain impairment (Filskov and Goldstein, 1974). The agreement in diagnosis of neuropsychological test results and more conventional neurological techniques is quite high (Filskov and Goldstein, 1974; Schrieber et al., 1976).

Localized Dysfunctions

Spellacy (1977, 1978) assessed neuropsychological functioning in violent and nonviolent juvenile and adult males. Performance by violent patients was poorer on approximately two-thirds of 31 test variables. Berman (1978) reports impairments of verbal, perceptual, and nonverbal functioning indicative of neuropsychological deficiency among violent males.

Yeudall (1977) provides neuropsychological test results for various criminal groups classified according to their past offenses. Discriminant function analyses were used to distinguish criminal subtypes from controls. Thirty neuropsychological test measures were used to compare psychopaths to controls (sample sizes for different analyses varied, but were generally 25 subjects per group). Approximately 91 percent of psychopaths exhibited significant neuropsychological dysfunction. Neuropsychological abnormalities were detected in 94 percent of those convicted of homicide, 87 percent of those convicted of physical assault, and 100 percent of those convicted of rape. The results have not yet been replicated. Performance deficits exhibited by psychopaths suggest frontal and temporal brain area dysfunction.

Although conventional EEG studies do not typically include neuropsychological evaluations, many tabulate information pertaining to localization of EEG abnormalities. The EEG localization results may be profitably compared to neuropsychological assessment results. Williams (1969) reports that about 80 percent of all EEG abnormalities detected were localized to anterior (frontal and temporal) brain regions. Bach-y-Rita et al. (1971) report that 20-37 percent exhibit abnormalities localized to temporal regions. Although EEG abnormalities in other brain regions are also identified, the majority of findings implicate frontotemporal brain dysfunction in violent individuals (Blumer et al., 1974; Hill and Pond, 1952).

Yeudall (1977) thinks that, by utilizing neuropsychological test findings, four types of criminals can be identified:

(1) those with temporal-limbic dysfunction
(2) those with dorsal-lateral frontal lobe impairments
(3) those with frontal-limbic dysfunction
(4) those with neocortical dysfunction

The means for identification and behavioral concommitants distinguishing these four neuroanatomical groups from one another are not entirely clear; however, Yeudall (1977) does explicate some behavioral deficits likely to characterize two groups.

Criminals with dorsal-lateral impairments of frontal lobes should exhibit deficiencies in concentration, abstract ability, and use of language. The frontal-limbic criminal is, according to Yeudall, characterized by a proclivity to engage in psychopathic behavior, is prone to affective disturbances, hypersexuality, and increased aggression, and may manifest extreme sensitivity to alcohol.

Lateralized Deficits

Studies in the difference of functioning of the left and right brain hemispheres have provoked efforts to identify a lateralized focus for brain dysfunction in violent individuals. Flor-Henry (1979) proposes a theory relating psychopathology to lateral dysfunction. According to Flor-Henry, psychopaths (and schizophrenics) suffer from irregularities of the dominant (left, in most right-handed individuals) hemisphere. Yeudall and Flor-Henry (1975) studied neuropsychological profiles of 25 aggressive psychopaths. Of the 25, 15 exhibited impairments and the majority of these suggest deficits localized in the dominant frontal-temporal region. Further attempts to establish a relationship between violent behavior and lateral dysfunction have been more equivocal (Andrew, 1980; Fitzhugh, 1973; Hare, forthcoming). Krynicki (1978) compared six adolescents suffering from organic brain impairments to eight who had committed assault. These subjects' neuropsychological test performances were quite similar; both groups exhibited deteriorated performance in two tasks lateralized to the left hemisphere. It has also been reported that delinquents and criminals tend to be left-handed more frequently than controls (Gabrielli and Mednick, 1980). Such results are compatible with Flor-Henry's hypothesis.

The neuropsychological evidence suggests the hypothesis that violent individuals predominantly suffer impairment of frontal and temporal brain regions. Dysfunction in these brain regions (especially in the frontal lobes) is associated with impaired self-control and inability to comprehend the consequences of one's own actions (Pincus and Tucker, 1978). These characteristics are compatible with our expectations regarding violent individuals.

IMPLICATIONS OF NEUROPSYCHOLOGICAL AND NEUROPHYSIOLOGICAL STUDIES

The evidence reviewed indicates that some violent individuals are characterized by abnormal EEGs and neuropsychological test profiles.

(1) The majority of EEG evidence indicates that some violent individuals are cortically underaroused, or suffer from a maturational lag in cerebral development, as demonstrated by excessively slow EEG activity (Hill and Pond, 1952; Monroe, 1978; Williams, 1969).

(2) Aggressive individuals exhibit impaired neuropsychological performance in a variety of tasks (Berman, 1978; Spellacy, 1977, 1978).

(3) Among violent individuals, dysfunction involving anterior brain regions is implicated by both EEG (Williams, 1969) and neuropsychological findings (Yeudall, 1977).

Though less definitive, the evidence reviewed also suggests that

(1) some subgroup of violent individuals may be cortically "overaroused," as demonstrated by excessive EEG beta (Lorimer, 1972); and

(2) neuropsychological test-performance deficits imply dominant hemisphere dysfunction (Yeudall, 1977; Flor-Henry, 1979).

Head Injury

Estimates of elevated abnormal neurologic histories among violent individuals are consistently rather high. Yeudall (1977) reports that over 70 percent of aggressive individuals examined had a history of head injury. In two separate reports, Bach-y-Rita et al. (1971, 1974) provide evidence that over half those examined had experienced loss of consciousness due to illness or injury. Approximately 75 percent of 400 violent adult prisoners studied by Mark and Ervin (1970) had histories that included loss of consciousness from head injury.

Additional studies provide comparable estimates of past injuries or illnesses likely to affect central-nervous-system functioning among violent individuals (Lidberg, 1971; Lorimer, 1972). It should be noted that closed cerebral injury may specifically affect anterior and temporal brain regions (Ommaya and Gennarelli, 1976).

Perinatal Factors in Violence

Damage to the brain has been suggested as a possible factor in the etiology of violence in several sections of this chapter. In view of the fact that aggressive behavior is a consistent pattern for some boys from early childhood, we might entertain the possibility that the brain damage occurs early in life. Perinatal difficulties could be an important source of such damage. We have examined this possibility in a longitudinal study of a birth cohort in Copenhagen, Denmark. The population (N = 9,125) consists of all children born at the University Hospital between September, 1959 and December, 1961. They form the cohort of a Danish perinatal project studying the long-term consequences of pregnancy, delivery, and neonatal difficulty. Their delinquency was ascertained in 1978. While the delinquents experienced poorer *social* conditions during their pregnancies, their medical, physical, and neurological progress in the pregnancy, delivery, neonatal period and at one year of age were *superior* to that of the nondelinquent. The more offenses with which an adolescent was credited, the better was his perinatal and one-year status. This finding is consistent with other data we have observed in longitudinal research.

When one examines the perinatal data for the Copenhagen delinquents who manifested violence, the picture changes somewhat. Like the other delinquents, they evidence poorer social conditions during pregnancy. But at one year of age, those individuals who have committed more than one violent offense have a significantly worse one-year physical status and worse neurological status. The most severe neurological problems are observed in those recidivistic violent offenders whose social conditions were more stable (parents married). This type of biosocial interaction has been observed before. Where the social experiences of an antisocial individual are not especially criminogenic, biological factors should be examined. The value of the biological factors is more limited in predicting antisocial behavior in individuals who have experienced criminogenic social conditions in their rearing.

These findings emphasize the likelihood that organic factors assume some role in the etiology of violence. However, not all violent individuals have sustained conditions likely to affect central-nervous-system (CNS) functioning, and not all exhibit EEG abnormalities. Such considerations highlight the importance of studying subtypes of violent individuals and interactions with social factors.

CLASSIFICATION OF VIOLENT OFFENDERS
BASED ON NEUROPHYSIOLOGICAL
AND NEUROPSYCHOLOGICAL FINDINGS

Monroe (1978) has attempted to devise a classification scheme for identifying types of violent offenders. The sample he studied and the scheme he used to identify subtypes of violent individuals are unique and will be briefly described. The prisoners he studied were quite homogeneous with respect to their criminal histories. The sample consisted of 93 adult male recidivists incarcerated for crimes of violence. Over 90 percent of the subjects had committed crimes that "resulted in at least work incapacity, incarceration or permanent damage to self or others." The most frequent types of crime committed were armed robbery, rape, assault, murder, and burglary.

Monroe used a two-dimensional classification system. One dimension comprised a measure of psychological impulse control (high or low). A second dimension was determined by amount of EEG theta activity (high or low). Since these two measures were not highly correlated (r = .14), Monroe was able to identify four types of violent individuals. Although the four groups did not differ substantially in the types of crimes they committed, marked behavioral tendencies distinguished these groups from one another.

Low Impulse Control

With Elevated EEG Theta. According to Monroe, it is likely that these individuals suffer organic brain dysfunction because the members of this group report medical histories likely to be detrimental to CNS functioning, such as birth trauma, head injuries, and excessive drug use. It is interesting that, behaviorally, this group of persons was aggressive and more sexually perverse than any other group, both in and out of prison.

With Lower EEG Theta. Although the behavior of these individuals was as aggressive as that of the first group, these persons lack medical histories suggesting neurological impairment. Behaviorally, this group was distinguished by their proclivity to exhibit neurotic symptoms.

High Impulse Control

With Elevated EEG Theta. The number and severity of psychiatric symptoms exhibited by these individuals exceeded those of any other group. Many had psychiatric histories, and evidenced very poor life adjustment. These persons appeared emotionally unresponsive and exhibited impaired judgment.

With Lower EEG Theta. According to the two-dimensional classification system, these individuals were essentially normal. They demonstrated some evidence of antisocial behavior but, overall, demonstrated less psychopathology than any other group.

The use of this classification scheme deserves further study in a broader sample of subjects with more varied criminal histories. Since their histories are so similar, it is not surprising that no consistent associations relating types of crimes to specific EEG and impulse-control measures emerged in this study. The classification scheme utilized was based purely on measures of individuals in this sample *relative* to the other members of this prison sample. If comparisons of these four groups to normal persons were obtained, we might find that all prisoners studied in this sample display elevations of EEG theta and impulse control, but that the prisoners differ in the degree of elevations in these measures.

Yeudall (1977) has also attempted to derive a classification scheme for categorizing types of criminal offenders. Yeudall thinks that ultimately he can identify four types of violent offenders, utilizing neuropsychological assessments. Monroe (1978) suggests a similarity relating two of Yeudall's "neuroanatomical" groups to two he describes.

Yeudall proposes that one group of criminals suffers from symptoms suggesting impairments of limbic projections to the frontal lobes. Monroe points out the basic behavioral similarities of these criminals to those with elevated EEG theta and poor impulse-control measures. Persons with limbic frontal-lobe impairments should, according to Yeudall, exhibit increased aggressive and sexual drives and poor impulse control. Yeudall also describes a second group of violent offenders, who are characterized by symptoms suggesting dorsal-lateral frontal-lobe impairments. Monroe points out that this group is behaviorally similar to persons characterized by adequate impulse control but elevated EEG theta. According to Yeudall, dorsal-lateral frontal-lobe dysfunction results in reduced abstract-reasoning ability, reduced concentration and motivation, and impaired ability to forsee consequences of actions. The foregoing descriptions are highly speculative insofar as the association between types of violent individuals and their behavioral tendencies are concerned. These speculations suggest three important issues subsequent research ought to address:

(1) Are those individuals who exhibit EEG abnormalities also those who demonstrate deficits in neuropsychological performance, or do these two assessment techniques identify different subgroups of violent individuals, some of whom exhibit EEG abnormalities, neuropsychological impairments, or both?

(2) Can the types of crimes committed be related to neuropsychophysiological functioning? How are types of criminal activity related to EEG findings?

(3) What proportions of those neuropsychologically impaired in the general population exhibit violent behavior? The answer to this question would require a popula-

tion study such as that reported above on the XYY violence issue (Witkin et al., 1977).

A careful consideration of previous research reports suggests to us two potential sources of bias that subsequent neuropsychophysiological research should attempt to avoid. First, quantitative EEG techniques may provide more reliable assessments of brain function than can be achieved by qualitative EEG evaluation; quantitative EEG methods should therefore be included in studies of violent individuals. Second, many of the subjects studied in these reports are drawn from prisons. The criteria for selection of these individuals is often not specified. The types of crimes for which these individuals were convicted are often not mentioned in the reports.

PHARMACOLOGICAL AND BIOCHEMICAL FACTORS IN VIOLENCE

In this section we shall review some exogenous and endogenous substances that may be related to violence. Among the exogenous substances we shall discuss are alcohol, amphetamines, phencyclidine, marijuana, and opiates. The endogenous substances include testosterone and glucose.

Alcohol

Alcohol is the substance for which a relation to violence has been demonstrated in extensive and long-term studies including large numbers of subjects. Reviews of that research are available (Tinklenberg, 1973; Moyer, 1976; Pernanen, 1976; Mendelson and Mello, 1979).

One of the best-known and largest studies is that of Wolfgang (1958), who analyzed 588 homicides and reported that the offender had been drinking just prior to the crime in 55 percent of the cases. Tinklenberg et al.(1974) studied drug involvement in criminal assaults by adolescents. In 23 of 56 assaults studied, the assailant was reported to be under the influence of alcohol (alone or in combination with other drugs). These thorough studies also exemplify a principal problem of this type of research: They rely only on reports of alcohol use rather than on measurements of alcohol levels in the blood. More direct evidence linking alcohol ingestion with crime was provided by Shupe (1954), who studied urine or blood samples obtained from suspects immediately after their arrests. Alcohol was detected in 144 of 163 suspects charged with violent crimes. This study also shows that the likelihood of arrest for violent crime under the influence of alcohol is an inverted-U-shaped function of the blood alcohol concentration (BAC). The likelihood increases from zero BAC up to 0.20-0.29 percent, and then decreases with increasing BAC. This goes along with the severe impairment of motor coordination at higher BAC; such impairment reduces the capability of the subject to cause bodily harm to others.

The usual dose-response relationships do not apply in cases of "pathological intoxication," which is characterized by an acute disruption of behavior (and sometimes violence) elicited by a small quantity of alcohol. The suddenness of the onset, disorientation, impairment of consciousness, and subsequent loss of memory of the attack make this phenomenon clinically similar to psychomotor epilepsy. Whether paroxysmal EEG discharges can be triggered in these cases by drinking alcohol is a controversial issue. It seems that persons prone to temporal-lobe dysfunction may be at high risk for EEG and clinical manifestations of pathological intoxication. The proneness to such dysfunction may be due, for example, to a head injury. A large collection of clinical cases supports this notion (Marinacci and Von Hagen, 1972).

Bach-y-Rita et al. (1970) studied ten men who received the diagnosis of pathological intoxication. None of these ten patients had a history of epilepsy. The experimenters administered alcohol intravenously while scalp EEG was being recorded, and no paroxysmal features were detected in any of the ten subjects. Two additional subjects were studied; both of them were known to have temporal-lobe epilepsy. EEGs in these two patients were recorded simultaneously from depth (amygdala), nasopharyngeal, and surface electrodes. Alcohol infusion increased the preexisting EEG abnormalities; this effect was most expressed in (but not limited to) the depth electrodes. In this experiment, pathological intoxication was not elicited in any of the twelve subjects. This study therefore cannot provide any answer to the question of possible epileptiform mechanisms of pathological intoxication. The most interesting implication of these observations is that internal and external cues (perhaps alcohol taste and a social setting) may be needed to trigger the syndrome of pathological intoxication.

It is not clear whether alcohol induces violent behavior directly or whether it acts primarily as a disinhibitor of preexisting aggressive tendencies. The latter hypothesis is perhaps supported by the notion that some perpetrators "drink for courage" prior to committing crimes against persons (Blumer, 1973). Wife-battering is accompanied by alcohol use in up to 93 percent of the cases Hilberman and Munson (1977-1978) studied, and it has been hypothesized that at least some of the batterers became intoxicated for the specific purpose of assaulting their wives. These issues are reviewed by Hilberman (1980).

Attempts to explain the relationship between alcohol and violence must therefore account for the expectation or even planning of the consequences of alcohol use by the user. Lang et al. (1975) demonstrated the important rule of expectancy for aggressive behavior in drinking situations. Some of Lang's subjects were told that they would receive alcohol; others were told that they would receive tonic. Half of each group was actually given alcohol and the other half was given tonic. Aggression was measured by the duration and intensity of shocks delivered by the experimental subjects to another person. Those subjects who expected to receive alcohol exhibited more aggression than those who expected tonic. The number and duration of shocks did not depend on whether alcohol was actually consumed.

The ingenious experimental study we have just reviewed set up the victim as a passive recipient of punishment. In real life, the victims interact with the aggressors. The study of such interactions is difficult and is further complicated by the fact that a proportion of victims are found to have been drinking prior to becoming targets of violence (Pernanen, 1976: 361-362).

No available study provides proof that alcohol ingestion alone elicits violent behavior. In Shupe's (1954) study, 88 percent of the suspects (144 of 163) used alcohol prior to the offense. However, how many law-abiding citizens of the same socioeconomic class, race, age, and sex also used alcohol at the same time of day? Alcohol use (or abuse) may be related to the same social or other environmental factors that cause the individual to engage in violent behavior.

Amphetamines

Chronic abusers of amphetamines frequently become irritable and suspicious. These features may range from mild uneasiness to a paranoid psychosis accompanied by outbursts of rage and counterattacks against imagined enemies. Violent behavior of amphetamine abusers was reported by Connel (1958), Angrist and Gershon (1969), and many others, as reviewed by Moyer (1976). Ellinwood (1971) reported histories of thirteen amphetamine abusers who committed homicide. In eight of these cases, the murderers acted under the influence of paranoid delusions. These subjects took unusually high doses of amphetamines before committing murder, but it is difficult to be sure how much time elapsed between the last dose of amphetamine and the murder. These murders may have taken place during an actual intoxication or in a period of drug withdrawal. Ellinwood concluded that amphetamine abusers move through several phases leading to a violent act. Chronic amphetamine abuse causes gradual personality change with paranoid thinking and fears. During this period the abuser frequently obtains a weapon. The next phase involves a sudden increase of amphetamine dosage, use of other drugs, and loss of sleep. Paranoid tendencies are suddenly expressed much more, and this results in increased anxiety. Under these conditions, a minor incident can trigger violence.

At the present time, we have no basis for an estimate of the relative importance of amphetamine abuse in violent behavior. Ellinwood's suggestion that every person arrested for a violent crime should have a urine test for drugs of abuse is certainly worthwhile.

Phencyclidine

Phencyclidine (PCP) is emerging as a major drug of abuse in the United States. Violent behavior may occur as a part of acute PCP toxicity (within three days after the administration) or during a PCP toxic psychosis, which may last several weeks (Smith, 1980). Fauman and Fauman (1979) summarized the relevant literature and presented case reports including a case of murder associated with chronic PCP abuse. The report exemplifies one of the main methodological problems of this type of research: All of the sixteen subjects were polydrug users and the man who committed murder drank beer and wine while injecting himself with PCP.

Many violent acts committed after the administration of PCP appear to be unmotivated, unprovoked, and gruesome. Some of the violence is self-directed. In the Fauman and Fauman (1979) study, twelve of the sixteen PCP users reported a history of PCP-related violence. We do not know how representative their subjects were of the population of PCP users. However, violence seems to be one of the hallmarks of the PCP effect.

Marijuana

There is a long history of allegations connecting marijuana and other cannabis preparations (e.g., hashish) with violent crime (Kaplan, 1970). Such allegations have been used to support the prohibition of marijuana. "How many murders, suicides, robberies, criminal assaults, holdups, burglaries, and deeds of maniacal insanity it causes . . . can only be conjectured," asserted Harry J. Anslinger, Commissioner of Narcotics, in 1937 (Kaplan, 1970: 89). We are still waiting to see the deeds of maniacal insanity caused by marijuana. The acute effect of marijuana on mood can be described as a "high" or as pleasant euphoria. Marijuana-smoking may elicit anxiety, particularly in higher doses (Volavka et al., 1973). However, feelings of hostility or overt aggression are not caused by marijuana under either experimental or "real-life" conditions. Criminal violence is not increased in chronic hashish users (Boulougouris et al., 1976).

Opioids

The notion that opioid (e.g., heroin) addiction is a major cause of violent crime is very popular. Opioids are seen as intrinsically criminogenic. We believe that the latter notion is untrue and that the former one is questionable.

More than 50 percent of heroin addicts have been arrested before they become addicted, but studies indicate a rise in the rate of *nondrug* arrests and self-reported criminality after the onset of addiction (Weissman et al., 1976). Comparisons of heroin addicts with nonaddict arrestees show that the addicts have a lower proportion of violent crimes against persons (and a higher proportion of property crimes) than the nonaddict arrestees (McGlothlin, 1979). These data do not necessarily mean that the heroin addicts are less likely to commit violent crimes than are nonaddict criminals. It is possible that they commit more of *both* types of crime. Definitive data on this problem are not yet available. There is a consensus that opioid addiction increases the frequency of crime in those individuals who use crime to support their heroin habits. This does not seem to apply to those addicts who are able to obtain drugs through legitimate channels and who have adequate funds; such persons may function reasonably well in social and occupational situations. Cutting (1942) described a physician who was functioning well both physically and mentally after 62 years of addiction. That opioid analgesics are not intrinsically criminogenic can be demonstrated by the example of methadone. Gearing and Schweitzer (1974) studied 17,500 patients who were maintained on methadone. The maintenance treatment was associated with a decrease in antisocial behavior and increased social productivity. It should be noted that heroin and methadone have very similar pharmacological effects. Both substances produce physical dependence, and a very unpleasant withdrawal syndrome develops when they are suddenly discontinued. Methadone has a longer duration of action than heroin and it produces less of a "high"; this difference is mainly due to the fact that it is given by mouth, whereas heroin is self-administered intravenously. However, the main difference is in the attitude of our society. Heroin is a "drug"; methadone is "medication." Heroin use is a disease; methadone use is a treatment. A heroin habit may cost several hundreds of dollars a day; methadone is free.

In contradistinction to alcohol, the acute administration of opiates does not increase aggressivity. An intravenous injection of heroin into an addict usually elicits mental clouding, euphoria, sedation, relaxation, talkativeness, and reduction of respiratory rate. We have administered heroin to ex-addicts on hundreds of occasions in our laboratory (Volavka et al., 1974, 1976, 1978) and have never observed increased hostility or aggression. If there was any effect in this respect, heroin made these persons more friendly.

The addicts' lives revolve around the drug in a cyclic fashion. The cycle of addiction starts when tolerance (and drug dosage) is increasing. This is followed by a plateau phase and then dose reduction with an attendant withdrawal syndrome. The dose is then increased again (or the drug is restarted), and the cycle goes on.

The withdrawal syndrome from opiates is unpleasant. The symptoms include loss of appetite, insomnia, fatigue, and irritability (Jaffe, 1975). The irritability in the withdrawal stage is frequently too pronounced to be explained as an epiphenomenon of physical discomfort. Workers in drug-abuse treatment programs are familiar with irritable, hostile, and sometimes aggressive clients in withdrawal. Occasionally, a psychotic episode accompanied by rage may develop. These manifestations disappear when opiates are administered.

An ex-addict schizophrenic patient who showed attacks of rage failed to respond to routine antipsychotic treatment; she improved dramatically on methadone (Berken et al., 1978).

Other Drugs

Barbiturates may elicit irritability, hostility, and overt aggression. Tinklenberg et al. (1974) reported on drug involvement in criminal assaults by adolescents. In all ethnic groups, alcohol and secobarbital, used alone or in combination with other drugs, were most often implicated in assaults. These adolescents overwhelmingly selected secobarbital as the drug most likely to enhance assaultive tendencies.

Benzodiazepines (marketed as Librium, for instance) usually reduce anxiety and hostility, but in some individuals they paradoxically increase hostility. The reaction is sometimes quite pronounced, and the term "paradoxical rage" has been used for it. This was reviewed by Moyer (1976).

Testosterone

Testosterone is the principal androgenic steroid hormone. Preliminary evidence suggests that its plasma levels and production rate may be related to criminal aggressive behavior in human males. Kreuz and Rose (1972) studied a sample of prisoners and reported that the plasma testosterone levels were higher in those men who had committed violent offenses than in the other men. Similar results were obtained by Rada et al. (1976), who classified rapists and child molesters according to the degree of violence manifested while committing their offenses. The more violent rapists had higher testosterone plasma levels than the less violent ones or the child molesters.

Various psychological tests purporting to measure aggression or hostility were administered to prisoners and nonprisoner control subjects, and the results of such tests were compared with the plasma testosterone levels. Some of these experiments suggested a positive relationship between aggressivity, hostility, and testosterone (Persky et al., 1971; Ehrenkranz et al., 1974). However, other studies did not confirm the existence of such a relationship (Kreuz and Rose, 1972; Meyer-Behlberg et al., 1974; Doering et al., 1975; Rada et al., 1976; Monti et al., 1977).

Hypoglycemia

Under normal conditions the plasma levels of glucose are maintained within a certain range (70-115 mg%, depending on the assay method). The brain is dependent on blood glucose for its energy supply. If the glucose in the blood decreases to an abnormally low level (that state is called hypoglycemia), brain function will be altered. Hypoglycemia may be induced by an injection of insulin; it develops during starvation; it may be a symptom of various (mostly endocrinological) diseases; and sometimes it occurs without any apparent cause. The initial effects of hypoglycemia include fatigue, irritability, aggressivity, and sometimes rage. Various types of criminal behavior may occur under the influence of hypoglycemia; this relationship was reviewed by Wilder (1947).

Hill and Sargant (1943) described a murderer whose EEG showed paroxysmal features only when he became hypoglycemic. It is well known that hypoglycemia may elicit a variety of other EEG abnormalities (Dawson and Greville, 1963). It is possible that hypoglycemia exerts some of its behavioral effects by means of the epilepsy-like mechanisms discussed in the preceding section on neurophysiology.

It is difficult to estimate the relative importance of hypoglycemia as a causative or contributory factor in the development of violent crime. There is no doubt that certain crimes occur under the partial influence of hypoglycemia, but there is little evidence that this biochemical abnormality represents a major threat to law and order.

Pharmacological and biochemical factors play a role in violence by several mechanisms. These involve the effects on drives, weakening of impulse control, generation of hostility and aggression, psychotic reactions, or drug-craving and withdrawal. There is no question that these factors do contribute to violence, but their importance (relative to social and other environmental factors) has yet to be established. No drugs or endogenous substances are intrinsically criminogenic; they elicit antisocial behavior in a set of cultural, social, and personal circumstances. Interactions between biochemical (or pharmacological) and socioeconomic factors are incompletely understood.

These complex interactions and their development in time cannot be explained successfully by only continuing and repeating cross-sectional or retrospective studies. Longitudinal prospective studies of drug use and delinquency (e.g., Johnston et al., 1978) represent a potentially fruitful avenue for future research.

TREATMENT

Pharmacological treatments and destruction of certain brain structures or regions are both strategies that have been employed in attempts to control violent behavior. The information gleaned from such research implicates the importance of brain functioning in violence.

Pharmacological Strategies

Phenytoin (Dilantin) is an anticonvulsant. It has been used in the treatment of various behavior disorders with mixed outcomes. Reductions in aggressive behavior subsequent to phenytoin administration have been reported for both men and women (Monroe and Wise, 1965; Pinto, 1975). Haward (1969) administered phenytoin to psychiatric patients and reported reductions in their aggressive behaviors. Maletsky (1973) reports reduced frequency and severity of outbursts in 19 of 22 violent subjects after phenytoin.

Another anticonvulsant, primidone, has been administered to aggressive persons (Dalby, 1971; Monroe, 1978). Preliminary research suggests that primidone is not particularly efficacious as a treatment for aggression; further research on its clinical utility seems warranted (Monroe, 1978). In general, neither antipsychotic nor anticonvulsant medications administered to aggressive persons who are not psychotic or epileptic are effective in controlling violent behavior (Goldstein, 1974).

Benzodiazepines include drugs such as diazepam (Valium) and chlordiazepoxide (Librium). These drugs are known to produce certain EEG effects. Rickels (1974) reports improvement in aggressive women after treatment with chlordiazepoxide (although, as mentioned in the previous section, these drugs can also precipitate "paradoxical rage").

Lithium has been widely used in the treatment of certain affective disorders. Lithium specifically affects aggressive and impulsive symptoms (Altschuler, 1977). In a literature review, Tupin (1972) reports that patients with recurrent aggressive symptoms respond to lithium.

Morrison and Minkoff (1975) administered tricyclic antidepressants to "explosive personality" subjects and obtained favorable responses. Morrison and Minkoff also suggest that the same brain defects responsible for explosive personality characterize hyperactivity in children. Since hyperactivity can be successfully treated by CNS stimulants (Shetty, 1971), it might be possible that aggressive individuals manifest "paradoxical" but favorable responses to these drugs. To our knowledge, such a strategy has not been tried.

There are reports that describe specific surgical or stimulation techniques to reduce aggressive behavior (Brown, 1977; Heath, 1977). However, the majority of research seems to be based on animal studies. Only studies with humans receive attention here.

Surgical Intervention

Brain surgery is a radical technique used in extreme cases where control of epileptic seizure is necessary or where good evidence exists that behavioral deviance (e.g., aggression or mental retardation) is directly the result of a circumscribed lesion. In certain of these surgical cases reported in the literature, mention is made of a reduction in aggressive behavior following the surgical procedure. In other cases the surgical procedure was instituted specifically to treat highly chronic aggressive and destructive behavior.

The results are of interest since if surgery in a specific brain region could have a dramatic effect on the likelihood of aggressive behavior, this finding would have relevance to biological theories of the origins of aggression. Because of its nature, this research is still in its infancy.

Surgical treatment of lesions of the amygdala and hypothalamus have yielded suggestive reductions in aggressive behavior (Mark and Ervin, 1970; Narabayashi, 1975; Schvarz et al., 1972). The results of surgical intervention in other brain areas have been mixed (Falconer, 1973; Kiloh, 1974; Ramamurthi, 1970; Vernet and Madsen, 1970).

CONCLUSIONS

We have reviewed the research literature linking biological factors to manifestations of criminality, especially violent behavior. The evidence suggests the following conclusions:

Genetic Factors

Sex-Chromosome Anomalies. Definitive research with a large representative population indicates that XYY men are not more likely to be involved in violent crime than are XY males. The evidence suggests that XYYs are, however, more likely to commit nonviolent criminal offenses.

Genetic Transmission. Evidence exists for genetic transmission of biological characteristics that predispose individuals to criminal behavior; the evidence with respect to violent behavior must be considered inconclusive. Due to the infrequent incidence of violence reported by authors of twin and adoption studies of criminality, this evidence does not permit conclusions to be drawn.

Sex Differences

Males are much more likely to commit crimes of violence than are females; similarly, boys are much more likely to behave aggressively than girls, even under the age of 6 years. These data have suggested the hypothesis that male-female differences in aggression may be related to biological as well as social determinants. Research findings suggest that testosterone levels may explain some of the male-female differences in aggression.

Autonomic Nervous System

There are a large number of reliable reports that recidivistic criminals exhibit diminished autonomic-nervous-system responsiveness. Violent individuals whose violence appears in the context of a career of property crimes tend to share this characteristic of ANS insensivity. Some research suggests that those whose violence appears within contexts involving family and friends may be quite different in their ANS response patterns.

Neurophysiological Features

A high prevalence of EEG abnormalities exists among persons convicted of violent crimes; this is especially true of recidivistic offenders. Violent criminals also exhibit impaired neuropsychological performance indicative of brain dysfunction. Both of those research leads implicate anterior brain regions. What is needed at this point is a study of brain dysfunction (neuropsychological and EEG) in a total population in order to determine whether those individuals exhibit an increased probability of violent behavior.

The study of elicited brain activity may also prove useful in diagnosis and detection of violent persons. For example, Monroe used the drug alpha chloralose as an EEG activator. This technique elicited more EEG abnormalities among violent criminals, but controls did not exhibit more EEG abnormalities after drug use.

Drugs and Alcohol

Opiate and marijuana ingestion is not associated with violent behavior. Syndromes of irritability and aggressiveness, however, are part of the consequences of opiate withdrawal. Criminal behavior may be instrumental in obtaining support for an opiate habit. Preliminary evidence suggests that some violent behavior may be a direct consequence of phencyclidine (PCP) intake.

Alcohol use is frequently associated with criminal and violent behavior. There is, however, no reason to believe that alcohol directly stimulates violent behavior. Social circumstances may mediate the relation between alcohol intake and manifestations of aggression.

SUMMARY

The aspects of central- and autonomic-nervous-system functioning discussed in this review are, in part, genetically determined (Zuckerman et al., 1980). The literature reviewed strongly suggests that many violent offenders suffer organic brain dysfunction. The evidence, however, does not imply that the origins of this dysfunction are genetic; rather, it is likely that organic impairments resulted from environmental events that induced cerebral trauma.

The interaction of sociocultural and biological factors is important in the study of the etiology of violence. Although it is clear that some violent offenders exhibit behavioral deficits indicative of underlying organic impairments, environmental events will moderate and mediate expression of violent behavior. Perhaps, as Sellin (1938) has suggested, in cases where aggressive criminal behavior is manifested by an individual reared in noncriminogenic social conditions, we must look to individual (biological) characteristics for the bases of deviance. Our research in Copenhagen supports this idea. The utility of aberrant biological features as predictors of antisocial behavior among persons who experience criminogenic social conditions are limited; however, biological features may be useful in understanding the resistance to commit criminal behavior.

These findings emphasize the importance of an interdisciplinary approach to understanding the etiology of criminal and violent behavior.

REFERENCES

Allen, H., Dinitz, S., Foster, T. W., Goldman, H., and Linder, L. A. Sociopathy: An experiment in internal environmental control. *American Behavioral Scientist,* 1976, 20, 215-226.

Altschuler, K. F., Abdullah, S., and Rainer, J. D. Lithium and aggressive behavior in patients with early total deafness. *Diseases of the Nervous System,* 1977, 38, 521.

American Psychiatric Association. *Diagnostic and statistical manuals for mental disorders.* Washington, DC: American Psychiatric Association, 1968.

Andrew, J. M. Are left handers less violent? *Journal of Youth and Adolescence,* 1980, 9, 1.

Angrist, B. M. and Gershon, S. Amphetamine abuse in New York City. *Seminars in Psychiatry, 1966 to 1968,* 1969, 1(2), 195-207.

Aniskiewicz, A. Autonomic components of vicarious conditioning and psychopathy. Ph.D. dissertation, Purdue University, 1973.

Arthurs, R. G. S., and Cahoon, E. B. A clinical and electroencephalographic survey of psychopathic personality. *American Journal of Psychiatry,* 1964, 120, 875.

Bach-y-Rita, G., Lion, J. R., Climent, C. E., and Ervin, F. Episodic dyscontrol: A study of 130 violent patients. *American Journal of Psychiatry,* 1971, 127(11), 1473-1478.

Bach-y-Rita, G., Lion, J. R., and Ervin, F. R. Pathological intoxication: Clinical and electroencephalographic studies. *American Journal of Psychiatry,* 1970, 127(5), 698-703.

Bach-y-Rita, G., and Veno, A. Habitual violence: A profile of 62 men. *American Journal of Psychiatry,* 1974, 131, pp. 1015-1017.

Bader-Bartfai, A., and Schalling, D. Recovery time of skin conductance response as related to some personality and physiological variables. Stockholm: Psychological Institute, University of Stockholm, 1974.

Bell, B., Mednick, S. A., Gottesman, I. I., and Sergeant, J. Electrodermal parameters in young, normal male twins. In S. A. Mednick and K. O. Christiansen (Eds.), *Biosocial bases of criminal behavior.* New York: Gardner Press, 1977.

Bender, L. Children and adolescents who have killed. *American Journal of Psychiatry,* 1959, 116, 510.

Berken, G. H., Stone, M. M., and Stone, S. Methadone in schizophrenic rage: A case study. *American Journal of Psychiatry,* 1978, 135(2), 248-249.

Berman, A. Neuropsychological aspects of violent behavior. Paper presented at the Symposium of Adolescent Murderers at the Annual Convention of the American Psychological Association, Toronto, Canada, 1978.

Blackburn, R. Aggression and the EEG: A quantitative analysis. *Journal of Abnormal Psychology,* 1975, 84(4), 358-365.

Blackburn, R. Cortical and autonomic arousal in primary and secondary psychopaths. *Psychophysiology,* 1979, 16, 143-150.

Blankenstein, K. R. Patterns of autonomic functioning in primary and secondary psychopaths. M. A. thesis, University of Waterloo, 1969.

Block, R. *Violent Crime: Environment, Interaction and Death.* Lexington, MA: D. C. Heath, 1977.

Blumer, D. Neuropsychiatric aspects of violent behavior. *Proceedings of the National Symposium on Medical Sciences and the Criminal Law,* 1973, 73-87. (Centre of Criminology, University of Toronto)

Blumer, D., and Migeon, C. Treatment of impulsive behavior disorders in males with medroxyprogesterone acetate. Presented at the annual meeting of the American Psychiatric Association, 1973.

Blumer, D., Williams, H. W., and Mark, V. H. The study and treatment on a neurological ward of abnormally aggressive patients with focal brain disease. *Confinia Neurologica,* 1974, 36(3), 125-176.

Bohman, M. Some genetic aspects of alcoholism and criminality. *Archives of General Psychiatry,* 1978, 35, 269-276.

Borgström, C. A. Eine Serie von kriminellen Zwillingen. *Archiv für Rassenbiologie,* 1939.

Borkovec, T. Autonomic reactivity to sensory stimulation in psychopathic, neurotic and normal juvenile delinquents. *Journal of Consulting and Clinical Psychology,* 1970, 35, 217-222.

Boulougouris, J. C., Laikos, A., and Stefanis, C. Social traits of heavy hashish users and matched controls. *Annals of the New York Academy of Sciences,* 1976, 282, 168-172.

Brown, M. H. Multi-target neurosurgery in the treatment of schizophrenia and violence. *Psychiatric Journal,* University of Ottawa, 1977, 2, 29.

Bundy, R. S. Electrodermal activity as a unitary phenomenon. Paper presented at the meeting of the Society for Psychophysiological Research, Philadelphia, 1977.

Buss, A. *Psychopathology.* New York: John Wiley, 1966.

Cadoret, R. J. Psychopathology in adopted-away offspring of biologic parents with antisocial behavior. *Archives of General Psychiatry,* 1978, 35, 176-184.

Carlsson, G. Crime and behavioral epidemiology: Concepts and applications to Swedish data. In S. A. Mednick and K. O. Christiansen (Eds.), *Biosocial bases of criminal behavior.* New York: Gardner Press, 1977.

Chesno, F., and Kilman, P. Effects of stimulation intensity on sociopathic avoidance learning. *Journal of Abnormal Psychology,* 1975, 84, 144-150.

Christiansen, K. O. A review of studies of criminality among twins. In S. A. Mednick and K. O. Christiansen (Eds.), *Biosocial bases of criminal behavior.* New York: Gardner Press, 1977. (a)

Christiansen, K. O. A preliminary study of criminality among twins. In S. A. Mednick and K. O. Christiansen (Eds.), *Biosocial bases of criminal behavior.* New York: Gardner Press, 1977. (b)

Cleckley, H. *The mask of sanity* (5th ed.). St. Louis: C. V. Mosby, 1976.

Cobb, W. A. The normal adult EEG. In J. D. N. Hill and G. Parr (Eds.), *Electroencephalography* (2nd Ed.). London: MacDonald, 1963.

Comte, A. *The positive philosophy of Auguste Comte* (H. Martineau, trans.). New York: Blanchord, 1855.

Connel, P. H. *Amphetamine psychosis.* London: Chapman & Hall, 1958.

Craft, M. J. *Ten studies into psychopathic personality.* Bristol: John Wright, 1965.

Crowe, R. An adoptive study of psychopathy: Preliminary results from arrest records and psychiatric hospital records. In R. Fieve, D. Rosenthal, and H. Brill (Eds.), *Genetic research in psychiatry.* Baltimore: Johns Hopkins University Press, 1975.

Currie, S., Heathfield, K., Henson, R., and Scott, D. Clinical course and prognosis of temporal lobe epilepsy: A survey of 666 patients. *Brain,* 1971, 94, 173.

Cutting, W. C. Morphine addiction for 62 years. *Stanford Medical Bulletin,* 1942, 1, 39-41.

Dalby, M. A. Antiepileptic and psychotropic effects of carbamazepine in the treatment of psycho-motor epilepsy. *Epilepsia,* 1971, 14, 105.

Dalgaard, O. S., and Kringlen, E. A. A Norwegian twin study of criminality. *British Journal of Criminology,* 1976, 16, 213-232.

D'Artri, D. A. *Psychophysiological responses to crowding determinants of criminal behavior* (L. Otten, Ed.). Rosslyn, VA: Mitre Corporation, 1978.

Dawson, M. Can classical conditioning occur without contingency learning? A review and evalua-tion of the evidence. *Psychophysiology,* 1973, 10, 82-86.

Dawson, M., and Faredy, J. The role of awareness in human differential autonomic classical conditioning: The necessary gate hypothesis. *Psychophysiology,* 1976, 13, 50-53.

Dawson, M., and Greville, G. D. Biochemistry. In J. D. N. Hill and G. Parr (Eds.), *Electroenceph-alography* (2nd ed.). London: MacDonald, 1963.

DeBaudouin, Haumonte, Bessing, and Geissman, P. [Study of a population of 97 confined mur-derers . . .]. *Annales Medico-Psychologiques,* 1961, 119(1), 625, 686.

Dengerink, H. A., and Bertilson, H. S. Psychopathy and physiological arousal in an aggressive task. *Psychophysiology,* 1975, 12, 682-684.

Dobbs, D. S., and Speck, L. B. Visual evoked response and frequency density spectra of prisoner-patients. *Comprehensive Psychiatry,* 1968, 9(1), 62-70.

Doering, C. H., Brodie, H. K. H., Kraemer, H. C., Moos, R. H., Becker, H. B., and Hamburg, D. A. Negative affect and plasma testosterone: A longitudinal human study. *Psychosomatic Medicine,* 1975, 37(6) 484-491.

Douglas, J. W. B., and Blomfield, J. M. *Children under five.* London: Allen & Unwin, 1958.

Driver, M. V., West, L. R., and Faulk, M. Clinical and EEG studies of prisoners charged with murder. *British Journal of Psychiatry,* 1974, 125, 583-587.

Ehrenkranz, J., Bliss, E., and Sheard, M. H. Plasma testosterone: Correlation with aggressive behavior and social dominance in man. *Psychosomatic Medicine,* 1974, 36(6), 469-475.

Eisenberg, J. Criminality and heart rate: A prospective study. Ph.D. dissertation, New School for Social Research, New York, 1976.

Ellinwood, E. H., Jr. Assault and homicide associated with amphetamine abuse. *American Journal of Psychiatry,* 1971, 127(9), 1170-1175.

Elliott, F. A. Neurological aspects of psychopathic behavior. In W. H. Reid (Ed.), *The psychopath: A comprehensive study of sociopathic disorders and behaviors,* forthcoming.

Falconer, M. A. Reversibility by temporal lobe resection of the behavioral abnormalities of tempo-ral lobe epilepsy. *New England Journal of Medicine,* 1973, 289, 451.

Falconer, M. A., et al. Clinical, radiological, and EEG correlations with pathological changes in temporal lobe epilepsy and their significance in surgical treatment. In M. Baldwin and P. Bailey (Eds.), *Temporal Lobe Epilepsy,* Springfield, IL: Charles C Thomas, 1958.

Farrington, D. P. Longitudinal research on crime and delinquency. In N. Morris and M. Tonry (Eds.), *Crime and justice: An annual review of research.* Chicago: University of Chicago Press, 1979, 289-348.

Fauman, M. A., and Fauman, B. J. Violence associated with phencyclidine abuse. *American Journal of Psychiatry,* 1979, 136, 1584-1586.

Fenton, G. W., Tennent, T. G., Fenwick, P. B. C., and Rattray, N. The EEG in antisocial behavior: A study of posterior temporal slow activity in special hospital patients. *Psychological Medi-cine,* 1974, 4, 181-186.

Filimonova, T. D. [Features of the dynamics of evoked cerebral electrical activity in psychopathic personalities . . .]. *Zhurnal Nevropatologii i Psikhiatrii Imeni, S. S. Korsakova,* 1978, 78(2), 222-227.

Filskov, S. B., and Goldstein, S. G. Diagnostic validity of the Halstead-Reitan neuropsychological battery. *Journal of Consulting and Clinical Psychology,* 1974, 42, 382.

Fitzhugh, K. B. Some neuropsychological features of delinquent subjects. *Perceptual Motor Skills*, 1973, 36, 474.

Flor-Henry, P. Laterality, shifts of cerebral dominance, sinistrality and psychosis. In J. Gruzelier, and P. Flor-Henry (Eds.), *Hemisphere asymmetries of function in psychopathology*. Amsterdam: Elsevier, 1979.

Forssman, H., and Frey, T. S. Electroencephalograms of boys with behavior disorders. *Acta Psychologica et Neurologia Scandinavica*, 1953, 28, 61-73.

Fox, R., and Lippert, W. Spontaneous GSR and anxiety level in sociopathic delinquents. *Journal of Consulting and Clinical Psychology*, 1963, 27, 368.

Gabrielli, W. F., and Mednick, S. A. Sinistrality and delinquency. *Journal of Abnormal Psychology*, 1980, 89(5), 654-661.

Gearing, F. R., and Schweitzer, M. D. An epidemiologic evaluation of long-term methadone maintenance treatment for heroin addiction. *American Journal of Epidemiology*, 1974, 100, 101-112.

Georgetown Law Journal. Note: The XYY chromosome defense. 1969, 57, 892-922.

Gibbs, F. A., Bagchi, B. K., and Bloomberg, W. Electroencephalographic study of criminals. *American Journal of Psychiatry*, 1945, 102, 294-298.

Gibbs, F. A., and Gibbs, E. L. *Atlas of electroencephalography, Volume 1: Methodology and controls* (2nd ed.). Cambridge, MA: Addison-Wesley, 1950.

Gibbs, F. A., and Gibbs, E. L. *Atlas of electroencephalography, Vol. III: Neurologic and psychiatric disorders*. Reading, MA: Addison-Wesley, 1964.

Giove, G., and Gastaut, H. Epilepsie alcoolique et declenchement alcoolique des crises chez les epileptiques. *Revue Neurologique* (Paris), 1965, 113, 347.

Goldstein, A. Opioid peptides (endorphins) in pituitary and brain. *Science*, 1976, 193, 1081-1086.

Goldstein, M. Brain research and violent behavior: A summary and evaluation of the status of biomedical research on brain and aggressive violent behavior. *Archives of Neurology*, 1974, 30(1), 1, 35.

Goodwin, D. W., Schulsinger, F., Knop, J., Mednick, S. A., and Guze, S. B. Alcoholism and depression in adopted-out daughters of alcoholics. *Archives of General Psychiatry*, 1977, 34, 751-755.

Goodwin, D. W., Schulsinger, F., Moller, N., Hermansen, L., Winokur, G., and Guze, S. B. Drinking problems in adopted and nonadopted sons of alcoholics. *Archives of General Psychiatry*, 1974, 30(1), 1, 35.

Gunn, J. *Violence*. New York: Praeger, 1973.

Gunn, J., and Bonn, J. Criminality and violence in epileptic prisoners. *British Journal of Psychiatry*, 1971, 118, 33f.

Haller, M. H. Social science and genetics: A historical perspective. In D. Glass (Ed.), *Genetics*. New York: Rockefeller University Press, 1968.

Hare, R. D. Temporal gradient of fear arousal in psychopaths, *Journal of Abnormal Psychology*, 1965, 70, 442-445.

Hare, R. D. Psychopathy, autonomic functioning and the orienting response. *Journal of Abnormal Psychology*, Monograph Supplement, 1968, 73, 1-24.

Hare, R. D. *Psychopathy: Theory and research*. New York: John Wiley, 1970.

Hare, R. D. Psychopathy and physiological responses to adrenalin. *Journal of Abnormal Psychology*, 1972, 79, 138-147.

Hare, R. D. The origins of confusion. *Journal of Abnormal Psychology*, 1973, 82, 535-536.

Hare, R. D. Psychophysiological studies of psychopathy. In D. C. Fowles (Ed.), *Clinical applications of psychophysiology*. New York: Columbia University Press, 1975.

Hare, R. D. Psychopathy and crime. In L. Otten (Ed.), *Colloquium on the correlates of crime and the determinants of criminal behavior*. Rosslyn, VA: Mitre Corporation, 1978. (a)

Hare, R. D. Electrodermal and cardiovascular correlates of psychopathy. In R. D. Hare and D. Schalling (Eds.), Psychopathic behavior: Approaches to research. London: John Wiley, 1978. (b)

Hare, R. D. Biological and behavioral correlations of criminal psychopaths. In L. Beliveau et al. (Eds.), *Today's problems in clinical criminality—Research on diagnosis and treatment*, 1979.

Hare, R. D. Psychopathy and violence. In J. R. Hayes, K. Roberts, and K. Soloway (Eds.), *Violence and the violent individual*. New York: Spectrum, n.d.

Hare, R. D. A longitudinal study of the criminal history of male psychopaths. In *Proceedings of the Life History Research Conference*. Boston: Kluwer Niejoff, forthcoming.

Hare, R. D., and Craigen, D. Psychopathy and physiological activity in a mixed-motive game situation. *Psychophysiology,* 1974, 11, 197-206.

Hare, R. D., and Quinn, M. J. Psychopathy and autonomic conditioning. *Journal of Abnormal Psychology,* 1971, 77, 223-235.

Hare, R. D., Cox, D. N., and Frazelle, J. Psychopathy and electrodermal responses to nonsignal stimulation. *Biological Psychology,* forthcoming.

Hare, R. D., Frazelle, J., and Cox, D. N. Psychopathy and physiological responses to threat of an aversive stimulus. *Psychophysiology,* 1978, 15, 165-172.

Haward, L. R. C. Differential modifications of verbal aggression by psychotropic drugs. In S. Garattini, and E. B. Sigg, (Eds.), *Aggressive Behavior*. New York: John Wiley, 1969.

Hawke, C. C. Castration and sex crimes. *American Journal of Mental Deficiency,* 1950, 55, 220-226.

Heath, R. G. Modulation of emotion with a brain pacemaker. *Journal of Nervous and Mental Disorders,* 1977, 165, 300.

Heath, R. B., and Mickle, W. A. Evaluation of seven years experience with depth electrode studies in human patients. In F. R. Ramey and D. S. O'Doherty (Eds.), *Electrical studies on the unanesthesized brain*. New York: P. B. Hoeber, 1960.

Heilbrun, A. B. Psychopathy and violent crime. *Journal of Counseling and Clinical Psychology,* 1979, 47(3), 509-516.

Hemming, H. Comparison of electrodermal indices theoretically relevant to antisocial behavior in a selected prison sample and students. Paper presented to the British Psychophysiological Association, Exeter, 1977.

Henry, C. E. Positive spike discharges in the EEG and behavior abnormality. In G. H. Glaser (Ed.), *EEG and behavior*. New York: Basic Books, 1963.

Hilberman, E. Wife-beater's wife reconsidered. *American Journal of Psychiatry,* 1980, 137, 1336-1347.

Hilberman, E., and Munson, M. Sixty battered women. *Victimology: An International Journal,* 1977-1978, 2(3/4), 460-471.

Hill, D. EEG in episodic psychotic and psychopathic behavior. *Electroencephalography and Clinical Neurophysiology,* 1952, 4(4), 419-442.

Hill, D. The EEG in psychiatry. In J. D. N. Hill and G. Parr (Eds.), *Electroencephalography* (2nd Ed.). London: MacDonald, 1963.

Hill, D., and Pond, D. A. Reflexions on 100 capital cases submitted to electroencephalography. *Journal of Mental Science,* 1952, 98(410), 23-43.

Hill, D., and Sargant, W. A case of matricide. *Lancet,* 1943, 244(1), 526-27.

Hill, D., and Watterson, D. Electro-encephalographic studies of psychopathic personalities. *Journal of Neurology and Psychiatry,* 1942, 5(1/2), 47-65.

Hinton, J., and O'Neill, M. Pilot research on psychophysiological response profiles of maximum security hospital patients. *British Journal of Social and Clinical Psychology,* 1978, 17, 103.

Hinton, J., O'Neill, M., Hamilton, S., Burke, M. Psychophysiological differentiation between psychopathic and schizophrenic abnormal offenders. *British Journal of Social and Clinical Psychology,* 1980, 19, 257-269.

Hinton, J., O'Neill, M., and Webster, S. Electrodermal indicies of psychopathic recidivism and schizophrenia in maximum security patients. Paper presented to the British Psychological Society, Exeter, 1977.

Hitchcock, E., and Carins, V. Amygdalotomy. *Postgraduate Medical Journal,* 1973, 49, 894.

Hodgins-Milner, S. Psychopathy: A critical examination. Ph.D. dissertation, McGill University, 1976.

Holden, C. The criminal mind: A new look at an ancient puzzle. *Science,* 1978, 199, 511-514.

House, T. H., and Milligan, W. L. Autonomic responses to modeled distress in prison psychopaths. *Journal of Personality and Social Psychology,* 1976, 34, 556-600.

Hughes, J., Smith, T. W., and Kosterlitz, H. W. Identification of two related pentapeptides from the brain with potential opiate agonist activity. *Nature,* 1975, 258(18), 577-579.

Hutchings, B. Genetic and environment factors in psychopathology and criminality. M. Phil. thesis, University of London, 1972.

Hutchings, B., and Mednick, S. A. Criminality in adoptees and their adoptive and biological parents: A pilot study. In S. A. Mednick and K. O. Christiansen (Eds.), *Biosocial bases of criminal behavior.* New York: Gardner Press, 1977.

Itil, T. M., Hsu, W., Saletu, B., and Mednick, S. A. Computer EEG and auditory evoked potential investigations in children at high risk for schizophrenia. *American Journal of Psychiatry,* 1974, 131(8), 892-900.

Ivanitskii, A. M. Nekotorye mekhanizmy narusheniia otsenki vneshnikh signalov pri psikhopa-tiiakh. *Zhurnal Nervoropatologii i Imeni, S. S. Korsakova* (Moskva), 1976, 76(11), 1669-1673.

Jaffe, J. H. Drug addiction and drug abuse. In I. Goodman and A. Gilman (Eds.), *The pharmacological basis of therapeutics.* New York: Macmillan, 1975.

Jenkins, R. L., and Pacella, B. L. Electroencephalographic studies of delinquent boys. *American Journal of Orthopsychiatry,* 1943, 13, 107-120.

Johnston, L. D., O'Malley, P. M., and Eveland, L. Drugs and delinquency: A search for causal connections. In D. B. Kandel (Ed.), *Longitudinal research on drug use.* Washington, DC: Hemisphere, 1978, 137-157.

Kaplan, J. Marijuana and aggression. In J. Kaplan (Ed.), *Marijuana: The New Prohibition.* New York: World Publishing Company, 1970.

Kessler, S., and Moos, R. H. The XYY karotype and criminality: A review. *Journal of Psychiatric Research,* 1970, 7, 153-170.

Kety, S. S. The types and prevalence of mental illness in the biological and adoptive families of adopted schizophrenics. In S. A. Mednick, F. Schulsinger, J. Higgins, and B. Bell (Eds.), *Genetics, environment and psychopathology.* Amsterdam: Elsevier North-Holland.

Kety, S. S., Rosenthal, D., Wender, P. H., and Schulsinger, F. The types and prevalence of mental illness in the biological and adoptive families of adopted schizophrenics. In D. Rosenthal and S. S. Kety (Eds.), *The transmission of schizophrenia.* Oxford: Pergamon, 1968.

Kido, M. An EEG study of delinquent adolescents with reference to recidivism and murder. *Folia psychiatrica et neurologia japanica,* 1973, 27(2), 77-84.

Kiloh, L. G. Sterotactic amydaloidotomy for aggressive behavior. *Journal of Neurology, Neurosurgery, and Psychology,* 1974, 37, 437.

Klingman, D., and Goldberg, D. A. Temporal lobe epilepsy and aggression. *Journal of Nervous and Mental Disease,* 1975, 160(5), 324-341.

Knott, J. R. Electroencephalograms in psychopathic personality and in murderers. In W. P. Wilson (Ed.), *Applications of electroencephalography in psychiatry.* Durham, NC: Duke University, 1965.

Knott, J. R., Lara, R. T., Peters, J. F., and Robinson, M. D. EEG findings in 73 persons accused of murder. In B. Burch and H. I. Altschuler (Eds.), *Behavior and brain electrical activity.* New York: Plenum Press, 1975.

Kooi, K. A., Tucker, R. R., and Marshall, R. E. *Fundamentals of electroencephalography* (2nd. ed.). Hagerstown, MD: Harper & Row, 1978.

Kotses, H., Glaus, K. D., and Freese, F. J. Skin conductance response frequency of incarcerated individuals differing in previous criminal behavior. *Psychophysiology,* 1977, 14, 101.

Kranz, H. *Lebensschicksale krimineller Zwillinge.* Berlin: Springer Verlag, 1936.

Kreuz, L. E., and Rose, R. M. Assessment of agressive behavior and plasma testosterone in a young criminal population. *Psychosomatic Medicine,* 1972, 34(4), 321-332.

Krynicki, V. E. Cerebral dysfunction in repetitively assaultive adolescents. *Journal of Nervous and Mental Disease,* 1978, 166(1), 59-67.

Lang, A. R., Goeckner, D. J., Adesso, V. J., and Marcatt, G. A. Effects of alcohol on aggression in male social drinkers. *Journal of Abnormal Psychology,* 1975, 84, 508-518.

Lange, J. *Verbrechen als Schicksal.* Leipzig: Georg Thieme. English edition, London: Unwin, 1931.

Laschet, U. Antiandrogen in the treatment of sex offenders: Mode of action and therapeutic outcome. In J. Zubin and J. Money (Eds.), *Contemporary sexual behavior: Critical issues in the 1970's.* Baltimore: Johns Hopkins University Press, n.d.

Legras, A. M. Psychese en criminalitet bij twellingen, utrech: Kemink en Zonn [German summary]. *Psychosen und Kriminalitat bei Zwillingen, Zeitschrift für die gesamte Neurologie und Psychiatrie,* 1933, 198-228.

Levander, S. E., Lidberg, L., Schalling, D., and Lindberg, Y. Electrodermal recovery time, stress, and psychopathy. Unpublished manuscript, 1977.

Levander, S. E., Schalling, D., Lidberg, L., Bader-Bartfai, A., and Lidberg, Y. Skin conductance and personality in a group of criminals. *Psychophysiology,* 1980, 17, 105-111.

Levy, S., and Kennard, M. A. A study of the electroencephalogram as related to personality structure in a group of inmates of a state penitentiary. *American Journal of Psychiatry,* 1953, 109, 832.

Lewis, D. O. Delinquency, psychomotor epileptic symptomatology and paranoid ideation. *American Journal of Psychiatry,* 1976, 133, 1395.

Lidberg, L. Frequency of concussions and types of criminality. *Acta Psychiatrica Scandinavica,* 1971, 47, 452.

Lidberg, L., Levander, S., Schalling, D., and Lidberg, Y. Necker cube reversals, arousal and psychopathy. *British Journal of Social and Clinical Psychology,* 1977.

Lidberg, L., Levander, S., Schalling, D., and Lidberg, Y. Urinary catecholamines, stress and psychopathy—A study of arrested men awaiting trial. *Psychosomatic Medicine,* forthcoming.

Lindsley, D. G. A longitudinal study of the occipital alpha frequency in normal children: Frequency and amplitude standards. *Journal of Genetic Psychology,* 1939, 55, 197-213.

Lippert, W. W., and Senter, R. J. Electrodermal responses in the sociopath. *Psychonomic Science,* 1966, 4, 24-26.

Loeb, J., and Mednick, S. A. A prospective study of preductors of criminality: 3 electrodermal response patterns. In S. A. Mednick and K. O. Christiansen (Eds.), *Biosocial bases of criminal behavior.* New York: Gardner Press, 1977.

Loomis, S. D., Bohnert, P. J., and Huncke, S. Prediction of EEG abnormalities in adolescent delinquents. *Archives of General Psychiatry,* 1967, 17, 494.

Lorimer, F. M. Violent behavior and the electroencephalogram. *Clinical Electroencephalography,* 1972, 3, 193.

Lykken, D. T. A study of anxiety in the sociopathic personality. *Journal of Abnormal and Social Psychology,* 1957, 55, 6-10.

Maccoby, E. E., and Jacklin, C. N. Sex differences in aggression: A rejoinder and reprise. *Child Development,* 1980, 51, 964-980.

Maletsky, B. M. Episodic dyscontrol syndrome. *Diseases of the Nervous System,* 1973, 34, 178.

Maletsky, B. M. The alcohol provocation test. *Journal of Clinical Psychiatry,* 1978, 39(5), 403-411.

Marinacci, A. A. Special type of temporal lobe seizures following ingestion of alcohol. *Bulletin of the Los Angeles Neurological Society,* 1963, 28, 241.

Marinacci, A. A., and Von Hagen, K. O. Alcohol and temporal lobe dysfunction. *Behavioral Neuropsychiatry,* 1972, 3(11/12), 2-11.

Mark, V. H., and Ervin, F. R. *Violence and the brain.* New York: Harper & Row, 1970.

Mathis, H. Emotional responsivity in the antisocial personality. Ph.D. dissertation, George Washington University, 1970.

Matousek, M., and Petersen, I. Frequency analysis of the EEG in normal children and adolescents. In P. Kellaway and I. Petersen (Eds.), *Automation of clinical electroencephalography.* New York: Raven Press, 1973.

Matousek, M., Volavka, J., Roubicek, J., and Roth, Z. EEG frequency analysis related to age in normal adults. *Electroencephalography and Clinical Neurophysiology,* 1967, 23, 162-167.

McCallum, C. The CNV and conditionability in psychopaths. *Electroencephalography and Clinical Neurophysiology,* 1973, 33, 337-343.

McClintock, F. H. *Crimes of violence.* London: Macmillan, 1963.

McGlothlin, W. H. Drugs and crime. In R. L. DuPont, A. Goldstein, and J. O'Donnell (Eds.), *Handbook on drug abuse.* Washington, DC: Government Printing Office, 1979, 357-364.

Mednick, S. A. Schizophrenia: A learned thought disorder. In M. Nielsen (Ed.) *Clinical psychology: Proceedings of the XIV International Congress of Applied Psychology.* Copenhagen: Munksgaard, 1962.

Mednick, S. A. *Learning* (2nd Ed.). Englewood Cliffs, NJ: Prentice-Hall, 1973. (1st Ed., 1964)

Mednick, S. A. Electrodermal recovery and psychopathology. In S. A. Mednick, F. Schulsinger, J. Higgins, and B. Bell (Eds.), *Genetics, environment and psychopathy.* Amsterdam: North-Holland, 1974.

Mednick, S. A. A bio-social theory of the learning of law-abiding behavior. In S. A. Mednick and K. O. Christiansen (Eds.), *Biosocial bases of criminal behavior.* New York: Gardner Press, 1977.

Mednick, S. A., Higgins, J., and Kirschenbaum, J. An exploration of *behavior and experience.* New York: John Wiley, n.d.

Mednick, S. A., and Hutchings, B. Some considerations in the interpretation of the Danish adoption studies. In S. A. Mednick and K. O. Christiansen (Eds.), *Biosocial bases of criminal behavior.* New York: Gardner Press, 1977.

Mednick, S. A., and Schulsinger, F. A preschizophrenic sample. *Acta Psychiatrica Scandinavica,* 1964, 40, 135-139.

Mednick, S. A., and Volavka, J. Biology and Crime. In N. Morris and M. Tonry (Eds.), *Crime and justice: An annual review of research* (Vol. II). Chicago: University of Chicago Press, 1980, 85-158.

Mednick, S. A., Volavka, J., Gabrielli, W. F., and Itil, T. EEG as a predictor of antisocial behavior. *Criminology,* 1981, 19, 219-231.

Mendelson, J. H., and Mello, N. K. Biologic concomitants of alcoholism. *New England Journal of Medicine,* 1979, 301, 912-921.

Meyer-Bahlburg, H. F. L., Nat, D. R., Boon, D. A., Sharma, M., and Edwards, J. A. Aggressiveness and testosterone measures in man. *Psychosomatic Medicine,* 1974, 36(3), 269-274.

Money, J. Use of an androgen-depleting hormone in the treatment of male sex offenders. *Journal of Sex Research,* 1970, 6, 165-172.

Monroe, R. R. *Episodic behavioral disorders: A psychodynamic and neurophysiologic analysis.* Cambridge: Harvard University Press, 1970.

Monroe, R. R. Maturational lag in central nervous system development as a partial explanation of episodic violent behavior. *Psychopharmacology Bulletin,* 1974, 10(4), 63-64.

Monroe, R. R. *Brain dysfunction in aggressive criminals.* Toronto: Lexington, 1978.

Monroe, R. R., Hulfish, B., Balis, G., Lion, J., Rubin, J., McDonald, M., and Barcik, J. D. Neurological findings in recidivist aggressors. In C. Shagass, S. Gershon, and A. J. Friedhoff (Eds.), *Psychopathology and brain dysfunction.* New York: Raven Press, 1977.

Monroe, R. R., and Wise, S. Combined phenothiazine, chordiazapoxide and primidone therapy for uncontrolled psychotic patients. *American Journal of Psychiatry,* 1965, 122, 694.

Monti, P. M., Brown, W. A., and Corriveau, D. P. Testosterone and components of aggressive and sexual behavior in men. *American Journal of Psychiatry,* 1977, 134(6), 692-694.

Morrison, J. R., and Minkoff, K. Explosive personality as a sequel to the hyperactive child syndrome. *Comprehensive Psychiatry,* 1975, 16, 343.

Mothers Aid Organization for Copenhagen, Copenhagen County and Frederiksberg County. Annual report for 1946-47.

Moyer, K. E. *The psychobiology of aggression.* New York: Harper & Row, 1976.

Mulvihill, D., Tumin, M., and Curtis, L. *Staff report to the National Commission on the Causes and Prevention of Violence.* Washington, DC: Government Printing Office, 1963.

Mundy-Castle, A. C. The EEG in twenty-two cases of murder or attempted murder: Appendix on possible significance of alphoid rhythms. *Journal of the National Institute of Personnel Research,* 1955, 6, 103.

Narabayashi, H. Sterotoxic amygdalotomy. In B. E. Eleftheriou (Ed.), *The neurobiology of the amygdala.* New York: Plenum Press, 1975.

Newman, G. *Understanding violence.* Philadelphia: Lippincott, 1979.

Neziroglu, F. Behavior and organic aspects of aggression. In J. Obiols, C. Ballees, E. Dongalex, M. Monclus, and J. Pujol (Eds.), *Biological psychiatry today* (Vol. B). Amsterdam: Elsevier North-Holland, 1979.

Okasha, A., Sadek, A., and Moneim, S. A. Psychosocial and electroencephalographic studies of Egyptian murderers. *British Journal of Psychiatry,* 1975, 126, 34-40.

Olweus, D. Testosterone, aggression, physical and personality dimensions in normal adolescent males. *Psychosomatic Medicine,* forthcoming.

Olweus, D. Bullies and whipping boys. In J. DeWit & W. W. Hartup (Eds.), *Determinants and origins of aggressive behaviour.* The Hague: Mouton, 1975.

Ommaya, A. K., and Gennarelli, T. A. A physiopathologic basis for noninvasive diagnosis and prognosis of head injury severity. In R. L. McLaurin, *Head injuries. Proceedings of the Second Chicago Symposium on Neural Trauma.* New York: Grune & Stratton, 1976.

Ounsted, C. Aggression and epilepsy. *Journal of Psychological Researches,* 1969, 13, 237.

Parker, D. S., Syndulko, R., Maltzman, I., Jens, R., and Ziskind, E. Psychophysiology of sociopathy: Electrocortical measures. *Biological Psychology,* 1975, 3, 198-200.

Pernanen, K. Alcohol and crimes of violence. In B. Kissin and H. Begleiter (Eds.), *The biology of alcoholism.* New York: Plenum, 1976, 351-444.

Persky, H., Smith, K. D., and Basu, G. K. Relation of psychologic measures of aggression and hostility to testosterone production in man. *Psychosomatic Medicine,* 1971, 33(3), 265-277.

Petersen, I., Matousek, M., Volavka, J., Mednick, S. A., and Pollock, V. E. EEG antecedents of thievery. *Acta Psychiatrica Scandinavica,* forthcoming.

Pincus, J. H. Can violence be a manifestation of epilepsy? *Neurology,* 1980, 30, 305.

Pincus, J. H., and Tucker, G. J. *Behavioral neurology.* New York: Oxford University Press, 1978.

Pinto, A., Simopoulos, A. M., Uhlenhuth, E. H., and DeRosa, E. R. Responses of chronic schizophrenic females to a combination of diphenylhydantoin and neuroleptics: A double blind study. *Comprehensive Psychiatry,* 1975, 16, 529.

Plovnick, N. Autonomic nervous system functioning as a predisposing influence on personality, psychopathy and schizophrenia. Ph.D. dissertation, New School for Social Research, New York, 1976.

Rada, R. T., Laws, D. R., and Kellner, R. Plasma testosterone levels in the rapist. *Psychosomatic Medicine*, 1976, 38(4), 257-268.

Ramamurthi, B. Sterotaxic ablation of the irritable forces in temporal lobe epilepsy. *Confinia Neurologia*, 1970, 32, 316.

Ratcliff, K. S., and Robins, L. N. Risk factors in the continuation of childhood antisocial behavior into adulthood. *International Journal of Mental Health*, 1979, 7, 96-116.

Rickels, K., and Downing, R. Chlordiazepoxide and hostility in anxious outpatients. *American Journal of Psychiatry*, 1974, 131, 442.

Riley, T. L. The electroencephalogram in patients with rage attacks or episodic violent behavior. *Military Medicine*, 1979, 144(8), 515-517.

Robins, L. N. *Deviant children grown up*. Baltimore: Williams & Wilkins, 1966.

Rodin, E. A. Psychomotor epilepsy and aggressive behavior. *Archives of General Psychiatry*, 1972, 29, 210-213.

Rosanoff, A. J., Handy, L. M., and Rosanoff, F. A. Criminality and delinquency in twins. *Journal of Criminal Law and Criminology*, 1934, 24, 923-934.

Rosen, A., and Schalling, D. Probability learning in psychopathic and non-psychopathic criminals. *Journal of Experimental Research in Personality*, 1971, 5, 191-198.

Sandberg, A. A., Koepf, G. F., Ishihara, T., and Hauschka, T. S. An XYY human male. *Lancet*, 1961, 488-489.

Sarbin, T. R., and Miller, J. E. Demonism revisited: The XYY chromosomal anomaly. *Issues in Criminology*, 1970, 5, 195-207.

Sayed, Z. A., Lewis, S. A., and Brittain, R. P. An electroencephalographic and psychiatric study of thirty-two insane murders. *British Journal of Psychiatry*, 1969, 115, 115-124.

Schachter, S. *Emotion, obesity and crime*. New York: Academic Press, 1971.

Schachter, S. and Latané, B. Crime, cognition and the autonomic nervous system. In M. R. Jones (Ed.), *Nebraska symposium on motivation*. Lincoln: University of Nebraska Press, 1964.

Schalling, D. The role of heart rate increase for coping with pain as related to impulsivity. Unpublished manuscript, University of Stockholm, 1975.

Schalling, D., and Levander, S. Spontaneous fluctuations in EDR during anticipation of pain in two delinquent groups differing in anxiety proneness. University of Stockholm Psychological Laboratory Report 238, 1967.

Schalling, D., Levander, S., and Dahlin-Lidberg, Y. A note on the relation between spontaneous fluctuations in skin conductance and heart rate, and scores on the Gough delinquency scale. Unpublished manuscript, University of Stockholm, 1975.

Schalling, D., Lidberg, L., Levander, S. E., and Dahlin, Y. Relations between fluctuations in skin resistance and digital pulse volume and scores on the Gough delinquency scale. Unpublished manuscript, University of Stockholm, 1968.

Schalling, D., Lidberg, L., Levander, S. E., and Dahlin, Y. Spontaneous autonomic activity as related to psychopathy. *Biological Psychology*, 1973, 1, 83-97.

Schmauk, F. J. Punishment, arousal and avoidance learning in sociopaths. *Journal of Abnormal Psychology*, 1970, 76, 325-335.

Schoenherr, J. C. Avoidance of noxious stimulation in psychopathic personality. Ph.D. dissertation, University of California, Los Angeles, 1964.

Schrieber, D. J., Goldman, H., Kleinman, K. M., Goldfather, P. R., and Snow, M. Y. The relationship between independent neuropsychological and neurological detection and localization of cerebral impairment. *Journal of Nervous and Mental Disorders*, 1976, 162, 360.

Schulsinger, F. Psychopathy: Heredity and environment. In S. A. Mednick and K. O. Christiansen (Eds.), *Biosocial bases of criminal behavior*. New York: Gardner Press, 1977.

Schvarcz, J. R., Driollet, R., Rios, E., and Betti, O. Sterotactic hypothalactomy for behavior disorders. *Journal of Neurology, Neurosurgery, and Psychology*, 1972, 35, 356.

Schwade, E. D., and Geiger, S. G. Severe behavior disorders with abnormal EEGs. *Diseases of the Nervous System,* 1960, 21, 616.

Sellin, T. *Culture, conflict and crime.* New York: Social Science Research Council, 1938.

Shah, S. A., and Roth, L. H. Biological and psychophysiological factors in criminality. In D. Glaser (Ed.), *Handbook of Criminology.* Chicago: Rand McNally, 1974.

Shetty, T. Photic responses in hyperkinesis of childhood. *Science,* 1971, 174, 1356.

Shupe, L. M. Alcohol and crime. *Journal of Criminal Law, Criminology and Police Science,* 1954, 44, 661-664.

Siddle, D. A. T. Electrodermal activity and psychopathy. In S. A. Mednick and K. O. Christiansen (Eds.), *Biosocial bases of criminal behavior.* New York: Gardner Press, 1977.

Siddle, D. A. T., Mednick, S. A., Nicol, A. R., and Foggitt, R. H. Skin conductance recovery of antisocial adolescents. In S. A. Mednick and K. O. Christiansen (Eds.), *Biosocial bases of criminal behavior.* New York: Gardner Press, 1977.

Siddle, D. A. T., Nicol, A. R., and Foggit, R. H. Habituation and over-extinction of the GSR component of the orienting response in antisocial adolescents. *British Journal of Social and Clinical Psychology,* 1973, 12, 303-308.

Silver, L. B., Dublin, D. D., and Lourie, R. S. Does violence breed violence? Contributions from a study of the child abuse syndrome. *American Journal of Psychiatry,* 1969, 126, 404-407.

Silverman, D. The electroencephalogram of criminals. *Archives of Neurology and Psychiatry,* 1944, 52(1), 38-42.

Slater, E. The incidence of mental disorder. *Annals of Eugenics,* 1934-1945, 6, 172-186.

Small, J. G. The organic dimension of crime. *Archives of General Psychiatry,* 1966, 15, 82-89.

Smith, D. E. A clinical approach to the treatment of phencyclidine (PCP) abuse. *Psychopharmacology Bulletin,* 1980, 16, 67-70.

Smith, S. M., Honigsberger, L., and Smith, C. A. EEG and personality factors in baby batterers. *British Medical Journal,* 1973, 7, 20-22.

Spellacy, F. Neuropsychological differences between violent and nonviolent adolescents. *Journal of Clinical Psychology,* 1977, 33, 966.

Spellacy, F. Neuropsychological discrimination between violent and nonviolent men. *Journal of Clinical Psychology,* 1978, 34, 49-52.

Spencer, H. *Social statistics.* New York: Appleton-Century-Crofts, 1878.

Stafford-Clarke, D., and Taylor, F. H. Clinical and EEG studies of prisoners charged with murder. *Journal of Neurological and Neurosurgical Psychiatry,* 1949, 12, 35.

Strasburg, P. *Violent delinquents.* New York: Monarch, 1978.

Stumpfl, F. *Die Ursprunge des Verbrechens. Dargestellt am Lebenslauf von Zwillingen.* Leipzig: Georg Thieme, 1936.

Sutker, F. Vicarious conditioning and sociopathy. *Journal of Abnormal Psychology,* 1970, 76, 380-386.

Syndulko, K., Parker, D. A., Jens, R., Maltzman, I., and Ziskind, E. Psychophysiology of sociopathy: Electrocortical measures. *Biological Psychology,* 1975, 3, 185-200.

Syndulko, K., Parker, D., Maltzman, I., and Ziskind, E. Central and autonomic nervous system measures of conditioning in sociopaths and normals. Presented at the Science Fair of the Society for Psychophysiological Research, Toronto, Canada, 1975.

Szpiler, J. A., and Epstein, S. Availability of an avoidance response as related to autonomic arousal. *Journal of Abnormal Psychology,* 1976, 85, 73-82.

Tharp, V., Syndulko, K., Maltzman, I., and Ziskind, E. Skin conductance and heart rate measures of the gradient of fear in non-institutionalized compulsive gambler socio-paths, 1978.

Tinklenberg, J. R. Alcohol and violence. In P. G. Bourne and R. Fox (Eds.), *Alcoholism: Progress in research and treatment.* New York: Academic Press, 1973.

Tinklenberg, J. R., Murphy, P. L., Murphy, P., Darley, C. F., Roth, W. T., and Kopell, B. S. Drug involvement in criminal assaults by adolescents. *Archives of General Psychiatry,* 1974, 30(5), 685-689.

Trasler, G. Criminal behavior. In H. J. Eysenck (Ed.), *Handbook of abnormal psychology* (2nd Ed.). London: Putnam, 1972.

Tupin, J. P. Lithium use in nonmanic depressive conditions. *Comprehensive Psychiatry,* 1972, 13, 209.

Venables, P. H., and Christie, M. J. Mechanism, instrumentation, recording techniques and quantification of responses. In W. F. Prokasy and D. C. Raskin (Eds.), *Electrodermal activity in psychological research.* New York: Academic Press, 1973.

Venables, P. H., and Christie, M. J. *Research in psychophysiology.* New York: John Wiley, 1975.

Verdeaux, G. Electroencephalography in criminology. *Medecine Legale et Dommage Corporel* (Paris), 1970, 3(1), 39-46.

Verebey, K., Volavka, J., and Clouet, D. Endorphins in psychiatry: An overview and a hypothesis. *Archives of General Psychiatry,* 1978, 30, 677-681.

Vernet, K., and Madsen, A. Sterotaxic amygdalotomy and basofrontal tractotomy in psychotics with aggressive behavior. *Journal of Neurology, Neurosurgery, and Psychiatry,* 1970, 33, 858.

Volavka, J., Crown, P., Dornbush, R., Feldstein, S., and Fink, M. EEG, heart rate and mood change (high) after cannabis. *Psychopharmacologia* (Berlin), 1973, 32, 11-25.

Volavka, J., Levine, R., Feldstein, S., and Fink, M. Short-term effects of heroin in man. *Archives of General Psychiatry,* 1974, 30, 677-681.

Volavka, J., Matousek, M., Feldstein, S., Roubicek, J., Prior, P., Scott, D. F., Brezinova, V., and Synek, V. The reliability of EEG assessment. *Z EEG-EMG,* 1973, 4(3), 123-130.

Volavka, J., Mednick, S. A., Rasmussen, L., and Teasdale, T. EEG response to sine wave modulated light in XYY, XXY, and XY men. *Acta Psychiatrica Scandinavica,* 1979, 59, 509-516.

Volavka, J., Mednick, S. A., Rasmussen, L., Teasdale, T., and Owen, D. Evoked potentials in XXY and XYY men. In preparation.

Volavka, J., Mednick, S. A., Sergeant, J., and Rasmussen, L. Electroencephalograms of XYY and XXY men. *British Journal of Psychiatry,* 1977, 130, 43-47. (a)

Volavka, J., Mednick, S. A., Sergeant, J., and Rasmussen, L. EEG spectra in XYY and XXY men. *EEG and Clinical Neurophysiology,* 1977, 43, 798-801. (b)

Volavka, J., Mednick, S. A., Sergeant, J., and Rasmussen, L. EEGs of XYY and XXY men found in a large birth cohort. In S. A. Mednick and K. O. Christiansen (Eds.), *Biosocial bases of criminal behavior.* New York: Gardner Press, 1977. (c)

Volavka, J., Resnick, R., Kestenbaum, R., and Freedman, A. Short-term effects of naltrexone in 155 heroin ex-addicts. *Biological Psychiatry,* 1976, 11, 679-685.

Volavka, J., Verebey, K., Resnick, R., and Mule, S. Methadone dose, plasma level and cross-tolerance to heroin in man. *Journal of Nervous and Mental Disease,* 1978, 166(2), 104-109.

Wadsworth, M. Delinquency in a national sample of children. *British Journal of Criminology,* 1975, 15, 167-174.

Wadsworth, M. Delinquency, pulse rates and early emotional deprivation. *British Journal of Criminology,* 1976, 16, 245-256.

Wahlstrom, G. Inhibitor(s) of narcotic receptor binding in brain extracts and cerebral spinal fluid. *Acta Pharmacologia et Toxicologica,* 1974, 35 (Supplement 1), 55.

Waid, W. M. Skin conductance to both signalized and unsignalized noxious stimulation predicts level of socialization. *Journal of Personality and Social Psychology,* 1976, 34, 923-929.

Weissman, J. C., Marr, S. W., and Katsampes, P. L. Addiction and criminal behavior: A continuing examination of criminal addicts. *Journal of Drug Issues,* 1976, 6, 153-165.

Wilder, J. Sugar metabolism in its relation to criminology. In S. Linduer and B. J. Selinger (Eds.), *Handbook of correctional psychology.* New York: Philosophical Library, 1947.

Williams, D. Temporal lobe syndromes, In P. J. Vinken and G. W. Bruyn (Eds.), *Handbook of clinical neurology, Volume 2: Localization in clinical neurology.* Amsterdam: Elsevier North-Holland, 1962.

Williams, D. Neural factors related to habitual aggression-consideration of differences between those habitual aggressives and others who have committed crimes of violence. *Brain,* 1969, 92, 503-520.

Winkler, G. E., and Kove, S. S. The implication of electroencephalographic abnormalities in homicide cases, *Journal of Neuropsychiatry,* 1962, 3, 322.

Witkin, H. A., Mednick, S. A., Schulsinger, F., Bakkestrom, E., Christiansen, K. O., Good-enough, D. R., Hirschhorn, K., Lundsteen, C., Owen, D. R., Philip, J., Rubin, D. B., and Stocking, M. Criminality, aggression and intelligence among XYY and XXY men. In S. A. Mednick and K. O. Christiansen (Eds.), *Biosocial bases of criminal behavior.* New York: Gardner Press, 1977.

Wolfgang, M. E. *Patterns in criminal homicide.* Philadelphia: University of Pennsylvania Press, 1958.

Wolfgang, M. E. Foreword. In S. A. Mednick and K. O. Christiansen (Eds.), *Biosocial bases of criminal behavior.* New York: Gardner Press, 1977.

Wolfgang, M. E. Violence in the family. In I. Kutash, S. Kutash, and L. Schlesinger (Eds.), *Violence: Perspectives on murder and aggression.* San Francisco: Jossey-Bass, 1978.

Wolfgang, M. E., and Ferracuti, F. *The subculture of violence.* London: Tavistock, 1967.

Wolfgang, M. E., Figlio, R. M., and Sellin, T. *Delinquency in a birth cohort.* Chicago: University of Chicago Press, 1972.

Yeudall, L. T. Neuropsychological assessment of forensic disorders. *Canadian Mental Health,* 1977, 25, 7.

Yeudall, L. T., Fedora, O., Fedora, S., and Wardell, D. A neurosocial perspective on the assessment and etiology of persistent criminality. In C. Roy (Ed.), *Perspectives in prison psychiatry.* London: Oxford University Press, 1979.

Yeudall, L. T., and Flor-Henry, P. Lateralized neuropsychological impairments in depression and criminal psychopathy, 1975. (Cited by Yeudall, L. T., 1977)

Yoshimasu, S. The criminological significance of the family in the light of the studies of criminal twins. *Acta Criminologiae et Medicinae Legalis Japanica,* 1961, 27.

Ziskind, E., Syndulko, K., and Maltzman, I. Aversive conditioning in the sociopath. *Pavlovian Journal,* 1978, 13, 199-205.

Zuckerman, M., Buchsbaum, M., and Murphy, D. Sensation seeking and its biological correlates. *Psychological Bulletin,* 1980, 88, 187-214.

2

Psychological Determinants and Correlates of Criminal Violence

Edwin I. Megargee

In this chapter we focus on the psychological factors that are currently thought to be involved in criminal violence. In the first section of the chapter, criminal violence will be set in the broader context of aggression and violence, and some of the problems in doing research will be briefly mentioned. The second section will take up the major crimes of violence directed primarily at people (assault, homicide, familial violence, rape, kidnapping, and terrorism) and the major violent crimes directed primarily at property (bombing, arson, and robbery). Some of the factors involved in each of these offenses will be discussed and typologies of violent offenders in each offense category will be reviewed, partly to illustrate the diversity of personality factors and motivations thought to contribute to these offenses and partly to acquaint the reader with some of the explanatory hypotheses that have implicitly been offered.

The third section will attempt to bring some order to the kaleidoscopic array of interpretations presented in the preceding section by presenting a conceptual framework for the study of aggressive behavior in general and violence in particular. It will be suggested that some of the apparent differences and contradictions stem from the fact that different theorists have focused on different components of the violent act, such as instigation, inhibitions, habit strength, and situational factors. It is hoped that this conceptual framework will assist the reader in evaluating the literature and doing research.

Author's Note: Preparation of this chapter was supported in part by grant MH 13202-08, National Institute of Mental Health, Center for Studies of Crime and Delinquency. The writer wishes to thank Susan McDonald for her assistance in preparing this chapter and David Farrington and Lewis Goldberg for their critical comments on a draft.

This chapter does not attempt to present a review of the major theoretical explanations that have been offered to account for criminal violence, such as the ethological, psychoanalytic, or social-learning views. For such an analysis, the reader is referred to earlier works by the writer (Megargee, 1969, 1972) on psychological theories of violence and aggression.

Given the focus on *psychological* determinants and correlates of criminal violence, this chapter will necessarily appear rather parochial, since biological and physiological determinants will not be discussed and sociological, political, and situational determinants will be touched on only tangentially. The reader should remain aware that a person's genes, endocrinological system, musculature, nervous system, and blood chemistry all influence aggressive proclivities, as do the external determinants (such as climate or political structure), situational factors (such as the presence of a bystander or the availability of a weapon), and specific stimuli (such as a punch in the nose). It is to be hoped that the other chapters in this collection will provide this breadth and compensate for this chapter's necessary preoccupation with nonbiological intraindividual determinants.

In addition to the narrowness of focus in its subject matter, this chapter will reflect a certain ethnocentrism, since the primary focus is on the psychological factors currently associated with violent crime in Western society; the reader should therefore be cautious in generalizing to other cultures and other periods in history.

AGGRESSION AND CRIMINAL VIOLENCE: DEFINITIONAL ISSUES

William Colby has been quoted as remarking, "I have definitional problems with the word 'violence.' I don't know what the word 'violence' means" (Peter 1977: 483). Unlike Colby, most of us think we know exactly what it means; the problem is that our definitions may not agree with anyone else's. Before proceeding with an exploration of the psychological correlates of criminal violence, it is best to explore what criminal violence is; in the process we shall touch on some of the problems that have plagued those who attempt to do research on this complex set of phenomena.

Although "criminal violence" refers to an extremely heterogeneous array of behavior, it is nonetheless a subcategory of a subcategory of a general category of behavior. We shall begin with the general category, aggression, and then attempt to narrow the focus until we come to "criminal violence."

Aggression

"Aggression" refers to agonistic or injurious behavior. Buss (1961) defined aggression as "a response that delivers noxious stimuli to another organism";

Berkowitz (1962) used the term to "denote behavior aimed at the injury of some object." However, so many issues cloud the definition of aggression that it has become commonplace to begin books on the subject with a list of twenty or so behavioral vignettes that the reader is to classify as aggressive or nonaggressive (Baron, 1977; Johnson, 1972). Johnson (1972: 8) concluded, "Perhaps . . . the most important thing which can be said about defining aggression [is] . . . there is no single kind of behavior which can be called 'aggressive' nor is there any single process which represents 'aggression.'"

One issue that quickly emerges is intentionality. Is injury to the victim the goal of the perpetrator, or is such injury a by-product of some other goal-seeking behavior? Students in seminars on aggression readily agree that knocking out someone's tooth in a fight is an example of aggressive behavior. There is less unanimity when the tooth is lost as a result of a body check in a hockey game, and considerable disagreement when the tooth is removed by a dentist.

The issue of intentionality centers on (1) whether the perpetrator had a reasonable expectation that his or her behavior would injure the victim, and (2) whether such injury was in fact desired by the offender. Kaufmann (1970) would not consider an act aggressive unless the person performing it had some expectation that the behavior would deliver noxious stimulation to the recipient. Berkowitz (1962) maintained that for an act to be considered aggressive, the injury to the victim had to be reinforcing.

Another issue is whether the act succeeds in injuring the victim. Those definitions that limit aggression to acts that physically injure the victim have the advantage of being precise and operational, avoiding the fuzzy concept of "psychological" injury. However, according to such a definition, the behavior of a would-be assassin such as Lynette (Squeaky) Fromme would have to be labeled nonaggressive, since she was prevented from firing her pistol at President Ford.

As might be anticipated, a third issue concerns "psychological" injury. Should verbal disparagement, scolding, passive injury, coercion, sexual harassment, and a variety of other nonphysical agonistic behaviors be considered aggression? Growling and ritualized aggressive displays on the part of animals and a variety of verbal and passive-aggressive behavior patterns by humans are included in most definitions of aggression, but there is less consensus on these behaviors than there is on physical aggression. Some scientists separate physical and nonphysical aggression in their theories and research. Most students of criminal violence do not study such acts as obscene phone calls, sexual coercion, blackmail, and extortion threats, although these behaviors undoubtedly deliver "noxious stimulations" to the goal objects.

A fourth issue is whether acts of *omission* that lead to injuries should be considered aggressive. The failure of bystanders to call police undoubtedly contributed to the death of Kitty Genovese. Should their behavior be regarded as aggressive? What of the legislator who votes against a three-day "cooling off" period for purchasing handguns? This issue was central to the recent criminal prosecution of the Ford Motor Company for failure to correct design features in the Ford Pinto fuel tank placement that allegedly resulted in a number of deaths. Although individuals (and corporations) can be prosecuted for criminal negligence, most students of criminal violence exclude injuries resulting from such acts of omission.

Buss (1961) distinguished "angry aggression," behavior that is reinforced by pain or injury to the victim, from "instrumental aggression," in which the aggression is a means to some other end. (Despite the terminology, it is not necessary to demonstrate the emotional state of anger in the case of "angry aggression.") A dog that attacks an intruder and breaks off his attack when the offending animal leaves its territory would be an example of instrumental aggression, whereas a pit dog that fights another to the death would be an example of angry aggression. Both instrumental and angry motivation will be considered in this chapter. As we shall see, in some violent crimes, such as familial violence, angry motivation is thought to predominate, while in others, such as arson, instrumental motives are more often found.

Milder forms of aggressive behavior, such as the delivery of electric shock or verbal criticism, can be studied in the laboratory, and a large body of experimental literature has accumulated on mild forms of both instrumental and angry aggression. In the case of instrumental aggression, a typical research paradigm has been for the experimenter to require the subject to deliver punishment in the form of mild electric shocks to another person, ostensibly to determine whether this helps the other person learn to peform a task more efficiently. Some people question whether this constitutes *real* (i.e., angry), aggression since the subject's primary motives are to comply with the experimenter's instructions and to help the other person learn the material. To meet this objection, some "aggression machines" are designed so that the subject can adjust the intensity and the frequency of the shock, the higher settings being interpreted as evidence of stronger aggressive tendencies.

Milgram's (1965) investigations of obedience and conformity represent the most extreme and controversial use of shock in the laboratory setting. In these studies the subjects were told to deliver what they were led to believe were potentially injurious and even lethal doses of shock to the ostensible victim, an impression that was reinforced by the victim's simulated reactions. There was some question of whether even this paradigm constituted true aggressive behavior, since the experimenter rather than the subject assumed responsibility for the conduct of the study and the victim's suffering was not reinforcing to the subjects.

The use of the experimental method permits some definitive statements to be made about the "psychological correlates and determinants" of the milder forms of aggressive behavior that can be studied in the laboratory. The question is the degree to which these findings can be generalized to the more extreme forms of aggressive behavior that are subsumed under the term "violence."

Violence

The term "violence" is reserved for the more extreme forms of aggressive behavior that are likely to cause significant injuries to the victim. Although violence typically refers to physical aggression, it can also be applied to psychological stress that causes suffering or trauma. The National Commission on the Causes and Prevention of Violence (see Megargee, 1969) defined violence as the "overtly threatened or overtly accomplished application of force which results in the injury or destruction of persons or property or reputation, or the illegal appropriation of property." By including the word "threatened," this definition permits classifying behavioral sequences clearly aimed at injuring others that fail in their objective as violent. Similarly, armed robberies in which weapons are used to intimidate and control the victims would be regarded as violent, even though no one was actually injured.

There is a question of where one draws the line between aggression and violence. The rapist, for example, uses coercion to obtain sexual relations from a nonconsenting victim. When that coercion involves the overt or threatened use of physical force, it clearly constitutes violence. But what of psychological coercion? In a prison, a "wolf" may offer "protection" to a younger, weaker inmate in return for sexual relations. An adult may use his authority to coerce a child to submit to fondling. In the workplace a man or woman in a position of authority may use the implied threat of dismissal to obtain sexual favors. What is the distinction between rape and sexual harassment? Should any sexual relations that involve coercion be considered acts of violence? People disagree on these questions.

Some writers attempt to resolve the issue by making a distinction between force and violence. Hofstadter (1970: 9) defined acts of force as "those which inhibit the normal free action of movement of other persons, or which inhibit them through the threat of violence," and Luckenbill and Sanders (1977: 146) wrote, "Some actions, for instance rape, are considered violent yet may involve only force." This would exclude kidnapping, hostage-taking, and robbery from the roster of violent crimes, unless the victim was injured. In contrast, the present writer considers threats of injury as violent acts, especially when they result in trauma.

Like aggression, violence can usefully be subdivided into "angry" and "instrumental" categories. The former has the injury of the target as the primary objective; to use Berkowitz's criterion, it is reinforced by the suffering inflicted upon the victim. Instrumental violence, on the other hand, is extreme aggression employed in accomplishing some other end. Arson may be committed to defraud an insurance company or conceal evidence of another crime; terrorism, to accomplish political goals.

Some regard destructive behavior directed against animals as constituting violence. This is especially true when the animal is not slain for food or sport, as in the annual clubbing of baby seals in Nova Scotia or the proposed shooting of wild burros in the Grand Canyon. Sadistic behavior directed at domestic animals or pets is prohibited by law and may be labeled violent by some. Nevertheless, most reserve the term "violence" for aggression by and against humans; ranchers who castrate or slaughter their cattle and hunters who shoot large or small game are not generally regarded as violent people.

Just as the definition of aggression raises the issue of intentionality, the definition of violence brings up the question of legality. Commenting on the Violence Commission's definition, the present writer noted:

> This definition would include acts that everyone would classify as violent, such as murder, rape, robbery, arson and gang fights. However, it could also include such legal acts as executions, injuries inflicted during a football game, or a parent spanking his child. Although many would object to classifying socially sanctioned aggressive behavior in the same category with criminal behavior, the alternative would be to classify as *nonviolent* the Roman gladiator who plunged a sword through the opponent's chest in response to Caesar's downturned thumb [Megargee, 1972: 2].

Criminal Violence

This leads us at last to criminal violence, a subcategory of the subcategory of violence. Criminal violence is extreme aggressive behavior that is prohibited by the statutes enforced in the particular culture or society. Restricting our attention to criminal violence appears to resolve our problems with respect to legality, since one safe generalization that can be made about criminal behavior is that it is illegal. Or is it?

By focusing on criminal violence, we are moving away from a behavioral definition that can be operationalized toward a social definition that is culture-specific. In previous writings on deviance, the writer has distinguished *"latitudes of acceptance"* from *"latitudes of rejection"* (Megargee, 1973). Within the former are behaviors the society "prescribes" and those which the society actually "prefers." With respect to aggressive behavior, for example, the Christian ethic *prescribes* nonviolence. However, historically, Western society has *preferred* aggressive behavior in defense of self, home, and country. Instead of "turn the other cheek" we prefer "don't tread on me." The writer recently examined a man who had stabbed a young girl to death and removed her still-beating heart: bizarre criminal behavior, clearly proscribed in twentieth-century America, but not especially deviant if it had occurred in fifteenth-century Meso-America. In our own culture, dueling was once prescribed in certain situations, was later merely permitted, and is now proscribed under any circumstances.

Within a particular society, some acts of violence are accepted, even prescribed, such as fighting the enemy in time of war. Unfortunately, not all groups agree on the identity of the enemy or the location of the war. In the 1960s, the elected officials of the United States defined the enemy as the dark-skinned Viet Cong and the place as Vietnam, but for other groups in our society, the enemy was the white-skinned police and the place, the streets. An act that is considered murder by one group may be justifiable homicide to another.

The waters grow even murkier if we shift our attention from "What is criminal violence?" to "Who is a violent criminal?" because the latter issue involves the whole social labeling process from the initial behavior through the process of arrest, prosecution, and imprisonment. In terms of discussing the psychological determinants and correlates of violent behavior, the biases introduced by plea bargaining and the like are of little concern, but to the extent that our knowledge of criminal violence stems from the study of those who have been convicted of violent crimes, such selective biases are highly relevant.

A Working Definition of Criminal Violence. "Criminal violence" for the purpose of this chapter will mean engaging in or threatening behavior that is (1) directly injurious or destructive, or potentially injurious or destructive, to persons or property, and (2) currently prohibited by state and/or federal laws and statutes. The purpose of stipulating that the behavior is "directly" injurious or destructive is to exclude a variety of offenses including, but not limited to, distribution and sale of drugs, narcotics, weapons, and other potentially harmful items; negligence in the design or construction of buildings, automobiles, airplanes, and the like; violations of environmental protection laws, such as dumping toxic wastes; and a number of other, similar offenses that are potentially threatening to lives and property but do not involve the direct application of force or violence by the offender on the victim.

The National Crime Information Center (NCIC) has published a comprehensive list of offenses. A list of those that the present writer regards as violent can be found in the appendix to this chapter. In essence, my list includes all forms of homicide, kidnapping, robbery, and arson; those types of extortion involving threats to persons or property (but not reputation); and all forms of sexual assault except nonforcible statutory rape. A few of the specific offenses within other broad NCIC categories are also regarded as violent; within the category of "damaging property," the specific offenses related to bombing have been included; within "weapons offenses," the use or threatened use of incendiary devices or explosives has been included; within "public peace," rioting or inciting to riot have been included; within "traffic offenses," hit and run has been included; and within "sovereignty offenses," sabotage has been included. It can be seen from this list that the term "violence" is reserved for acts that involve relatively serious physical or psychological injury or property destruction. Minor acts of malicious mischief or vandalism are excluded, as are highly injurious or destructive acts that are not prohibited by law.

When writing about criminal violence, many behavioral scientists have focused their attention on specific offenses: homicide, rape, arson, and the like. Others have treated a variety of offenses directed at certain targets, such as familial violence or terrorism. Within these broad categories they have made finer distinctions based on such factors as the relative responsibility of the offender and victim for the behavior in question (compare "victim-precipitated" versus "nonvictim-precipitated"), the relative ages of the victim and offender (e.g., peer rape, child rape, elderly rape), and, most relevant for our purposes, the apparent etiology of the offense and motivation of the offender. These considerations have formed the basis for a wide variety of typologies of violent offenders. In the next section a number of these typologies will be surveyed to provide us with some hypotheses as to the psychological correlates and determinants of criminal violence. The primary emphasis will be on those developed in the last five years in the United States.

Unlike aggression, criminal violence cannot be studied experimentally in a laboratory. Instead, we must rely on correlational and case studies and on naturalistic observations so that it is difficult to make causal inferences. As already noted, some of our knowledge comes by extrapolation from experiments on milder forms of aggressive behavior and on infrahuman species. Some comes from personality research on that subsample of criminals who have been convicted of violent crimes and, in all likelihood, changed to some extent by the offense and the subsequent judicial and correctional procedures. And some comes from study of the violent events themselves, typically reconstructed imperfectly after the act by interviewing victims and witnesses or interpreting physical evidence. Because of these constraints, it is better to regard treatises such as this one on the "psychological causes and determinants of *criminal violence*" as constituted more of educated opinions and reasonable deductions than of "scientific knowledge." Most of these hypotheses still require rigorous empirical verification.

TYPOLOGIES OF CRIMINAL VIOLENCE

Although there is a substantial experimental literature on the causes and determinants of milder forms of aggression, the problems of performing rigorous research on criminal violence have prevented the growth of an extensive experimentally based body of knowledge on extreme forms of aggression. Not surprisingly, most of the studies in the literature have applied correlational techniques to the most readily available source of data, routinely collected statistical data on convicted offenders. These data have been used to delineate the demographic characteristics of those arrested or convicted of violent crimes, and the incidence of such offenses has often been related to other measures such as mean income, population density, and the like.

The second modal group of studies have concerned the psychological characteristics of violent offenders. These have typically been based on the clinical study of small groups of violent criminals, usually in connection with pretrial psychiatric examinations or postconviction treatment. Some of the most significant research on rapists, for example, has been performed at centers for the confinement and treatment of mentally disordered sex offenders. The price for the richer data base of these idiographic studies has been decreased generalizability, for they have been subject to all the selective biases involved in apprehension, arrest, plea bargaining, conviction, and referral for psychiatric examination.

The variables chosen for investigation have typically been those that are most readily available and those that the researcher's theoretical frame of reference has suggested might have causal significance. Nomothetic researchers have focused on such variables as social disorganization and alcohol usage. Psychoanalytically oriented idiographic investigators have been more concerned with the role of early childhood experiences and sexual disturbances in violent crime, whereas those sharing a social-learning orientation have investigated the role played by aggressive models and the degree to which violent criminals experienced or witnessed violence as children. Many such investigators have found the relationships they sought. Unfortunately, the absence of adequate control groups in many of the studies of violent offenders makes it impossible to determine whether the factors cited are in fact significantly more frequent among violent criminals than among other offender populations, or among other groups matched for age, socioeconomic status, ethnic background, and the like.

The emerging interest in victimology and the "scenario of violence" has led some investigators such as Wolfgang (1958), Toch (1969), and Luckenbill (1977) to concentrate on the behavioral patterns of the victim that may contribute to the violent resolution of an interaction. The victim's role has come under closest scrutiny in cases of spouse abuse, partly because violence in the context of an ongoing relationship naturally raises questions regarding the role of the victim as well as the offender, and partly because it is often the victim who seeks psychological treatment and is therefore available for study by mental health professionals (Steinmetz, 1978a, 1979b; Star, 1977; Star et al., 1979; Segal, 1976; Symonds, 1979; Shainess, 1977). On the other hand, those writing from a radical feminist perspective have denied that it is the battered wife's masochism or behavior that contributes to the battered-spouse syndrome, instead attributing the crime to a male-dominated social structure and gender-role inequities (Warrior, 1974; Walker, 1979; Gingold, 1976).

Does the fact that clinicians and researchers have filtered their observations through their own theoretical and social frames of reference, as illustrated above, invalidate their reports? No. The criminal offender's behavior and characteristics have generally contributed most of the variance, and the possibly distorting effects imposed by theoretical biases can be partly offset by contrasting the reports of observers representing differing schools of thought. For this reason it is wise to survey as broad a range of the literature as possible rather than to rely on a single authority. The present writer has attempted to do this in the present review.

What about the sampling biases, failure to include control or contrast groups, inadequate operational definitions, lack of quantitative measurements, and reliance on subjective impressions that has characterized many of these idiographic reports? Does this lack of rigor render them scientifically useless? Again, the answer is no. First, even though many of the descriptions of the motives of violent criminals have consisted of "armchair" heuristic reflections, these observations are by people who have often spent considerable time dealing with such offenders. Even though they may not be quantitative, they should not be dismissed as "unscientific." Instead they properly belong at the first stage of scientific inquiry, that of preliminary observation and hypothesis generation. Moreover, not all the clinical reports are impressionistic. Many, such as Toch's (1969), are based on systematically collected data on a number of cases, and a few, such as Megargee's (1966), have been systematically validated through quantitative empirical research. To the extent that researchers approaching the problem from differing perspectives using different techniques have arrived at similar formulations, we can place greater confidence in their descriptions.

Typologies, Taxonomies, and Syndromes. The more closely one studies any phenomenon, the more complex it becomes and the more refined are the questions posed. Initially criminologists set out to answer the questions, "What causes crime?" and "What are criminals like?" only to discover that the heterogeneity of those labeled "criminal" was too great to permit a simple answer. The next step was an attempt to subdivide criminals into smaller, more homogeneous subtypes (Megargee et al., 1979; Megargee, 1980). A natural basis for this was the criminal offense; therefore, the questions were refined so as to inquire into the causes of broad offense categories, such as crimes against persons. When these, too, proved too broad, they focused on specific offenses such as homicide, rape, and arson in the hope that these offense categories would provide homogeneous types.

It was soon found that a diverse array of people expressing a variety of motives engaged in each of these offenses. Faced with a heterogeneous array of objects, whether they be rocks, clouds, plants, or people, one of the scientist's first reactions is to attempt to formulate a typology into which they may be classified. So, too, with violent offenders. Beginning with murderers, who have always attracted more interest than their numbers justify, and on to other crimes of violence, experts from a variety of disciplines have suggested typologies and syndromes within each of the various crimes of violence.

Some of these typologies are of offenders, others of offenses. Generally they overlap considerably. The typologist who started out discussing the "sadistic rapist," for example, typically described the "sadistic rape" as well, and vice versa.

Most typologists have attempted to formulate *taxonomies,* sets of mutually exclusive categories, often hierarchically ordered, into which all the cases encountered could be classified. The present writer's MMPI-based system for classifying criminal offenders is an example of such a taxonomy (Megargee et al., 1979). Others have chosen to delineate *syndromes,* differentiating a group that appeared to be homogeneous with respect to behavior, psychodynamics, or motivation. In the latter approach, which is quite similar to the procedure physicians use in describing a possible new disease entity, there is no implication that all the individuals encountered will fall into the syndrome or syndromes described. When the present writer demonstrated the existence of undercontrolled and overcontrolled assaultive types, he was employing the syndrome approach, since he specifically stated at the time that other assaultive types no doubt existed (Megargee, 1966, 1971). The present chapter will review both taxonomies and syndromes of violent criminals, and, to a lesser extent, criminal violence.

Because most typologists have focused on specific offense categories more or less conforming to the criminal law (familial violence and terrorism being exceptions), this practice will be adopted in this chapter. We will first consider crimes of violence directed primarily at people: homicide, assault, familial violence, rape, kidnapping, and terrorism. Next we shall deal with violent crimes directed primarily at property, which nonetheless have a high risk of injuring people: bombing, arson, and robbery.

Crimes Against People

As we shall see in the pages that follow, a number of different organizing principles have been used to establish typologies of violent offenders. Perhaps the most common is the apparent motivation for the crime. Although he was not addressing criminal violence per se, Arnold Buss (1961, 1971) did propose a motivational distinction that has been adopted by a number of scholars, some explicitly and others implicitly. When we think of criminal violence, we typically focus on behavior aimed at injuring the victim. In addition to this type of aggression, which he labeled "angry aggression," Buss reminded us that aggression and violence, both legal and criminal, can also be used as means to achieving other ends, such as acquisition of money, property, status, power, safety, sexual gratification, and political change. Most typologies of violent offenders include categories representing both types of motivation. As might be expected, types manifesting angry motivation tend to be more prevalent among those convicted of offenses such as assault and homicide, whereas instrumental motivation is more often cited as a causal factor in offenses such as kidnapping and robbery. Some, such as arson, are almost equally divided between angry and instrumental types, and of course, the motivation can be mixed, as in many instances of rape and terrorism.

Another broad organizing principle has been the psychological condition of the violent offender. Some typologists, as we shall see, have contented themselves with two broad categories, roughly corresponding to "normal" versus "disturbed," although the specific terminology varies; others have differentiated various groupings within these broad categories with separate types corresponding to different psychiatric diagnoses and personality patterns. Of course, some writers have formulated taxonomies incorporating a combination of motivational and psychodynamic constructs. These principles are evident in the many typologies that have been offered for the first violent crime we shall consider, murder.

Murder

Murder is, of course, the unlawful taking of a human life or lives. It is a subcategory of homicide, which also includes lawful taking of human life, manslaughter, deaths resulting from criminal and noncriminal negligence, unpremeditated vehicular deaths, and the like. Our discussion will not include these other forms of homicide within its purview, but it will include, in addition to murder, killings by individuals who lack the capacity to form a criminal intent *(mens rea)* and are judged to be not guilty by reason of insanity (NGRI).

Taxonomies of Murderers. Ever since the first recorded homicide, attributed to sibling rivalry (Genesis 4:1-15), the crime of murder has played a prominent role in people's thinking on crime. This interest is reflected in the large number of typologies that have been devised for the classification of murderers and in the fact that such typologies have been offered for decades, in contrast to some of the more "recently discovered" crimes, such as child and spouse abuse. Some of these typologies are listed in Table 2.1.

Owing to the gravity of the charges, murderers are more likely to be referred for psychiatric examination and treatment than are most other offenders, and a number of taxonomies have been offered that reflect psychiatric and psychoanalytic frames of reference. Abrahamsen (1960) and Bromberg (1961) simply differentiated between murderers who did and did not manifest diagnosable psychiatric disorders. Glaser et al. (1968) made a similar broad distinction and then went on to describe several subtypes within each broad grouping. Within the "appropriate" murder category, Glaser et al. included people who were raised in a subculture in which violence was the norm ("ordinary" murderers), those who were compelled by social pressures to kill someone per-

TABLE 2.1 Taxonomies of Murderers

Banay (1952)	Jesse (1952)	Abrahamsen (1960)	Bromberg (1961)	Guttmacher (1960)	Glaser (1968)	Tanay (1969)	Morrison (1973)	Revitch and Schlesinger (1978)	Cole et al. (1968)
Subcultural	Gain	Manifest	Normal	Normal	*Appropriate*	Psychotic	*Square John*	*Motivated*	(Women)
Cultural	Revenge	Symptomatic	Psychopathic	Sociopathic	Ordinary	Ego Syntonic	Personal—one-time loser	Environmental	Masochistic
Supercultural	Elimination			Avenging	Cultural	Dissociative	Accidental	Situational	Overtly hostile
	Jealousy			Schizophrenic	Professional		*Subcultural*	Impulsive	Covertly hostile
	Lust			Temporarily psychotic	*Inappropriate*		Victim pre-cipitated	Catathymic	Inadequate
	Conviction			Symbolic suicide	Inadequate		Violent subculture	Compulsive	Amoral
				Gynocidal	Brain damaged		Mob riot	*Pathological*	Psychotic
				Homosexual	Psychopathic		*Deliberate*	Organic	
				Passive-aggressive	Psychotic		Antisocial	Toxic	
				Sadistic			Professional assassin	Paranoid	
							Political assassin		
							Felony homicide		
							Mentally ill		
							Psychopathic		
							Psychotic		
							Violent sex offender		

ceived to be an enemy of society ("cultural" murderers), and an instrumentally motivated group of hired killers ("professional" murderers). Within the "inappropriate" (i.e., pathological group), Glaser et al. described four subtypes conforming to different psychiatric diagnoses, the inadequate, the brain-damaged, the psychopathic, and the psychotic.

Like Glaser et al., Revitch and Schlesinger (1978) also distinguished normal ("motivated") from abnormal ("pathological") murderers. In the former category they delineated a continuum according to the degree to which the motivation was exogenous (outer) or endogenous (inner). The "environmental" and "situational" subtypes represented the exogenous extreme, the "impulsive" a mixture of endogenous and exogenous motivation, and the "catathymic" and "compulsive" groups appeared to be almost entirely endogenously motivated.

In contrast to these systems, in two of the earliest typologies, Jesse (1952) suggested that murderers be differentiated according to their apparent motivation (jealousy, gain, revenge, and so on), while Banay (1952) proposed that they be subdivided according to the degree to which they had assimilated cultural norms. Banay's "subcultural" type was composed of individuals with insufficient controls who were unable to conform to society's rules; his "cultural" group included normal individuals who killed someone in the course of another crime; and his "supercultural" group consisted of people too inhibited to express aggression normally who nevertheless responded violently when under stress. The subcultural and supercultural types closely resemble Megargee's (1966) undercontrolled and overcontrolled syndromes respectively.[1]

A similar tripartite distinction couched in psychodynamic terms was proposed by Tanay (1969), who divided murderers into "psychotic," "ego syntonic," and "dissociative" types; although somewhat more narrowly construed, it would appear that his "psychotic" type would be included in Banay's subcultural or inadequately controlled category, the ego syntonic in the cultural, and the dissociative in the supercultural.

The remaining two typologies proposed by Guttmacher (1960) and Morrison (1973) were both less parsimonious. Guttmacher employed a kaleidoscopic variety of explanatory constructs including psychiatric diagnosis ("schizophrenic type"), motivation ("avenging type"), and even sexual orientation ("homosexual type"). With no central organizing principle, it is unlikely that Guttmacher's system represents mutually exclusive types, even if the types could be operationally defined.

Based on their criminal careers, socialization, and mental conditions, Morrison (1973) divided murderers into four broad types, each with several subtypes. "Square Johns" were normal, ordinarily conforming members of society who committed murder accidentally or in response to strong situational provocation. "Subcultural assaulters" were people who accepted and approved of violence as a way of settling disputes. "Deliberately antisocial" murderers had chosen to maintain a violent antisocial lifestyle, while "mentally ill" offenders were people who, even though they might not be judged legally insane, were nonetheless driven to violence by compulsions stemming from personality imbalances. Probably the most comprehensive of the taxonomies we have considered, Morrison's four groups and their associated subtypes include virtually all of the types delineated by the other typologists we have examined.

Turning to women, Cole et al. (1968) consider their female murderers' relationships with others, including the victim, along with other variables in formulating six types. For example, the "masochistic" murderer was described as a stable, well-controlled woman married to an abrasive, unstable man. After putting up with years of abuse, she impulsively killed her mate, probably in the course of a violent quarrel in which she was being beaten or feared for her life. The "inadequate" murderer was portrayed as a woman who was unable to cope effectively; highly dependent on the man in her life, she killed because he told her to. Types such as these have not been described in the taxonomies of male murderers, although other types described by Cole et al., such as the "amoral" and the "psychotic," resemble male types that have been discussed.

Syndromes of Murderers. In addition to these typologies, syndromes of murderers have been described. We shall discuss three such syndromes, all of which involve rather bizarre and atypical forms of homicide. Although (fortunately) rare, these syndromes are useful in testing the generality of theoretical explanations of homicide.

Wilson (1972) identified a group of alienated individuals who killed without apparent reason or provocation. They regarded murder as a creative means of self-fulfillment in an otherwise boring and meaningless life, and killed to express their individuality and independence in a tedious, repressive, suffocating society that blocked legitimate avenues for creative self-expression. Wilson termed this the "assassin" syndrome, although it has none of the political overtones typically associated with this label.

A second syndrome, the "lust murderer," has been described by several authors (DeRiver, 1949; Hazelwood and Douglas, 1980). According to De-River (1949: 40), the lust murderer characteristically maims the victim's body by slashing the parts that have strong sexual significance. Typically a man, the offender prefers to use his hands or sharp, pointed objects, rather than "neater" weapons such as guns.

Hazelwood and Douglas (1980) recently differentiated two subtypes of lust murderers. The "organized nonsocial" was described as a totally egocentric, amoral individual. Although he disliked people he could be superficially charming and manipulative of others for his own ends. The crime was committed in a methodical and cunning fashion, usually on a stranger some distance from his home. Part of his gratification was thought to be the impact of the crime on the community. The "disorganized asocial" type was described as a loner who had great difficulty in interpersonal relationships and felt rejected and alienated. The crime exhibited less cunning and was typically committed in an impulsive, frenzied fashion in an area close to his home where he apparently felt more secure and at ease. Whereas the nonsocial type was likely to rape the victim before or after death, the asocial type rarely did so, although he sometimes inserted foreign objects into bodily orifices. Both types were thought to engage in a great deal of sexually sadistic fantasy prior to acting out these fantasies in the offense. The lust murderer usually selected female strangers as victims, although male victims were not unknown.

A third bizarre homicidal syndrome is "Amok," a phenomenon peculiar to Southeast Asia. In the typical form of Amok, a young man launches a sudden, indiscriminate attack on all those around him. The attack occurs without warning or apparent cause in a crowded place, resulting in numerous casualties. Like ordinary homicides in that region, Amok has typically been precipitated by a serious loss, such as the termination of a relationship or serious financial reverses, often through gambling. Some have suggested it is a way of saving face, and it is often followed by suicide (Westermeyer, 1972).

The twentieth-century modernization of Southeast Asia has apparently influenced this ancient cultural pattern. Although custom long dictated that those who "run Amok" should use edged weapons, a recent study by Westermeyer revealed that 90 percent had abandoned the old patterns and instead used hand grenades, a barbaric innovation that will be deplored by those who value the importance of tradition and the proper way of doing things.

Surveying these taxonomies and syndromes, it is clear that much more effort has gone into formulating than into validating them. There is little empirical evidence available testing the implicit hypotheses that the various types of murderers differ in their etiology, personality dynamics, or responses to different management or treatment strategies. Indeed, one of the few quantitative studies carried out indicated that there was little difference between Laotians who engaged in the exotic syndrome of Amok and ordinary murderers (Westermeyer, 1972).

Many behavioral scientists from a variety of disciplines have focused on murder; even though it is among the least frequent of the violent offenses we shall consider, it is one of the most dramatic. Moreover, there is a natural inclination to write up the most unusual (i.e., least typical) cases. Whole books have been written about mass and multiple murderers—Jack the Ripper, William Hierens, Richard Speck, and Theodore Bundy—although the less exotic barroom cuttings or domestic quarrels culminating in homicide are far more common. This predilection for the dramatic and exotic, coupled with the fact that murderers are more likely to be examined psychiatrically, may partly account for the emphasis on complex psychodynamics and psychopathology in the typologies we have examined.

The greater pathology reported among murderers may also be partly a result of the offense. The difference between an assault and a murder is often simply a matter of whether a bullet or blade happens to strike an artery or vital organ, but the consequences to the perpetrator are significantly different and can be expected to influence his or her emotional status. Killing a human being and being charged with a capital offense should have considerably greater emotional impact and induce greater stress than being apprehended for a simple assault. This, in turn, should increase the likelihood that pathological symptomatology will be noted at the time of the clinical examination.

As already noted, most of the typologies of general violence and assault include murder, as well as less violent offenses within their purview, and they, too, should be considered when discussing types of homicidal offenders. We shall turn to them in the next section.

Assault and General Violence

By assault, we are referring to the unlawful use of force or violence on the person of another. Some typologists have focused on assault in the narrow sense in which it is used in the criminal code; others have dealt with violence in the more general sense, including homicide, sexual assault, and similar offenses within their purview. The typologies of assault and general violence resemble those for murder, except that there is less emphasis on psychopathology (see Table 2.2).

Conrad (cited by Spencer, 1966) and Ochberg (1980) have set forth quite similar taxonomies, each containing six types. Conrad's system emphasized social learning ("culturally violent"), psychopathology ("pathologically violent"), and situational factors ("situationally," "accidentally," and "institutionally" violent). Interestingly, Conrad delineated no types motivated by simple anger or rage. Ochberg (1980) did include such a group ("explosions of affect"). In place of Conrad's institutionally violent type, Ochberg included a "sexually motivated" group; his remaining four types ("accidental," "group sanctioned," "instrumental," and "explosions of assault" stemming from mental or neurological illness) were essentially the same as Conrad's groups, except Ochberg focused on offenses rather than offenders.

Williams (1972) distinguished people involved in group violence from those who acted individually. Within the latter category he discussed four types similar to those later identified by Ochberg ("instrumental," "situational-alcohol inspired," "sexual," and "psychotic").

Ochberg's (1980) and Williams's (1972) inclusion of sexually assaultive people as a type within a general typology of assaultive or violent offenders illustrates the leveling and sharpening that will take place as we move from one offense category to the next. Whereas sexually assaultive people are grouped as a presumably homogeneous category when we are studying general violence,

TABLE 2.2   Taxonomies of Assault

Buss (1961)	Conrad*	Toch (1969)	Williams (1972)	Ochberg (1980)
Instrumental	Cultural	*Self-Preserving*	*Individual*	Instrumental
Angry	Criminal	Rep. defending	Instrumental	Accidental
	Pathological	Norm-enforcing	Psychotic	Group-sanctioned
	Situational	Self-image compensating	Situational/Alcohol	Sexual violence
	Accidental	Defending	Sexual	Explosion of affect
	Institutional	Promoting	*Group*	Explosions of assault
		Pressure-removing		(mental/neurological)
		Needs Promoting		
		Bullying		
		Exploitation		
		Self-indulging		
		Catharting		

*Cited by Spencer, 1966.

when we consider forcible rapists we shall discover that a number of types have been formulated within this category.

Based on extensive interviews with prisoners and police officers who had engaged in violence, Hans Toch (1969) formulated a typology that focused on the functional use of violence in interpersonal relations. He distinguished two broad categories, each with several subtypes. The first ("self-preserving") comprised the use of violence to preserve an individual's reputation or self-concept, a motive particularly important to both police and convicts, who are more likely than most to encounter frequent threats to their pride and persons. The second broad category ("needs-promoting") was comprised of egocentric people who "see themselves (and their own needs) as being the only fact of social relevance. Other people are viewed as objects rather than as persons" and violence is used to manipulate their behavior or, by some, as simply an enjoyable activity in and of itself.

Syndromes of Assault and General Violence. In addition to the taxonomies described above, several investigators have delineated specific syndromes of violence-prone individuals (see Table 2.3). The present writer suggested and gathered evidence to demonstrate that within Buss's angry aggression category it is possible to differentiate those whose violent acts stem from inadequate control over aggressive drives from those whose violence paradoxically stems from excessive controls over aggression (Megargee, 1966). Within the undercontrolled type are habitually aggressive people who have not learned the inhibitions and taboos against violent behavior that are common in our society; within the overcontrolled category are those who are rarely aggressive and whose hostility builds up to the point where it overwhelms even their massive defenses so that an extremely violent act occurs.

Since the initial research successfully testing predictions made from this model (Megargee, 1966) and the subsequent derivation of a personality scale that appeared to identify the overcontrolled type (Megargee et al., 1967), an extensive literature has accumulated verifying the existence of these two syndromes and, to a lesser extent, validating the Overcontrolled-Hostility Scale of the MMPI (Lane, 1978).

Shotland (1976) recently delineated a syndrome of violent individuals whom he termed "spontaneous vigilantes," normally law-abiding people who apprehend and punish wrongdoers on the spot rather than waiting for the criminal justice system to take its course. According to Shotland, this type of spontaneous retribution is most likely to occur in a disadvantaged, high-crime area whose residents are frustrated with the perceived inadequacy of the criminal justice system. Often bound together by a common ethnic background that fosters community cohesion, these people are most likely to mete out retribution when there is unanimous agreement that a crime has occurred and the individual they have apprehended is the perpetrator.

TABLE 2.3   Syndromes of Assault and Murder

Wilson (1972)
Assassin syndrome

DeRiver (1949), Hazelwood and Douglas (1980)
Lust murderer syndrome
Organized nonsocial
Disorganized asocial

Westermeyer (1972)
Amok

Megargee (1966)
Chronically overcontrolled assaultive type
Undercontrolled assaultive type

Shotland (1976)
Spontaneous vigilante syndrome

Rosenbaum and Sederburg (1976)
Crime control vigilantes
Political vigilantes
Social-group control
Regime-control

Pursuing the vigilante syndrome one step further, Rosenbaum and Sederberg (1976) described three subtypes of vigilantes. The first, "crime control," would include not only the spontaneous vigilantes described by Shotland (1976), but also well-organized groups such as the Jewish Defense League and Spades Unlimited in the United States and the Esquadrao de Morte in Brazil, the latter rumored to be composed largely of police officers, frustrated by the judicial system, who "execute" alleged criminals the law is unable to deal with to their satisfaction. Types of "political vigilantes" depicted by Rosenbaum and Sederberg (1976) included "social-group control" vigilantes such as the Ku Klux Klan, who attempt to suppress rising minority groups whose values challenge their way of life, and "regime-control" vigilantes who attempt to preserve the status quo, even going so far as forming a coup to resist change. The Movimiento Costa Rica Libre, a group of middle- and upper-class Costa Rican businessmen with a private army prepared to control the regime in power, is such a group. Although groups such as these are far removed from the popular image of the violent criminal, nevertheless, they engage in violent crimes and exemplify the heterogeneity of motivations and personalities that must be addressed in a comprehensive study of criminal violence.

Familial Violence

Unlike murder and assault, violence directed at family members is not a separately defined criminal offense. In the eyes of the law, a murder is a murder and an assault is an assault no matter what the relationship is between the offender and the victim. However, in recent years a literature on violence directed at family members has rapidly accumulated. Given the long-standing and intimate nature of the relations between offenders and victims, it is natural to suppose that to some degree the familial violence stems from these relationships and constitutes an episode in a continuing pattern of interactions. This sets familial violence apart from most other violent offenses and makes it worthy of study in its own right.

Until recently there was a tendency for familial violence to be overlooked or "swept under the carpet." The feminist literature, focusing on wife abuse, has attributed this to the indifference of a male-dominated criminal justice system in which the wife and children are still viewed as the husband's chattel (Walker, 1979; Warrior, 1974; Gingold, 1976). However, it is also true that the victims in familial violence, who include parents, husbands, and siblings as well as wives and children, are locked into long-standing and typically dependent relationships with their attackers and are often less willing to press charges and prosecute the perpetrators than are the victims of assaults committed by strangers.

Spouse and child abuse, the most common forms of familial violence, have received the most attention in the literature. Parent abuse is beginning to be recognized as another form of familial violence; other types such as sibling violence has thus far been almost totally ignored, although Gelles (personal communication, 1981) suspects that sibling violence is the most common type of family violence.

Spouse Abuse. Not too long ago, spouse abuse was regarded as such a rare event that it hardly deserved scientific study. Although this is still true of husband abuse, wife-beating has become recognized as a serious social problem. With the growth of the feminist movement, victims of "crimes against women" such as rape and wife abuse have been encouraged by their peers to report these offenses and prosecute the perpetrators. Shelters for battered women have been established in some cities to assist those women who wish to leave violent husbands, but have no place to go. With the increased visibility of spouse abuse, a literature on the subject has rapidly accumulated in the last few years.

Professional personnel are more likely to treat the abused wife than the abusive husband, if only because the wife is more often the one to seek help. As a result, many articles have been written on the characteristics of abused wives (Hanks and Rosenbaum, 1977; Segal, 1976; Shainess, 1977; Steinmetz, 1978a, 1978b; Star, 1977; Star et al., 1979). Dewsbury (1975) wrote that battered wives seen by five English doctors often exhibited psychiatric problems, entered mental hospitals, abused drugs, received abortions, and made frequent attempts at separation followed by reunion. Professional personnel have described abused wives as lacking self-esteem, as often having witnessed or experienced violence as children, as passive and overly dependent on their husbands, and as placing a greater value on the maintenance of their marriage than on preservation of their safety. The victims of spouse abuse have even been depicted as masochistic, consciously or unconsciously precipitating the violence to which they have been subjected.

Feminists have reacted strongly against this negative stereotype, likening it to the way the female victim has often been blamed for being raped (Pagelow, 1977). Some writers have gone to the other extreme, denying the victim plays any role in precipitating these violent encounters despite the fact they occur in the context of long-term relationships that typically continue after the first assault.

Based on interviews with 420 women, Walker (1978b, 1979) described a recurring three-phase cycle in wife abuse. In the first phase, tension escalates and the husband engages in sporadic hostility followed by apologies as the wife attempts to placate him. This tension-building phase culminates in a short phase of overt wife abuse that is almost welcomed by both parties since it dissipates the tension and is followed by a third phase of loving and contrite behavior, which continues until the first phase begins again.

Walker (1979) maintained that it is a myth that all abused wives are masochistic, mentally ill, uneducated, unskilled women who deserve being beaten or that all abusive husbands are alcoholics or psychopaths. Instead, Walker (1979) described the wives as having low self-esteem, accepting responsibility for being beaten, suffering from guilt and severe stress reactions, and presenting a passive face to the world in the belief that no one can help them. The husbands were described as being possessive and jealous, coming from violent homes, and having had love-hate relationships with their mothers.

Rounsaville (1978), who studied 31 battered wives, listed eight specific causal factors: (1) pathological conflicts over autonomy and dependency, with the men engaging in paranoid controlling behavior and the women alternating between dependency and counterdependent, passive-aggressive behavior; (2) the husband's deficiency in impulse control, exacerbated by alcohol and/or drugs; (3) a paralyzing learned-helplessness syndrome among the women; (4) pressured, early marriage; (5) distorted views of marital roles learned as children; (6) severe, continuing social stress; (7) status inconsistencies between husband and wife; and (8) society's failure to recognize wife abuse as a serious problem. This viewpoint, involving the interaction among social factors and pressures on the one hand and attitudes, behavior patterns, and personality conflicts on the other, is one of the more balanced analyses in the literature.

Several writers have discussed general factors conducive to familial violence. The most common characteristic, noted by dozens of authorities, is a history of the abusers having been physically abused and neglected as children. This can lead to residual rage displaced to family members, and also to the cognitive belief that physically disciplining wives and children is appropriate and even necessary masculine behavior. Stress and financial problems are also conducive to violence, as are feelings of weakness, vulnerability, and insecurity, especially in the area of sexual adequacy. The latter can lead to paranoid suspicions of the wife's infidelity (Segal, 1976; Strauss, 1978).

Taxonomies of Spouse (Wife) Abuse. Five typologies of spouse-abusing men are presented in Table 2.4. Shainess (1977) and Tracey (1978) both formulated typologies based on the husband's psychopathology; Shainess added that these predisposing personality patterns are exacerbated by jealousy and by alcohol or drug addiction.

Elbow (1977) also focused on the personality of the abusive husband, but instead of describing it in terms of psychiatric diagnosis, Elbow focused on the abusive husband's distorted perception of his wife's role. Some ("controllers") were described as seeing their wives as objects to be controlled; others ("defenders") expected love and forgiveness despite their abuse; some ("incorporators") viewed their wives as extensions of themselves; and still others ("approval seekers") responded violently because they were insecure and threatened by the possibility that the wife might leave.

Symonds (1979) and Steinmetz (1978b) shifted the focus to patterns of familial violence and described two similar dichotomies. The first was a pattern of long-term, habitual abuse beginning early in the relationship, even during the courtship, and escalating throughout the marriage.

Whereas habitual violence was seen as stemming from the husband's pathology and the wife's acquiescence, the second type was thought to be precipitated by chronic quarreling between the spouses. Steinmetz (1978b), describing this as "the Saturday Night brawl," noted that either or both partners could end up as victims. Symonds (1979), referring to this as the "neurotic interaction" pattern, portrayed the violence as a last-ditch effort at communication after prolonged quarreling by people who are not normally prone to violence.

Child Abuse. Like spouse (and parent) abuse, violence against children has only recently emerged in the literature as a serious social problem. Although some regard any physical discipline of children as constituting child abuse, most reserve the term for serious nonaccidental injuries of children, up to and including homicide. Since children are often unable or unwilling to report such abuse (and their parents are understandably less than cooperative), national campaigns have been undertaken to educate physicians, nurses, teachers, and others in a position to observe such injuries about the signs of child abuse so that they may report such cases to the proper authorities.

Brandon (1976) described the typical abusive family as made up of young parents with longstanding emotional difficulties; small families with pregnancies occurring close together were common. Many of the families were highly mobile and the mothers were often rigid and overcontrolling and had experi-

TABLE 2.4   Taxonomies of Familial Violence

SPOUSE ABUSE

Elbow (1977)	Shainess (1977)	Symonds (1979)	Steinmetz (1978)	Tracey (1978)
Wife-controlling	Sadistic	Habitual	Chronic (habitual)	Bullies
Forgiveness-seeking	Obsessive-compulsive	Neurotic-interaction	"Saturday night brawl"	Alcoholics
Approval-seeking	Paranoid			Psychopaths
Incorporator	Passive-aggressive			Psychotics

CHILD ABUSE

Walters (1975)	Brandon (1976)	Kent et al. (1978)	Allan (1978)	Blehar (1979)
Socially-parentally incompetent	Disorganized-violent family pattern	Incompetent child rearers	Learned violent behavioral patterns	Flashpoint—Impulsive middle-class abusers
Frustration displacing	Immature-unsupported women under stress	Economically distressed	External pressures	"Spare the rod"—Teach child "respect for authority"
Situational	Explosive-impulsive	Pathological/conflicted	Emotional deficits and egocentricity	"You asked for it"—Mostly male abusers of young children; often immigrants or new arrivals
Accidental	Hysterical	Feeling of inadequacy and worthlessness	Mentally ill	"Who needs it?"—Mostly women involved in series of unstable relations with abusive men
Neglectful	Sadistic			
Victim-precipitated	Mentally ill or subnormal			
Subcultural				
Mentally ill				
Institutionally pre-scribed (caretakers)				
Self-identified				

enced deprivation, lack of love, and abuse as children. Violence toward the children appeared chronic; many of the children seen had been injured before, and 70 percent were subsequently injured again. Attacks on children often occurred in concurrence with wife-beating and alcohol abuse.

The literature on child abuse consistently reports that parents who abuse their children frequently, perhaps even typically, have been found to have suffered abuse and neglect or to have witnessed violence when they themselves were children (National District Attorneys' Association, 1980; Ross, 1979; Segal, 1976, 1979; Somerset Area Review Committee, 1977; Strauss, 1978; Varma, 1977; Yahraes et al., 1979). Unfortunately, it is not always clear how a history of "neglect" or "child abuse" was operationally defined, some authorities apparently viewing any form of corporal punishment as constituting abuse. Moreover, such retrospective studies too often lack proper controls or contrast groups, and independent verification of the parents' reports of experiencing neglect or violence as children is rare. Nevertheless, because of the frequency of the reports or the plausibility of the relationship, it has become almost axiomatic that "violence begets violence" across generations. Perhaps follow-up studies of children who have been independently identified as having suffered child abuse can test this hypothesis more adequately in the future.

As might be expected, familial stress has been found to be associated with abusive behavior (Gil, 1979; Strauss, 1978; Varma, 1977). Poverty, unemployment, unwanted pregnancies, and differing religious values are among the stressors that have been cited as conducive to familial child abuse.

Taxonomies of Child Abuse. Five taxonomies of child abusers that have been suggested in recent years are presented in Table 2.4. Some, such as Allan's (1978), are frankly a priori; others, such as Blehar's (1979), were based on observations of cases of child abuse; and one (Kent et al., 1978) was derived from statistical analyses. Despite the diversity in approach and in the number of types suggested, some common threads are evident. Most of the typologists described one group as socially and parentally incompetent parents who learned inappropriate child-rearing practices, such as burning a child's hand on the stove, from their parents or grandparents when they themselves were children. A somewhat similar group consisted of parents who had introjected the belief that severe Old Testament discipline was essential to child rearing. A third commonly described group were young, immature parents frustrated by economic pressures and familial responsibilities who displaced their aggressive feelings onto their children, who were regarded as partly responsible for the situation. A fourth modal pattern consisted of parents suffering from various forms of psychopathology including mental illness, psychopathy, and drug or alcohol addiction. Of course, these factors are not mutually exclusive and one would suppose that the more causal elements that are present, the greater is the likelihood of familial violence.

Parent Abuse. Harbin and Madden (1979) maintained that abuse of parents by adolescents and young adults involves dynamics different from those of spouse or child abuse. Violence is used by the children to establish independence and, obviously, represents serious authority problems. Elderly individuals also experience abuse in institutions and homes for the aged in which they have been placed by children who are ignorant of, or choose to ignore, their physical maltreatment. Parents frequently sanction such violence by remaining silent.

Violence Among Siblings. It has been suggested that violence among siblings may be the most frequent form of familial violence, but there is a dearth of literature on the subject. When thinking of sibling violence, there is a tendency to recall harmless childhood scuffles that are a normal part of growing up, but siblings can and do inflict serious injuries on one another, up to and including death. Although it is reasonable to suppose that the dynamics of sibling violence differ from those reported in other forms of family violence, this remains an area that is wide open to research.

Concluding Comments on Familial Violence. The causes and determinants of familial violence that have been hypothesized differ in certain respects from those suggested for assault and murder. The complex psychodynamics that were attributed to murderers and the deliberate, rational use of violence to further instrumental goals found in some typologies of murder and assault were notably lacking.[2] Even though it has been suggested that spouse abuse is used by men to control their wives and consolidate their power in the family, nevertheless spouse abuse is generally regarded as primarily an act of angry rather than instrumental aggression, with any instrumental reinforcement reduced to the status of a secondary reinforcer.

The analyses of familial violence also differed from those of assault and murder in their consistent emphasis on situational stresses—unemployment, crowded quarters, and the like. It may be that this difference in emphasis reflects a real difference between "street crimes" and "family crimes," but it seems equally likely that it is due to the facts that (1) family violence occurs in the home, where the influence of these environmental variables is more readily apparent, and (2) those who have written about family violence have often been more interested in marital dynamics than in criminal behavior per se. However, without systematic controlled comparisons of those who direct their violent behavior at relatives rather than strangers, these issues will remain unresolved.

Forcible Rape

By forcible rape, we mean a nonconsenting sexual encounter in which the victim is threatened with or experiences bodily harm or injury as an explicit or implicit consequence of resistance or refusal to participate. Although forcible rape is typically thought of as a crime by men against women, involving some form of penile insertion, we will include within our purview the other possible combinations of victim and offender (male victim-male rapist, male victim-female rapist, and female victim-female rapist) and forcible sexual acts that do not involve penile insertion.

In contrast to familial violence, rape can occur between strangers who have no preexisting relationship. The victims may be chosen not because of their personality characteristics or behavior but merely because they have a body that the rapist wishes to use. This, is, of course, not always the case; people have raped friends, lovers, and even marital partners.

Since victims are usually the only witnesses in a rape, favorite legal defense tactics are to attempt to impeach their credibility by attacking their character and reputation, or to deny that a rape took place, instead characterizing the event as a consenting, or at least unresisted, sexual encounter. In addition, victims must cope with the social stigma often associated with having been raped, especially the myth that anyone who *really* wanted to could have avoided it.

As a result of this stigmatization of the victim, rape remains one of the most underreported crimes of violence, and only the rare or foolish rapists who are actually identified, arrested, prosecuted, convicted, and sentenced become subjects for study by behavioral scientists. As a result, convicted rapists are probably less representative of the largely undetected population of rapists than convicted murderers are of the total population of murderers.

The incidence of reported rapes has increased dramatically in recent years. In part this is probably due to an increased willingness of victims to come forward as law enforcement and court personnel, in response to pressures from the women's movement, have attempted to make the criminal justice system more responsive to the needs of rape victims and ease the trauma associated with the legal process. However, it is likely that this also reflects a real increase stemming from demographic and social forces. Most rapists are young males, and the baby boom of the 1950s has resulted in an unprecedented number of young men (and women) at the most critical age period.

Social as well as demographic changes would also be likely to yield more rapes. Three elements are necessary for a rape to take place: a potential victim, a potential rapist in the vicinity of the victim, and an absence of protection or "guardians" (physical barriers or people who would be likely to intervene if an attack were to take place). Modern women live significantly less sheltered lives than their predecessors. They are more likely to live alone and move freely about the community, so there are more opportunities available for would-be rapists to encounter unguarded potential victims.

It has also been alleged that mass media, especially television, emphasizing sex and violence operate to lessen inhibitions on the part of would-be rapists. (This, as we shall see, is different from the argument that the media act to stimulate sexual and aggressive drives.) Although the Surgeon General's Report indicated a link between televised and real-life violence, the networks naturally deny that there is a causal relationship (Cater and Strickland, 1975). Although there is no definitive experimental evidence that TV causes rape and other serious crimes of violence, it appears inconsistent to this writer for the networks to argue that TV has sufficient impact on viewer behavior to justify charging sponsors millions of dollars for brief commercial messages while maintaining that the dramatic content of broadcasts has no effect on behavior.

Although the social context undoubtedly plays a role in the commission of any violent crime, it is difficult to do rigorous research on such pervasive influences; not surprisingly, the bulk of the literature on the psychological determinants of rape have focused on the characteristics of rapists who have been identified by the criminal justice system.

Taxonomies of Forcible Rape. Seven taxonomies of forcible rape and/or rapists are presented in Table 2.5. It can be seen that in recent years the role ascribed to sexual motivation has decreased and forcible rape is increasingly viewed as primarily an act of aggression motivated by anger and hostility.[3]

Sadistic rape, which in its most extreme form becomes the lust-murder syndrome described earlier, is also motivated by hostility and anger and their more extreme cousins, hatred and rage. However, the bizarre, gratuitous violence seen in sadistic rape and lust murder strongly indicates the presence of serious psychopathology as well.

Not all rapes are motivated by anger. Instrumental motivation is also evident in most of the typologies. Groth (1979) recently maintained that "power rape," in which the rapist wishes to possess and control rather than harm the victim, is the most frequent type he has observed among the many rapists he has treated. Such rapists, according to Groth, are acting out sexual fantasies; since the actual experience rarely measures up to the fantasy they often feel compelled to rape again and again. Since repeated offenses naturally increase the likelihood of apprehension, prosecution, and conviction, this repetitive aspect of their behavior might well lead to their being overrepresented in treatment programs for sex offenders such as the one Groth directed.[4]

Whereas some typologists focused on the rapists' apparent motivation, such as anger or power, others were more concerned with the perpetrators' apparent lack of inhibitions or controls. They described types with chronic superego deficiencies ("psychopathic," "amoral," or "criminal" types) as well as those with temporary lapses ("impulsive" or "alcohol-inspired"). In the third major section of this chapter, in which a dynamic framework for analyzing criminal violence is presented, we shall see that it is essential to consider both motivational and inhibitory factors.

All of the typologies in Table 2.5 deal with the most frequent type of forcible rape, adult men raping adult women. In addition to this pattern, men also rape

TABLE 2.5 Taxonomies of Forcible Rapists

Guttmacher (1951)	Amir (1971)	Cohen et al. (1971)	Bromberg (1974)	Astor (1975)	Becker & Abel (1978)	Groth (1979)
True sex offender	Rule-supportive	Sexual aim	Immature adolescent	Amoral	Aggressive	Angry
Sadistic	Role-expressive	Aggressive aim	Gang-rapist	Aggressive	Sexual	Power-oriented
Aggressive criminal	Idiosyncratic/ symptomatic	Sex-aggression defusion	Adult-sadistic	Alcohol inspired	Sexual-aggressive	Sadistic
		Impulsive	Lonely	Explosive	Criminally sadistic	
			Destroyer	Double-standard		
				Mentally defective or psychotic		

other men and women rape other women. In the case of male homosexual rape, power and dominance are the most frequently described motives, especially in prison rape (which will be discussed below as a separate syndrome).

Rape of women by other women occurs in both prison and community settings. The dynamics of female prison rapes are probably similar to those for males. In the community some women have assisted men in raping female victims by arranging for a "double date" in which the female rapist knows that the other woman will be required to engage in sexual relations whether or not she is willing (Astor, 1975). Women may or may not participate actively in the sexual assault, but in either case they can be charged with the offense. Although there are no data available, the dynamics are probably similar to gang rape, with the women involved being motivated to enhance or maintain their relationships with their male partners as well as by hostility toward the victims.

Women acting alone, or, more often, with other women have also raped men (Astor, 1975; Groth, 1979). The extent of such rapes by women is unknown; it seems likely that male victims of rape by women would be especially reluctant to report such crimes, since the macho stereotype dictates men should always welcome heterosexual relations.

Groth (1979: 192) suggested that the dynamics of the female rapist were probably the same as those of the male (i.e., anger, power, and sadism), but admitted that because of the rarity of reported rapes by women, "the female offender . . . remains an incompletely studied and insufficiently understood subject."

Syndromes of Rape. Several syndromes of rapists and rape have been described, some of which differ from ordinary rapes in the apparent motivation and characteristics of the perpetrators (see Table 2.6). One such syndrome is *gang* or *group* rape. In gang rape, each codefendent may play a different role, but the overall effect of the group is to diminish each member's individual inhibitions and feelings of personal responsibility. The person who initiates the rape, according to Groth (1979), satisfies needs for power and control, not only over the victim but also over the other members of the group. Most of the leaders in gang rapes studied by Groth had previously committed individual, solitary rapes. The follower in a gang rape "seeks to find or confirm his masculinity, achieve recognition, and/or retain his acceptance with his co-offenders" (Groth, 1979: 113). Groth (1979: 115) points out that "one of the unique dynamics in gang rape is the experience of rapport, fellowship, and cooperation with the co-offenders. . . . It appears [the offender] is using the victim as a vehicle for interacting with other men . . . behaving . . . in accordance with what he feels is expected of him . . . validating himself and participating in a group activity."

The *prison rape* (typically of a man by other men, but also of women by other women) is regarded by many as a unique rape syndrome (Davis, 1968;

TABLE 2.6   Syndromes of Rape

Brownmiller (1975)
Wartime rape
Groth (1979)
Gang rape
Rape of the elderly
Rape of children
Marital rape
Prison rape (also described by Davis, 1968; Scacco, 1975; Lockwood, 1979)
Homosexual rape
Rape by women (also discussed by Astor, 1975)

Scacco, 1975; Lockwood, 1979). Although one might suppose that it results from sheer heterosexual deprivation, this does not appear to be the case. Unlike most rapes, which are intraracial encounters, prison rapes more often involve blacks raping young, slightly built whites; they appear to be motivated by hostility, racial antagonism, and the need to assert dominance and power. In many jails and some prisons it has become almost an initiation rite and is frequently a group rape, with all of the dynamics associated with that syndrome.

According to Groth (1979), the purposes of male homosexual rape are to conquer, control, degrade, and humiliate the victim, ideally forcing him to ejaculate involuntarily, parodoxically proving the victim's homosexuality and thereby legitimizing the assault in the mind of the perpetrator. Homosexual rapes can be motivated by desires for revenge and retaliation (often mixed with racial antagonism) and may enhance the offender's status in his peer group, but they also serve to reassure the offender of his strength and authority and compensate for unconscious feelings of weakness and vulnerability.

Another syndrome is *rape of the elderly,* whom Groth operationally defined as victims at least twice as old as the offender. Groth (1978) found that men who raped significantly older women were characterized by their alienation from both their parents, coming from unhappy homes in which love, trust, respect, and security were notably lacking. Most such offenders were suffering psychological stress at the time of their offense, usually involving an emotional crisis with some significant woman in their lives. The older woman symbolized an authority figure and the predominant motivation was rage; typically the offenders engaged in considerable violence, 60 percent seriously injuring their victims.

The final syndrome described by Groth (1979) is *marital rape,* an offense that is rarely reported or prosecuted, especially if the couple is not separated at the time of the offense. Instrumental motivation predominated in the cases Groth studied, the husband using forcible sexual relations to (1) reassure himself of his virility; (2) assert his power and dominance in the marriage; (3) convince himself that his wife loves him; (4) degrade, humiliate, or punish the wife; or (5) resolve the couple's marital conflicts or problems.

Concluding Comments on Rape. Historically, rape was viewed as motivated primarily by sexual motives; indeed, some regarded it as a normal response to female provocation, an attitude that is far from extinct. Later, anger and hostility were viewed as the primary motives for forcible rape, and more recently needs for power, dominance, and affiliation have been elucidated.

The typologies of rape stand in marked contrast to the typologies of murder, assault, and familial violence in the notable absence of a category for the mentally ill or neurologically impaired, despite the fact that mentally disordered sex offender (MDSO) statutes are on the books in a number of states and men institutionalized under these laws were the subjects studied by some of the taxonomists.

Another category that is notable by its absence is the "subcultural" or "learned-deviant-values" group postulated for murder, assault, and familial violence. Although some writers have suggested that social values dictated by men condone rape (Brownmiller, 1975) and others have cited rape as symptomatic of the subculture of violence, none of the typologies reviewed by the present writer delineated a group reared with the belief that rape is acceptable.

Kidnapping and Hostage-Taking

In contrast with the crimes we have reviewed thus far, kidnapping and hostage-taking are more likely to involve instrumental than angry motivation. Kidnapping, which involves the forcible or coercive abduction of an individual, has historically been associated with the extortion of ransom. Although ransom is still a motive, especially in cases of "diplonapping" and "skyjacking," in recent years political motives have come to the fore as terrorists have used kidnapping to force governments to do their bidding and to publicize their causes. Hostage-taking, which does not necessarily involve the transportation of the victim or victims to a different location, has also increasingly come to be used as a means of political extortion, the most notable example being the prolonged captivity of American Embassy personnel in Iran to force the United States to return the late Shah and his wealth. Hostages are also taken to facilitate the commission of other crimes. Armed robbers may take hostages to help deter pursuit, and a rapist may abduct a victim to a lonely area where he is able to proceed without interruption.

Even when instrumentally motivated, kidnapping and hostage-taking are still acts of criminal violence. As in the cases of robbery and rape, there is an implicit or explicit threat that resistance, attempts to escape, or efforts to free the victims will result in their physical injury or death, a threat that has been carried out in cases ranging from the infant son of Charles Lindbergh to former Italian Premier Aldo Moro.[5]

The selection of the victim in kidnapping and hostage-taking differs somewhat from that in the other crimes of violence discussed thus far. In homicide, assault, and familial violence, the violent behavior often grew out of the interpersonal relationship or the ongoing interactions between the offender and the victim. In kidnapping, which is typically a premeditated crime, victims are rarely chosen on the basis of personal characteristics or behavior but instead because of their wealth or position, as in the cases of heiresses Barbara Mackel and Patricia Hearst. Hostage-taking is more likely to be an impulsive offense, with victims selected on the basis of availability. Of course, the more leverage the hostage will provide the offender, the better. In the Middle Ages, when hostages were often exchanged to seal diplomatic agreements, princes were preferred to peasants.

Taxonomies of Kidnapping and Hostage-Taking. These varied motivations are reflected in the typologies in Table 2.7. Miron and Goldstein (1978) reduced these offenders to two broad types, the "instrumental," who sought tangible rewards such as ransom, and the "expressive," who craved power, control, and significance. Whereas publicity is anathema to the former type, it is craved by the latter. In some instances, a kidnapping that began for instrumental reasons was continued for expressive purposes after the tangible goal became impossible to obtain. This sort of a progression has been observed in some skyjackings and prison takeovers.

Schlossberg (1979) and Dawe (1979) each preferred similar tripartite taxonomies. Both had categories for professional criminals who kidnapped for ransom and for mentally disturbed individuals acting out conflicts and deriving gratification from the kidnap situation. Both also differentiated "group" kidnappers, including terrorists or self-proclaimed revolutionaries such as the Brigate Rosse, which has claimed responsibility for many abductions in Italy. In addition to well-organized cadres such as these, Schlossberg also pointed to "undisciplined mobs," such as the hostage-taking rioters at Attica prison.

Syndromes of Kidnappers. Baumann (1973) delineated a syndrome that she dubbed "diplonapping," the kidnapping of a foreign diplomat to secure ransom. Since her report, other diplomats have been taken in order to effect the release of "political prisoners," typically fellow terrorists already apprehended and imprisoned.

TABLE 2.7   Taxonomies of Kidnappers and Hostage-Takers

Miron and Goldstein (1978)	*Schlossberg (1979)*	*Dawe (1979)*
Instrumental	Professional '	Professional criminals
Expressive	"Psycho"	Psychotics
	Group hostage-taker	"Rebels" seeking social justice
	Disorganized mob	
	Tightly organized terrorist	

"Skyjacking," or air piracy, is another definable syndrome with several subtypes (Hubbard, 1971). Perhaps the earliest recorded case of skyjacking was carried out in 1941 when Deputy Führer Rudolph Hess flew to Scotland in a stolen Luftwaffe fighter. Later, during the Cold War, freedom-selecting Eastern Europeans flew or commandeered planes to escape from the Iron Curtain countries. The refusal of the Western Allies to return them to the Communists left these countries in a dubious moral position when they later requested the return of people who hijacked airliners to fly to Communist Cuba after scheduled commercial flights to that nation had been halted (Hubbard, 1971). People who are seeking transportation to a country to which they are unable to travel legally might constitute one skyjacker syndrome.

A second syndrome, "hijacking for extortion" was inaugurated by D. B. Cooper who commandeered a plane, successfully demanded ransom, and parachuted out in midflight, apparently to his death. His *modus operandi* was widely publicized and quickly emulated (Hacker, 1976). Skyjacking has also come to be used to extort political concessions or to force governments to free prisoners.

A third syndrome is the skyjacking by confused or pathological individuals such as Hess. Some have appeared to be committing an expressive sort of suicide, some have been seeking power and publicity, and some have been acting out other psychological conflicts. David Hubbard (1971) and Frederick Hacker (1976), psychiatrists who have examined a number of skyjackers, have reported that all those they examined were "severely neurotic or psychotic individuals, with or without criminal tendencies" (Hacker, 1976: 95). Both authorities noted that the airplane had strong symbolic value for these disturbed skyjackers and that the skyjacking itself, aided and abetted by media coverage, induced feelings of omnipotence. The possibility of death, according to Hacker, was actually an incentive rather than a deterrent.

Terrorism

We are inclined to think of political terrorism as a relatively recent phenomenon, and indeed international terrorist activity has become increasingly well publicized and visible in recent years. However, the use of terror to accomplish political goals such as the "liberation of an oppressed people" has a long tradition, especially in the Middle East. Long before Anwar Sadat attempted to negotiate peace with the Israelis, a previous ruler of Egypt who was less enlightened was subjected to a systematically escalating campaign of terror that began with the pollution of the rivers and escalated through successive plagues of frogs, lice, boils, and locusts, culminating in the death of the Egyptians' firstborn sons (Exodus 7-14). Those of today's urban revolutionaries who assiduously study the writings of Mao and Che would also do well to add Machiavelli and Robespierre to their libraries.

Modern technology has brought about changes in terrorism, however. Lacking Moses' powerful ally, terrorists of the past typically had to be able to command a number of followers to carry out their schemes. This meant that the effective use of terror was restricted to the wealthy or those in positions of political and/or religious power. Thus, terror was generally used by the civil establishment to help suppress dissident elements in the populace, as in the case of Pompey, whose legions crucified 6,000 survivors of Spartacus's slave revolt in 71 B.C., or by religious authorities to discourage deviant beliefs, as in the Spanish Inquisition under Tomas de Torquemada in the fifteenth century.

Revolutions provided the apparent exception to this general rule. The Reign of Terror in France in 1793 and 1794 was directed against, rather than by, the aristocracy and their sympathizers, but by this time the common people or "citizens," as represented by the Committee of Public Safety, had become the new establishment, a pattern similar to that noted in Iran after the Ayatollah Khomeini's Islamic Revolution.

True democratization in the use of terror had to await the technological advances in weapons, communications, and transportation of the twentieth century. As Hacker (1976: ix) noted, "The practice of intimidation, at one time a luxury reserved for the powerful few, has now become a common custom among the many would-be powerful." These technological "advances" have made it possible for small groups to terrorize society at large, and in the process derive for themselves individual significance and power otherwise denied them in a complex society (Hacker, 1976).[6] Of course, terror also continues to be used by the establishment, Idi Amin and Pol Pot being two of the most recent infamous examples.

Although terrorism involves most of the violent crimes discussed in this chapter—murder, assault, kidnapping, robbery, bombing, and arson—the modal personality characteristics of many terrorists have been observed to differ from those of other criminals who commit these offenses. Hacker (1976: xiii) noted that this type of violence "seemingly produces not guilt but pride, not anxiety but self-confidence, not remorse but enhanced self-righteousness." Since "ideological crimes," as Verin (1971) labels them, proceed from a cognitive belief structure in which the end justifies the means, it would logically follow from Festinger's (1957) theory of cognitive dissonance that these effects would be observed, especially when we consider the fact that Hacker could clinically examine only those who had been apprehended for their crimes. Cognitive dissonance theory would predict that the prospect of punishment would strengthen the beliefs.

Consistent with our cognitive dissonance interpretation, a number of authorities have maintained that terrorists lack conventional guilt feelings (Hacker, 1976; Verin, 1971). According to Davis (1978), dissident terrorists are typically social misfits who, after being recruited into the group, are exposed to rhetoric and propaganda to neutralize their guilt feelings. Through mutual coercion, sometimes assisted by drugs, members of the group reinforce loyalty to the cadre rather than external society. Eventually the groups' values and goals are totally incorporated, guilt is felt only for disloyalty to the group, and the individual is willing to kill or be killed to further the group's goals.

Although this analysis may be applicable to many members of groups whose terrorist activities are rejected by the larger society, such as the Brigate Rosse and Baader-Meinhof groups in Europe and the Weather Underground in the United States, the present writer feels it is less descriptive of establishment terrorists and members of quasi-military groups who have been raised since childhood in an environment that accepts terroristic activities against perceived foreign enemies. The young man or woman reared in Bogside in Belfast or in a Palestinian refugee camp in Lebanon might well join the Provisional Wing of the IRA or the Palestinian Liberation Organization respectively as a normal response to an abnormal environment, and, if subjected to clinical examination, appear less deviant or disturbed than the alienated youths Davis described.

It would be naive to suppose that all terrorists are motivated solely by abstract political ideals. In addition to the group acceptance that has already been cited, O'Brien (1977) described the glamour, power and prestige that accrue from carrying a gun in the name of a cause, as well as the freedom from conventional routines and restraints, not to mention the money. May (1974) has written of the "ecstasy of terrorism," noting that terrorist activities that originally may have begun to achieve well-defined political goals have been known to be continued as ends in themselves after the terrorists' activities have become politically counter-productive.

Taxonomies of Terrorists. Several authorities have formulated typologies of terrorism and terrorists. Most typologies of "terrorism" simply differentiate terror used by the establishment to suppress the people from terror used by dissidents against the established order, so in this section we shall limit our discussion to the classification of dissident terrorists.

The typologies in Table 2.8 typically focus on role definitions and motivations in typing terrorists. The FBI's SOARS group (1978) used the structure of the so-called Symbionese Liberation Army (SLA) to illustrate differences in the roles, expectation, and personalities of the members of this and other similar groups such as the Baader-Meinhof band. The "leader," a role occupied in the SLA by Nancy Ling Perry and in the Baader-Meinhof gang by Ulrike Meinhof, supplies the group with its theoretical rhetoric and its rationale for rebellion. Both Perry and Meinhof were described as middle-class, perfectionistic paranoid personalities with well-developed delusional systems who exercised control through the "opportunist," a criminal psychopathic personality who supplied the group with tactical knowledge and muscle in return for a hedonistic criminal lifestyle justified by the revolutionary rationalizations of the leader. In

TABLE 2.8   Taxonomies of Terrorists

Hacker (1976)	SOARS (1978)	Milte et al. (1976)
Crusaders	Leader	Political existentialist
Criminals	Opportunist	Freedom fighter
Crazies	Idealist (gofer)	

the SLA this position was occupied by Donald David DeFreeze, a.k.a. General Field Marshall Cinque. The rest of the cadre is made up of "gofers" or "idealists," naive, alienated middle-class losers deluded by the leader and the opportunist into believing their lives will have meaning if they serve as cannon fodder. (It is this latter group that Davis was apparently describing.)

The typology proposed by Hacker was somewhat similar; the "crusaders" were the rebels with a cause, motivated by abstract ideals, while the "criminals" were concerned solely with material gain and self-interest. In Hacker's typology, the "crazies" were acting out their mental aberrations.

Milte et al. (1976) approached the classification from a somewhat different stance in differentiating between "political existentialists," who continually redefine themselves through redemptive acts of violence, and "freedom fighters," who work within established organizations to liberate those they regard as subjugated by repressive regimes.

Crimes Directed at Property

Despite the fact that the destruction or acquisition of property is the primary goal of bombers, arsonists, and robbers, these individuals nevertheless kill and injure many people each year. As this chapter was being prepared, four fires, at least three of which were set by arsonists, were responsible for the deaths of over a hundred people, as well as the destruction of hundreds of millions of dollars worth of property.[7] Clearly, any discussion of violent crime would be incomplete without a consideration of these offenses.

Bombers

The incidence of bombing varies widely from place to place and from time to time. In 1975, bombings were responsible for less than 1 percent of the homicides in the United States, in marked contrast to Northern Ireland, in which 29 percent of the murders resulted from bombings that year. This country was not always so fortunate. In one six-month period in 1928, Chicago experienced 62 bombings as Al Capone's "bomb squad," headed by James "King of the Bombers" Belcastro, tried to create a favorable business climate by blowing up stills and speakeasies producing and selling rival brands of beer. Even Eliot Ness, leader of the "Untouchables," found a dynamite bomb wired to his car's engine. Bombings by Prohibition gangs became such a political issue that the Chicago election became known as the "Pineapple Primary" (MacDonald, 1977). The recent assassination of investigative reporter Don Bolles by means of a bomb wired to the starter of his automobile demonstrates that hired killers still resort to bombs on occasion, while the recent outbreak of explosions in and around New York City is evidence that political terrorists use bombs in the United States as well as Europe.

Aside from John MacDonald (1977), whose book is the primary source of information for this section, behavioral scientists in this country have devoted little attention to bombers. There are no nomothetic studies known to this writer and the few idiographic case reports have concentrated on highly publicized or sensational cases such as those of George Metesky, the "Mad Bomber" of New York City (MacDonald, 1977), Muharem Kurbegovic, the "Alphabet Bomber" of Los Angeles (Hacker, 1976), and John Gilbert Graham, who, in an extreme case of parent abuse, placed a time bomb with 25 sticks of dynamite in his well-insured mother's suitcase, destroying her and her fellow plane passengers (Galvin and MacDonald, 1959).[8]

Part of the problem appears to be the difficulty of apprehending and convicting bombers. Whereas most violent criminals must have direct contact with their victims, thus facilitating their recognition, time delay mechanisms make it possible for the bomber to be long gone from the scene and the bomb, when it explodes, leaves only "fragmentary" physical evidence.

Discussing the motivation of bombers, MacDonald (1977: 59) pointed out that "bombing like other behavior is complex and does not lend itself to neat, psychological, sociological, or biological explanations. The bomber who seeks financial gain may also be motivated by other factors, possibly beyond his awareness. His need for attention, for power, or for gratification of sadistic impulses may also determine his behavior." With this caveat, MacDonald proceeded to describe some of the modal motivational patterns as follows:

(1) financial gain, including extortion, insurance fraud and, paradoxically, the efforts of some bomb-disposal officers to convince the local city fathers of the continuing need for their services;
(2) "settlement of disputes," including labor-management conflicts, racial strife connected with the civil rights movement and school busing, and disputes between religious groups;
(3) avoidance of punishment, including intimidation of witnesses, concealment of crimes, and escape from prison;
(4) personal motives, including revenge, jealousy, and hatred, as well as the resolution of marital problems (as in the case of a husband who detonated a bomb under the bed in which his wife was entertaining her lover).

Although MacDonald (1977) did not list individual psychopathology and sexual disturbances as modal motives, his taxonomy of bombers, to be discussed next, makes it clear that these, too, are often regarded as psychological determinants of bombing.

A Taxonomy of Bombers. Based on his studies, MacDonald (1977) described six types of bombers. The first (1) were the "compulsive bombers" who were fascinated and excited by the power, flames, and loud noise of the bombs they created. Similar to compulsive firesetters, some derived sexual excitement from bombs, one being quoted by MacDonald (1977: 42) as reporting, "I'd rather shoot a rifle and hear the sound of explosives than ball my old lady." Others used bombs to satisfy sadistic tendencies, to emphasize their masculinity, to satisfy their curiosity, or to obtain excitement through daredevil risk-taking. Other types were: (2) "psychotic bombers," typically suffering from paranoia (as in the case of George Metesky) or paranoid schizophrenia; (3) "sociopaths," who had no guilt or respect for life, as in the case of John Gilbert Graham; (4) "political bombers," who used the bomb as a tool for assassination; (5) "mafia bombers"; (6) "military bombers" or "fraggers," who found a fragmentation grenade placed under a cot an effective way of removing an incompetent or unpopular commanding officer; (7) "revolutionary bombers," a category subdivided into "terrorists," who wanted to effect political change, and "counter-revolutionaries," who wished to preserve the status quo; and (8) "bombers for profit," whose motives have already been discussed.

MacDonald (1977: 59) was the first to question the scientific adequacy of his typology, pointing out that not all bombers can be neatly classified into these types. He also cautioned, "The classification is open to the criticism that it does not have a single basis such as clinical diagnosis." This drawback is equally applicable to most of the other typologies we have reviewed, but few authors have been as candid as MacDonald about their systems' deficiencies.

Arson

Arson, like bombing, is rarely mentioned in behavioral scientists' discussions of violent crime. The psychological literature instead focuses on offenses in which there is a direct confrontation between the offender and victim and in which personal injury rather than property damage is the ostensible primary motivation.

MacDonald (1977) maintained that there are numerous parallels between arsonists and bombers. Indeed, some bombers are also firesetters. He also asserted that many of the motives he ascribed to bombers apply equally well to firesetters. This would be especially true of those whose offenses are motivated by profit, personal animosity, and psychopathology. On the other hand, fires are less useful than bombs in assassination attempts, burglaries, and armed robberies. Perhaps because less technical skill and fewer exotic ingredients are required to start a fire than to build a bomb, arson is more widespread, with juveniles constituting a significant proportion of the incendiary population.

Taxonomies and Syndromes of Firesetters. Different typologists have postulated the existence of anywhere from three to nine different types of arsonists. There is general agreement on certain broad patterns; the chief differences are in the number of subcategories within these patterns that the typologist choses to define (see Table 2.9).

One broad, generally agreed-on category is the arsonist for profit. Within this category, Levin (1976) differentiated between the businessman who arranges for the fire to collect on insurance and the "torch," who actually sets the blaze. In discussing specific syndromes of torches, Karchner (1977) described the "Mafia" arsonist, who is able to offer a complete package deal including insurance arrangements, while Stevenson (1976) detailed the use of arson as a device for intimidating builders employing nonunion labor.

Another broad category is the juvenile firesetter. Within this group, Barlay (1976) focused on children who set fire to schools to destroy records, cover up petty offenses, or simply relieve boredom, while Vernon (1972) differentiated young children experimenting with fire from older youths acting out stress induced by family conflicts or school problems.

The mentally disturbed or pathological adult arsonist is another frequently described general type. Included within this category are compulsive firesetters or "pyromaniacs," who are thought by MacDonald (1977) to obtain sexual gratification and feelings of power from setting fires; psychotics whose firesetting is a symptom of a broader and more profound disturbance such as a psychotic depression or chronic brain syndrome; and alcoholics who inadvertently set fires while intoxicated (MacDonald, 1977).

There is also general agreement that some people set fires out of revenge or for spite; indeed, revenge was cited as the motive for at least half of the 8,000 cases of arson processed in New York City (Milliken, 1979). This can be either a solitary or a group pattern; anger and frustration are probably the predominant motives for fires set in conjunction with riots, especially in urban ghettos. Similar motivation may be present in the fires set by political dissenters, another type delineated by some authorities.

Fires can also be set by guards, watchmen, and volunteer firemen who wish to demonstrate their alertness, pose as heroes, or try out some new firefighting equipment. Indeed, the person who first reports a blaze is often one of the first to be investigated.

Instrumental motivation is also evident in MacDonald's (1977) description of the "female firesetter," a syndrome apparently peculiar to the nineteenth century when the typical arsonist was often described as a homesick serving girl who hoped she could return home if her employer's house burned down. According to MacDonald (1977), some women also set fires so they could be rescued by handsome young firemen. Insurance companies are no doubt relieved that modern women can find less drastic ways of meeting firemen who attract their attention.

TABLE 2.9 Taxonomies of Bombers and Arsonists

BOMBERS	ARSONISTS			
MacDonald (1977)	*MacDonald (1977)*	*Barlay (1976)*	*Levin (1976)*	*Milliken (1979)*
Compulsive	Compulsive	Schoolchildren	*Arson for profit*	*Pathological firesetters*
Psychotic	Psychotic	Criminals	Businessmen	*Juvenile firesetters*
Sociopathic	Juvenile	Political dissenters	Torches	*General Arsonists*
Political (assassin)	Female	Professionals	*Solitary*	Revenge
Mafia	Fireman/watchman		Revenge and spite	Profit
Military (fragger)	Alcoholic		Would-be hero	
Revolutionary	Professional		*Group*	
Terrorist			Political	
Counterrevolutionary			Vandal	
Profit-seeking			Riot	
			(Added to Levin's list by	
			Vreeland and Waller, 1978)	
			Female	
			Youthful	

SYNDROMES OF ARSONISTS

Vernon (1972)
Subtypes of juvenile firesetters:
  Children experimenting with fire
  Youths reacting to stress or conflict

Karchner (1977)
  Mafia arsonist

Stevenson (1976)
  Labor union firesetters

Robbery

According to John Conrad, "Robbery is a perfectly rational transaction which includes the assumption that violence will be exercised if compliance to the robber's will is not forthcoming" (quoted by MacDonald, 1975: 135). Al Capone put it more succinctly: "You can get much farther with a kind word and a gun than you can with a kind word alone" (Peter, 1977: 141).

Material gain is the ostensible motive for armed robbery; when asked why he robbed banks, the late Willie (The Actor) Sutton was supposed to have responded, "Because that's where the money is." (In fact, a reporter made up the quotation, but Willie always wished he had said it.) Money is only part of the motivation, however. Some people simply enjoy playing cops and robbers with real guns and real cars. Some become cops, others become robbers. A graduate student who had formerly served thirteen years for armed robbery and murder nostalgically described the "adrenaline high" he had gotten when robbing a bank, and the heady feeling of power that came from being in total command of the situation with the omnipotent power of life or death in his trigger finger.

Nevertheless, most robbers downplay the role of violence, insisting it is used only to achieve control of the situation and force compliance. One robber was quoted by MacDonald (1975: 143) as stating, "So violence is wrong, on a fundamental level, I admit that. But on a day-to-day level it just happens that it's a tool of my trade and I use it—like an engineer uses a slide rule or a bus driver the handbrake, or a dentist the drill. Only when necessary and only when it can't be avoided. . . . I don't indulge in it, you know, for the sheer pleasure of the thing. I'm no sadist."

The fact that more victims are injured by unarmed (strong-arm) robbers than by armed robbers tends to support this statement. People are more likely to resist an unarmed robber who must then exercise force to achieve control. Of course, when an armed robber does inflict injuries, they are more serious. Injuries in an armed robbery come about not only as a result of resistance by the victims but also as a result of impulsive explosions of affect on the part of the robber (Petty and Mason, 1978). When one mixes high excitement and loaded weapons, accidents can occur. More than one robber has managed to shoot himself, his partners, or their car in the course of a robbery.

A Taxonomy of Robbers. Conklin (1972) postulated four types of robbers: (1) the "professional," who has a long-term commitment to a criminal career to support a playboy lifestyle, works with accomplices who have specialized roles, and carries out robberies that are carefully planned; (2) the "opportunist," a young, inexperienced amateur who steals small sums from targets of opportunity and rarely plans his jobs; (3) the "addict," who robs to support a habit and engages in more planning than the opportunist but less than the professional; and (4) the "alcoholic," who engages in drunken assaults and takes the victim's money as an afterthought.

Bartol (1980) recently criticized the completeness of Conklin's typology, suggesting the possibility of at least four other types of robbery: (1) robbery for social protest; (2) robbery for attention or excitement, (3) robbery as a form of suicide, and (4) robbery to gain control of social status.

Some Conclusions

It is clear after surveying this array of typologies of violent crimes and criminals that there is no simple single cause of criminal violence. To be sure, some of the diversity stems from the differences between assault and robbery, familial violence, and political terrorism, and some reflects the different frames of reference brought to the task by the typologists themselves. However, most of the variance seems due to the fact that there are a number of different causes of violent crime, both situational and personal.

Despite this diversity, there are a number of broad areas of agreement that cut across the array of violent offenses. Different observers with different perspectives studying different offenses have consistently reported finding certain modal groups of offenders. These include:

(1) Normal, adequately socialized people exposed to extremely provocative or frustrating situations or circumstances. In some instances, their violent tendencies are exacerbated by inhibition-lowering drugs, notably alcohol.

(2) A group committed to a violent lifestyle with supporting attitudes and values. This includes both normal people who learn that violence is expected in certain circumstances by being reared in a subculture that rewards violent behavior, and psychopaths who fail to develop adequate inhibitions against violent behavior because of disturbed developmental patterns.

(3) Individuals whose inhibitions against violence are impaired by functional or organic pathology.

(4) Overcontrolled offenders whose violence paradoxically stems from excessive, inflexible inhibitions against the expression of normal aggressive behavior.

(5) A group characterized by high instigation to aggression or anger for a variety of reasons, including, but not limited to, frustration, revenge, jealousy, and oppression.

(6) Instrumentally motivated offenders who engage in violence as a necessary means to achieve certain goals and fulfill needs other than injuring the victim.

Obviously there is some overlap among these categories and some syndromes may not fit neatly into any other types. Nevertheless, it appears that most of the types discussed could be included in these six broad categories.

What is the relative importance of these six broad categories? Our review indicated some differences across offense categories. Instrumental motives such as seeking profit or excitement were more apparent in arson than in homicide, and anger was more often cited as a motive for rape than for kidnapping. However, this must remain a matter for speculation, because there is no reasonably rigorous literature on the incidence of these various types across offenses. Indeed few of the typologists surveyed have ever attempted to classify actual offenders into types, and, given the dearth of adequate operational definitions, reliable typological classification would be virtually impossible with most systems.

The primary value of these types is heuristic. They represent the first important stage in scientific inquiry, preliminary observation and hypotheses formation. Faced with this diversity, it is necessary to derive a conceptual scheme to organize these heterogeneous observations and cope with this complexity. In the next section such a framework will be provided.

VARIABLES ASSOCIATED WITH CRIMINAL VIOLENCE

The previous section demonstrated the complexity associated with aggressive behavior in general and criminal violence in particular. Clearly, violence is a multidimensional rather than a unitary phenomenon. The survey of typologies made it apparent that there are a variety of personality patterns associated with each of the major violent crimes; less apparent was the fact that there are also a variety of motives and factors, often in conflict with one another, within each violent offender.

The present writer has long maintained that the only sound strategy for the theorist or researcher is to recognize and deal with this complexity; attempts at oversimplification are likely to distort the facts and leave us further from the truth than we were at the outset. For this reason, in his writing and teaching over the years, he has set forth what he has termed the "algebra of aggression," a rather abstract, sometimes symbolic, conceptual framework that can be used to organize most of the explanatory principles that have been proposed for aggression and violence. In this section, this conceptual framework will be introduced; then each of the component variables will be examined in light of the typologies reviewed in the preceding section.

The "Algebra of Aggression"[9]

Most human behavior, including violent behavior, is performed fairly automatically. As response follows response in a smooth-flowing, often automatic sequence, it is easy to lose sight of its complex determinants. However, when we analyze a single response we become aware that each act results from the interaction of many factors and comprises dozens of often unconscious choices.

In most situations, you can make any one of a number of different responses. If you are threatened, you can fight, run away, or attempt to make some conciliatory gesture. If you choose to attack, you can do so verbally or physically, with vigor or with restraint, within certain limits or with no holds barred.

How do you choose? Typically, you select the response that appears to offer the maximum satisfactions and the minimum dissatisfactions in that particular situation. This rather obvious statement conceals a rapid but extremely complex internal bargaining process in which the capacity of a given response to fulfill many different drives and motives is weighed, often subconsciously, against the pain that might result from that response, as well as from the postponement of the satisfaction of other competing drives. In some situations, flight might best satisfy your need for safety, but only at the expense of humiliation over what might be regarded as cowardly behavior. Attack might satisfy your aggressive needs, but at the expense of possible injury. By means of this internal algebra, which occurs so rapidly you are often unaware of it, you calculate the net strength of each possible response, compare it with all other responses, and select the strongest.

What determines the net strength of a response? In the case of an aggressive or violent response, we can isolate four broad factors that interact to determine response strength. The first of these is *instigation to aggression*. By instigation to aggression, we mean the sum of all the internal factors that motivate a person to commit a violent or aggressive act. This includes not only any desire to injure or kill the victim, but also any wish for other outcomes that the violent act might effect, such as economic gain in the case of a strong-arm robbery.

We shall designate instigation to aggression by the symbol A and use subscripts to differentiate the strength of motivation for different aggressive acts directed at various targets. Thus, $A_{j \cdot t-1}$ will denote the instigation for an aggressive act j directed at target 1. This might be the motivation for stabbing (j) a particular individual (t - 1). $A_{k \cdot t-1}$ would indicate the motivation for some other aggressive act (k) directed at the same target (t - 1) such as striking him instead of stabbing him. Similarly, $A_{j \cdot t-2}$ would denote the amount of instigation for stabbing some other person (t - 2) while $A_{k \cdot t-2}$ would mean the motivation for hitting some other victim.

The second class of factors we shall term *habit strength*. Aggressive habit strength in this formulation refers to preferences for the use of certain forms of aggressive behavior in certain situations that are learned by rewarded experience.

Thorndike, in his classic Law of Effect, stated that behavior that is rewarded will tend to be repeated. As social learning theorists have pointed out, some individuals are reinforced for aggressive behavior patterns and thereby develop aggressive habits; other things being equal, the stronger the habit strength, the more likely it is that an individual will choose an aggressive as opposed to a nonaggressive response.

Aggressive habits, which we will denote by the symbol H (a simplification of Hull's sHr, although the construct is the same), can be generalized or fairly specific. Because of their experience with different reinforcement schedules over the course of learning, individuals differ in the degree to which they are predisposed to behave aggressively toward others. They also develop preferences for different types of aggressive behavior. For example, women in our culture have historically been taught as girls that verbal aggression and passive-aggressive behavior are the most appropriate ways to express their hostility. Boys, on the other hand, are trained to fight and are given toy weapons with which to play; later as youths they are more likely to receive military training during which they are taught to rely on real weapons. Given these cultural influences, it is not surprising that men are more likely than women to choose physical violence as a way to express instigation to aggression.[10]

The third major construct is *inhibitions against aggression*. These too are learned, generally through punishment rather than reward. Inhibitions against aggression include the sum of all internal factors opposing a particular aggressive act directed at a given target. Included within this construct would be moral prohibitions, such as conscience or superego, learned taboos, and any internal inhibitions that might stem from the fact that the individual may regard the act as unwise. Thus, a man's inhibitions against punching a woman in the jaw could stem from the feeling that any violence is wrong, the belief that although punching a man is all right, punching a woman is taboo, or the judgment that while it is all right to punch a woman, it would be unwise in this case since the lady has a black belt in karate. We shall denote the strength of inhibitions against aggression by the letter I. As with instigation to aggression, the subscripts $j, k \ldots n$ will be used to denote inhibitions against particular aggressive acts, and the subscripts $t - 1, 2 \ldots n$ will designate the different targets of the various possible aggressive acts.

Instigation, habit strength, and inhibitions are all characteristics of individuals. Behavior, however, results from people interacting with their milieus. The final class of variables, *stimulus factors,* will encompass those immediate environmental factors that may facilitate or impede aggressive behavior. Among the external stimulus factors that might facilitate aggressive behavior are the availability of a weapon, the presence of other people urging violence, and aggressive gestures or behavior on the part of an antagonist. Such facilitating stimuli will be designated S_a. Stimuli that inhibit violence might include people who will arouse guilt over aggression, such as parents or clergy, or people who promise swift retribution for violent behavior, such as police, as well as those who may decrease aggressive instigation by pacifying an opponent or by relieving tension through humor. Stimuli that thus impede aggressive behavior will be designated S_i.

Let us analyze in a molar fashion some of the dynamics involved in the expression of a particular aggressive act j directed at a certain target $t - 1$. First, the strength of the instigation for this behavior ($A_{j \cdot t-1}$) plus habit strength (H) as well as any facilitating stimuli in the environment (S_a) must exceed the total strength of internal inhibitions against the commission of this act against this target ($I_{j \cdot t\text{-}1}$)—as well as any environmental stimuli which may impede the expression of this behavior (S_i). Symbolically:

$$(A_{j \cdot t\text{-}1}) + (H) + (S_a) > (I_{j \cdot t\text{-}1}) + (S_i)$$

A professional bank robber recently described this internal algebra. Pursued by the police, he had ditched the loot and a stash of drugs but decided to keep his gun, having decided he would rather take his chances on a shoot-out than be returned to prison. "If they wanted me they would have to work for it," he phrased it. A man who had killed before, his instigation, both angry and instrumental, plus his habit strength clearly exceeded his minimal inhibitions.

When the police ran his car off the road, however, his weapon flew onto the floorboards; by the time he had grabbed it and lifted his head back up, every window of the car was occupied by a loaded revolver or shotgun trained on his head, and he was informed that he had the choice of dropping the gun or dying. He briefly and consciously debated the issue. Since he had made his initial decision, his chances of successfully completing his aggressive intention had decreased to zero and the value of the inhibiting stimulus factors (S_i) had risen markedly. The sum total of the factors now outweighed the motivating ones; he dropped the gun.

When the sum of the motivating factors exceeds the sum of the inhibitory factors for a given aggressive or violent act, then that act is *possible*. However, before that possibility becomes an actuality, it must compete with all other possible responses. A man who is insulted by another man in a honky-tonk may be sufficiently angry and uninhibited to respond with extreme violence. He can (1) go to his pickup truck and get his shotgun and blow the other man away, (2) reach for the Buck knife at his belt and stab the pest, (3) take a swing at the offending individual, (4) reply with a verbal insult, or (5) choose to ignore it. His anger will have to compete with his thirst, for a shooting or cutting could conceivably end his drinking for the evening. The response that will meet the most needs—anger, reputation, thirst, and so on—at the least cost will be chosen. This response *competition* is the fifth and final element in the algebra of aggression.

In this overview, we have analyzed the dynamics at a single point in time. In real life, of course, one response follows another in a complex interplay, and the eventual victim usually has a decisive role to play in the outcome (Luckenbill and Sanders, 1977; Toch, 1969). In the example above, the insulted individual may first attempt to overlook the insult so as to continue with his drinking in peace; continued harassment by the other party may convince him that this is no longer a viable option, limiting the choices to violence or abject retreat. As Luckenbill and Sanders (1977: 113) pointed out, in many cases of assault and homicide, "the offender, victim, and, when present, audience, forge an explicit or implicit agreement that physical violence is a suitable if not required means for resolving questions of face." Nevertheless, at each step of what Toch referred to as the "scenario of violence," the parties involved are consciously or unconsciously making decisions, and at each choice point the equations generated by the algebra of aggression are entering into the response competition, which determines the outcome. In the pages that follow, each of the major variables we have identified will be discussed in more detail and the psychological factors that augment or diminish them reviewed.

Instigation to Aggression

"Instigation to aggression" refers to all those internal factors that may motivate an individual to respond aggressively to a given stimulus in a particular situation. Different theorists have referred to this construct as "aggressive drive," "aggressive motivation," and "need for aggression." Buss (1961, 1971), as we have noted, differentiated two broad types of instigation to aggression: (1) "instrumental" or "extrinsic" motivation, in which the aggressive or violent behavior serves as a means to some end, and (2) "angry" or "intrinsic" motivation, in which the injury to the victim is an end in itself. "Anger," "rage," "hostility," and "hatred" are popular synonyms for the latter type of instigation.

Instrumental (Extrinsic) Motivation

Although most psychological theorists have focused on angry motivation, instrumental motives can result in the full range of crimes of violence and are particularly common in such offenses as kidnapping, arson, and robbery. Even violence occurring in the context of a longstanding and ongoing interpersonal relationship, such as spouse or child abuse, is now recognized as having instrumental components, such as maintenance of status or power within the family structure or, in the case of child abuse, simply an attempt to halt aversive stimulation (e.g., crying). On the other hand, rape, once considered an instrumental offense aimed at securing sexual gratification, is now typically thought of as motivated by both angry and instrumental drives, the instrumental goals being interpreted as needs for power and for group status more than sex per se (Groth, 1979).

Based on our survey of the typologies of violent offenders that have been hypothesized, as well as the general literature on the psychology of crime, it is possible to formulate a list of some of the more common instrumental motives that have been suggested. This list certainly does not exhaust the range of possibilities, since violence can be used as a means of securing virtually any goal, including, paradoxically, peace.

Personal Gains or Satisfactions. Violence is often mentioned as a means for achieving personal goals or satisfying personal needs. Among the most common needs that people attempt to satisfy through violence are *acquisition, excitement, enhancing the self-concept,* and *affection.*

ACQUISITION. One way to secure something that is desirable is by taking it. People do not always cooperate freely in these endeavors, so violence may be used to persuade them. *Money, drugs, territory,* and *sexual gratification* are among the commodities most often acquired via violence.

Money. The desire to acquire money or other objects of value motivates considerable violence. Money may be secured directly from the victim, as in robbery, indirectly through a third party, as in kidnapping for ransom, or through arson, as a part of an insurance fraud. (In the latter instance, the value of the property to be burned is often artificially enhanced as the owner, operating through a series of dummy corporations, buys and sells dilapidated property from and to himself at steadily increasing prices over a period of months prior to the fire.)

Drugs. Although drugs can lead to violent crime directly through their effects on hypothalamic rage and inhibition centers, they can also indirectly motivate violence. People who are addicted to or dependent on scarce and expensive drugs may attempt to steal the drugs or money needed to satisfy their habit.

Drugs are also valuable commodities, and many individuals who are not themselves drug users will engage in robbery, assault, and homicide in an attempt to secure them. Southern Florida, a center for much of the drug-smuggling trade in recent years, has experienced a wave of drug-related homicides that may eclipse the body count recorded in Chicago during the height of Prohibition.

Territory. Ethologists such as Ardrey (1966) maintain that humans, like many other animals, have an innate need to defend their territory. Whether innate or acquired, the reciprocal needs of acquiring and defending territory have motivated many of the world's wars, including the recent conflicts in Iran and Afghanistan. Whether or not this violence is regarded as "criminal" depends on whether one is a Persian or an Arab, an Afghan or a Russian. On a less global level, the so-called territorial imperative has also motivated many individual acts of violence, ranging from the householder shooting a trespasser to the urban ghetto gang defending its "turf."

Sexual gratification has been suggested as a motive for many crimes of violence. This includes the direct use of force to obtain sexual relations with the victim in forcible rape, as well as the sexual gratification obtained from setting fires or exploding bombs.

ENHANCEMENT OF THE SELF-CONCEPT. A variety of personal motives can be loosely aggregated under this general heading. These include *proving one's manhood, seeking excitement, demonstrating courage and smartness,* and *obtaining attention.*

Proving one's manhood. A number of cultures place great emphasis on *machismo,* a stubborn masculine sense of honor.[11] An essential element of *machismo* is never retreating in the face of a challenge (Rosenquist and Megargee, 1969). Although there is no comparable feminine term, women, too, may seek to prove their toughness through aggressive behavior. Machismo may lead to violence when two adversaries agree that violence is preferable to backing down and losing face. Proving one's masculinity (and unconsciously denying one's homosexuality) has also been cited as a latent motive for forcible rape, especially the "power rape" described by Groth (1979).

Excitement. Seeking excitement, kicks, or, as one bank robber phrased it, an "adrenaline high" can also motivate crimes of violence. Indeed, that bank robber described it as addictive, a characterization reminiscent of May's (1974) discussion of the "ecstasy" of terrorism in which violence becomes an end in itself. Quay (1965) suggested that pathological sensation-seeking might be the root cause of psychopathy. He suggested that without engaging in such daring behavior, psychopaths might experience a condition akin to sensory deprivation; they might not merely enjoy but actually crave the "kicks" or excitement they experience in the course of criminal violence.

Demonstrating courage is used here for ego-enhancing, risk-taking behavior such as playing "cops and robbers." Such behavior not only generates the excitement noted above but also serves to convince the offender that he or she is braver and smarter than ordinary, square, conventional citizens. This motivational pattern has been associated with armed robbery, hostage-taking, and skyjacking.

Obtaining attention. Attention-seeking can also motivate criminal violence. The more notable the victim of a homicide, for example, the more one must consider attention-seeking as a possible cause. Some primitive cultures used to believe that by killing an individual one assumed that person's characteristics; by assassinating a noted or public figure a person who has been a nonentity can inherit that importance and prove that he or she is even more powerful than the person who was slain. Attention-seeking can also motivate highly publicized crimes such as skyjacking or hostage-taking. Such personal attention-seeking must be distinguished from group attention-seeking or "media-terrorism" (Bell, 1978), in which an individual or group may engage in violence in order to seek publicity for their cause rather than for themselves as individuals. Among the ranks of would-be assassins, Arthur Bremer, who shot George Wallace, would be an example of a person who was motivated in part by personal needs for attention and self-fulfillment, whereas Oscar Collazo and Griselo Torresola, the Puerto Rican nationalists who attempted to kill President Harry Truman, would be examples of people who wished to publicize a cause.

NEED FOR AFFECTION. A need for affection can also be a motive for some acts of criminal violence. This can be conceptually divided between those who, paradoxically, seek the affection of the victim and those who use the violence to obtain the affection of some third party.

Seeking the victim's affection through violence has been cited as a motivational factor in several typologies. This pattern appeared in some of the fight-and-make-up scenarios of familial violence, in some rapes, and apparently in a significant number of cases of nonforcible pedophilia, although the last are not treated as violent crimes in this chapter.

Seeking another's affection has been cited as a neurotic motive for instrumental violence, a sort of knight-errant syndrome in which the offender goes forth to slay whatever latter-day dragon he feels will win the respect and affection of the person he wishes to impress. For example, John W. Hinckley apparently felt that slaying President Reagan would impress actress Jodie Foster. Some cases in which jealousy appears to be the primary motive may also have affection-seeking as a secondary motive.

Removal of Problems, Impediments, or Annoyances. The first broad category listed a variety of instrumental motivations that had in common the use of violence to obtain various positive goals or rewards. In this second broad category, the emphasis shifts to the use of violence to eliminate various undesirable factors that threaten the individual's lifestyle. This includes the use of violence to *facilitate other crimes*, to *eliminate or neutralize people blocking goal achievement*, to *eliminate threats to security*, and even to *eliminate the self*.

USE OF VIOLENCE TO FACILITATE OTHER CRIMES. One of the most common instrumental uses of violence is to facilitate the commission of other crimes. The use of violence to achieve control, intimidate victims, and abet escape in a robbery has already been discussed. Violence may also be used to intimidate victims or eliminate witnesses to other criminal activities. Extortion, loan-sharking, gambling, white slavery, "protection," and similar rackets rely on the use or threat of violence, and arson and bombing are used to destroy evidence and to conceal the fact that a crime has taken place.

ELIMINATION OF PEOPLE WHO BLOCK GOALS. A common motive in mystery novels, the use of violence to eliminate people who stand in one's way or block certain goals, also occurs in real life. Violence of this type may accompany struggles for power in organized crime and is alleged to have been a motive for some of the more notable murders of labor-union officials.

ELIMINATION OF THREATS, ENHANCEMENT OF SECURITY. Self-defense is a classic instrumental motive for violence; indeed, if it can be proven that sufficient threat has existed, the violence is no longer classified as criminal. However, the threat that the perpetrator perceives often does not legally justify violent behavior; for example, "fragging" an officer who orders too many combat patrols is not regarded as a "legitimate" act of self-defense by the military.

Violence is used not only to remove those who may threaten the offender's security directly, but also to intimidate others who may be inclined to follow suit. If a key witness is attacked or killed prior to testifying, other witnesses become reluctant to get involved. Criminals as well as courts believe in deterrance, although its effectiveness remains an empirical question to criminologists.

ELIMINATION OF THE SELF. In expressive forms of suicide, an individual may commit violence to others in order to effect his or her own death. It is unlikely that Charles Whitman ever thought that he would survive the Texas Tower incident, and some cases have been recorded of individuals who committed murder in order to be executed by the state, suicide being contrary to their religion.

Achievement of Personal Social Goals. The first two broad categories dealt in a crude way with individual goals and motives. In this category we place the instrumental use of violence to achieve certain social goals, such as *approval or acceptance by a group, maintenance of group solidarity,* and *acquisition of power, control, or dominance over others.*

APPROVAL OR ACCEPTANCE BY THE GROUP. Wolfgang and Ferracuti (1967) have defined a "subculture of violence" in which social mores dictate the use of violence in certain defined circumstances. Prison is another example of a setting in which one must "scuffle to survive." Violence may be necessary to obtain or maintain the acceptance or respect of a reference group in such settings. Gang rape, both in the community and in prison, is an offense often attributed to the male peer group.

MAINTENANCE OF GROUP SOLIDARITY. Violence has been used by some deviant groups such as the Manson family to establish and maintain group cohesion and solidarity. According to Teresa (1973), an act of violence ("making his bones") was necessary for initiation into the Mafia, and although Teresa had a tendency to sensationalize, cultural anthropologists can cite many tribes in which some form of violence against an enemy was a basic requirement for warrior status.

Taking a broader perspective, maintenance of group solidarity and group values in the face of perceived threats by outsiders has been one of the chief causes of social group conflicts ranging from struggles between rival street gangs to the civil rights struggles in the United States.

POWER, CONTROL, OR DOMINANCE OVER OTHERS. Many individuals have found violence to be an effective means of achieving power, dominance, and control over others. Groth (1979) reported that power was one of the principle causes of rape, and, as we have seen, Brownmiller (1975) maintained that the male need to subjugate women was responsible for all rapes. Power is frequently one of the major issues in marital and familial violence, and dominance and control are necessary elements in successful extortion and robbery attempts.

Just as violence can be a means to the end of obtaining power, power, in turn, can be a means to other ends, such as acquisition, as well as a goal in itself. As MacDonald (1975) pointed out, bank robbers need to achieve control over the situation through the threat of violence, but readers will recall the bank robber discussed earlier who found life-and-death power over others was intensely satisfying and fulfilling.

Achieving Political or Religious Goals. Not all social goals are of a personal nature. Individuals may also commit acts of criminal violence to further group-defined goals that go beyond maintaining membership in a group or preserving group solidarity. Throughout history, political and religious groups have used violence as a means of obtaining or maintaining political power. Through violence, groups can eliminate key people in the opposition, attack supporters of the opposition to intimidate and thereby neutralize them, create a climate of chaos receptive to change, extract information, and finance their activities. Although distinctions are probably arbitrary insofar as any observable personality differences are concerned, two broad types of political-religious violence are often distinguished, *violence to maintain the established power structure* and *violence aimed at overthrowing it.*

VIOLENCE AIMED AT MAINTAINING THE ESTABLISHED STRUCTURE. Violence can be used by the establishment to eliminate or neutralize leaders of the opposition, to intimidate their followers, and to extract, through the use of torture, information about dissident activities. The establishment typically has more resources at its command. When it does not it is replaced by a new establishment. Therefore, it is capable of much greater violence than any private citizen or group of dissidents. As a result, it is likely that violence aimed at preserving the prevailing political and/or religious autocracy and values has resulted in more casualties than any other single form of violent activity.

To the extent that the established power structure makes and enforces the laws, violence by the establishment on its behalf may not be considered "criminal" according to a strict construction of local laws. Revolutionary violence by a new regime aimed at eliminating the last remnants of the old regime, such as occurred in France during the Terror and in Iran following the fall of the late Shah Mohammed Reza Pahlavi, was specifically sanctioned by revolutionary tribunals operating under revolutionary law. Nevertheless, in addition to the proclaimed goal of redressing crimes committed during the past regime, this violence also had the instrumental function of eliminating potential dissident elements that might seek a restoration of the previous monarchies.

Violence can also be used to preserve the religious establishment. Partly to preserve pagan values, the Roman Empire attempted to suppress Christianity with violence, beginning with Christ's crucifixion and continuing for three centuries until the reign of Constantine I. When Christianity replaced paganism, violence was used to preserve the Christian establishment from deviant or heretical elements. Despite the difference in goals—suppression versus maintenance of the Christian Church—the violence in both instances was legal.

In the Nuremberg war crimes trials, the court appealed to "universal" laws of human conduct that supersede the statutes operating in a given time or place.

Violence that contravened these universal principles, such as that involved in the Holocaust, could be deemed criminal even if it was permitted or required by local laws. To use Megargee's (1973) terminology, the court shifted the boundaries between the "latitudes of acceptance and rejection" and proscribed acts that had been permitted and even prescribed under the Third Reich.

VIOLENCE AIMED AT REPLACING OR OVERTHROWING THE POWER STRUCTURE. Violence by dissidents does not differ greatly from violence by the establishment. The goals of eliminating rival leaders, intimidating their followers, and obtaining information remain the same. This was particularly evident in South Vietnam during the early 1960s when Viet Cong cadres killed village leaders who supported the Saigon government and terrorized their followers.

Dissident groups must also finance their activities and arm themselves; this leads to robberies and raids or attacks aimed at securing weapons and supplies, activities the Establishment generally does not need to engage in. Indiscriminant terrorism, including bombings, hostage-taking, arson, and sabotage, are also more likely to be used by dissident groups. Those that seek a complete change in societal values (as opposed to a simple replacement of the leadership) often feel that total destruction of the social and political structure is necessary; anarchy and chaos must prevail before society can be restructured.

In contrast to establishment violence, which is often kept secret, dissident groups are more likely to seek maximum publicity for their causes through suicidal but highly visible terrorist activities, such as the Munich attack on the Israeli Olympic team and the subsequent hostage-taking aimed at freeing those imprisoned as a result of the attack.

It should be pointed out that not all political or religious violence is instrumental. Although some of the individuals involved in racial, religious, and political violence are motivated by instrumental goals, hatred and other forms of angry aggression are often the primary motives.

Altruism. The catalogue of instrumental motivation presented thus far has involved some of humankind's baser and less noble drives. Greed, lust, and personal power have been the motives most frequently cited. Although none of the typologies reviewed in the second section of this chapter listed altruistic or loving types of violent offenders, such individuals do exist. Here we are not talking about those who delude themselves by rationalization that the violence is really for the victim's own good—the parent who grossly abuses a child so he or she will "learn respect for authority" or the rapist who is convinced that once he overcomes a woman's resistance she will experience unsurpassed sexual fulfillment. Instead, the small group in this category consists of those who commit euthanasia or mercy killing, often at the behest of the victims, to relieve them from the intractable pain of a terminal illness or to spare them from having to live out their days in an institution. These offenses typically involve familial homicide and are frequently followed by the suicide of the offender. Sometimes it involves the murder/suicide of an elderly couple, one of whom is suffering from a terminal illness or both of whom are suffering from terminal poverty. At other times a seriously depressed parent who has decided to end his or her life will first murder the children so they do not have to cope with the manifold problems the suicide will engender. Although the thinking may sometimes be misguided, the motivation in such cases is clearly instrumental rather than angry and involves a sincere judgment that the violent act, typically homicide, is in the victim's best interest.

These five broad categories of instrumental motivation (personal gains, removing impediments, achieving social goals, fulfilling political objectives, and altruism) are based primarily on the typologies presented in the second section, which in turn were based for the most part on case studies, clinical experience, and "common sense." They are obviously not mutually exclusive; in any given crime of violence several instrumental motives may be operating along with angry motivation. Nor have they been subjected to anything approximating rigorous scientific scrutiny.

The second major type of instigation, "angry" instigation, occupies a different status, since numerous experimental studies have been performed on this type of aggressive behavior. Most of this research has involved the milder forms of aggressive behavior that can be studied in the laboratory; hence it is necessary to extrapolate from these investigations when discussing criminal violence. Nevertheless, the psychological determinants of intrinsic "angry" instigation, which we will discuss next, have been much more extensively and rigorously investigated than the instrumental motives we have just surveyed.

"Angry" (Intrinsic) Motivation

Intrinsic motivation to hurt or injure someone is popularly termed "anger" if it is short-lived and moderate in degree, "rage" if it is transitory and intense, "hostility" if it is long-term and moderate, and "hatred" if it is chronic and extreme. These motivating emotional states can be diffuse and generalized or focused on a specific target.

Some theorists have maintained that instigation to aggression is an innate human characteristic. Lorenz (1966), for example, viewed aggressive instigation as analogous to hunger, thirst, or sexual drives, steadily accumulating in the absence of need satisfaction. Freud (1955) postulated that the aggressive drive or "death instinct" (popularly referred to as *thanatos*) was one of the two central motives governing human behavior. Selective breeding for aggressiveness or docility has been successfully carried out on a number of species, including dogs, chickens, cattle, and fish. Theories and research on a possible genetic basis for aggressive instigation are beyond the scope of this chapter. However, in considering the "psychological" determinants that will be discussed, the reader should bear in mind the likelihood of genetic differences in the capacity to be angered.

Frustration-Aggression Theory. The best-known and most thoroughly explored theory of environmental causation was originally proposed by a group of psychologists at the Institute of Human Relations at Yale University in 1939. In the true behaviorist tradition, the Yale group stated their hypotheses in clear and unambiguous prose. While this may have oversimplified the problems inherent in the study of aggression, particularly since aggression was treated as a unidimensional construct, it did have the advantage of permitting the various formulations to be empirically tested.

The first basic assumption of the Yale group was as follows:

> This study takes as its point of departure the assumption that *aggression is always a consequence of frustration*. More specifically the proposition is that the occurance of aggressive behavior always presupposes the existence of frustration and, contrariwise, that the existence of frustration always leads to some form of aggression [Dollard et al., 1939: 1].

The Yale group did not offer an opinion as to whether this inevitable relationship was innate or learned; they simply hypothesized that it was a necessary relationship, no matter what its origin.

What did they mean by frustration? In the initial formulation of the theory, a frustration was defined as something that interferes with an ongoing goal response. A mother who stops a child reaching for a cookie would thus be regarded as having frustrated the child. As we shall see, other theorists have attempted to extend the definition of frustration to include other behavior, such as being injured, criticized, or physically attacked. Berkowitz (1962: 30), for example, suggested that one becomes angry after one's toes are stepped on, because having one's toes stepped on frustrates one's need to maintain security and comfort. The present writer feels that, given such extension, the term "frustration" loses any explanatory power, so for the present we shall simply treat frustration as it was originally defined.

The major criticism leveled at the frustration-aggression hypothesis concerned the notion that frustration *always* leads to aggression. While a number of studies indicated that aggression *may* follow frustration, a variety of other studies have suggested that overt aggression is not the inevitable consequence. Consequently, this formulation was changed to read, "Frustration produces instigation to a number of different types of responses, one of which is an instigation to some form of aggression" (Miller, 1941: 338). Whether or not this instigation results in *overt* aggressive behavior depends on other factors, such as internal inhibitions and external stimulus events (Miller, 1941).

The Yale theorists then went on to hypothesize that the strength of instigation to aggression varies directly with the amount of frustration. The greater the frustration, the greater the instigation to aggression. They postulated that the amount of frustration, and hence the strength of instigation to aggression, is a function of three factors. The first is the drive strength of the frustrated goal response. Let us suppose you go into a bar and order a beer only to be told that there is no more. Your frustration, and consequently your instigation to aggression, will be greater if it is a hot day, you are very thirsty, and you have been looking forward to a beer for some time. The second factor is the degree of interference with the frustrated response. According to this postulate, your frustration will be greater if there is no other place nearby where you can get a beer. The third factor is the number of frustrated response sequences. According to this principle, "the amount or strength of aggressive response will depend in part on the amount of residual instigation from previous or simultaneous frustrations, which instigation summates to activate the response under observation. Minor frustrations add together to produce an aggressive response of greater strength than would normally be expected from the frustrating situation that appears to be the immediate antecedent of the aggression" (Dollard et al., 1939: 31). This important principle states essentially two things: first, that frustration can remain active over a period of time, and second, that the frustration from different events can summate. Returning to our example, if you have also been refused service in three or four other bars prior to entering this one, you will be angrier than if this is the first such refusal.

The postulate also states that different kinds of frustrations can add up to yield greater instigation to aggression. If you are tired and hungry, as well as thirsty, and in addition to not being served a beer, you are told that you cannot sit down or get anything to eat, you will be even angrier as the frustrations from failure to satisfy your needs for rest, hunger, and thirst combine.

Instigation to aggression can also stem from chronically recurring or generalized frustrations. Being trapped in a second-rate job because of one's skin color or gender, experiencing chronic hunger, and living in substandard conditions are among the frustrating conditions that can yield chronic instigation to aggression. These generalized sorts of frustrations, as we have seen, have frequently been mentioned as antecedents of child and spouse abuse.

Since instigation to aggression from a number of sources can summate, it might be expected that someone who is chronically frustrated would require less immediate provocation to elicit overt aggressive behavior because the instigation to aggression stemming from some relatively minor incident could summate with the chronic instigation to aggression stemming from the general frustrations of everyday life. Indirect support of this formulation can be found in the work of Hovland and Sears (1940) and Henry and Short (1954), who demonstrated significant correlations between economic conditions and violence.

Subsequent research on the frustration-aggression theory has suggested that there are other factors that may influence the amount of perceived frustration and the subsequent instigation to aggression. Pastore (1952) suggested that the more arbitrary the frustration, the greater is the resulting instigation to aggression. According to this formulation, if you went into a bar and asked, "May I have a beer?" and the bartender simply responded, "No," you would feel more frustrated and angry than if the bartender said, "No, because we can't sell beer on Election Day."

While research has indicated less overt aggression following nonarbitrary as opposed to arbitrary frustration, it is difficult to establish whether this was because the arbitrary frustration elicited more instigation to aggression or the nonarbitrary condition aroused greater inhibitions against the overt expression of aggression. The latter possibility was pointed out by Rothaus and Worchel in 1960, and subsequently Kregarman and Worchel (1961) obtained data they felt supported the hypothesis that arbitrariness influences inhibitions rather than instigation.

This ambiguity of interpretation illustrates one of the major difficulties in doing research on the frustration-aggression hypothesis. Typically all one can measure is the overt behavior that results from a given situation, and often there is no way of determining whether the experimental manipulations have influenced the instigation, the inhibition, or the stimulus factors.

Turning now from the factors that have been suggested as influencing the amount of instigation to aggression, let us examine briefly the status of the theory itself. Some social learning theorists have disagreed with the frustration-aggression hypothesis, preferring to regard aggressive behavior as simply another habit that is learned through reinforcement. The present writer does not view the two positions as incompatible; indeed, one purpose of the conceptual framework proposed herein is to help integrate such conflicts. The frustration-aggression theory is focusing on the motivational aspect of the aggressive response. This does not minimize the effects of reinforcement, which are specifically acknowledged in the construct of habit strength (H).

Learning can also influence instigation. It is in the process of acculturation that we develop our expectancies; it is when these expectancies are not met that we experience frustration. An American who has been acculturated to expect promptness and punctuality is more likely to become frustrated and angry when kept waiting for an hour or two than a person from a country where such delays are commonplace. Expectations also account for the paradox that there is more rioting and social unrest among disadvantaged people when conditions are improving than there was before. The explanation appears to be that, with improvement, expectations rise dramatically, leading to a greater discrepancy and, hence, more frustration and aggression than there was previously (Feierabend and Feierabend, 1966). Thus one can acknowledge the importance of learning without necessarily rejecting the frustration-aggression formulation.

Other Environmental Causes of Instigation. Classical frustration-aggression theorists have maintained that frustration was the *only* cause of instigation to aggression. This position has the advantage of parsimony, but to account for the available data it is necessary to redefine the definition of frustration to such an extent that it loses its original meaning. Among the other sources of instigation are *attack, jealousy, revenge,* and *reminiscence.* Of these, attack has been most thoroughly studied.

ATTACK. Buss (1961) has suggested that attack can also elicit instigation to aggression. A number of studies on animals have shown that stimuli that elicit pain—such as electrical shock, intense heat, physical blows, tail pinches, and even, in one study of killer whales, depth charges—can result in intra- and/or interspecies aggression in a variety of creatures (Ulrich et al., 1965). Research on humans has been hampered by the ethical prohibitions against inflicting injury on subjects as well as by the fact that the research designs used in many studies often confound frustration with attack. However, laboratory and field data indicate that among humans, attacks elicit aggressive behavior and, by inference, instigation to aggression.

Frustration-aggression theorists who uphold the notion that *only* frustration leads to aggression redefine frustration to include the types of painful stimuli described above. According to this argument, if you become angry when you are punched in the nose, it is not because such attacks elicit instigation to aggression but instead because the punch in the nose frustrated your need for respect. If we stretch the term "frustration" to encompass any antecedent event that elicits aggression, then the term loses its meaning and its explanatory value. It appears more parsimonious simply to include attack as one of the variables that, along with frustration, can elicit aggressive instigation.

JEALOUSY. There is little scientific literature on the role of jealousy in causing instigation to aggression, although it has been a classic motive for violence since Cain slew Abel. Although frustration-aggression theorists would redefine jealousy as a particular type of frustration (e.g., blocking the goal of having exclusive possession of a loved one), it seems better to treat it as a distinct motivational construct, since actual blocking is not necessary to produce jealousy.

Almost by definition, jealousy occurs in the context of a relationship that is important to the jealous party. Although in the case of individuals suffering from a paranoid disorder this relationship may in fact be imaginary, as when a disturbed person forms a fixation on a public figure, it is more often an actual, ongoing relationship, such as that between lovers or marital partners. The real or imagined infidelity of one arouses jealous feelings in the other. The jealous party is apt to seek confirmation and overinterpret minor events; as Shakespeare noted, "Trifles light as air are to the jealous confirmations strong as proofs of holy writ" (*Othello,* III, 3, 1. 323). Given the nature of the relationship, crimes such as assault and homicide are most likely to occur, although cases of kidnapping or abduction are not unknown. The victim may be the individual who is the object of the jealous person's affection, that person's new lover, or both. In cases of murder, suicide may follow if the jealous party feels he or she cannot live without the other person.

REVENGE. Revenge involves retaliation against another party for some real or imagined wrong. In some cultures such responses are expected; in others they are socially deviant.

The perceived need for revenge can be an immediate response to real or imagined provocation; in such instances it is more likely to be termed retaliation. However, feelings of vengefulness can be extraordinarily long-term, breeding chronic instigation to aggression. This was well illustrated by George Metesky, who exploded a series of bombs in New York City over a seventeen-year period in order to obtain revenge on the Consolidated Edison Company, which had rejected his claims for compensation for an alleged industrial accident. Except for case studies such as this and surveys of self-reported motivation, revenge has not been studied intensively in the psychological literature on violence, although it is regarded as a popular motive for a number of violent offenses, especially arson.

There is a considerable literature in social psychology involving "aggression" machines. In a typical paradigm, one subject has the option of responding to another subject with aggressive or nonaggressive responses of varying degrees of intensity (Hokanson, 1970). One finding that has emerged is, not surprisingly, that subjects are more likely to deliver aggressive stimuli such as shocks to fellow subjects who aggress against them. Although the levels of emotional arousal and aggression are too mild to justify the term "revenge," nevertheless these findings do lend some scientific underpinnings to the popularly observed phenomenon.

REMINISCENCE AND RESIDUAL INSTIGATION. Thus far we have been discussing the events and factors that can arouse aggressive instigation in an ahistorical context. A person is confronted with a situation, weighs the factors, and chooses whether or not to respond aggressively. In actual life the situation does not end at that point. If inhibitions outweigh instigation so that an aggressive or violent response is prevented from occurring, the instigation may still remain active. It may summate with additional instigation so as to elicit aggressive behavior at some later time, it may motivate lesser aggressive responses (response substitution), or it may lead to aggression directed at a "safer" target with fewer inhibitions attached (displacement).

Even if a violent act does take place, thereby discharging the hostility, people, by virtue of their unique verbal capabilities, can reminisce and recall frustrating and provocative incidents, thereby arousing renewed aggressive instigation. George Metesky's protracted vendetta against Consolidated Edison is a case in point.

Dissipation of Instigation to Aggression

This leads us to the question of the dissipation of aggressive instigation. Once an individual has become aroused, what happens? Although the psychological and criminological literature has concentrated on the factors that yield instigation, the question of dissipation is equally important. An analogy can be made to the pharmacological study of the effects of a drug. The investigation of the factors that lead to instigation is analogous to the question of how a drug is ingested and its effective dosage. However, this cannot be separated from the question of how long the drug remains active in the body. Some of the differences between violent criminals and other people may be in the degree to which the two groups can effectively dissipate their feelings of anger and hostility. Studies of prison violence typically focus on the frustrations associated with being imprisoned and the aggressive instigation that results; few consider the fact that prison also denies individuals normal, socially acceptable outlets for expressing and discharging aggressive instigation. The research already cited on the chronically overcontrolled violent individual (Megargee, 1966; Lane, 1978) suggested that these people may become violent because their personality structures do not permit them to discharge their instigation to aggression as it is aroused so that it can summate to the point where an act of extreme violence results.

The present writer does not subscribe to a closed hydraulic model and all of the theoretical ramifications it entails (Megargee, 1969). It appears that in many individuals aggressive instigation can dissipate over time to some extent, just as it can be rearoused through reminiscence, phenomena that a closed hydraulic model finds difficult to explain. Nevertheless, there is evidence that aggressive instigation can summate over time, and differences in the ability to discharge such instigation should be considered by psychologists concerned with criminal violence.

A variety of instigation-reducing behaviors or factors have been proposed that can be divided into three broad categories: (1) reduction of instigation to aggression by need satisfaction, (2) reduction of instigation through expression of aggressive behavior, and (3) reduction of instigation through cognitive redefinition of the situation. We shall deal with each of these in turn.

Reduction of Instigation to Aggression Through Need Satisfaction. By far the most effective way of reducing environmentally caused instigation to aggression is simply to remove those environmental conditions that elicit it. If frustration of a goal-oriented response results in instigation to aggression, then eliminating the frustration should reduce the instigation.

Similarly, instrumental aggression and violence should be diminished if alternative, nonaggressive means for accomplishing the same goals can be provided. Some evidence for the need-satisfaction hypothesis is available from criminal case studies; professional robbers, for example, typically take a vacation and live a playboy life after a successful job, not performing new robberies until they again need funds (MacDonald, 1977). Unfortunately, except for politics, there are few alternative occupations that will provide an armed robber with as big a score for as little effort.

Reduction of Instigation Through Overt Aggression and Catharsis. Most theorists agree that the overt expression of aggression is one way of reducing instigation. If for some reason you want to hit someone in the nose, then you should be able to satisfy this need by doing so. Such overt expression of aggressive instigation is typically referred to as "catharsis," a term applied by psychoanalysts, who derived it from the Greeks.

There is considerable controversy over the effectiveness of aggression in reducing instigation. The issue has been clouded in part by the association of the catharsis hypothesis with a rather unwieldy closed hydraulic model. Moreover, experimental research on the hypothesis has been hindered by problems of operationally defining the independent and dependent variables as well as the interpolated aggressive tasks.

It is the present writer's conclusion that aggression undoubtedly can reduce instigation. However, this is neither inevitable nor necessarily the most effective way of reducing instigation. Over a long period of time the problem is complicated by the facts that (1) subsequent stimuli, or the individual's own reminiscenses, can rearouse the instigation despite catharsis, and (2) while the catharsis may lower instigation, it may also lower inhibitions and increase habit strength so that the individual has an even greater propensity for aggressive behavior after the catharsis than prior to it.

Displaced Aggression. Aggressive behavior directed toward other targets may also reduce aggressive instigation. If inhibitions exceed instigation so that it is not possible to make a particular aggressive response (k) toward the original target (t-1), it may still be possible to make that aggressive response (k) toward some other target (t-2) toward whom fewer inhibitions are felt. This phenomenon of expressing aggression against a substitute target is called "displacement."

The mechanism of displacement is used by many to help account for child abuse. People frustrated by poor marital situations and difficult financial circumstances accumulate considerable instigation to aggression. A crying child may trigger the release of these chronic feelings of frustration and hostility, especially if the parent is able to rationalize the act as "discipline," thereby reducing inhibitions. Some terrorists and assassins also appear to be displacing instigation accumulated as a result of lifelong patterns of maladjustment to society.

Response Substitution. Another way to cope with the situation of having an aggressive response toward a particular target blocked by inhibition is to change the response rather than the target. Sometimes verbal aggression can be used in place of physical aggression, or a hostile letter in place of direct verbal aggression. A particular type of response substitution in which aggressive instigation is redirected into constructive paths is called "sublimation." If Jack the Ripper, for example, had sublimated his homicidal tendencies he might have become a gifted surgeon specializing in tracheotomies.

In some situations the algebra of aggression may be such that both response substitution and displacement work together so that a different aggressive response is directed at some other target. The classic example of this would be honking your horn at another driver on your way home from work when you would really prefer to punch your boss in the nose.

Vicarious Expression of Aggressive Instigation. It has been suggested that aggressive instigation can also be reduced by watching someone else perform an aggressive act. A small boy beaten up by a larger child would, according to this analysis, have his anger reduced by watching his big brother thrash the bully.

Generally, two types of vicarious aggression have been described. The first is the type noted above, in which the angered person watches someone else attack his or her tormentor. The second is simply watching aggressive behavior that is not specifically directed against the frustrating agent. According to this analysis, the boy who was beaten up by the neighborhood bully might have at least some of his instigation reduced if he watched a violent TV show. It is on the basis of the latter theory that media representatives have often attempted to justify violence in films and television.

A number of experiments have been performed in an effort to shed light on these issues. The results are equivocal, but it can be concluded that those who would advocate vicarious participation in violence and aggression as an antidote for aggressive behavior have a weak case on which to base their argument. While some experiments have obtained data consistent with the hypothesis that vicarious aggression reduces instigation to aggression, it appears that many subtle factors operate to determine whether or not this takes place. There is also a considerable body of evidence, as we shall see, that suggests that although instigation may be lowered, inhibitions may also be decreased so that the net effect might be an increased tendency toward aggressive behavior.

Cognitive Redefinition of the Situation. In addition to discharging aggressive instigation through some form of aggressive behavior or satisfaction of whatever need has been frustrated, one may also reduce it through a cognitive redefinition of the original situation. If you are jostled roughly while waiting for a bus, you may become angry until you notice that the person who bumped you is blind. You cognitively redefine the situation from a rude attack to an unavoidable accident. Similarly, an apology, a "soft word," or a joke can dissipate aggressive tension.

Habit Strength

The second major construct in the algebra of aggression is habit strength, a Hullian concept that refers to the degree to which the individual has been positively reinforced for behaving aggressively in the past. In previous theoretical writings, the present writer did not treat habit strength as one of the major constructs along with instigation and inhibition; instead, a history of reinforced aggressive responding was treated as one of the factors that would contribute to aggression by decreasing inhibitions (Megargee, 1969, 1971, 1972).

Further reflection has suggested that this formulation missed the mark. In the limiting case, if two people with equal instigation had no inhibitions against a particular aggressive act, the one with the greater habit strength would be more likely to select an aggressive or violent response. If so, then habit strength should be treated as an independent construct, just as it was in Hull's writings.

Habit strength is postulated to operate according to Thorndike's Law of Effect. If a violent act is rewarded, the habit strength will increase according to the laws governing operant learning. Instrumentally motivated aggressive behavior would be reinforced by achieving the extrinsic goal, such as money in the case of a robbery, and aggression motivated by anger should, by definition, be intrinsically reinforced by the injury to the victim.

Additional unanticipated sources of reinforcement that serve to strengthen aggressive or violent habits may also be forthcoming. The original motive for a robbery might have been to secure money, but the robber may also find the excitement and power gratifying. A murderer reported that when he was a teenager he had impulsively shot a person. At first he was terrified, but as weeks passed and he was not apprehended, he experienced a tremendous exhilaration when he realized he had "gotten away with it." The satisfaction derived from beating the system and outsmarting the police motivated much of his subsequent criminal behavior.

The successful performance of an aggressive or violent act should strengthen the tendency to repeat that specific response, and the effect of the reinforcement should also generalize to other, similar behavior. Thus, a person who has been reinforced for engaging in moderately aggressive behavior would be more likely to commit a violent act than someone who had not experienced such reinforcement, other factors such as instigation, inhibitions, and situational factors being equal.

The above analysis was drawn from the literature on principles of learning and applied to aggression and violence. However, according to Akers (1977: 261-262), there is evidence that violent and aggressive habits are no exceptions to these principles:

> Of course no one has produced homicide, either "senseless" or otherwise, in a controlled situation in order to study the variables leading to its occurrence. But

experimental research has shown that very aggressive behavior, which on the surface could be described as equally impulsive and uncontrolled, although not as destructive, is acquired and extinguished through the social reinforcement contingencies surrounding it. Both physical and verbal aggression have been conditioned, inhibited, and reproduced by manipulating reinforcement and punishment. It has been found that violent and aggressive people have had such behavior reinforced in the past or have imitated it after observing that it was rewarded when practiced by others. Studies have discovered that aggressive adolescents have parents who actively encouraged and rewarded their children's violence. Nonaggressive people have not been exposed to violent models and had parents who responded with approval to nonviolent acts. Both the intensity of violence and the situation in which it is likely to occur may be manipulated through social reward [Bandura, 1973].

Acquisition of Aggressive and Violent Habits

Aggressive and violent habits are learned through direct experience in which a person is reinforced for aggressive behavior and through observational or imitation learning in which a person observes violent behavior.

Acquisition Through Direct Experience. In our culture, many parents deliberately raise their children, especially boys, to be aggressive. They tell their sons, "Don't let anyone push you around," and inculcate them with cultural myths extolling the virtues of physical courage and denigrating nonviolence. Although the dominant Christian ethic prescribes "turning the other cheek," counteraggression is preferred (Megargee, 1973). Parents want their children to be able to "handle themselves," and most fathers and mothers, given the choice, would prefer to have a son who is a bully ("a little too rough at times") than one who is a "wimp."

Even if the parents succeed in reinforcing aggressive behavior only in the context of self-defense or in sports, it is not surprising that the aggressive habits that are learned generalize to other situations. As McNeil (1959: 227) pointed out,

Since a child will learn whatever responses are rewarded by others or bring gratification of his needs, it is easy to see how he can grow in sophistication in the use of aggressive devices. When other individuals are blocking the child's way and frustrating him, he can, by accident, learn that an aggressive attack will remove them and free the path to gratification. . . . When the child discovers the benefit of hurting others and he gains experience and learns more about the motivation of others, he'll become more and more skilled in using this knowledge of motivation as a means of controlling them and getting what he wants.

This is particularly true in the culture of poverty. McCandless (1967: 587) has described rewards for aggressiveness in the world of a lower-class child as follows:

He has learned that he had better grab while the grabbing is good, because if he doesn't, one of his brothers and sisters, or his parents, or his peers, will grab instead. Reason has never won a street fight nor enabled him to get the biggest share of the can of beans, nor served to keep his father from beating his mother when he got drunk. . . . Without immediate action and intense drive, the child may not survive the tooth-and-claw existence that for him is almost routine. . . . When one is battling for survival—for his fair share of the limited supply of food in the window cooler or ice box, for his turn with the local girl who will let the boys go as far as they want—intense emotion facilitates and spurs action. Standing back, thinking, and suppressing result in failure to reach the goal. Striking out, yelling, and pushing cause others to stand back so that you can go ahead.

Given such a milieu the child learns that aggression can satisfy a variety of needs in addition to whatever satisfactions are to be gained through violence itself. It is, therefore, not surprising that investigators such as McKee and Leader (1955) have observed more aggressiveness on the part of lower-class children. Goldfarb's (1943a, 1943b, 1944, 1945) studies showed children reared in an institutional setting learned aggressive habits to compete successfully for adult attention. Thus, environmental deprivation can produce aggression not only through frustration, but also by teaching the child that aggression is the best way to satisfy needs for attention, food, safety, and the like, in addition to the reinforcement stemming from injuries to the victim.

The effects of reinforcement on milder forms of aggressive behavior have been studied in a number of laboratory studies of children. Bandura and Walters (1963; reprinted in Megargee and Hokanson, 1970: 37) summarized their evidence as follows:

The influence of positive reinforcement on the acquisition and maintenance of aggressive behavior has been investigated in a number of controlled laboratory experiments. It has been demonstrated that positive reinforcement in the form of verbal approval or material rewards will increase the frequency of children's aggressive responses; that reinforcement of one class of aggressive responses may result in an increment in another class of aggressive responses; and that the effects of rewarding aggression in relatively impersonal play situations are transferred to new social situations in which interpersonal aggression may be displayed.

Ethical (and practical) constraints have naturally prohibited the controlled laboratory study of extreme forms of aggressive behavior such as violence. Anthropology, however, has provided cogent "experiments of nature" through ethnological research in other societies. According to Bandura and Walters (1963; reprinted in Megargee and Hokanson, 1970: 36-37),

There is considerable evidence, however, from cross-cultural and field studies that aggressive habits are acquired largely through the direct reinforcement of aggressive responses. In the culture of the headhunting Iatmul (Bateson, 1936), the scalping of enemies is reinforced not only by the prestige that accrues to the possessor of the scalp, but also, more immediately and tangibly, by the dances and celebrations that follow the decapitation. . . . The child and adolescent in this society are constantly surrounded by aggressive models and . . . when the occasion comes for them to reproduce the aggressive behavior of the adults, their imitative responses are socially approved, while failure to behave aggressively is negatively reinforced. . . .

In contrast, among the Hutterites (Eaton and Weil, 1955), who stress pacifism as a style of life, aggressive behavior goes consistently unrewarded. Despite the fact that children in this subculture are subjected to relatively severe and presumably frustrating socialization pressures, they show virtually no interpersonal aggression.

The dominant Western culture falls between these extremes, but is probably closer to the Iatmul than the Hutterite pattern. The number of statues and plaques erected honoring military heroes or warriors far exceeds the number commemorating any other occupational group. Indeed, in some sports individuals known as "headhunters" have achieved folk-hero status; during Bubba Smith's playing days, whole stadiums full of people would chant, "Kill, Bubba, kill!" and Jack Tatum's autobiography was appropriately titled *They Call Me Assassin*.

Acquisition Through Observation or Imitation. Even in the absence of direct reinforcement for aggressive or violent behavior, habit strength can be acquired vicariously by observing others being rewarded intrinsically or extrinsically for aggressive behavior (Akers, 1977; Bandura, 1978). An English robber quoted by Parker and Allerton (1952) graphically described how his values regarding violence had been shaped by being raised in what Wolfgang and Ferracuti (1967) would no doubt call a violent subculture:

Violence is in a way like bad language—something that a person like me's been brought up with, something I got used to very early on as part of the daily scene of childhood, you might say. I don't at all recoil from the idea, I don't have a sort of inborn dislike of the thing, like you do. As long as I can remember I've seen violence in use all around me—my mother hitting the children; my brothers and sister all whacking one another, or other children; the man downstairs bashing his wife, and so on. You get used to it, it doesn't mean anything in these circumstances [MacDonald, 1975, p. 143].

As already noted, a history of witnessing or experiencing familial violence is one of the most common characteristics found among those who engage in familial and other forms of violent behavior (Anderson, 1977; Steele, 1970).

For those not reared in the "subculture of violence," aggressive habit strength can be obtained vicariously through the media. Televised dramatizations of violent behavior can alter attitudes toward violence, making it more acceptable as a solution to interpersonal problems (Menzies, 1972), and a number of laboratory studies have demonstrated that children will imitate aggressive models (Walters, 1966).

Imitative learning can also influence the form that aggressive or violent behavior will take. In their studies of imitative aggression by children, Bandura et al. (1961, 1963) noted their subjects repeated the highly distinctive aggressive acts performed by the models; turning to violence, we have noted distinctive culturally conditioned forms of violence such as headhunting among the Iatmul and Amok among the Laotians. Perhaps the most vivid examples of media influence on the forms of violent behavior were the imitations of the skyjacking technique devised by D. B. Cooper and the fictional extortion scenario involving an altimeter-activated bomb placed in an aircraft described in Rod Serling's TV drama "Doomsday Flight."

Decreasing Aggressive Habits

Numerous studies of learning in people and other animals have demonstrated that the only effective way to decrease or eliminate habit strength is through extinction. This involves the repeated unrewarded performance of the particular behavior.

By their nature, aggressive habits are extremely difficult to extinguish. Intrinsic aggressive behavior is, by definition, rewarded immediately by the injuries inflicted on the target, and it is virtually impossible in our culture to arrange the environmental contingencies so that no extrinsic rewards are forthcoming for aggressive behavior. Partial reinforcement only makes habits more resistant to extinction.

Punishment may block or suppress aggressive or violent behavior by increasing inhibitions against aggression, but it does not appear to affect aggressive habit strength per se. At best it may promote discrimination learning, guiding individuals to select aggressive acts that are less likely to be punished. To the extent that this strategy succeeds, these unpunished acts will acquire greater habit strength. Recently, the writer asked a prisoner who was about to complete a prison sentence for bank robbery what he had learned from the experience. He replied that he had learned it didn't pay to rob banks with a revolver. In the future he would use a submachine gun. If this technological advance proves to be successful in helping him avoid prison, we can expect that carrying a machine gun will become a regular part of his *modus operandi*.

Inhibitions Against Aggression

Thus far we have discussed the major psychological factors that lead to the commission of a violent act, instigation and habit strength. If these were the only variables operating, we could expect everyone to respond to provocation with aggression or violence. Obviously this is not the case; despite the impression this chapter may have given the reader thus far, most people in our society do not engage in criminal violence. The reason is to be found in the third major variable, inhibitions against violence and aggression.

Although some theorists have postulated innate inhibitions against aggression, and indeed, animal husbandrymen have produced docile as well as aggressive strains of animals, most psychologists maintain that inhibitions against aggressive behavior are environmentally acquired through socialization. (Since the focus of this chapter is on "psychological" determinants of aggressive behavior, we shall not discuss physiologically induced inhibitions such as those obtained by the administration of drugs or through surgical procedures, although, strictly speaking, these too are environmental determinants.)

As already noted, inhibitions can be both general and specific. Specific inhibitions may be attached to certain acts, such as homicide, or to particular targets, such as one's mother. This makes them difficult to assess and complicates the thorny problem of attempting to predict violent tendencies.

A detailed discussion of the acquisition of inhibitions would involve a consideration of the whole process of development and socialization, which fortunately is beyond the scope of this chapter. Instead we shall content ourselves with mentioning some of the ways whereby inhibitions are thought to be acquired and lost.

Acquisition of Inhibitions Against Violence and Aggression

Surveying the theoretical and empirical literature, it is possible to discern four broad, somewhat overlapping, determinants of inhibitions against aggression: (1) anxiety or conditioned fear of punishment, (2) learned values and attitudes, (3) empathy or identification with the potential victim, and (4) utilitarian concerns.

Anxiety or Conditioned Fear of Punishment. In their classic monograph *Frustration and Aggression,* the Yale group maintained that inhibitions stemming from conditioned fear of punishment are the reason that frustration does not inevitably lead to aggression:

> The basic variable that determines the degree to which any specific act of aggression will be inhibited appears to be anticipation of punishment. Provisionally it may be stated that *the strength of inhibition of any act of aggression varies positively with the amount of punishment anticipated to be a consequence of that act. . . .*

In essence this principle derives from the law of effect; those actions cease to occur which, in the past, have been followed by punishment. It may be supposed that each frustration acts as an instigator to a great variety of aggressive responses. Some of these are overt in the sense that other persons can perceive them and some are so minimal (nonovert) that only the subject himself is aware of them. If past experience has taught him that certain of these aggressions are followed by punishment, those forms will tend to be eliminated and there will remain a residue of the forms that have not been punished [Dollard et al., 1939: 33].

In addition, they postulated, "Two occurrences not ordinarily considered under the rubric of punishment may be added to the terms mentioned above. (1) *Injury to a loved object is punishment*. . . . (2) *Anticipation of failure is equivalent to anticipation of punishment*" (1939). In short, they held that inhibitions stemmed from negative consequences accruing to the aggressive act.

Although the Yale group postulated a simple operant conditioning mechanism, one can assume that verbal warnings or threats could also lead to anticipations of punishment. Few of us are inhibited from committing murder because we have killed someone and been punished for it. To the extent that anticipation of punishment is the primary deterrent for our homicidal inclinations, we can attribute it to vicarious learnings, gleaned from media sources and verbal injunctions, of the fate that supposedly befalls killers.

Ignoring for the moment other ways of acquiring inhibitions, most theorists would attribute individual differences in inhibitions to differences in reinforcement schedules. The less inhibited child, according to this formulation, would have had fewer aggressive acts punished. Eysenck (1960), however, maintained that people and animals differ in conditionability, and that that least inhibited of individuals, the psychopath, suffers from a low level of conditionability so that punishment is less effective than with the normal person.

Assuming that the Yale group was correct in suggesting that inhibitions are acquired according to the laws governing operant conditioning, we might expect that generalization and discrimination would take place. The initial effect of punishing a given aggressive act should make the reoccurrence of that act and others similar to it less likely. If, however, a different aggressive act should occur and go unpunished, then discrimination should take place and the child should acquire inhibitions that are specific to the punished act. Through this mechanism, people might learn that some aggressive acts are taboo whereas others are acceptable, that it is forbidden to be aggressive against some targets, such as the members of one's own clan or tribe, but permissable to attack others, such as members of an alien tribe or race. Such discriminations would lead to the mechanisms of response substitution and displacement described earlier.

Given the punishment-leads-to-inhibitions formulation, the most likely discrimination that one would expect is between situations in which punishment is likely (i.e., in the presence of an authority figure) and those in which one can be aggressive with relative impunity. Thus, a child might learn to refrain from hitting his little brother when their mother is present and instead attack him when she is in another room.

As long as punishment depends on external authority figures, discriminations like this one will be formulated and inhibitions will be very situation-specific. In the course of socialization, however, most people acquire a new and omnipresent authority figure, themselves. Whether one labels this self-evaluating tendency the "conscience" or the "superego," the punishment it inflicts is the same . . . guilt. The acquisition of this self-monitoring tendency is the second major source of inhibition.

Inhibitions Stemming from Learned Values and Attitudes. Different theorists have postulated various explanations for the processes of identification and socialization, ranging from secondary reinforcement to the resolution of the Oedipal conflict, theoretical analyses that are beyond the scope of this discussion (see Megargee, 1969, 1972). Suffice it to say that in the course of development, children introject social values acquired from their parents, peers, schools, churches and various other reference groups. These values consist of sets of "thou shalts" and "thou shalt nots," and when children and adults fail to live up to these various injunctions, not all of which are mutually consistent, they will punish themselves with feelings of guilt for their self-perceived sins of omission or commission. The learned inhibitions are, of course, specific to the cultures, subcultures, and family units involved. When it comes to headhunting behavior, we might expect Iatmul and Hutterite adolescents to differ significantly in their guilt reactions, the former feeling pangs of remorse if they fail to behead an opponent, and the latter suffering from guilt if, in an unaccustomed fit of pique, they should decapitate an adversary.

Consistent, stable value systems are most likely to develop when the primary agents of acculturation share similar codes of ethics and morality. On the other hand, inconsistency among primary identification figures or reference groups can lead to conflicting values. A son born from the unlikely union of an Iatmul father with a Hutterite mother could be expected to have some major psychological conflicts regarding scalp-taking behavior. Unless he can somehow integrate these disparate values (perhaps sublimating them by becoming a barber), psychological stress and inconsistent behavior patterns can be expected. The so-called double bind, in which a parent simultaneously imparts conflicting behavioral prescriptions is a classic cause of psychopathology.

Whatever theoretical frame of references one adopts, there is general agreement that strong identification with parental values is most likely to develop in the context of a stable, warm, mutually supportive family system. The more the family and other reference groups uniformly oppose aggression, the stronger will be the inhibitions against violence that the child will develop. (A solid, affectionate family structure also decreases the likelihood of violent behavior by meeting the child's basic needs, thereby minimizing frustration-produced instigation to aggression, and by providing the child with altruistic, rather than aggressive, models to imitate.)

Empathy or Identification with the Victim. As we have seen, the Yale group maintained that injury to a love object constitutes punishment. This principle can be extended to anyone with whom the individual identifies. The more one empathizes with another, the more one will suffer should harm befall the other, and the less likely one will be to aggress against them.

This principle would at first appear contrary to the observation that much violent behavior takes place between intimates and family members. Again, we must turn to our conceptual framework for an explanation. Love, empathy, and compassion serve to increase inhibitions against aggression and violence. At the same time, family members, lovers, and friends are usually the principal individuals in our lives, serving to satisfy some of our primary needs for security, affection, and self-esteem. When such important people fail to meet these needs, it is extremely frustrating and threatening to our psychological equilibrium. Intimates are thus in a position to arouse much more instigation to aggression than strangers by virtue of their importance to us. Moreover, people are frequently locked into these unsatisfactory relationships. Unable to leave, they are trapped in classic approach-avoidance conflicts, subjected to repeated arousal of instigation that would not occur in less intense relationships. The result may be instigation that periodically overpowers the inhibitions, leading to the recurring cycles of familial violence described by Walker (1978a, 1978b, 1979).

A number of factors determine how much empathy one person feels for another. The first is proximity. The more remote people are in time or place, the less empathy one feels for them. When viewing the body of a recent homicide victim or even photographs of the crime scene, the author typically experiences strong feelings of compassion and empathy; but when, on an archaeological expedition to Oaxaca, he unearthed the skull of a man who had apparently been killed by a blow to the head some 1,200 years before, such feelings were minimal.

The second factor is similarity. Because they could identify more closely with the 52 American hostages in Iran, most Americans felt more concern for their plight in 1980 than they did for the 200 Syrians who were machine-gunned by governmental security forces in the town square of Aleppo, even though both events were equally remote geographically.

A third factor is familiarity. The more familiar or better known people are to us, the more we empathize with them. A recent newscast announced an all-points bulletin for an armed convict who had made his escape by stealing a car and kidnapping the driver, John Freeman, Jr. Having a nephew named John Freeman, Jr., who was scheduled to be driving in that vicinity, the writer was greatly alarmed until it was ascertained that the hostage was a different John Freeman, Jr., whereupon his concern diminished.

Proximity, similarity, and familiarity all operate to humanize people; the more people are humanized, the more empathy and compassion is felt toward them and the greater are the inhibitions against injuring them. One reason hostage negotiators stall for time is in hope that kidnappers will develop feelings of compassion for their victims that will lessen the likelihood of further violence.

Empathy does not, of course, depend solely on the characteristics of potential victims. People differ in their capacity to feel compassion for others. Hogan (1973) included this empathic ability as one of the criteria by which he evaluated individuals' moral development. Other factors (such as socialization) being equal, the greater the capacity to empathize with others, the less a person will engage in antisocial behavior (Hogan, 1973).

Utilitarian Concerns. Thus far we have focused on inhibitions that are relatively enduring characteristics of people, inhibitions stemming from childhood conditioning, value systems, and identification with potential victims. In a given situation, utilitarian factors can also influence inhibitions.

These utilitarian concerns fall into two general categories: (1) the degree to which violence is likely to result in adverse consequences for the offender and/or those he cares about, and (2) the likelihood that the aggressive behavior will fail in its objective of injuring the victim or accomplishing the relevant extrinsic goals.

These factors are similar to, but conceptually distinct from, situational factors inhibiting aggression or violence. For example, you may be involved in a dispute with someone who invites you to "step outside" to settle it. If you are on parole, engaging in a fight might result in your being returned to prison. This added risk could increase your inhibition level. If your potential adversary had a weapon, this external factor would be considered a situational variable.

Factors Decreasing Inhibitions

Inhibitions can be decreased in a number of ways, thereby increasing the likelihood of aggression or violence. If anticipation of punishment, values and attitudes opposed to violence, empathy for the victim, and utilitarian concerns foster inhibitions, as described in the previous section, changes in these factors can also decrease inhibitions.

Anticipation of Punishment. The Yale group maintained that anticipation of punishment through direct experience or vicarious learning is a primary factor leading to inhibitions against aggressive behavior. Conditioned anxiety responses like these have been found to be extraordinarily resistant to change, because people and animals avoid performing acts that have been punished in the past. However, if the instigation to aggression is so great that the aggressive act is, nevertheless, performed and the anticipated punishment does *not* occur, then the strength of the inhibitions associated with that act on that target will diminish, thereby making it easier for the individual to repeat this behavior.

Learned anxiety responses are also subject to response generalization. If inhibitions block a particular aggressive act directed at a certain target, the individual may discharge his or her hostility by means of response substitution, replacing aggressive act j with aggressive act k or, by displacement, substituting target t-2 for target t-1, or both. If the resulting aggressive behavior is successful, it will naturally strengthen the tendencies to perform the substituted aggressive act k, or to choose target t-2, by increasing the habit strength and decreasing any associated inhibitions. In addition, however, this successful aggression should, by means of response generalization, also decrease somewhat the inhibitions associated with the original suppressed aggressive response j directed at the original target t-1.

In addition to direct experiences in which the anticipated punishments for aggressive behavior are not forthcoming, inhibitions can also be decreased vicariously when people observe others performing aggressive acts with impunity. This phenomenon may account for the mixed literature regarding catharsis. It will be recalled that much of the debate regarding the effects of media violence centered on the apparent conflict between those who maintained that viewing violent films and television shows decreased violence by providing a harmless vicarious outlet through which aggressive instigation could be discharged, and those who maintained these shows fostered aggressive tendencies. Both sides could be correct. Viewing televised violence could simultaneously decrease both instigations and inhibitions. Unfortunately, the dependent variables studied in most investigations have been too crude to resolve this issue empirically. Most studies have simply measured input (the amount of violence viewed) and output (amount of overt aggressive behavior) and have not assesed the intervening variables of instigation, habit strength, and inhibitions.

In short, reinforcement schedules in which aggressive responses are reinforced rather than punished, either directly or vicariously, should diminish inhibitions. Such schedules are specifically emphasized in military training. Recruits, who presumably have the normal culturally induced prohibitions against killing, are trained to stick bayonets into lifelike dummies not only to achieve technical proficiency with the weapon, but also to overcome inhibitions that could lead to fatal hestitations in combat.

Values and Attitudes. Inhibitions can also be lessened by altering attitudes and values or by convincing people that certain specific situations are exceptions to the general taboo. If a society maintains that killing fellow humans is wrong, their warriors can be taught that the current enemies are less than human, so these prohibitions do not apply. Self-defense is one of the most nearly universal justifications for violence; most violent groups, ranging from street gangs to nation-states, attempt to justify their violent behavior, and lessen their members' inhibitions, by maintaining that they are responding to actual or imminent aggression from the enemy. Hitler used both of these tactics—dehumanization of the Polish people and a trumped-up border incident—to justify to the German people the invasion of Poland in September 1939.

Conflicts in values can also be used by individuals and groups to justify the use of force or violence. Sykes and Matza (1957) wrote of "techniques of neutralization," rationalizations whereby juvenile delinquents and criminals justify acts of violence and social deviance that would otherwise be contrary to their moral codes. A person may sincerely believe that assault is wrong, but maintain that in a particular case, such as a gang fight, the moral duty to "help a friend" takes priority. As we have seen, many rapists maintain that rape is wrong but that their particular offense does not constitute rape because the victim "really wanted it." Groth (1979) noted that in a homosexual rape, the offender often does his best to get the victim to ejaculate. This neutralization technique serves two functions: (1) it convinces the offender that the victim really "enjoyed it" and that the offense therefore did not constitute rape, and (2) it demonstrates that the victim was basically homosexual and therefore a legitimate victim (Sykes and Matza, 1957).

Once a person has been a victim, it is often easier to become a perpetrator of violence, as if the victimization justifies the subsequent aggression. This writer recently evaluated a multiple murderer and rapist who had killed several women by stabbing them in the heart, just as he himself had once been stabbed adjacent to his heart. Despite a long history of antisocial behavior, he had never raped a woman until after he, himself, had been raped in prison. He agreed that experiencing these assaults had decreased his inhibitions against assaulting others. (Undoubtedly they also increased his instigation to violence.)

Empathy for the Victim. Inhibition can also be diminished by decreasing the empathy felt for the victim. Lorenz (1966) maintains that humankind's unique propensity for intraspecific aggression (i.e., homicide) stems from technological advances that enable people to kill one another at a distance. As you read these words, hundreds of airmen in missile sites sit poised before control panels ready to launch, upon command, unparalleled nuclear devastation on millions of distant people. How many of them would be able to kill or maim three, two, or even one of these unarmed noncombatants in a face-to-face encounter, even if ordered to do so? It is somehow easier to incinerate thousands of unseen children than it is to strangle a single individual infant.

Decreasing proximity is not the only way to diminish empathy and lower inhibitions. Emphasizing other peoples' differences rather than their similarities is also effective. One of the reasons both racial and religious violence are so widespread is that it is always easier to attack someone who is clearly one of "them" rather than one of "us," whoever "them" and "us" may be.

Inhibitions can also be decreased by lessening the offender's personal responsibility and decreasing his or her humanity. The classic film *The Ox Bow Incident* dramatically depicted how individuals could participate in a lynching that was acceptable to the group although abhorrent to many of the individual members of that group. How many of the National Guardsmen who fired on student demonstrators at Kent State University could have done so if they had not been part of a group, clothed in identical uniforms, with their faces concealed behind gas masks?

Utilitarian Factors. Just as utilitarian factors increasing the risk or lessening the rewards can increase inhibitions, decreasing the risks or increasing the likelihood of reinforcement can diminish inhibitions. This is especially evident in prison insurrections and terrorist attacks. When rioting prisoners are granted amnesty or imprisoned terrorists are released in exchange for civilian hostages, the risks, and therefore the inhibitions, associated with participating in such violence are decreased. Although this strategy may lead to a resolution of the immediate confrontation, it probably leads to an increase in the future use of such tactics.

Physiological Factors and Psychopathology. Not all of the factors that can reduce inhibitions against aggression and violence are mirror images of inhibition-producing mechanisms. Humankind's ethical sensitivity and moral prohibitions develop relatively late in the course of maturation and socialization. In physiological terms, they depend upon sound cortical functioning; in psychoanalytic terminology, on the emergence and development of the superego and ego. Anything that intereferes with cortical functioning on the one hand or impairs ego or superego functioning on the other can decrease ethical functioning and inhibitions against taboo behavior.

Although physiological mechanisms are beyond the scope of this chapter, it should be mentioned that inhibitions can be decreased chemically. Alcohol acts to diminish ethical prohibitions and inhibitions. This characteristic is one of its chief attractions for humankind—as Ogden Nash once remarked, "Candy's dandy but liquor's quicker." Unfortunately its effects are not specific; it acts to diminish the obstacles not only to social intercourse but also to violence.

Other drugs, notably phencyclidine (PCP), have also been associated with violent behavior (Astill, 1979; Nakamura and Noguchi, 1979; Luisada, 1978; Siegel, 1978), but it is less clear whether they operate to decrease inhibitions or increase instigation.

Chemical substances can produce acute brain syndromes. Chronic brain syndromes stemming from disease, aging, trauma, and the like can also interfere with sound cortical functioning. Impulsivity, irritability, poor judgment, and diminished ethical sensitivity are among the symptoms associated with many chronic organic disorders, and can lead to reduced inhibitions against aggressive and violent behavior. Focal lesions in the hypotholamic and limbic regions and temporal-lobe tumors have been implicated in the violence displayed in some well-documented clinical cases (Mark and Ervin, 1970).

Major mental illnesses such as functional psychoses can impair ego and superego functioning, leading to diminished reality-testing and decreased ethical sensitivity. Psychotics are typically so preoccupied with their own problems that they lack the capacity to empathize with or relate to others. Paranoid delusions may convince them they are the victims of plots that threaten their very existence if a violent counterresponse is not forthcoming. Hallucinations may call for the performance of forbidden acts including violence. Major depressive disorders may induce a belief that life is not worth living, either for the patient or his or her loved ones. The impaired judgment, lack of control, and diminished reality-testing common to many psychotic and extremely disturbed individuals can lead to diminished inhibitions against a variety of behaviors, including violence.

Situational Factors

The final variables that enter into the equations in the algebra of aggression are the situational factors, which may operate to increase or decrease the likelihood of a violent response. Situational factors are, by definition, characteristics of the milieu rather than the organism; therefore they are somewhat beyond the scope of this discussion of the intraindividual or "psychological" determinants of violence and will be discussed in less detail than the other variables analyzed thus far.

Perhaps the most cogent situational factor in the scenario of violence is the behavior of the other people involved, the victim or victims and any codefendants, or bystanders. A number of observers of criminal homicide and other forms of violence have commented on the important role played by the eventual victim (Luckenbill and Sanders, 1977; Toch, 1969; Wolfgang, 1958). Most violent crimes that focus on people (as opposed to property) involve complex interpersonal interactions between the offender and the victim, and case studies and analyses of violent and potentially violent interactions have begun to investigate the role played by the victim. Was the victim's behavior a situational factor that facilitated or impeded violent behavior? What are the best strategies for people involved in potentially violent encounters such as confrontations with a possible rapist, armed robber, or hostage taker? How can they decrease instigation and increase inhibitions? Perpetrators of violent crimes as well as victims have served as subjects in such studies.

The behavior of fellow offenders is another important situational factor. As we have seen, many authorities have indicated that affiliation with the group is a primary motive in gang rapes. The "contagion" of aggression behavior has been well documented (Redl and Wineman, 1957; Wheeler and Caggiula, 1966). Laboratory studies of conformity, obedience, and group decision-making performed by social psychologists, such as Asch (1951), Milgram (1965), and Myers and Lamm (1977), should provide valuable insights and hypotheses for behavioral scientists interested in the group dynamics of antisocial behavior and violence.

Bystanders, if present, can also facilitate or impede violent behavior. Their behavior can escalate a confrontation, forcing the adversaries to feel they will lose face if they disengage or retreat. Any police officer knows that a person arrested in the presence of his friends is more apt to resist than if he is apprehended alone. Bystanders' disapproval or intervention can also help defuse a situation. Unfortunately, the effect of intervention can be to unite the quarreling parties against the would-be peacemaker. More police officers have been seriously injured attempting to quell domestic disputes than in any other single situation (Bard, 1971).

Weapons are another important stimulus factor. Berkowitz (1968) maintained that the presence of weapons, in and of themselves, increases arousal levels and stimulates violent behavior. Whether or not this is the case, the ready availability of weapons makes it possible to translate intention into action with minimal reflection and maximum injury. They can thus facilitate violent behavior.

Weapons can also serve to inhibit violence. An unarmed person will often think twice before attacking an armed opponent, and MacDonald (1975) reported there were fewer, albeit more serious, injuries resulting from armed than from strong-arm robberies, presumably because the victims were less likely to provoke violence by resisting.

The effect of architecture on antisocial behavior and violence is also receiving increasing attention. As already noted, for a violent crime to take place there must be a possible victim in the immediate proximity of a potential offender, in the absence of effective guardians. Architectural design can provide real or symbolic barriers between victims and offenders and increase the availability of potential guardians through lighting, alarm systems, and other security measures.

These are only a few of the situational factors that can facilitate or impede violent behavior. Although the primary focus of this chapter has been on psychological characteristics of violent individuals, this does not mean that the importance of situational factors should be underestimated. It is essential that situational as well as personal factors should be considered in predicting the likelihood of violent behavior and crime-prevention measures aimed at environmental factors may well be more cost-effective than person-centered techniques.

Response Competiton

Response competition is the final element in the algebra of aggression. The algebraic sum of instigation, habit strength, inhibitions, and situational factors facilitating and impeding a particular aggressive act directed at a given target determine its "reaction potential" (sEr). If the reaction potential is zero or less—perhaps because there is no instigation or because inhibitions are too high—then that act of violence against that target will not occur at that time or place. If, on the other hand, the reaction potential is greater than zero—if the forces favoring the violent response outweigh those opposing it—then that act is *possible*. Before it can actually be performed, it must compete with other possible responses, some violent and others nonviolent, that may lead to greater satisfactions with fewer costs.

The phenomenon of response competition and, indeed, the author's whole "algebra of aggression" complicate the interpretation of research findings. If, after a series of manipulations, a research subject makes an aggressive response, the experimenter can conclude that the factors favoring an aggressive response outweighed the factors inhibiting it. The reverse is not true. Failure to act aggressively does not necessarily mean that the inhibitory factors outweighed the excitatory ones; it may simply mean that some other response was selected in the response competition.

Response competition does, however, broaden the range of techniques available to those who are interested in preventing violent behavior. In our microscopic analysis of a particular violent act, it appeared the ways to decrease violence were limited to decreasing instigation to aggression, habit strength, and situational factors facilitating violent behavior and/or increasing inhibitions and situational factors impeding violence. However, response competition makes it possible to avert violence by strengthening competing nonviolent response alternatives.

For example, a paroled bank robber and murderer who enrolled in one of my seminars has had the reaction potential of his violent response tendencies decreased significantly by virtue of thirteen years of hard time; however, despite his protestations to the contrary, it is doubtful that their potential is zero. He has, however, learned that nonviolent behavior can satisfy many of his other nonaggressive needs more effectively. His "war stories" in class bring him considerable attention, and although it is undoubtedly less intense than the attention he received when he held people at gunpoint, it is longer lasting. The ego satisfaction derived from outwitting the police has been sublimated into outsmarting professors, at considerably less personal risk. His needs for companionship, security, and sexual gratification are more easily satisfied as a student than as a robber on the run (or as a prisoner). There is, of course, less money and less excitement in academe, and if the chance for an easy score should come along he might well be tempted, but so far the strength of the competing nonviolent responses has apparently been sufficiently strong for them to be chosen.

Strengthening competing responses has been a well-recognized behavioral technique. Reinforcement for "on-task" behavior has replaced punishment for aggressive attention-seeking in some classrooms (Brown and Elliott, 1965), and similar management techniques have been adopted in some psychiatric settings. Attempts to apply behavioral techniques in correctional settings have been quite controversial, however.

It would appear that strengthening competing responses would be more effective in instances involving instrumental rather than angry aggression. When violence is used as a means to some other end (such as acquisition), alternative, nonviolent, techniques have a better chance of succeeding than in cases where the only goal is injury to the victim.

CONCLUDING REMARKS

H. L. Mencken, as usual, said it best, "There's always an easy solution to every human problem—neat, plausible and wrong" (quoted in Peter, 1977: 410). So, too, with violence. In these pages we have surveyed many types of human violence. Some are exotic, such as. the terrorist plotting a political assassination or the Laotian soldier "running Amok" with hand grenades in the village square. Others are ordinary, such as the drunken father beating his children or a young man with a pistol holding up a convenience store. The only common denominators are that the victims were injured or threatened with injury and the acts were illegal.

Some recurring patterns were noted in the types of people who engage in homicide, rape, robbery, arson, and the other violent offenses surveyed; some groups of people are more often involved in violence than others. No group, however, has an exclusive franchise on violent behavior, and the causes of violence are as varied as the human condition itself. If the reader has been left with an appreciation of the complexity of violent behavior and a skeptical attitude toward easy, neat, plausible explanations, one of the objectives of this chapter has been accomplished.

The second major objective has been to set forth a conceptual framework for the study of violence and the evaluation of the violent individual. Like most models, it involves some distortions and fits some observations better than others. Being multivariate, it reflects the complexity of the phenomenon and encompasses the wide variety of people who engage in various types of violent behavior. At the same time, as with most multivariate models, it is probably better suited to explaining what *occurred* in an experiment or a violent encounter than it is to predicting what *will occur* in the future.

The major deficiency of the model for research or clinical application is that the major constructs that have been postulated—instigation, habit strength, inhibitions, and situational factors—were not operationally defined. Some analogues have been developed, such as Hokanson's (1970) use of blood pressure to assess instigation, but our current level of sophistication in assessment does not allow us to quantify these variables rigorously or precisely. At this point, the major contribution of this model is a conceptual framework that will help us sort out the various observations and theories, assist us in discussing the issues, and guide the direction of future research. If it has done this, then the second major objective of this discussion has been achieved.

To conclude on a somewhat encouraging note, Edward Searles once remarked, "It is in the realm of uncertainties that progress, if it is ever encountered, must lie" (quoted by Peter, 1977: 410). If this is the case, then our review indicates that criminal violence is an area in which progress can be made.

NOTES

1. Banay's typology also illustrates not only that different typologists use different labels to refer to the same construct, but also that the same label can mean different things in different systems. "Subcultural" to Banay meant "undersocialized," whereas in other systems it typically refers to a group that is adequately socialized into a deviant value system, as in Wolfgang and Ferracuti's (1976) "subcultures of violence."

2. Child abusers who belong to the Old Testament "spare-the-rod" group would be exceptions to this generalization.

3. When sexual motivation is attributed, rape is rarely viewed as the act of a deprived, inadequate person with no other sexual outlets; indeed, the rapists treated by Groth (1979) typically had consenting sexual partners available. Instead, rape with a sexual aim is more likely to be attributed to an amoral or psychopathic individual who simply takes what he wants when and where he wants it.

4. Brownmiller maintained that power has always been one of the primary, if not *the* primary, motivations for rape. She wrote (1975: 5), "Man's discovery that his genitalia could serve as a weapon to generate fear must rank as one of the most important discoveries of prehistoric times, along with the use of fire and the first crude stone axe. From prehistoric times to the present, I believe, rape has played a critical function. It is nothing more or less than a conscious process of intimidation by which *all men* keep *all women* in a state of fear."

5. Parental abduction of children in custody disputes is an exception to this general rule and will not be regarded as a violent crime in this section.

6. The abortive Gunpowder Plot to blow up the British Houses of Parliament while they were being addressed by King James I on November 5, 1605, illustrates how technology has aided the modern terrorist. To accomplish their objective, Guy Fawkes and his fellow conspirators had to place *36 barrels* of gunpowder surrounded by iron bars and firewood in a rented cellar beneath the House of Lords. The number of people who had to be recruited to carry out this massive operation made secrecy impossible and the plot was thwarted. With modern high explosives, a much smaller cadre might well have succeeded, as illustrated by the recent bombing of the Islamic Party Headquarters in Teheran in which a 30-kilo bomb killed over 70 highly placed Iranian government officials.

7. These fires included (1) the MGM Grand Hotel, Las Vegas, Nevada; (2) Stouffer's Inn, Harrison, New York; (3) the Professional Development Center, Tallahassee, Florida; and (4) hundreds of homes and thousands of acres of vegetation in a "brush" fire in Los Angeles, California.

8. Aside from case studies such as these, the chief "contribution" of psychologists to the field appears to be the alleged invention of an ingenious timing device by an experimental psychologist with a Ph.D. from Stanford. Using this device, he was able to place bombs timed to explode seven

months later in safe-deposit boxes of nine major banks in New York, Chicago, and San Francisco (MacDonald, 1977).

9. The material in this section is adapted from Megargee (1969).

10. The reader should not infer from the use of these examples that social learning is a necessary or sufficient explanation of gender differences in aggression. The effects of testosterone on both males and females of many species have been well documented, for example. However, as noted at the beginning of the chapter, the task assigned this writer was to grapple with "psychological" rather than physiological or situational determinants.

11. "Machismo" comes from the Spanish noun "macho" which means "male" but can also refer to a "he-mule" (Castillo and Bond, 1950). As Rosenquist and Megargee (1969: 66) noted, "By keeping in mind a rather mulish masculinity, we can closely approach the concept of machismo."

REFERENCES

Abrahamsen, D. *The psychology of crime*. New York: John Wiley, 1960.

Akers, R. L. *Deviant behavior: A social learning approach* (2nd ed.). Belmont, CA: Wadsworth, 1977.

Allan, L. J. Child Abuse: A critical review of the research and the theory. In J. P. Martin (Ed.), *Violence and the family*. New York: John Wiley, 1978.

Amir, M. *Patterns in forcible rape*. Chicago: University of Chicago Press, 1971.

Anderson, G. M. Child abuse. *America*, 1977, 136, 428-442.

Ardrey, R. *The territorial imperative*. New York, Atheneum, 1966.

Asch, S. E. Effects of group pressure upon the modification and distortion of judgment. In N. H. Guetzkow (Ed.), *Groups, leadership and men*. Pittsburgh: Carnegie Press, 1951.

Astill, K. S. Phencyclidine (PCP)—"Angel dust" alias "the embalmer." *Australian Police Journal*, 1979, 33, 211-224.

Astor, G. *The charge is rape*. Chicago: Playboy Press, 1975.

Banay, R. S. Study in murder. *The Annals*, 1952, 284, 26-34.

Bandura, A. *Aggression: A social learning analysis*. Englewood Cliffs, NJ: Prentice-Hall, 1973.

Bandura, A. Social learning perspective: Mechanisms of aggression. In H. Toch (Ed.), *The ecology of crime and criminal justice*. New York: Holt, Rinehart & Winston, 1978.

Bandura, A., Ross, D., and Ross, S. Transmission of aggression through imitation of aggressive models. *Journal of Abnormal and Social Psychology*, 1961, 63, 575-582.

Bandura, A., Ross, D., and Ross, S. Imitation of film-mediated aggressive models. *Journal of Abnormal and Social Psychology*, 1963, 66, 3-11.

Bandura, A., and Walters, R. H. *Social learning and personality development*. New York: Holt, Rinehart & Winston, 1963.

Bard, M. The study and modification of intra-familial violence. In J. L. Singer (Ed.), *The control of aggression and violence: Cognitive and physiological factors*. New York: Academic Press, 1971.

Barlay, S. Firebugs and their fearless victims. *Top Security*, 1976, 2(6), 195-197.

Baron, R. A. *Human aggression*. New York: Plenum Press, 1977.

Bartol, C. R. *Criminal behavior: A psychosocial approach*. Englewood Cliffs, NJ: Prentice-Hall, 1980.

Bateson, G. *The Naven*. Stanford: Stanford University Press, 1936.

Baumann, C. E. *Diplomatic kidnappings—A revolutionary tactic of urban terrorism*. The Hague, Netherlands: Martinus Nijhoff, 1973.

Becker, J. R., and Abel, G. G. Men and the victimization of women. In J. R. Chapman and M. R.

Gates (Eds.), *Victimization of women*. Beverly Hills, CA: Sage Publications, 1978.

Bell, J. B. *Time of terror: How democratic societies respond to revolutionary violence*. New York: Basic Books, 1978.

Berkowitz, L. *Aggression: A social psychological analysis*. New York: McGraw-Hill, 1962.

Berkowitz, L. Impulse, aggression and the gun. *Psychology Today*, 1968, 2, 18-22.

Blehar, M. C. Helping abused children and their parents. In E. Corfman (Ed.), *Family violence and child abuse*. Rockville, MD.: U.S. Department of Health, Education and Welfare, ADAMHA, 1979.

Brandon, S. Physical violence in the family: An overview. In M. Borland (Ed.), *Violence in the family*. Atlantic Highlands, NJ: Humanities Press, 1976.

Bromberg, W. *The mold of murder*. New York: Grune & Stratton, 1961.

Bromberg, W., and Coyle, E. Rape! A compulsion to destroy. *Medical Insight*, 1974, April, 21-22, 24-25.

Brown, P., and Elliott, R. Control of aggression in a nursery school class. *Journal of Experimental Child Psychology*, 1965, 2, 103-107.

Brownmiller, S. *Against our will: Men, women and rape*. New York: Bantam Books, 1975.

Buss, A. H. *The psychology of aggression*. New York: John Wiley, 1961.

Buss, A. H. Aggression pays. In J. L. Singer (Ed.), *The control of aggression and violence: Cognitive and physiological factors*. New York: Academic Press, 1971.

Castillo, C., and Bond, O. (Eds.). *The University of Chicago Spanish Dictionary*. New York: Pocketbooks, 1950.

Cater, C., and Strickland, S. *TV violence and the child: The evolution and the fate of the Surgeon General's report*. New York: Russell Sage Foundation, 1975.

Cohen, M. L., Garofalo, R., Boucher, R., and Seghorn, T. The psychology of rapists. *Seminars in Psychiatry*, 1971, 3(3), 307-327.

Cole, K., Fisher, G., and Cole, S. Women who kill. *Archives of General Psychiatry*, 1968, 19, 1-8.

Conklin, J. E. *Robbery and the criminal justice system*. Philadelphia: Lippincott, 1972.

Davis, A. J. Sexual assaults in the Philadelphia prison system and sheriff's vans. *Transaction*, 1968, December, 8-16.

Davis, J. R. Typical terrorism. In J. R. Davis (Ed.), *Terrorists: Youth, biker, and prison violence*. San Diego, CA: Grossmont Press, 1978.

Dawe, D. Police problems of the future: Terror—Future trends in hostage taking and violence. *Canadian Police College Journal*, 1979, 3(1), 44-54.

DeRiver, P. *The sexual criminal*. Springfield, IL: Charles C Thomas, 1949.

Dewsbury, A. R. Battered wives: Family violence seen in general practice. *Royal Society of Health Journal*, 1975, 95, 290-294.

Dollard, J., Doob, L. W., Miller, N. E., Mowrer, O. H. and Sears, R. R. *Frustration and aggression*. New Haven: Yale University Press, 1939.

Eaton, J. W., and Weil, R. J. *Culture and mental disorders*. New York: Free Press, 1955.

Elbow, M., Theoretical considerations of violent marriages. *Social Casework*, 1977, 58, 515-526.

Eysenck, H. J. *Behavior therapy and the neuroses*. New York: Pergamon Press, 1960.

Feierabend, I.K., and Feierabend, R.L. Aggressive behaviors within polities, 1948-1962: A cross-national study. *Journal of Conflict Resolution*, 1966, 10, 249-272.

Festinger, L. *A theory of cognitive dissonance*. Stanford, CA: Stanford University Press, 1957.

Freud, S. Beyond the pleasure principle. In J. Strachey (Ed.), *The standard edition of the complete psychological works of Sigmund Freud* (Vol. 18). London: Hogarth, 1955. (Originally published in 1920.)

Galvin, J. A., and MacDonald, J. N. Psychiatric study of a mass murderer. *American Journal of Psychiatry*, 1959, 115, 1057-1061.

Gil, D. G. Unraveling child abuse. In D. G. Gil (Ed.), *Child abuse and violence*. New York: AMS Press, 1979.

Gingold, J. One of these days—Pow! Right in the kisser: The truth about battered wives. *Ms.*, August 1976, pp. 51-54, 94.

Glaser, D., Kenefick, D., and O'Leary, V. *The violent offender.* Washington, DC: U.S. Department of Health, Education and Welfare, Social Rehabilitation Service, Office of Juvenile Delinquency and Youth Development, 1968.

Goldfarb, W. The effects of early institutional care on adolescent personality. *Journal of Experimental Education,* 1943, 12, 106-129. (a)

Goldfarb, W. Infant rearing and problem behavior. *American Journal of Orthopsychiatry,* 1943, 13, 249-266. (b)

Goldfarb, W. Infant rearing as a factor in foster home placement. *American Journal of Orthopsychiatry,* 1944, 14, 162-167.

Goldfarb, W. Psychological privation in infancy and subsequent adjustment. *American Journal of Orthopsychiatry,* 1945, 15, 247-255.

Groth, A. N. The older rape victim and her assailant. *Journal of Geriatric Psychiatry,* 1978, 11, 203-215.

Groth, A. N. *Men who rape: The psychology of the offender.* New York: Plenum Press, 1979.

Guttmacher, M. S. *Sex offenses.* New York: Norton, 1951.

Guttmacher, M. S. *The mind of the murderer.* New York: Farrar, 1960.

Hacker, F. J. *Crusaders, criminals, crazies: Terror and terrorism in our time.* New York: Norton, 1976.

Hanks, S. E., and Rosenbaum, C. P. Battered women: A study of women who live with violent alcohol abusing men. *American Journal of Orthopsychiatry,* 1977, 47, 291-306.

Harbin, H. T., and Madden, D. J. Battered parents: A new syndrome. *American Journal of Psychiatry,* 1979, 136, 1288-1291.

Hazelwood, R. R., and Douglas, J. E. The lust murderer. *FBI Law Enforcement Bulletin,* 1980, 49(4), 18-22.

Henry, A. F., and Short, J. F., Jr. *Suicide and homicide.* New York: Free Press, 1954.

Hofstadter, R. Reflections on violence in the United States. In R. Hofstadter and M. Wallace (Eds.), *American violence: A documentary history.* New York: Random House, 1970.

Hogan, R. Moral conduct and moral character: A psychological perspective. *Psychological Bulletin,* 1973, 79, 217-232.

Hokanson, J. E. Psychophysiological evaluation of the catharsis hypothesis. In E. I. Megargee and J. E. Hokanson (Eds.), *The dynamics of aggression: Individual, group, and international analyses.* New York: Harper & Row, 1970.

Hovland, C. I., and Sears, R. R. Minor studies of aggression: VI, Correlation of lynchings with economic indices. *Journal of Psychology,* 1940, 9, 301-310.

Hubbard, D. G. *Skyjacker—His flights of fantasy* (Rev. ed.). New York: Collier Books, 1971.

Jesse, F. T. *Murder and its motives* (Rev. ed.). London: Harrar, 1952.

Johnson, R. N. *Aggression in man and animals.* Philadelphia: W. B. Saunders, 1972.

Karchner, C. L. Arson and the mob: Special report. *Firehouse,* August 1977, pp. 22-27, 68-69.

Kaufmann, H. *Aggression and altruism.* New York: Holt, Rinehart & Winston, 1970.

Kent, J., Weisber, H., Lamar, B., and Marx, T. Physical abuse of young children: A preliminary typology of cases. In *House Committee on Science and Technology, Research into Violent Behavior: Domestic Violence.* Washington, DC: U.S. Congress, 1978.

Kregarman, J. J., and Worchel, P. Arbitrariness of frustration and aggression. *Journal of Abnormal and Social Psychology,* 1961, 63, 183-187.

Lane, P. J. Annotated bibliography of the overcontrolled-undercontrolled assaultive personality literature and the overcontrolled-hostility (O-H) scale of the MMPI. *JSAS Catalog of Selected Documents in Psychology,* 1978. (JSAS Ms. No. 1760)

Levin, B. Psychological characteristics of firesetters. *Fire Journal,* 1976, 70(2), 36-40.

Lockwood, D. *Prison sexual violence.* New York: Elsevier North-Holland, 1979.

Lorenz, K. *On aggression.* New York: Bantam Books, 1966.

Luckenbill, D. F. Criminal homicide as a situated transaction. *Social Problems,* 1977, 25(2), 176-186.

Luckenbill, D. F., and Sanders, W. B. Criminal violence. In E. Sagarin and F. Montanino (Eds.), *Deviants: Voluntary actors in a hostile world.* Morristown, NJ: General Learning Press, 1977.

Luisada, P. V. Phencyclidine psychosis: Phenomonology and treatment. In R. C. Peterson and R. C. Stillman (Eds.), *Phencyclidine (PCP) abuse: An appraisal.* Rockville, MD: U.S. Department of Health, Education and Welfare, Food and Drug Administration, 1978.

MacDonald, J. M. *Armed robbery: Offenders and their victims.* Springfield, IL: Charles C Thomas, 1975.

MacDonald, J. M. *Bombers and firesetters.* Springfield, IL: Charles C Thomas, 1977.

Maier, H. W. Über Katathyme Wahnbildung und Paranoia. *Zeitschrift für neurologie und psychiatrie,* 1912, 15, 555.

Mark, V. H., and Ervin, S. R. *Violence and the brain.* New York: Harper & Row, 1970.

May, W. F. Terrorism as strategy and ecstasy. *Social Research,* 1974, 41, 277-298

McCandless, B. B. *Children: Behavior and development* (2nd ed.). New York: Holt, Rinehart & Winston, 1967.

McKee, J. P., and Leader, F. B. The relationship of socioeconomic status and aggression to the competitive behavior of preschool children. *Child Development,* 1955, 26, 135-142.

McNeil, E. B. Psychology and aggression. *Journal of Conflict Resolution,* 1959, 3, 195-293.

Megargee, E. I. Undercontrolled and overcontrolled personality types in extreme antisocial aggression. *Psychological Monographs,* 1966, 80 (3, Whole No. 611).

Megargee, E. I. The psychology of violence: A critical review of theories of violence. In D. J. Mulvihill and M. M. Tumin (Eds.), *Crimes of violence: A staff report to the National Commission on the causes and prevention of violence.* NCCPV Staff Report Series Vol. 13. Washington, DC: Government Printing Office, 1969.

Megargee, E. I. The role of inhibition in the assessment and understanding of violence. In J. L. Singer (Ed.), *The control of aggression and violence: Cognitive and physiological factors.* New York: Academic Press, 1971.

Megargee, E. I. *The psychology of violence and aggression.* New York: General Learning Press, 1972.

Megargee, E. I. The heuristic value of the concept of "social deviance" for psychologists. *Representative Research in Social Psychology,* 1973, 4, 67-81.

Megargee, E. I. Psychological classification of criminals in differential management and treatment. In D. E. Silver (Chair), *Is there value in a psychological classification system of offenders?* Symposium presented at the 88th Annual Convention of the American Psychological Association, Montreal, Québec, Canada, September 1980.

Megargee, E. I., and Bohn, M. J., Jr., with Meyer, J., Jr., and Sink, F. *Classifying criminal offenders: A new system based on the MMPI.* Beverly Hills, CA: Sage Publications, 1979.

Megargee, E. I., Cook, P. E., and Mendelsohn, G. A. Development and validation of an MMPI scale of assaultiveness in overcontrolled individuals. *Journal of Abnormal Psychology,* 1967, 72, 519-528.

Megargee, E. I., and Hokanson, J. E. (Eds.). *The dynamics of aggression: Individual, group and international analyses.* New York: Harper & Row, 1970.

Menzies, E. S. Effects of repeated exposure to televised violence upon attitudes toward violence among youthful offenders. *FCI Research Reports,* 1972, 4(5). (Federal Correctional Institution, Tallahassee, Florida 32304)

Milgram, S. Some conditions of obedience and disobedience to authority. In I. D. Steiner and M. Fishbine (Eds.), *Current studies in social psychology.* New York: Holt, Rinehart & Winston, 1965.

Miller, N. E. The frustration-aggression hypothesis. *Psychological Review,* 1941, 48, 337-342.

Milliken, J. Up in smoke. *Law Enforcement Communications,* 1979, 6(1), 12-15.

Milte, K. L., Bartholomew, A. A., O'Hearn, D. J., and Campbell, A. Terrorism: Political and psychological considerations. *Australian and New Zealand Journal of Criminology,* 1976, 9, 89-94.

Miron, M. S., and Goldstein, A. P. *Hostage.* Kalamazoo, MI: Behaviordelia, 1978.

Morrison, W. A. Criminal homicide and the death penalty in Canada: Time for reassessment and new directions: Toward a typology of homicide. *Canadian Journal of Criminology and Corrections,* 1973, 15, 267-396.

Myers, D. G., and Lamm, H. The polarizing effect of group discussion. In I. L. Janis (Ed.), *Current trends in psychology.* Los Altos, CA: William Kaufmann, 1977.

Nakamura, P. R., and Noguchi, T. T. PCP (Phencyclidine): A drug of violence and deaths. *Journal of Police Science and Administration,* 1979, 7, 459-466.

National District Attorneys' Association. *Prosecutor's responsibility in child abuse cases.* Washington, DC: U.S. Department of Justice, Law Enforcement Assistance Administration, 1980.

O'Brien, C. C. On violence and terrorism. *Dissent,* 1977, 24, 433-436.

Ochberg, F. M. On preventing aggression and violence. *Police Chief,* 1980, 67(2), 52-56.

Pagelow, M. D. *Blaming the victim: Parallels in crimes against women: Rape and battering.* Paper presented at the annual meeting of the Society of the Study of Social Problems, Chicago, September 1977.

Parker, T., and Allerton, R. *The courage of his convictions.* London: Hutchinson Publishing Group, 1952.

Pastore, N. The role of arbitrariness in the frustration-aggression hypothesis. *Journal of Abnormal and Social Psychology,* 1952, 47, 728-731.

Peter, L. J. *Peter's quotations: Ideas for our time.* New York: William Morrow, 1977.

Petty, C. S., and Mason, J. K. Robbery with violence. In J. K. Mason (Ed.), *Pathology of violent injury.* London: Edward Arnold Publishers, 1978.

Quay, H. C. Psychopathic personality as pathological stimulation seeking. *American Journal of Psychiatry,* 1965, 122, 180-183.

Redl, F., and Wineman, D. *The aggressive child.* New York: Free Press, 1957.

Revitch, E., and Schlesinger, L. B. Murder: Evaluation, classification and prediction. In I. L. Kutash, S. B. Kutash, and L. B. Schlesinger and Associates (Eds.), *Violence: Perspectives on murder and aggression.* San Francisco: Jossey-Bass, 1978.

Rosenbaum, H. J., and Sederberg, P. C. *Vigilante politics.* Philadelphia: University of Pennsylvania Press, 1976.

Rosenquist, C. M., and Megargee, E. I. *Delinquency in three cultures.* Austin: University of Texas Press, 1969.

Ross, R. R. *Violence in, violence out: Child abuse and self-mutilation in adolescent offenders.* Unpublished paper, 1979. (NCJRS Document No.09900.00.065227)

Rothaus, T. and Worchel, P. The inhibition of aggression under nonarbitrary frustration. *Journal of Personality,* 1960, 28, 108-117.

Rounsaville, B. J. Theories in marital violence: Evidence from the study of battered women. *Victimology,* 1978, 3, 11-31.

Scacco, A. M. *Rape in prison.* Springfield, IL: Charles C Thomas, 1975.

Schlossberg, H. Police response to hostage situations. In J. T. O'Brien and M. Marcus (Eds.), *Crime and justice in America: Critical issues for the future.* Elmsford, NY: Pergamon, 1979.

Segal, J. Violent men: Embattled women. *Cosmopolitan,* 1976, 180(5), 238-241.

Segal, J. Child abuse: A review of research. In E. Corfman (Ed.), *Family violence and child abuse.* Rockville, MD: U.S. Department of Health, Education, and Welfare, ADAMHA, 1979.

Shainess, N. Psychological aspects of wifebeating. In M. Roy (Ed.), *Battered women—Psychosociological study of domestic violence.* New York: Van Nostrand Reinhold, 1977.

Shotland, R. L. Spontaneous vigilantes. *Society,* 1976, 13(3), 30-32.

Siegel, R. K. Phencyclidine, criminal behavior, and the defense of diminished capacity. In R. C. Peterson and R. C. Stillman (Eds.), *Phencyclidine (PCP) abuse: An appraisal*. Rockville, MD: U.S. Department of Health Education, and Welfare, Food and Drug Administration, 1978.

SOARS. The terrorist organization profile: A psychological evaluation. Quantico, VA: FBI Academy, 1978. (Unpublished training materials.)

Somerset Area Review Committee for Non-Accidental Injury to Children. *Report of the review panel*. Taunton, Somerset, England: Somerset Area Review Committee, 1977.

Spencer, C. *A typology of violent offenders*. Working paper, California Department of Corrections, Crimes Studies Section, Research Division, January 1966.

Star, B. *Treating the battered women*. Paper presented at the 5th NASW Professional Symposium on Social Work, San Diego, California, November 1977.

Star, B., Clark, C. G., Goetz, K. M., and D'Malia, L. Psychosocial aspects of wife beating. *Social Casework*, 1979, 60, 479-487.

Steele, B. F. Violence in our society. *Pharos*, 1970, 33(2), 42-48.

Steinmetz, S. K. *Family violence: The silent crime*. Proceedings of the 13th Annual Interagency Workshop of the Institute of Contemporary Corrections and the Behavioral Sciences, Houston, Texas, 1978. Huntsville, TX: Criminal Justice Center, Sam Houston State University, 1978. (a)

Steinmetz, S. K. Wife beating: A critique and reformulation of existing theory. *Bulletin of the American Academy of Psychiatry and the Law*, 1978, 6(3), 322-334. (b)

Stevenson, C. Arson-to-order in the building trades. *Readers Digest*, March 1976, pp. 85-90.

Strauss, M. A. *Stress and assault in a national sample of American families*. Durham: University of New Hampshire, 1978.

Sutherland, E. H., and Cressy, D. R. *Principles of criminology* (7th ed.). Philadelphia: Lippincott, 1966.

Sykes, G. M., and Matza, D. Techniques of neutralization: A theory of delinquency. *American Sociological Review*, 1957, 22, 664-670.

Symonds, A. Violence against women: The myth of masochism. *American Journal of Psychotherapy*, 1979, 33(2), 161-173.

Tanay, E. Psychiatric study of homicides. *American Journal of Psychiatry*, 1969, 125, 1252-1258.

Teresa, V. *My life in the Mafia*. Garden City, NY: Doubleday, 1973.

Toch, H. *Violent men*. Chicago: Aldine, 1969.

Toch, H. The social psychology of violence. Invited address delivered to Division 8 of the American Psychological Association, New York, September 1966. Reprinted in E. I. Megargee and J. E. Hokanson (Eds.), *The dynamics of aggression*. New York: Harper & Row, 1970.

Tracey, R. *Battered wives*. London: Bow Publications, 1978.

Ulrich, R. E., Hutchinson, R. R., and Azrin, N. H. Pain-elicited aggression. *Psychological Record*, 1965, 15, 111-116.

Varma, M. Battered women—battered children. In M. Roy (Ed.), *Battered women: A psychological study of domestic violence*. New York: Van Nostrand Reinhold, 1977.

Verin, J. *Torture and hostage taking*. New York: United Nations Social Defense Research Institute, 1971.

Vernon, R. F. *Dimensions of juvenile arson and false fire alarms for the urban areas of San Diego*. Washington, DC: U.S. Department of Housing and Urban Development, 1972.

Vreeland, R. G., and Waller, M. B. *Psychology of firesetting: A review and appraisal*. Washington, DC: U.S. Department of Commerce, Bureau of Standards, Center for Fire Research, 1978.

Walker, L. E. *Treatment alternatives for battered spouses*. Testimony to House Committee on Science of Technology, Subcommittee on Domestic and International Scientific Planning Analyses and Co-operation, February 15, 1978. (a)

Walker, L. E. Treatment alternatives for battered women. In J. R. Chapman and M. Gates (Eds.), *Victimization of women*. Beverly Hills, CA: Sage Publications, 1978. (b)

Walker, L. E. *Battered women*. New York: Harper & Row, 1979.

Walters, D. R. *Physical and sexual abuse of children*. Bloomington: Indiana University Press, 1975.

Walters, R. H. Implications of laboratory studies of aggression for the control and regulation of violence. *The Annals*, 1966, 364, 60-72.

Warrior, B. *Battered wives*. Pittsburgh: Know, 1974.

Westermeyer, J. Comparison of Amok and other homicides in Laos. *American Journal of Psychiatry*, 1972, 129, 708-709.

Wheeler, L., and Caggiula, A. R. The contagion of aggression. *Journal of Experimental Social Psychology*, 1966, 2, 1-10.

Wilson, C. *Order of assassins—The psychology of murder*. London: Panther Books, 1972.

Williams, J. E. Treatment of violence. *Medicine, Science and the Law*, 1972, 12(4), 269-274.

Wolfgang, M. E. *Patterns in criminal homicide*. Philadelphia: University of Pennsylvania Press, 1958.

Wolfgang, M. E. and Ferracuti, F. *The subculture of violence*. London: Tavistock, 1967.

Yahraes, H., Strauss, M. A., and Gelles, R. J. Physical violence in families. In E. Corfman (Ed.), *Family violence and child abuse*. Rockville, MD: U.S. Department of Health, Education, and Welfare, ADAMHA, 1979.

APPENDIX

Offenses Considered Violent from NCIC Uniform Offense Codes

Homicide (0900)	NCIC Code Number
Homicide—willful killing—family—gun	0901
Homicide—willful killing—family—(other weapon)	0902
Homicide—willful killing—nonfamily—gun	0903
Homicide—willful killing—nonfamily—(other weapon)	0904
Homicide—willful killing—public official—gun	0905
Homicide—willful killing—public official—(other weapon)	0906
Homicide—willful killing—police officer—gun	0907
Homicide—willful killing—police officer—(other weapon)	0908
Homicide—negligent manslaughter—vehicle	0909
Homicide—negligent manslaughter—(other weapon)	0910
Homicide—willful killing—gun	0911
Homicide—willful killing—(other weapon)	0912

Kidnapping (1000)	
Kidnap minor for ransom	1001
Kidnap adult for ransom	1002
Kidnap minor to sexually assault	1003
Kidnap adult to sexually assault	1004
Kidnap minor	1005
Kidnap adult	1006
Kidnap hostage for escape	1007
Kidnap—hijack aircraft	1009

Sexual Assault (1100)

Rape—gun	1101
Rape—(other weapon)	1102
Rape—strong-arm	1103
Sex assault—sodomy—boy—gun	1104
Sex assault—sodomy—man—gun	1105
Sex assault—sodomy—girl—gun	1106
Sex assault—sodomy—woman—gun	1107
Sex assault—sodomy—boy—(other weapon)	1108
Sex assault—sodomy—man—(other weapon)	1109
Sex assault—sodomy—girl—(other weapon)	1110
Sex assault—sodomy—woman—(other weapon)	1111
Sex assault—sodomy—boy—strong-arm	1112
Sex assault—sodomy—man—strong-arm	1113
Sex assault—sodomy—girl—strong-arm	1114
Sex assault—sodomy—woman—strong-arm	1115
Sex assault—carnal abuse	1117

Sovereignty (0100)

Sabotage	0104

Robbery (1200)

Robbery—business—gun	1201
Robbery—business—(other weapon)	1202
Robbery—business—strong-arm	1203
Robbery—street—gun	1204
Robbery—street—(other weapon)	1205
Robbery—street—strong-arm	1206
Robbery—residence—gun	1207
Robbery—residence—(other weapon)	1208
Robbery—residence—strong-arm	1209
Forcible purse-snatching	1210
Robbery—banking-type institution	1211

Assault (1300)

Aggravated assault—family—gun	1301
Aggravated assault—family—(other weapon)	1302
Aggravated assault—family—strong-arm	1303
Aggravated assault—nonfamily—gun	1304
Aggravated assault—nonfamily—(other weapon)	1305
Aggravated assault—nonfamily—strong-arm	1306
Aggravated assault—public officials—gun	1307
Aggravated assault—public officials—(other weapon)	1308
Aggravated assault—public officials—strong-arm	1309
Aggravated assault—police officer—gun	1310
Aggravated assault—police officer—(other weapon)	1311
Aggravated assault—police officer—strong-arm	1312
Simple assault	1313
Aggravated assault—gun	1314

Aggravated assault—(other weapon)	1315
Intimidation	1316

Arson (2000)

Arson—business—endangered life	2001
Arson—residence—endangered life	2002
Arson—business	2005
Arson—residence	2006
Arson—public building—endangered life	2008
Arson—public building	2009

Extortion (2100)

Extort—threat injure person	2101
Extort—threat damage property	2102

Damage Property (2900)

Damage property—business—with explosive	2904
Damage property—private—with explosive	2905
Damage property—public—with explosive	2906

Weapon Offenses (5200)

Explosives—using	5206
Incendiary device—using	5208

Public Peace (5300)

Riot—inciting	5302
Riot—engaging in	5303
Riot—interfering firemen	5304
Riot—interfering officer	5305

Traffic Offense (5400)

Hit and run	5401

3

Longitudinal Analyses of Criminal Violence

David P. Farrington

DEFINITIONS

Criminal Violence

There is no agreed-upon definition of violence. Most definitions include acts that cause physical harm to some other person. Some also include acts that are intended to cause physical harm but do not succeed, acts that cause psychological harm (such as a wife not speaking to her husband), self-injurious acts, acts that cause damage to property or animals, and aggressive or threatening statements. Not all acts that cause physical harm would be defined as violent. This depends on the social context. Obvious examples of acts not necessarily regarded as violent are a doctor cutting open a patient, killings in war, violence in sport, and a parent smacking a child. The same physical act may be regarded as violent in some contexts but not in others.

These kinds of definitional problems are important, but they cannot be discussed in detail here. The focus of interest here is on *criminal* violence, that is, on violent acts that are prohibited by the (Anglo-American) criminal law. The most important of these acts are homicides, assaults, robberies, and forcible rapes. Focusing on legal categories does not avoid definitional problems. Why some violent acts in general are prohibited by the criminal law, and why some specific acts are followed by reactions by criminal justice agencies, are important questions, but again they cannot be discussed in detail here. This chapter is concerned primarily with why people commit acts of criminal violence, and in particular with the advances in our knowledge in this area that have accrued (and that might accrue) by the use of the longitudinal method.

Defining criminal violence according to processing by criminal justice agencies makes it difficult to disentangle factors associated with the commission of a violent act from those associated with selection for official processing. This is one of the reasons official records of violence should be supplemented by interview information (see "Interviews versus Records" in the methodology section of this chapter). Most of our knowledge about criminal violence is based on records, which in turn are based on legal categories. The problem is that the same legal category may include widely differing acts, just as the same act may lead to an entry in one of several different legal categories.

An example of the same legal category including widely differing acts is provided in English law by buggery (anal intercourse). Buggery of a nonconsenting female is similar in many respects to rape and therefore might be regarded as an act of criminal violence. Indeed, charges of multiple rapists (such as the famous Cambridge rapist, Peter Cook) often include one or more charges of buggery. On the other hand, buggery with a consenting male is quite different. The legal category of buggery in the English criminal statistics does not provide any information about whether the "victim" is male or female, consenting or nonconsenting. In a special analysis, Walmsley and White (1979) found that nearly 90 percent of buggeries leading to convictions in one particular year were carried out with males, suggesting that most buggeries are not violent crimes.

As an example of the same act leading to different legal classifications, consider a fight in the street between two youths. This may be regarded by a policeman as normal high spirits, and hence may not lead to any official action. Alternatively, it may lead to a prosecution for common assault, which is a nonindictable offense. (The more serious offenses, those conventionally regarded as "crimes" by the English police, are the indictable ones.) Again, it may lead to a prosecution for assault occasioning actual bodily harm (which is an indictable offense). Another possibility is that some form of plea bargaining may occur, so that, for example, the police drop an actual bodily harm charge in return for a plea of guilty to possessing an offensive weapon.

The inadequacies of legal categories as measures of actual behavior are so well known that they need not be discussed in detail in this chapter. More informative and realistic measures of criminal violence might be obtained by devising new behavioral categories, but these would inevitably raise the problem of comparison with previous research results. Another possibility would be to classify offenses according to seriousness ratings (for example, following Sellin and Wolfgang, 1964). This chapter will concentrate on the legal categories of criminal violence, since they are the ones used by most longitudinal (and other) researchers in the field.

An important question is the extent to which the legal categories of homicide, rape, robbery, and assault are related, and the extent to which there might be a developmental sequence between them. For example, people might graduate from assault to rape to robbery and finally to homicide. Alternatively, it may be that most people who commit homicide have not previously committed any other violent crime. Longitudinal research could throw light on this.

Longitudinal Analyses

The defining feature of a longitudinal survey is that it involves measures taken at two or more times based on the same people (or on samples from the same population). The measures taken at different times may be of the same or different theoretical constructs. For example, violence at one time may be compared with violence or intelligence at an earlier time. The measures need not necessarily be obtained from the same people. For example, a youth's violence at one time could be compared with his parents' child-rearing behavior at an earlier time.

Following the classification system of Robins (1978b), three kinds of longitudinal studies can be distinguished: real-time prospective, catch-up prospective, and follow-back studies. The real-time-prospective study selects a sample and measures them at one time, then waits to measure them again at some later time. The Cambridge Study in Delinquent Development (West and Farrington, 1973, 1977) is an example of this kind of project. The survey began in 1961-1962 and included all 411 boys aged 8-9 in six state primary schools in a working-class area of London. The boys were tested in their schools at ages 8, 10, and 14, and interviewed outside school at ages 16 and 18. Subsamples were also interviewed at 21 and 24. Their parents were interviewed in their homes about once a year from when the boys were 8 until their last year of compulsory schooling at age 15, and their teachers filled in questionnaires about them at ages 8, 10, 12, and 14. The complete criminal records of the boys from 10 to 25 have also been obtained, as well as criminal records of their parents and siblings up to the present time.

The catch-up-prospective study begins at a later time but identifies and measures the sample at an earlier one, using existing records. It is prospective in the sense that the record data were noted down before any outcomes of interest were known (e.g., which members of the sample were convicted of violent offenses). Most examples of this kind of survey that are concerned with criminal violence are primarily based on records spanning a long period, as in the Philadelphia cohort study of Wolfgang et al. (1972) and the Columbus research on violent juveniles of Hamparian et al. (1978).

The follow-back study begins with a sample identified at a later time and then tries to obtain retrospective information about members of the sample from records and/or interviews. For example, Goldstein and Kant (1973) interviewed rapists and other sex offenders, primarily to try to discover their preadolescent, adolescent, and adult exposure to erotic stimuli. Petersilia et al. (1978) interviewed 49 armed robbers to try to obtain information about their criminal careers during the juvenile, young adult, and adult years. These kinds of surveys are particularly susceptible to methodological difficulties such as retrospective bias and sampling problems. Therefore, the emphasis in this chapter will be on prospective surveys. The advantages and disadvantages of prospective versus retrospective surveys will be discussed in the methodology section of this chapter, together with those of longitudinal versus cross-sectional research and of interviews versus records.

The official criminal statistics might be regarded as longitudinal data, since they show changes over the years in the incidence of crimes known to the police and of convictions. However, the population at risk in any year is not the same as that in any other year, because of births, deaths, immigration, emigration, and institutionalization. Since criminal statistics do not in general show repeated measures on the same people, they will not be classified as longitudinal surveys. Similarly, any investigation of changes in crime rates over the years (e.g., Vigderhous, 1978) or of changes in other rates of offending (e.g., Megargee, 1976a) will be excluded.

Special attention will be given here to long-term longitudinal surveys, namely those spanning a period of five years or more. If the focus of interest is on convictions for criminal violence, it could be argued that long-term surveys are particularly important, since such convictions are relatively rare and are often separated by long intervals. For example, Van Dine et al. (1977) studied a sample of adults convicted of violent offenses and found that their average interval since a previous conviction for a felony was 5.6 years.

The primary use of longitudinal research is to investigate the course of development, the natural history and prevalence of a phenomenon at different ages, how phenomena emerge, and continuities and discontinuities from earlier to later ages. Longitudinal research has also been used to study the relationship between earlier and later events, the effects of particular events or life experiences on the course of development, and the transmission of characteristics from one generation to the next. Few long-term longitudinal studies of crime and delinquency have been carried out (see the review by Farrington, 1979) and fewer still have been concerned with criminal violence. The major long-term longitudinal surveys including at least some information about criminal violence are summarized in Table 3.1. These vary greatly in the extent to which they provide information about criminal violence. Some are centrally concerned with it (e.g., Hamparian et al., 1978), but others go little beyond a mention (e.g., McCord, 1980).

SPECIFICITY OR GENERALITY?
Violent and Other Crimes

It can be argued that violent crimes are behaviorally different from other kinds of offenses, and hence that it is reasonable to study criminal violence as a

(Continued on p. 178)

TABLE 3.1 Major Longitudinal Surveys Including Information about Criminal Violence

Principal Investigators	Sample
Anttila and Westling (1965)	All 542 persons serving a life sentence (most for homicide) in Finland at some time between 1929 and 1958. Followed up to 1958 and back in records.
Bachman, O'Malley, and Johnston (1978)	2,213 boys entering U.S. high schools in 1966 (random probability sample) followed up for 8 years by interviews and mail questionnaires (5 contacts).
Blumstein and Cohen (1979)	FBI Criminal History file: 5,338 adults arrested for serious crimes in 1973 in Washington, D.C. Followed back in records and up to 1975.
Brody and Tarling (1980)	1. Same as Phillpotts and Lancucki (1979). 2. Random sample of all males serving sentences in prisons in the Southeast of England in 1972 (N = 811). Followed back in records and up to beginning of 1979.
Buikhuisen and Jongman (1970)	All male 21-year-old recidivists convicted in the Netherlands in 1964-1965 (N = 848). Followed back in records.
Bursik (1980)	469 youths adjudicated delinquent at least 5 times in Illinois. Followed back in records.
Christiansen (1974)	3,586 twin pairs born in Denmark 1881-1910 and alive at least until 15. Followed up in records.
Christiansen, Elers-Nielsen, LeMaire, and Stürup (1965)	3,185 males convicted 1929-1939 in Denmark of sex offenses. Followed back and up in records until 1951-1953.
Hamparian, Schuster, Dinitz, and Conrad (1978)	811 persons born 1956-1958 and arrested for at least one violent offense in Columbus, Ohio. Followed up in records to age 18.
Kozol, Boucher, and Garofalo (1972)	435 male offenders (most convicted for violent sex offenses) released from Bridgewater institution. Followed up in records for nearly 5 years.

—continued on the following page

TABLE 3.1 Continued

Principal Investigators	Sample
McClintock (1963)	1. All 911 persons convicted of violence in London in 1950. 2. All 1,388 persons convicted of violence in London in 1957. 3. 464 persons convicted of violence in London in 1960. All followed back in records.
McCord (1980)	253 treatment and 253 control boys from Cambridge-Somerville Study. Chosen at average age 10 in 1937-1939, treatment group got average 5 years of help, contacted by mail questionnaire in 1975-1976.
Mulvihill, Tumin, and Curtis (1969)	FBI Careers in Crime file: 194,550 federal offenders arrested 1963-1967, followed back in records.
Petersilia, Greenwood, and Lavin (1978)	49 armed robbers in California prison, interviewed around 1975 about criminal career.
Phillpotts and Lancucki (1979)	Random sample of 5,000 persons convicted in England and Wales in January 1971. Followed back in records and up to 1976.
Rappeport and Lassen (1965)	708 men discharged in 1947 and 2,152 discharged in 1957 from Maryland psychiatric hospitals. Checked in records 5 years before and 5 years after hospitalization.
Robins (1966)	524 children treated in St. Louis child guidance clinic in 1924-1929, and 100 control public schoolchildren from the same period. Interviewed more than 30 years later.

Robins, West, and Herjanic (1975)	235 black males born in St. Louis in 1930-1934 and located in elementary school records. Interviewed in 1965-1966.
Shannon (1978)	1. 1,352 persons born in Wisconsin in 1942 who resided in Racine, Wisconsin.
	2. 2,099 persons born in Wisconsin in 1949 who resided in Racine, Wisconsin.
	3. 2,676 persons born in Wisconsin in 1955 who resided in Racine, Wisconsin.
	All followed up in records to 1974. Subsamples of first two cohorts interviewed.
Short and Moland (1976)	52 black male Chicago gang members interviewed in 1959-1965 and reinterviewed in 1971-1972.
Strasburg (1978)	Random sample of juveniles taken to court in New York and New Jersey in 1974 (N = 510). Followed back in records.
Van Dine, Dinitz, and Conrad (1977)	All 364 adults charged with violent offenses in Columbus, Ohio, in 1973. Followed back in records.
Wadsworth (1979)	5,362 children selected from all legitimate single births in England, Scotland, and Wales in one week of March 1946. Followed up to 21 in criminal records. Children of families contacted every 1-2 years since birth.
Walker, Hammond, and Steer (1967)	1. 4,301 males convicted for the first time in Scotland in 1947. Followed up in records for 11 years.
	2. 4,239 males convicted in London in March-April 1957. Followed back in records and forward for next 5 years.
West and Farrington (1977)	All 411 boys aged 8-9 in 1961-1962 in 6 London schools. Interviewed every 2-3 years up to age 24.
Witkin et al. (1976)	4,591 males born in Copenhagen in 1944-1947 with known adult height at least 6 feet. Seen at age 26.
Wolfgang, Figlio, and Sellin (1972)	9,945 boys born in 1945 and residing in Philadelphia at least from 10-18. Followed up in records to age 30. Interviewed 10 percent sample at age 26.

separate category and to suggest that it might require different explanations from other offenses. However, it is rare to find people who show a high degree of specialization in criminal violence. It is more common for people to commit a variety of different kinds of offenses. A possible implication of this is that, insofar as they concern the person rather than the situation, explanations of criminal violence need not necessarily be different from explanations of other kinds of offenses. Similarly, findings obtained with offenders in general may often apply to violent offenders.

Both official records and self-reports show that specialized violent offenders are rare. In England, West and Farrington (1977) reported 80 percent of adults convicted of violence also had convictions for dishonesty. McClintock (1963) found that nearly half of those first convicted for violent offenses had previous convictions for nonviolent offenses, and the same was true for 80 percent of those sustaining a second conviction for violence. Soothill et al. (1976) showed that the most common previous and subsequent convictions of rapists were for theft, and Christiansen et al. (1965) obtained the same result with a Danish sample of more than 3,000 sex offenders. In a sophisticated American longitudinal analysis of juveniles, Wolfgang et al. (1972) found that the probability of committing any kind of offense did not depend on the kind of offense committed on the last occasion of arrest, and Thornberry and Figlio (1978) showed that this result held up until the age of 30.

While it is rare to find a high degree of specialization, it is also rare to find complete generality. Usually, there is some degree of specialization superimposed on a high degree of generality, as Bursik (1980) reported in a replication of the analysis of Wolfgang et al. (1972). Phillpotts and Lancucki (1979) followed up a nationally representative sample of 5,000 convicted English offenders. They divided offenses into eight groups and found that, while it was unusual for a complete criminal career to consist of offenses from only one group, there was a significant degree of specialization. The probability of all offenses being drawn from the same group decreased with the number of offenses; for males, it was 46 percent for those with 2 convictions, 16 percent for those with 3-5 convictions, and 3 percent for those with 6 or more convictions. These figures, while well below 100 percent specificity, were significantly greater than chance expectation.

Similar results were obtained in the United States by Mulvihill et al. (1969) and Blumstein and Cohen (1979), and in Holland by Buikhuisen and Jongman (1970). Blumstein and Cohen were interested in the individual arrest rate, defined as the number of arrests per person per year in the community. They found that persons arrested at least once for aggravated assault had an arrest rate for aggravated assault of .19, for robbery of .14, for theft of .11, for drugs of .10, for burglary of .08, and a total arrest rate of 1.04. This again shows the large degree of generality in the offenses of those convicted for violence.

Perhaps the most unusual finding in the literature is the high degree of specialization in violent or property crimes reported in the American study by Peterson et al. (1962). This may be a function of the small sample and the restricted range of offenses included in it. The foregoing results were obtained with official records. Studies based on self-reports also show a great deal of generality. For example, Farrington (1973) reported that admissions of aggressive acts, such as fighting with police, were significantly correlated with admissions of acts of dishonesty, such as burglary, and status offenses, such as truancy and drinking under age. Hindelang (1971), Cernkovich (1978), and Johnson (1979) obtained similar results in the United States. Cernkovich related his results to the issue of whether status offenses should be decriminalized, in view of the similarity between status and other kinds of juvenile offenders (see, for example, Clarke, 1975; Thomas, 1976). Self-report studies with adults also show generality. Peterson et al. (1980) found that about half of their sample of incarcerated males reported crimes of at least four different types, and less than 10 percent were specialists in the sense of committing one type of crime several times. Studies based on reports of offending made by other people (e.g., by detached group workers; Short et al., 1963) also show generality.

Violent offenders tend to have more convictions than nonviolent offenders. For example, Farrington (1978) found that violent delinquents averaged 4.3 convictions each, in comparison with 2.7 for nonviolent delinquents. It seems that the more times a person is convicted, the more likely it is that at least one of these convictions will be for a violent crime. Walker et al. (1967) showed that the probability of committing a violent offense increased with the number of previous nonviolent offenses, and concluded that a conviction for violence was an occupational risk of a career of nonviolent crime. Similarly, Wolfgang et al. (1972) discovered that the chronic offenders (the 6 percent of their sample with five or more recorded delinquencies) committed 71 percent of the homicides, 73 percent of the rapes, 70 percent of the robberies, and 69 percent of the aggravated assaults.

From the foregoing, it might perhaps be expected that results obtained in comparisons between violent and nonviolent offenders might be similar to those obtained in comparisons between more and less persistent offenders (and hence might be relevant to predicting which criminal careers will continue and which will end). Osborn and West (1978) found that low family income, large family size, and convicted parents were among the best predictors of the persistence of criminal careers of recidivists. In the same project, Farrington (1978) showed that the best discriminators between violent and nonviolent delinquents were harsh parental attitude and discipline, low IQ, and separation from parents. Therefore, it is not necessarily true that differences between more and less persistent offenders are relevant to differences between violent and nonviolent offenders. Despite the generality of offending, unique results may still be obtained by isolating and studying special groups, such as those convicted of violence.

Violence and Other Deviance

Just as there is generality in offending, there is generality in deviant behavior. Violence is related not only to other kinds of criminal offenses but also to other kinds of deviance, such as heavy drinking, sexual promiscuity, heavy smoking, heavy gambling, hanging around with antisocial groups, and having an unstable job record (West and Farrington, 1977). The longitudinal surveys of Robins (1966, 1978a) show both the generality of deviance and its continuity from childhood to adulthood. In her 30-year follow-up of children referred to a child guidance clinic in St. Louis, she found that the children stole, were truants, ran away from home, were aggressive, were enuretic, had disciplinary problems in school, were pathological liars, and so on. As adults, they tended to be arrested, divorced, placed in mental hospitals, alcoholics, sexually promiscuous, vagrants, bad debtors, poor workers, and so on. Robins and Wish (1977) were also able to investigate how one deviant act led to another.

The generality of deviance means that it is important to investigate how far results obtained with criminal violence are specific to this act and how far they apply to other kinds of deviance. The answer to this question should be taken into account in formulating explanations of criminal violence. It may also have more practical implications, since attempts to prevent or treat other kinds of deviance may (if successful) lead to a reduction in criminal violence, and vice versa, depending on the precise theoretical linkages among the various deviant acts. Longitudinal research stands a better chance than cross-sectional research in elucidating such causal linkages (see the section on longitudinal versus cross-sectional research under "Methodological Issues").

Longitudinal Research on Aggression

Many longitudinal studies have been intended to investigate aggression or aggressiveness, variously defined. For example, Olweus (1979) was able to review 16 projects with independent samples of subjects (average number 116), in which the age at the time of the first measurement varied from 2 to 18 and the follow-up period from 6 months to 21 years. The results of some of these projects may be relevant to criminal violence.

Generally, measures of aggression in children predict arrests or convictions later on in life. This result has been obtained with peer and teacher ratings of aggression, in the United States (e.g., Feldhusen et al., 1973; Havighurst et al., 1962), England (e.g., Mulligan et al., 1963; West and Farrington, 1973), and other countries (e.g., Sweden; see Magnusson et al., 1975). Furthermore, the backgrounds of boys identified as aggressive are quite similar to those of convicted boys (see Farrington and West, 1971; McCord et al., 1963). Farrington (1978) showed that teacher ratings of aggressive behavior in class at age 8-10 significantly predicted convictions for assault or robbery, mostly occurring at age 17-18. Nearly half of the violent delinquents had been rated aggressive at 8-10, in comparison with about 20 percent of the remainder. This result, in particular, suggests continuity between rated aggressiveness and criminal violence.

The longitudinal surveys agree in showing consistency in aggressiveness over time. For example, Bachman et al. (1978) found a significant relationship between self-report measures of aggression at ages 15 and 23; Farrington (1978) obtained the same result for teacher-rated aggression at 8 and self-reported violence at 18; and Lefkowitz et al. (1977) showed that peer-rated aggression at 8 was the best predictor of peer-rated aggression at 19, independently of other factors such as intelligence and socioeconomic status. In a comprehensive review, Olweus (1979) reported that the average stability coefficient (correlation) in 16 surveys was .68. Furthermore, the stability coefficient decreased linearly with the time interval between measurements, according to the following equation:

$$y = .78 - .018x$$

where y = stability coefficient and x = time interval in years. Olweus concluded that relatively stable, internal reaction tendencies were important determinants of aggressive behavior, although he acknowledged that the stability may lie in environments rather than individuals.

Farrington (1978) attempted to study careers of aggressiveness by comparing measures of aggression at ages 8-10, 12-14, and 16-18 for 400 boys. In agreement with the idea of consistency, more boys were rated high in aggressiveness at all three ages than expected by chance (24 as opposed to 8.8), and more were rated low at all three ages (187 as opposed to 146.6). If a boy was rated low at 12-14, whether he had been rated high or low at 8-10 helped in predicting whether he would be rated high or low at 16-18. This suggests that history is important in aggressive careers and therefore that Markov models may not be appropriate. Farrington also found that most of the background factors that predicted violent delinquency (see the following section) were significantly related to aggressiveness at age 8-10. This suggested that these factors had already exerted their aggression-producing effects by age 8-10, and that they were related to violent delinquency because, as boys matured, there was a natural progression from aggressiveness in the primary school to assault and robbery.

Other results obtained in longitudinal surveys of aggression could be quoted here but will not, in view of the emphasis on criminal violence. One of the most interesting surveys is that of Lefkowitz et al. (1977), who compared factors measured at age 8 with self-reports and peer ratings of aggressiveness at age 19. Among their most important results were that a preference for violent television programs was the best predictor of peer-rated aggression for boys, but did not predict for girls; that the rated aggressiveness of the father predicted self-reported aggression for girls, while the rated aggressiveness of the mother predicted self-reported aggression for boys; and that one factor related to aggressiveness of boys and girls, and to peer-rated and self-reported aggression, was low IQ. These kinds of results might serve as starting points for theories of aggression and criminal violence.

The aim of this section is to draw attention to the overlap of and continuity between aggression and criminal violence, and to suggest that the volume of research on aggression should not be ignored by those who are interested in criminal violence.

SUBSTANTIVE RESULTS

Natural History of Criminal Violence

Longitudinal research can provide information about the incidence and prevalence of criminal violence at different ages, both for a general population and for a population of offenders. It is possible to estimate the prevalence of convictions for violence using official criminal statistics for one year, providing that the proportion of offenders in each category who are being convicted for the offense for the first time is known (for an example of this method, see Farrington, 1981). Unfortunately, this information is not usually given in official statistics, which are notoriously poor in linking records from one year with records from other years. Even if this information is available, a prevalence estimate from one year's statistics must be based on the doubtful assumption that the probability of a first conviction for violence has not changed over the years. This assumption would certainly be false in England, where the incidence of convictions for indictable offenses of violence has increased from 7,895 in 1958 to 39,996 in 1978 (Home Office, 1959, 1979).

Following steady-state assumptions, McClintock and Avison (1968) estimated that the prevalence of convictions for violence up to age 21 for English males was 1.2 percent, in comparison with 13.7 percent for theft and burglary and 0.5 percent for sex offenses. Estimates obtained in longitudinal surveys are likely to be more accurate for any given time period. In the national survey by Wadsworth (1979), which covered a period similar to that estimated by McClintock and Avison, the prevalence of officially recorded violent offenses for males was 2.2 percent up to age 21. Violent offenses constituted a small minority of all offenses, since the corresponding prevalence for all crimes was

17.7 percent. For females up to 21, the prevalence for all crimes was only 2.5 percent, and only 0.8 percent of convicted females had committed a violent offense.

There are difficulties in comparing prevalence estimates for violence, because of differing definitions of violence and of official reactions (e.g., arrests or convictions). In Ohio, Dinitz and Conrad (1980) estimated the prevalence of arrests for violence up to 18 as 1.6 percent of all youth, or 2.3 percent of all boys. In Wisconsin, Shannon (1978) followed three cohorts of people, born in 1942, 1949, and 1955, respectively, up to 1974. The prevalence of contact with the police for males (not necessarily arrest) for a felony offense against the person was 2.8 percent, 4.5 percent, and 8.8 percent, respectively, in the three cohorts (Petersilia, 1980). The prevalence of contact with the police for any nontraffic offense was 69 percent, 67 percent, and 59 percent, respectively. These very high figures are a function of the wide definition of official contact.

Most surveys report that only a small minority of official contacts for crime are for violence. However, the prevalence of a violent offense at some time can be considerable. For example, West and Farrington (1977) found that only 6.8 percent of juvenile convictions were for violence, and only 10.6 percent of young adult offenses. On the other hand, up to age 25, 23.5 percent of convicted youths (32 out of 136) had been convicted at least once for an offense that must have involved physical violence. This latter figure was based on a more restrictive definition of violence than the previous two, since robberies which merely involved jostling or snatching were not counted, nor was carrying an offensive weapon without actually using it, nor was threatening behavior that did not involve actual physical violence.

Estimates of the prevalence of violence among more extreme groups of offenders are often high. In a survey of adult male prisoners in the southeast of England, Brody and Tarling (1980) found that 14 percent were currently serving sentences for violence, 10 percent for robbery, and 4 percent for sexual offenses. However, 38 percent had been convicted at some time for violence, 18 percent for robbery, and 8 percent for sexual offenses. The majority of prisoners (52 percent) had been convicted for violence, robbery, or a sexual offense at some time. Similar results were obtained by Strasburg (1978) in a survey of more than 500 juveniles brought to court for delinquency in New York and New Jersey. While 28.6 percent had currently committed a violent offense, 43.5 percent were known to have committed one at some time.

Longitudinal surveys are useful in estimating the prevalence of criminal violence. With rare offenses, surveys may have to be based on large samples and cover long time periods. For example, Anttila and Westling (1965) were interested in recidivism rates among criminals sentenced to life imprisonment (mostly for homicide) in Finland. They followed up more than 500 offenders in records, and found that the average time served in prison was 13 years. The homicide rate after release was 2.3 per 1,000 man-years in the community, almost exactly the same homicide rate as when the men were in prison. This survey does not prove that life-sentence prisoners are just as likely to commit homicides inside prison as in the community, because those released probably differed in many ways from those still in prison. It does give an estimate of the prevalence of a very rare event in what is usually considered to be a relatively dangerous group.

Another example of a survey giving information over a long time period is the 22-year-records follow-up of English rapists by Soothill et al. (1976). About half were reconvicted, but the reconvictions were spread out over the long time interval. Only about a third of reconvicted persons were reconvicted within 5 years, and a quarter were not reconvicted until at least 10 years after the conviction for rape. The short follow-up period of two or three years used in most research on recidivism would have given a false picture of the prevalence of reconviction among these rapists.

Longitudinal surveys of criminal violence show that, while the incidence of official processing for violence is rare, the prevalence is not. Of course, offenses that are followed by official processing are only a minority of those committed (see the section on interviews versus records under "Methodology"). In longitudinal surveys, it is possible to investigate changes with age in incidence of offending by asking at regular intervals about offenses committed. For example, in the Cambridge Study in Delinquent Development, Knight et al. (1977) found that fewer fights were reported at age 21 than at age 18, and Osborn and West (1980) found that fewer still were reported at age 24. Repeated questions at regular intervals are likely to provide more accurate estimates than retrospective questions covering a long period. In a retrospective survey, Petersilia et al. (1978) interviewed 49 armed robbers about their criminal careers. They concluded that the robbers had committed about 200 crimes in an average 20-year career, half of which was spent in prison. The robbers had committed about 4 violent and 16 property offenses per year. Recalling crimes committed over a 20-year period seems to require a great feat of memory.

Longitudinal surveys are especially useful in providing information about careers of criminal violence: when they start, when they finish, and what is the peak age. The Uniform Crime Reports in the United States show that the peak ages for arrests for violence (24) and sexual offenses (26) are later than for property offenses such as burglary (17) and theft (17; see Cline, 1979). However, it is impossible on the basis of the official statistics to know whether the same individuals progress from property offenses to violence during the transition from adolescence to young adulthood, or whether the property offenders decline and different individuals embark on careers of violence. One of the most important contributions of longitudinal surveys is to demonstrate generality rather than specificity (see the preceding discussion on "Violence and Other Crime") and hence that the same individuals tend to be involved in both property crimes and violence.

An interesting question is whether the degree of specialization increases with age. This can be investigated using Table 4.3 of Phillpotts and Lancucki (1979), which shows the probability of one offense being followed by another at different ages. Collapsing the table into violence and sex versus burglary, robbery, theft, and handling, 38.5 percent of violent offenses were followed by violence under age 21, in comparison with 88.5 percent of the burglary group being followed by burglaries ($X^2 = 51.72$ with 1 df, p < .001). Over age 21, there was slightly more specialization, since 48.6 percent of violence was followed by violence and 87.1 percent of the burglaries were followed by burglaries ($X^2 = 74.90$ with 1 df, p < .001). The issue of generality versus specificity at different ages is one that deserves more detailed investigation.

In the survey of violent juveniles by Hamparian et al. (1978), the mean age for the first arrest for violence was 14.4, in comparison with the average of 13.3 for first arrests generally. Wadsworth (1979) in England also reported that first convictions for violence occurred at later ages than first convictions for other offenses. Given that violence is regarded as more serious than property offenses, it might be expected that offenses in general would become more serious as people become older, at least up to the peak for violence at about age 25. Whether this happens is uncertain. Wolfgang et al. (1972) found that later offenses were no more serious than earlier ones, and the same result was obtained by Shannon (1978).

Generally, those first convicted at the earliest ages tend to be the most persistent offenders. For example, West and Farrington (1977) showed that boys first convicted at age 10-12 were still committing more offenses at age 19-20 than boys first convicted at later ages. Hamparian et al. (1978) reported a beautiful straight-line relationship between the age of first arrest and the average number of arrests. The average number of arrests declined from 7.27 (first arrest at 10 or less) to 6.16 (first arrest at 11) to 5.25 (first arrest at 12) to 4.10 (first arrest at 13) and so on. Whether those with early first arrests for violence tend to be the most persistent violent offenders is less certain. Hamparian et al. were hindered in investigating this by the fact that there was only just over 1 violent offense per offender in their sample (985 offenses by 811 offenders). Consequently, it was not surprising that their relationship between mean number of violent arrests and age of first violent arrest was pretty flat (declining irregularly from 1.41 at age 10 or less to 1.01 at age 17). A sample with several violent offenses per offender would be required to investigate this relationship more fully.

Longitudinal surveys can also be used to investigate the relationship between juvenile and adult offenses, or the probability of one violent offense following another. For example, McCord (1980), in her 30-year follow-up, divided the adult offenders into those with both property and person offenses, those with property offenses only, those with person offenses only (rapes, assaults, and homicides), and those with only minor crimes. She found that the group who were violent offenders only were much less likely to have records of serious crimes as juveniles (31 percent) than those who were property offenders only (57 percent) or those with both property and violent offenses (63 percent). In agreement with these results, those convicted only for violence as adults tended to be older at the time of their first convictions than those of the other two groups.

In two studies of violent offenders, Walker et al. (1967) showed that the probability of a subsequent conviction for violence increased after each conviction for violence. In their Scottish sample, this probability was 14 percent after the first conviction, 40 percent after the second, 44 percent after the third, and 55 percent after four or more convictions for violence. They recommended that the number of previous convictions for violence should be taken into account when someone is sentenced for violence. In commenting on these results, Carr-Hill (1970) pointed out that the data were consistent with two different models, a static heterogeneity model (in which the population consists of individuals with varying degrees of violence-proneness) and a dynamic contagion model (in which the probability of being convicted for violence increases after each conviction for violence). The dynamic contagion model would be consistent with the ideas of labelling and stigmatization, assuming that the police tended to arrest people for violence partly on the basis of their past records. However, Levine (1976) argued that police selection was not very important in arrests for violence, because most assailants were identified by victims or witnesses.

One policy issue to which the natural history of criminal violence is very important is incapacitation. As policymakers have started to place more emphasis on incapacitation as a penal aim (coincidentally with the declining emphasis on rehabilitation), several researchers have tried to investigate how many crimes could be prevented by having mandatory sentences of imprisonment for certain classes of offenders. This topic has been reviewed several times (see Brody and Tarling, 1980; Cohen, 1978; Pease and Wolfson, 1979), and longitudinal data have been used by several researchers. For example, Clarke (1974) used the Philadelphia cohort data of Wolfgang et al. (1972) and concluded that the average period of incarceration of 9 months prevented only one index offense at an average cost of $1,100. Even if double the number of juvenile offenders had been incarcerated, the total decrease in index offenses would only have been on the order of 1-4 percent, so that the benefits of incarceration were outweighed by its costs. In one of the best-known incapacitation studies specifically concerned with criminal violence, Van Dine et al. (1977) concluded that a mandatory five-year prison sentence for all felony convictions would prevent only 4 percent of recorded violent crime.

One of the advantages of a longitudinal survey in investigating incapacitation is the greater possibility of establishing actual time incarcerated and actual time in the community at risk than in cross-sectional surveys. On the other hand, conclusions drawn from longitudinal surveys based only on official records of offending can be misleading (see also the discussion of interviews versus records, under "Methodology"). The problem is to establish how many of the total number of crimes committed in the community were committed by detected offenders and how many by undetected people. For example, in studying the effects of incapacitation for violent crimes, it is necessary to know how many violent crimes were committed by persons convicted for violence, how many were committed by persons convicted only for nonviolent crimes, and how many were committed by persons not convicted for any crimes. Only the first of these groups would be subject to special incapacitative measures designed to prevent violence. (This assumes that incapacitation would not be based on predicted violence; see the following section, "Predicting Criminal Violence").

A longitudinal survey of a random sample of the population, involving repeated interviews in which questions were asked about crimes committed, could provide valuable information about the natural history of violence (or any other crime) that would enable the benefits of incapacitation to be specified more realistically. It could show, for example, how rates of committing different kinds of crimes vary with age, and hence whether incapacitation has greater benefits if used relatively late in a criminal career (as at present) or relatively early. It could also show how arrest rates vary with age and with number of crimes committed, thereby showing how far those arrested at each age are indeed the most serious and persistent offenders. The self-report survey of Peterson et al. (1980) concluded that a group of 100 people convicted of robbery would have committed 490 robberies, 310 assaults, 720 burglaries, 70 car thefts, 100 forgeries, and 3,400 drug sales (the only acts inquired about) in the previous year at risk in the community. This kind of information, obtained longitudinally rather than cross-sectionally, might show that the benefits of incarceration are greater than had been thought previously.

On the other hand, it would be undesirable for a study of incapacitation to lose sight of other penal aims (such as general or individual deterrence or rehabilitation) and to ignore negative effects of imprisonment. For example, Farrington and Nuttall (1980) showed that prison-overcrowding rates were closely correlated with higher-than-expected reconviction rates. If mandatory prison sentences led to more overcrowded prisons, the benefits of incapacitation might be canceled out by the increased recidivism rates. It might be thought that mandatory prison sentences would have a general deterrent effect, but Schwartz (1968) could not demonstrate any such effect of minimum prison sentences for rape.

Longitudinal surveys that included interviews could provide information not only about the natural history of criminal violence but also about changes in factors correlated with criminal violence. Information on this topic will be discussed in the next two sections of this chapter. Long-term surveys could also provide information about the later lives of people who were violent at one point in time. For example, Short and Moland (1976) reinterviewed 52 former black gang members who were studied 12-15 years before in Chicago, and found that they had been more successful than might have been expected. Most were employed, and most disapproved of Black Power methods and riots.

Predicting Criminal Violence

Longitudinal surveys are useful in investigating how far the beginning and ending of careers of criminal violence can be predicted. Establishing factors that are correlated with violent careers should aid in the development and testing of theories of criminal violence. Farrington (1978) found that, when they were aged 8-10, youths subsequently convicted of an offense involving physical violence tended to have parents who were cold, harsh, disharmonious, poor supervisors, and convicted, tended to have low IQs, and tended to be rated daring and aggressive. Each of these factors predicted criminal violence independently of each other factor. Harsh parental attitude and discipline was the best predictor of criminal violence, and in fact was an even better predictor than rated aggressive behavior in school. The same factors predicted those youths who were high on self-reported violence at age 16-18. The precise theoretical meaning of these results is not clear. The major result showing the importance of harsh parental discipline is in agreement with the modeling theory of Bandura and Walters (1963) suggesting that children tend to imitate the aggressive behavior of their parents.

Farrington's results are in agreement with those of McCord et al. (1963), who found that, as children, violent delinquents tended to have parents who were in conflict, who supervised them poorly, who were rejecting and punitive, whose discipline was erratic, and who were aggressive, alcoholic, or convicted. In her later follow-up, McCord (1979) again showed that those convicted of violent crimes tended to have aggressive, conflicting parents. Farrington also tried to carry out some more specifically longitudinal analyses, and reported that the factors predicting the emergence of (self-reported) violence at age 16-18 among previously nonviolent youths were parental disharmony and convicted parents. Furthermore, there was some evidence that newly emerging parental disharmony at 14 predicted newly emerging self-reported violence at 16-18, although it is always difficult to be sure of causal order in this kind of nonexperimental research.

Most research on the prediction of criminal violence is not concerned with theory but with the policy issue of dangerousness. Dangerous behavior is usually defined in terms of criminal violence, and many researchers have argued that dangerousness either cannot be predicted or is greatly overpredicted (see Bottoms, 1977; Megargee, 1976b; Monahan, 1978; Wenk et al., 1972).

The overprediction argument concentrates on the high rate of false positives, although, as Gordon (1977) pointed out, it is desirable to consider the rate and social costs of false negatives as well as those of false positives. The unpredictability argument contrasts strangely with the results reviewed in our earlier discussion of longitudinal research showing the stability of aggressiveness.

As in many other instances, the conclusions drawn depend crucially on the definition of key variables such as "prediction" and "violence." If violence is defined as a recorded violent offense within 15 months of release from a juvenile facility, with a prevalence of 2.5 percent (Wenk et al., 1972), it will be very difficult to predict. As Monahan (1981) pointed out, small targets are harder to hit than big ones. If predictive power is evaluated according to the false positive rate in trying to predict a rare event, rather than according to the overall correlation between predicted and actual outcomes, conclusions will stress unpredictability or overprediction.

These issues can be illustrated using data from Farrington (1978). The prevalence of convictions for physical violence up to age 21 in this survey was 6.6 percent. These convictions could be predicted to a statistically significant degree by teachers' ratings of aggressive behavior in class at age 8-10. Of the quarter of the sample who were the most aggressive, 14 percent became violent delinquents, in comparison with 4.5 percent of the remaining three-quarters (χ^2 = 9.02 with 1 df, p < .005). This prediction had a very high false-positive rate of 86 percent. Turning the percentages around, nearly half of the violent delinquents, 48.1 percent, had been rated aggressive as children, in comparison with only 21.1 percent of those who were not violent delinquents. The percentage of violent delinquents who were not predicted, 51.9 percent, was considerably less than the percentage of predicted persons who were not violent delinquents. On the criterion of a statistically significant predictive relationship, convictions for criminal violence can be predicted. On the criterion of a low false-positive rate, they cannot.

Of course, it might be argued that what should be predicted is not convictions but violent behavior, and that the behavior is likely to be much more common than the convictions. Monahan (1978) is surely right to recommend self-report measures of violence. Farrington (1978) used them and investigated the extent to which the most violent quarter of the youths at 16-18 could be predicted by ratings of aggressiveness at 8-10. Once again, there was a statistically significant relationship between the two measures, with 40.4 percent of the most aggressive quarter at 8-10 being in the most violent quarter at 16-18. The false-positive rate is lower in this kind of a comparison.

More longitudinal research on criminal violence would help to establish its predictability under different definitions of "prediction" and "violence." Whether the predictability under any definition would justify incapacitative preventive measures is doubtful.

Effects of Specific Events

One of the most distinctive uses of a longitudinal survey is to investigate the effects of specific events on the course of development. Unfortunately, little of this kind of research has been done with criminal violence. Whatever is done needs to be theoretically guided.

As a example of the kind of research that could be done, Farrington (1977) studied the effects on self-reported delinquent behavior of being convicted. This research was intended to test labelling theory. Youths who were first convicted between ages 14 and 18 were matched on self-reported delinquency at age 14 with youths not convicted up to age 18, and a similar analysis was carried out between 18 and 21 (Farrington et al., 1978). During both time periods, youths who were convicted increased their delinquency in comparison with matched unconvicted youths, showing that the effects of official labelling were not reformative. In trying to investigate causal links between public labelling and delinquency, it was found that changes in hostile attitudes to the police were correlated with changes in self-reported delinquency. It may be that public labelling produces hostility to the police, which in turn produces increased delinquency, although other possible casual explanations cannot be ruled out.

Little research has been carried out in the Cambridge Study in Delinquent Development to investigate the effects of specific events on violence. In the preceding section on predicting criminal violence, it was noted that the emergence of violent behavior seemed to follow the onset of parental disharmony. Several analyses were carried out by Knight et al. (1977) to investigate the effects of getting married on delinquent behavior. Generally, getting married had little effect on official or self-report measures of delinquency, although it did reduce some of the behavior associated with delinquency (such as heavy drinking and sexual promiscuity). Getting married did not produce any reduction in self-reported violence.

More longitudinal analyses to study the effects of specific events on criminal violence should be carried out. It is surprising that there have been few attempts to study the effects of penal treatments on violence using an experimental design and a reasonably long follow-up period. Before-and-after measures of offending, such as those used by Empey and Erickson (1972) and Empey and Lubeck (1971), preferably based on self-reports as well as official records, are needed. The treatment of violence has not been studied in penal experiments partly because of the ethical, practical, and legal problems of randomly allocating persons convicted of violence to nonsecure facilities. Such persons are often eliminated from the pool of offenders eligible for random allocation (e.g., Palmer, 1971). There have been some nonexperimental follow-up studies on the effect of penal treatment on violent delinquents (e.g., Miller and Dinitz, 1973), but experimental studies would be more conclusive.

Intergenerational Transmission

Longitudinal research can also be used to investigate the transmission of criminal violence from one generation to the next. In the Cambridge Study in Delinquent Development, convicted parents tended to have convicted sons (Farrington et al., 1975; Osborn and West, 1979). However, in agreement with the generality of delinquency, there was no specific relationship between the types of crime committed by parents and the types committed by sons. Of fathers convicted for violence, 47 percent had a convicted son, in comparison with 53 percent of fathers convicted exclusively for crimes of dishonesty. Of fathers convicted for violence, 29 percent of their convicted sons had convictions for violence. Of fathers convicted for offenses not including violence, 23 percent of their convicted sons had convictions for violence. These results suggest general rather than specific transmission of delinquency.

The research of McCord (1977) shows that 28.6 percent of fathers convicted for violence had sons convicted for violence, in comparison with 11.7 percent of fathers not convicted for violence. However, this analysis included convicted and unconvicted fathers and sons. Therefore, it is difficult to know whether this result reflects the general relationship between convicted fathers and convicted sons or a specific tendency for fathers convicted for violence to have sons convicted for violence. Other research on the intergenerational transmission of delinquency (e.g., Robins et al., 1975) does not seem to have investigated the transmission of specific offense types.

In trying to study why convicted fathers tended to have convicted sons, Farrington et al. (1975) found no evidence that convicted fathers encouraged their sons to commit crimes or taught them criminal techniques. Very few of the convicted fathers were convicted together with their sons. The major difference between the convicted and unconvicted fathers was that the convicted fathers exercised poorer supervision over their sons. There was evidence that the sons of criminal fathers were more likely to be convicted, over and above their increased likelihood of committing delinquent acts (as measured by self-reports). It may be that when the police catch a youth committing an offense and know that he comes from a family containing other convicted persons, they are more likely to prosecute and secure a conviction than in other cases. This factor and the poor supervision were the major links Farrington et al. could find in the chain between convicted fathers and convicted sons.

Several researches have been designed to investigate biological mechanisms of intergenerational transmission of crime. Christiansen (1974) followed up all twin pairs born in Denmark in 1881-1910, where both twins survived at least to age 15, the age of criminal responsibility. He found that when one twin had been convicted, the other was much more likely also to have been convicted if the twins were identical than if they were fraternal. This result suggests a hereditary component in criminal behavior. Furthermore, the twin coefficients were higher for the more serious (violence or sex) offenses, suggesting that these offenses were most strongly influenced by similarities between the twins. Adoption studies (e.g., Hutchings and Mednick, 1975) also indicate genetic factors in crime.

Little of this research has been specifically on criminal violence. The one genetic abnormality that has been especially linked with violence is the XYY syndrome (see for example, West, 1969). The most exhaustive longitudinal survey to investigate this was carried out by Witkin et al. (1976), who followed up all males born in Copenhagen between 1944 and 1947. The Danish national register provided their current addresses at age 26, and the draft boards, to which all men were required to report by age 26, provided information about their adult heights. The XYY abnormality is known to be more prevalent among tall men, so the 4,500 males with heights exceeding six feet were identified. Attempts were made to visit every one of these men to take blood samples and buccal smears to determine chromosomal constitution, and this was done successfully in 91 percent of the cases. Unfortunately, only 12 XYY males were found. Five of these had been convicted, but they were not especially violent people. These results suggest that the XYY abnormality is not important in the explanation of criminal violence.

METHODOLOGICAL ISSUES

Longitudinal versus Cross-Sectional Research

In designing a longitudinal survey, a number of major choices have to be made. The two sections following this one will discuss some of the advantages of interviews as opposed to records, and of prospective versus retrospective designs. This section will discuss some of the general advantages and disadvantages of longitudinal versus cross-sectional methods. Many topics can be investigated both longitudinally and cross-sectionally, and a combination of methods is often desirable.

The longitudinal method is very useful in documenting changes over time directly, rather than inferring them from differences between groups in a cross-sectional survey. Cross-sectional surveys always have selection problems, whereas each person acts as his or her own control in a longitudinal survey. An advantage of a longitudinal survey is that with before-and-after measures it is easier to investigate causal hypotheses and to establish causal order. Causes are essentially hypotheses about changes in one factor producing changes in another, and the longitudinal method is ideal for detecting such changes. Random allocation experiments are especially useful in testing causal hypotheses, but even nonexperimental longitudinal research stands a better chance of establishing cause-and-effect relationships than cross-sectional research.

One problem with longitudinal research involving interviews is to control for testing effects: the effect of prior contacts on later ones. Bachman et al. (1978) and Douglas (1970) investigated these effects in longitudinal surveys by comparing tested and nontested groups, and found that they were negligible. In any quasi-experimental analysis, it is also desirable to control for other factors listed by Campbell and Stanley (1966), such as instrumentation and regression to the mean. It is impossible to separate maturation and period effects in one longitudinal survey. Farrington (1979) reported that the proportion of boys who admitted that they had taken illegal drugs increased from 0.5 percent at age 14 (in 1967) to 6.3 percent at age 16 (in 1969) and 31.4 percent at age 18 (in 1971). This increase could have been related to increasing age or to changes during the period 1967-1971. The period effects were probably more important. Gold and Reimer (1975) found that admitted drug use by American boys aged 13-16 increased by ten times between 1967 and 1972. In order to separate maturation and period effects, it is necessary either to study more than one cohort (see Shannon, 1978) or to have overlapping cross-sectional and longitudinal surveys.

One of the major problems of longitudinal research is attrition, or the loss of people from the sample for a variety of reasons, such as death, emigration, unknown address, and refusals. Attrition can be minimal even over lengthy periods. In the Cambridge Study in Delinquent Development, 95 percent of the original sample were reinterviewed ten years later at age 18 (West and Farrington, 1977). However, the loss of subjects over long periods has often been much greater than this. Lefkowitz et al. (1977) could interview only 427 out of the 875 original children (49 percent) ten years later. The missing subjects are often among the most interesting to criminological researchers. For example, the ones missing in the Lefkowitz et al. survey included a disproportionate number of the most aggressive children. An advantage of a longitudinal survey is that something is known about the missing subjects from earlier contacts, so that the maximum error introduced by attrition can sometimes be estimated.

Interviews versus Records

Most of the researches reviewed in this chapter have been based entirely on information available in criminal records. Records can be easily and cheaply available, can cover a lengthy period, and can be free from retrospective bias (where the information in them was recorded contemporaneously with the events). However, records have many limitations. One of the major problems is that officially recorded violent offenses are the tip of the iceberg of violent crimes committed. Peterson et al. (1980) found that only 10 percent of rapes, 10 percent of assaults, and 21 percent of armed robberies committed by their sample of male prisoners led to arrests. Violent offenses often have high clearance rates (see Monahan, 1978), but this is sometimes because they tend to be recorded by the police only when a suspect has been apprehended. Records are often incomplete, with an unsystematic coverage of topics of interest, and are usually compiled for administrative rather than research purposes. The advantage of interviews is that data can be collected for theoretical reasons rather than because they are available.

Records can be useful in checking the truthfulness of interviewees. For example, West and Farrington (1977) found that only 6 percent of convicted youths failed to admit a conviction, and only 2 percent of unconvicted youths claimed to have been convicted. However, Petersilia (1978) showed that only 60 percent of recorded convictions for violence (67 out of 112) were admitted by her sample of incarcerated armed robbers. Robins (1966) reported that the probability of not admitting an arrest that occurred between ages 18 and 30 was very low for those currently in prison but relatively high for those who had not been arrested since age 30 (perhaps because they wished to hide earlier offenses). It may sometimes be difficult to know whether discrepancies between interviews and records reflect inadequacies in the records or in the interviews.

It is desirable to collect data from a variety of sources, although direct observation of violence is rarely feasible. If a large number of variables are measured, it is possible to control statistically for many of them and hence to be more confident about conclusions than if only a small number of variables are controlled. With interviews, it is more possible to establish what a variable means and how it exerts its effect. The interviewee's version of a violent crime may fit in more neatly with other data than does the account in official records.

The argument here is not that records should not be used, but that both records and interviews should be used.

Prospective versus Retrospective Surveys

Prospective longitudinal surveys have many practical problems. The researcher ages at the same rate as the subjects, and theories and methodology may change so much over time that the value of the research is lessened. It could be argued that prospective surveys are unsuitable for rare phenomena like criminal violence, but this depends on the definition of violence (e.g., convictions or self-reports) and on the sample studied.

The major advantages of prospective surveys are that information can be collected contemporaneously with events of interest and uncontaminated by retrospective bias. Wadsworth (1979) reviewed a number of noncriminological studies that showed how people distorted past events in order to make sense of later ones. More research is needed to establish the precise nature and extent of retrospective bias in criminological investigations, so that workers can make an informed decision about when a prospective design is especially needed. The nearest approach to this research is probably the "reverse record check" used in victim surveys (see Sparks et al., 1977). Retrospective bias and other distortions and losses of memory may pose a special problem with more subjective, less factual information. It can be investigated in longitudinal surveys.

Prospective longitudinal surveys involving regular interviews and long-term records constitute probably the most adequate way of investigating criminal violence at present.

CONCLUSIONS

Longitudinal research on criminal violence has especially investigated the natural history of arrests or convictions for violence among officially processed groups and among more representative samples from the general population. This research shows that convicted offenders are versatile rather than specialized in the crimes they commit and that, while the incidence of violence convictions is low, the prevalence of offenders with at least one conviction for violence may be quite high. Convictions for violence begin later than those for other offenses, so that adults with only violence convictions are less likely to have been convicted as juveniles than adults with only property convictions. The probability of having a subsequent conviction for violence increases with each violence conviction.

Longitudinal research has also investigated the prediction of violence, the effects of specific events on it, and its intergenerational transmission. There is continuity between rated aggression at an early age and convictions for violence (and self-reports of violence) at a later age. Persons convicted for violence are more likely to have had cold, harsh, disharmonious parents who exercised poor supervision over them; are more likely to have had convicted parents; and more likely to have had low IQs. There is some evidence that the emergence of violence follows the emergence of parental disharmony and that violence is not reduced by getting married. While convicted parents tend to have convicted children, there is no specific relationship between violence convictions of parents and violence convictions of children.

Most longitudinal research on criminal violence has been based entirely on records and has been designed to investigate its natural history. More research should be carried out, using interviews as well as records with the aim to carry out specifically longitudinal analyses such as those studying the effects of specific events on the course of development. Most longitudinal research on criminal violence has been designed to collect basic information about careers of violence or has been inspired by policy issues such as incapacitation or dangerousness. More studies should be concerned with developing theories and testing hypotheses about violence.

While many studies have been designed to collect basic information about the natural history of criminal violence, their reliance on official records means that this basic information is still needed. A longitudinal survey from about age 17 to about age 29 with lower-class urban males, based on regular (yearly) interviews, is a necessary precursor of more theoretically guided research or studies of other groups. Ideally, such a project should be combined with cross-sectional surveys of 17-29-year-old males at its beginning and end, to give some chance of separating maturation and period effects. Criminal violence at present seems to be at the stage juvenile delinquency was 25 years ago, before the self-report revolution. Almost everything we know about it is based on official records.

Other researches would also be desirable. Since most studies are based on lower-class urban males, research on other groups should be carried out. Other groups have a very low incidence of official processing for violence, but they may not have such a low incidence of violent behavior. Random allocation experiments on penal treatments for violence, with before-and-after measures, are also desirable. The most urgent need is to embark on a prospective longitudinal survey of the natural history of criminal violence, with overlapping cross-sectional surveys, and with regular collection of record and interview data.

REFERENCES

Anttila, I., and Westling, A. A study in the pardoning of, and recidivism among, criminals sentenced to life imprisonment. In K. O. Christiansen (Ed.), *Scandinavian studies in criminology* (Vol. 1). London: Tavistock, 1965.

Bachman, J. G., O'Malley, P. M., and Johnston, J. *Youth in transition* (Vol. 6). Ann Arbor: University of Michigan Institute for Social Research, 1978.

Bandura, A., and Walters, R. H. *Social learning and personality development.* New York: Holt, Rinehart & Winston, 1963.

Blumstein, A., and Cohen, J. Estimation of individual crime rates from arrest records. *Journal of Criminal Law and Criminology,* 1979, 70, 561-585.

Bottoms, A. E. Reflections on the renaissance of dangerousness. *Howard Journal,* 1977, 16, 70-96.

Brody, S., and Tarling, R. *Taking offenders out of circulation.* London: Her Majesty's Stationery Office, 1980.

Buikhuisen, W., and Jongman, R. W. A legalistic classification of juvenile delinquents. *British Journal of Criminology,* 1970, 10, 109-123.

Bursik, R. J. The dynamics of specialization in juvenile offenses. *Social Forces,* 1980, 58, 851-864.

Campbell, D. T., and Stanley, J. C. *Experimental and quasi-experimental designs for research.* Chicago: Rand McNally, 1966.

Carr-Hill, R. A. Victims of our typologies. In *The violent offender—Reality or illusion?* Oxford: Blackwell, 1970.

Cernkovich, S. A. Delinquency involvement: an evaluation of the non-intervention strategy. *Criminal Justice Review,* 1978, 3, 45-51.

Christiansen, K. O. Seriousness of criminality and concordance among Danish twins. In R. Hood (Ed.), *Crime, criminality and public policy.* London: Heinemann, 1974.

Christiansen, K. O., Elers-Nielsen, M., LeMaire, L., and Stürup, G. K. Recidivism among sexual offenders. In K. O. Christiansen (Ed.), *Scandinavian studies in criminology* (Vol. 1). London: Tavistock, 1965.

Clarke, S. H. Getting 'em out of circulation: Does incarceration of juvenile offenders reduce crime? *Journal of Criminal Law and Criminology,* 1974, 65, 528-535.

Clarke, S. H. Some implications for North Carolina of recent research in juvenile delinquency. *Journal of Research in Crime and Delinquency,* 1975, 12, 51-60.

Cline, H. F. Criminal behavior over the life span. In O. G. Brim and J. Kagan (Eds.), *Constancy and change in human development.* Cambridge: Harvard University Press, 1979.

Cohen, J. The incapacitative effects of imprisonment. In A. Blumstein, J. Cohen and D. Nagin (Eds.), *Deterrence and incapacitation.* Washington, DC: National Academy of Sciences, 1978.

Dinitz, S., and Conrad, J. P. The dangerous two percent. In D. Shichor and D. H. Kelly (Eds.), *Critical issues in juvenile delinquency.* Lexington, MA: D. C. Heath, 1980.

Douglas, J. W. B. Discussion. In E. H. Hare and J. K. Wing (Eds.), *Psychiatric Epidemiology.* London: Oxford University Press, 1970.

Empey, L. T., and Erickson, M. L. *The Provo Experiment.* Lexington, MA: D. C. Heath, 1972.

Empey, L. T., and Lubeck, S. G. *The Silverlake Experiment.* Chicago: Aldine, 1971.

Farrington, D. P. Self-reports of deviant behavior: Predictive and stable? *Journal of Criminal Law and Criminology,* 1973, 64, 99-110.

Farrington, D. P. The effects of public labelling. *British Journal of Criminology,* 1977, 17, 112-125.

Farrington, D. P. The family backgrounds of aggressive youths. In L. Hersov, M. Berger, and D. Shaffer (Eds.), *Aggression and Anti-Social Behavior in Childhood and Adolescence.* Oxford: Pergamon, 1978.

Farrington, D. P. Longitudinal research on crime and delinquency. In N. Morris and M. Tonry (Eds.), *Crime and justice* (Vol. 1). Chicago: University of Chicago Press, 1979.

Farrington, D. P. The prevalence of convictions. *British Journal of Criminology,* 1981, 21, 173-175.

Farrington, D. P., Gundry, G., and West, D. J. The familial transmission of criminality. *Medicine, Science and the Law,* 1975, 15, 177-186.

Farrington, D. P. and Nuttall, C. P. Prison size, overcrowding, prison violence, and recidivism. *Journal of Criminal Justice,* 1980, 8, 221-231.

Farrington, D. P., Osborn, S. G., and West, D. J. The persistence of labelling effects. *British Journal of Criminology,* 1978, 18, 277-284.

Farrington, D. P., and West, D. J. A comparison between early delinquents and young aggressives. *British Journal of Criminology,* 1971, 11, 341-358.

Feldhusen, J. F., Thurston, J. R., and Benning, J. J. A longitudinal study of delinquency and other aspects of children's behavior. *International Journal of Criminology and Penology,* 1973, 1, 341-351.

Gold, M., and Reimer, D. J. Changing patterns of delinquent behavior among Americans 13 through 16 years old: 1967-72. *Crime and Delinquency Literature,* 1975, 7, 483-517.

Goldstein, M. J., and Kant, H. S. *Pornography and sexual deviance.* Berkeley: University of California Press, 1973.

Gordon, R. A. A critique of the evaluation of the Patuxent institution, with particular attention to the issues of dangerousness and recidivism. *Bulletin of the American Academy of Psychiatry and the Law,* 1977, 5, 210-255.

Hamparian, D. M., Schuster, R., Dinitz, S., and Conrad, J. P. *The Violent Few.* Lexington, MA: D. C. Heath, 1978.

Havighurst, R. J., Bowman, P. H., Liddle, G. P., Matthews, C. V., and Pierce, J. V. *Growing up in River City.* New York: John Wiley, 1962.

Hindelang, M. J. Age, sex, and the versatility of delinquent involvements. *Social Problems,* 1971, 18, 522-535.

Home Office. *Criminal statistics, England and Wales, 1958.* London: Her Majesty's Stationery Office, 1959.

Home Office. *Criminal statistics, England and Wales, 1978.* London: Her Majesty's Stationery Office, 1979.

Hutchings, B., and Mednick, S. A. Registered criminality in the adoptive and biological parents of registered male criminal adoptees. In R. R. Fieve, D. Rosenthal, and H. Brill (Eds.), *Genetic research in psychiatry.* Baltimore: Johns Hopkins University Press, 1975.

Johnson, R. E. *Juvenile delinquency and its origins.* Cambridge: At the Cambridge University Press, 1979.

Knight, B. J., Osborn, S. G., and West, D. J. Early marriage and criminal tendency in males. *British Journal of Criminology,* 1977, 17, 348-360.

Kozol, H. L., Boucher, R. J., and Garofalo, R. F. The diagnosis and treatment of dangerousness. *Crime and Delinquency,* 1972, 18, 371-392.

Lefkowitz, M. M., Eron, L. D., Walder, L. O., and Huesmann, L. R. *Growing up to be violent.* New York: Pergamon, 1977.

Levine, D. Careers of violence: Further comments. *British Journal of Criminology,* 1976, 16, 161-163.

Magnusson, D., Duner, A., and Zetterblom, G. *Adjustment: A longitudinal study.* Stockholm: Almqvist & Wiksell, 1975.

McClintock, F. H. *Crimes of violence.* London: Macmillan, 1963.

McClintock, F. H., and Avison, N. H. *Crime in England and Wales.* London: Heinemann, 1968.

McCord, J. A comparative study of two generations of native Americans. In R. F. Meier (Ed.), *Theory in criminology.* Beverly Hills, CA: Sage Publications, 1977.

McCord, J. Some child-rearing antecedents of criminal behavior in adult men. *Journal of Personality and Social Psychology,* 1979, 37, 1477-1486.

McCord, J. Patterns of deviance. In S. B. Sells, R. Crandall, M. Roff, J. S. Strauss, and W. Pollin (Eds.), *Human functioning in longitudinal perspective.* Baltimore: Williams & Wilkins, 1980.

McCord, J., McCord, W., and Howard, A. Family interaction as antecedent to the direction of male aggressiveness. *Journal of Abnormal and Social Psychology,* 1963, 66, 239-242.

Megargee, E. I. Population density and disruptive behavior in a prison setting. In A. K. Cohen, G. F. Cole, and R. G. Bailey (Eds.), *Prison violence.* Lexington, MA: D. C. Heath, 1976. (a)

Megargee, E. I. The prediction of dangerous behavior. *Criminal Justice and Behavior,* 1976, 3, 3-22. (b)

Miller, S. J., and Dinitz, S. Measuring institutional impact: A follow-up. *Criminology,* 1973, 11, 417-426.

Monahan, J. The prediction of violent criminal behavior. In A. Blumstein, J. Cohen, and D. Nagin (Eds.), *Deterrence and incapacitation.* Washington, DC: National Academy of Sciences, 1978.

Monahan, J. *The clinical prediction of violent behavior.* Rockville, MD: National Institute of Mental Health, 1981.

Mulligan, G., Douglas, J. W. B., Hammond, W. H., and Tizard, J. Delinquency and symptoms of maladjustment. *Proceedings of the Royal Society of Medicine,* 1963, 56, 1083-1086.

Mulvihill, D., Tumin, M., and Curtis, L. *Staff report to the National Commission on the Causes and Prevention of Violence.* Washington, DC: Government Printing Office, 1969.

Olweus, D. Stability of aggressive reaction patterns in males: A review. *Psychological Bulletin,* 1979, 86, 852-875.

Osborn, S. G., and West, D. J. The effectiveness of various predictors of criminal careers. *Journal of Adolescence,* 1978, 1, 101-117.

Osborn, S. G. and West, D. J. Conviction records of fathers and sons compared. *British Journal of Criminology,* 1979, 19, 120-133.

Osborn, S. G., and West, D. J. Do young delinquents really reform? *Journal of Adolescence,* 1980, 3, 99-114.

Palmer, T. B. California's Community Treatment Program for delinquent adolescents. *Journal of Research in Crime and Delinquency,* 1971, 8, 74-92.

Pease, K., and Wolfson, J. Incapacitation studies: a review and commentary. *Howard Journal,* 1979, 18, 160-167.

Petersilia, J. The validity of criminality data derived from personal interviews. In C. Wellford (Ed.), *Quantitative studies in criminology.* Beverly Hills, CA: Sage Publications, 1978.

Petersilia, J. Criminal career research: A review of recent evidence. In N. Morris and M. Tonry (Eds.), *Crime and justice* (Vol. 2). Chicago: University of Chicago Press, 1980.

Petersilia, J., Greenwood, P. W., and Lavin, M. *Criminal careers of habitual felons.* Washington, DC: U. S. Department of Justice, 1978.

Peterson, M. A., Braiker, H. B., and Polich, S. M. *Doing crime.* Santa Monica, CA: Rand Corporation, 1980.

Peterson, R. A., Pittman, D. J., and O'Neal, P. Stabilities of deviance: A study of assaultive and non-assaultive offenders. *Journal of Criminal Law, Criminology and Police Science,* 1962, 53, 44-48.

Phillpotts, G. J., and Lancucki, L. B. *Previous convictions, sentence and reconviction.* London: Her Majesty's Stationery Office, 1979.

Rappeport, J. R., and Lassen, G. Dangerousness—Arrest rate comparisons of discharged patients and the general population. *American Journal of Psychiatry,* 1965, 121, 776-783.

Robins, L. N. *Deviant children grown up.* Baltimore: Williams & Wilkins, 1966.

Robins, L. N. Aetiological implications in studies of childhood histories relating to antisocial personality. In R. D. Hare and D. Schalling (Eds.), *Psychopathic behavior.* New York: John Wiley, 1978. (a)

Robins, L. N. Longitudinal methods in the study of normal and pathological development. In K. P. Kisker, J. E. Meyer, C. Muller, and E. Stromgren (Eds.), *Psychiatric der Gegenwart* (Vol. 1). Heidelberg: Springer-Verlag, 1978. (b)

Robins, L. N., West, P. A. and Herjanic, B. L. Arrests and delinquency in two generations: A study of black urban families and their children. *Journal of Child Psychology and Psychiatry,* 1975, 16, 125-140.

Robins, L. N., and Wish, E. Childhood deviance as a developmental process: A study of 223 urban black men from birth to 18. *Social Forces,* 1977, 56, 448-473.

Schwartz, B. P. The effect in Philadelphia of Pennsylvania's increased penalties for rape and attempted rape. *Journal of Criminal Law, Criminology and Police Science,* 1968, 59, 509-515.

Sellin, T., and Wolfgang, M. E. *The measurement of delinquency.* New York: John Wiley, 1964.

Shannon, L. W. A longitudinal study of delinquency and crime. In C. Wellford (Ed.), *Quantitative studies in criminology.* Beverly Hills, CA: Sage Publications, 1978.

Short, J. F., and Moland, J. Politics and youth gangs: A follow-up study. *Sociological Quarterly,* 1976, 17, 162-179.

Short, J. F., Tennyson, R., and Howard, K. I. Behavior dimensions of gang delinquency. *American Sociological Review,* 1963, 28, 411-428.

Soothill, K. L., Jack, A., and Gibbens, T. C. N. Rape: A 22-year cohort study. *Medicine, Science and the Law,* 1976, 16, 62-69.

Sparks, R. F., Genn, H. G., and Dodd, D. J. *Surveying victims.* London: John Wiley, 1977.

Strasburg, P. A. *Violent delinquents.* New York: Monarch, 1978.

Thomas, C. W. Are status offenders really so different? *Crime and Delinquency,* 1976, 22, 438-455.

Thornberry, T., and Figlio, R. M. Juvenile and adult offense careers in the Philadelphia birth cohort of 1945. Paper presented at the annual meeting of the American Society of Criminology, Dallas, Texas, 1978.

Van Dine, S., Dinitz, S., and Conrad, J. The incapacitation of the dangerous offender: A statistical experiment. *Journal of Research in Crime and Delinquency,* 1977, 14, 22-34.

Vigderhous, G. Cyclical variations of monthly and yearly homicide rates in the United States and their relationship to changes in the unemployment rate. In C. Wellford (Ed.), *Quantitative studies in criminology.* Beverly Hills, CA: Sage Publications, 1978.

Wadsworth, M. E. J. *Roots of delinquency.* London: Martin Robertson, 1979.

Walker, N., Hammond W., and Steer, D. Repeated violence. *Criminal Law Review,* 1967, 465-472.

Walmsley, R., and White, K. *Sexual offenses, consent and sentencing.* London: Her Majesty's Stationery Office, 1979.

Wenk, E. A., Robison, J. O., and Smith, G. W. Can violence be predicted? *Crime and Delinquency,* 1972, 18, 393-402.

West, D. J. (Ed.). *Criminological implications of chromosome abnormalities.* Cambridge, England: Institute of Criminology, 1969.

West, D. J., and Farrington, D. P. *Who becomes delinquent?* London: Heinemann, 1973.

West, D. J., and Farrington, D. P. *The delinquent way of life.* London: Heinemann, 1977.

Witkin, H. A., et al. Criminality in XYY and XXY men. *Science,* 1976, 193, 547-555.

Wolfgang, M. E., Figlio, R. M., and Sellin, T. *Delinquency in a birth cohort.* Chicago: University of Chicago Press, 1972.

4

Domestic Criminal Violence

Richard J. Gelles

That the family has been a scene of interpersonal violence for as long as we have had written records of humankind and family life is a theory borne out by both anecdotal accounts and historical data (Bakan, 1971; DeMause, 1974, 1975; Radbill, 1974; Taylor and Newberger, 1979; Shorter, 1975). It would be equally fair to claim that for nearly that entire length of time violence between family members has suffered from "selective inattention" (Dexter, 1958; Straus, 1974a; Gelles, 1980b). The victims of family violence have been among the missing persons of the social problems literature and much of the literature on criminal violence.

As the victims of family violence came out from the closets and from behind the closed doors of the home in the late 1960s and early 1970s, the issue of family violence was transformed from a private issue into a public problem. Numerous social scientists have attempted to explain why both the public and scientific communities alike ignored for so long the varied evidence that the family was perhaps one of society's most violent social institutions. Star (1980) claims that the silence, which traditionally surrounded the issue of family violence, was attributable to three factors: (1) lack of awareness, (2) general acceptance, and (3) denial.

Official reporting systems for recording incidents of family violence were first nonexistent and then slow to develop. Thus, accurate statistical evidence on the existence and extent of family violence were largely unavailable. Whi'e the child welfare movement of the late nineteenth century uncovered incidents

Author's Note: This chapter was originally part of a research project on family violence carried out at the University of Rhode Island. Funding has been provided by the National Institute of Mental Health (MH-27557) and the National Center on Child Abuse and Neglect (#90-C-425).

of the abuse and exploitation of children (Taylor and Newberger, 1979), it was not until 1968 that all fifty states had legislated mandatory child-abuse-reporting statutes. Although evidence from official homicide statistics long indicated that intrafamilial murders were perhaps the modal form of homicides (Wolfgang, 1958; Palmer, 1962; Curtis, 1974; Steinmetz and Straus, 1974), other records of tabulating acts of criminal violence made no provision for measuring the extent of husband-wife assaults.

Star's second factor, general acceptance, actually contradicts the theory of lack of awareness. Rather than not knowing that violence occurs frequently in families, it could be that these acts are known but are not viewed as "violent" or deviant. Violence between family members has enjoyed a long tradition of legal legitimization. In 1824, the Mississippi Supreme Court was the first of several states to grant husbands immunity from assault and battery charges for moderately chastizing their wives (Calvert, 1974; Star, 1980). The California Penal Code provides that an injury to a wife must be *more* than what is required for battery (Calvert, 1974). Such legal support for domestic violence can be traced back to English common law, which gave husbands the right to strike their wives with sticks no wider than their thumbs—hence the classic "rule of thumb" (Calvert, 1974; Davidson, 1978). Similarly, historical evidence indicates legal precedents allowing for the mutilation, striking, and even killing of children as part of the legal parental prerogative (Radbill, 1974). Modern survey research points to the continued acceptance of the right of a parent to hit a child, or a husband to strike a wife (Stark and McEvoy, 1970; Straus et al., 1980).

Star (1980) believes that it was the third factor, denial, which was the most widely held defense against acknowledging either the prevalence or the severity of family violence. Doctors, lawyers, social workers, and teachers often preferred to see a child's injury as caused by a fall or accident rather than as inflicted by a parent or caretaker. Adult women victims of violence were frequently described as fantasizing or, worse, wanting or liking their own victimization.

FAMILY VIOLENCE AND THE LACK OF
A CRIMINAL PERSPECTIVE

Star's analysis of the tardy discovery of the problem of family violence and the analysis of legal precedents and public opinion which tended overtly or tacitly to support various levels of domestic violence lend support to a more general theory as to why both the public and the scientific community failed to recognize the extent and seriousness of the problem of domestic assault. The theory, briefly stated, is that the general acceptance of various types of family violence meant that it was not viewed as a *criminal* problem. Hence, violence was not labeled "criminal," no official records were kept, the public could nurture the myth that families were not violent, and no research needed to be carried out (which could provide the data to refute the myth of nonviolent families).

With the singular exception of intrafamilial homicides, violence between family members is rarely viewed as criminal. While the police spend more of their time investigating incidents of domestic violence than they do engaging in virtually every other type of police work (Bard, 1969; Parnas, 1967), most police departments continue to record these calls as "domestic disturbances" as opposed to criminal assaults. When I began my first empirical investigation of violence between spouses, I turned to a local police department to assist me in locating families where police had been called in to intervene in interspousal attacks (Gelles, 1974). Of 150 families identified over a five-year period, 149 were located under the heading of "domestic calls" and one was found under the heading of "assault."

The lack of a criminal violence perspective is evidenced in the way the issue of domestic violence is defined, the response of agencies of social control and social service, and the approach used by social scientists in studying the phenomenon.

Definitions: Violence and Abuse

The first form of domestic violence that was uncovered and recognized as a social problem was the abuse of children. While the victimization and exploitation of children was a problem seen and treated by members of the social service and child welfare community since the mid-nineteenth century, it was not until physician C. Henry Kempe and his colleagues published their seminal paper, "The Battered Child Syndrome," in 1962 that general attention was drawn to the problem of the abuse of children. Kempe and his colleagues narrowly defined the battered-child syndrome as willfully inflicted injury caused by a parent or caretaker. The definition was limited to acts of physical violence that produced injury and thus was consistent with the normal criminal definition of assault and battery. But the term "battered-child syndrome" quickly gave way to the terms "child abuse," "child abuse and neglect," and "child maltreatment." The definitions of these terms added conditions such as malnutrition, failure to thrive, sexual abuse, educational neglect, medical neglect, and mental abuse to Kempe's "willfully inflicted trauma." By 1973, the "official" definition of child abuse, stated in the Federal Child Abuse Prevention and Treatment Act of 1974 (PL 93-237), was as follows:

> Child abuse and neglect means the physical or mental injury, sexual abuse, negligent treatment, or maltreatment of a child under the age of eighteen by a person who is responsible for the child's welfare under circumstances which indicate that the child's health or welfare is harmed or threatened thereby.

The first federally funded national incidence study of child abuse and neglect mandated that the extent of the problem as defined in the Child Abuse Prevention and Treatment Act be measured (the study has recently been completed). The current concept of child abuse is perhaps more political than scientific (Gelles, 1980a). It implies behavior that is considered immoral or improper, but fails to provide a specific, precise definition of the nature of that behavior. The definition of child abuse has become increasingly broad since 1962, and has encompassed an extensive range of behaviors and misbehaviors by parents and caretakers. What has been lost from the definition is its early concern with behavior similar to criminal assault and battery. The consequences of this are that many if not most of the research investigations that measure the extent, patterns, and causes of child abuse are not suitable for obtaining an insight into the extent, patterns, and causes of criminal violence toward children—for acts of violence get lumped into the more general child welfare concerns with child abuse and neglect.

The same general pattern that occurred with the broadening and politicalization of the definition of child abuse also occurred with the definition of wife abuse. Initial definitions of wife abuse (Gelles, 1974; Martin, 1976) focused on acts of damaging physical violence directed toward women by their spouses or partners. As wife abuse became recognized as a social problem, the definition was sometimes broadened to include sexual abuse, marital rape, and even pornography (London, 1978). While this broadening and politicalization has been much less pronounced than it was in the case of child abuse, it still results in the concept of wife abuse referring to a much wider range of behavior than injurious violence. Consequently, the problems of abuse are viewed as wider concerns than simple criminal violence between family members.

There have been definitional problems at the opposite end of the scale from acts of injurious violence. When investigators attempt to apply the concept of violence to intrafamilial behavior, they confront the situation wherein many acts the investigator wishes to include under a definition of violence are accepted as normal and necessary aspects of family life. Some researchers attempt to distinguish between what they see as "legitimate" acts of force between family members and illegitimate acts of violence (see, for example, Goode, 1971). This is a direct consequence of the fact that much of the hitting in families is culturally approved and normatively accepted. Later investigators became troubled by this attempt to establish a dichotomy between legitimate and illegitimate acts of force and violence (Gelles, 1974). It is difficult to arrive at a consensus concerning what is legitimate force and what is illegitimate violence. Who should draw the line—the victim, the offender, the bystanders, agents of social control, or researchers? Perhaps the greatest objection arises when investigators attempt to include spankings, slappings, pushings, and grabbings of children under a definition of violence. So great is the cultural approval for spanking children that to include a spanking as an act of violence violates the sensibilities of many people. Clearly, no court or police officer would attempt negatively to sanction a parent who spanks a child, yet that same act, were it perpetrated by a stranger on a stranger, might well be considered criminal assault (Straus et al., 1980).

Thus, at one end of the spectrum of violence in the family the definition lacks a criminal violence perspective because the acts of criminal violence get lumped together with other harmful, but nonviolent, acts. At the opposite end of the scale, behavior which is clearly violent is not viewed as criminal due to the high level of cultural support for some types and forms of family violence.

Official Responses to Family Violence

The official response to instances of violence in the family has traditionally been noncriminal. In general, courts have taken a hands-off attitude toward the modern family. It would be unfair to say that the courts approve of all violence in the home, but courts generally agree with public opinion that certain types of violence are acceptable (for example, the rule of thumb).

For those acts of violence in the home that *are* generally viewed as deviant, the official response has tended to be noncriminal. This is most obvious in the case of violence toward and abuse of children.

Child Abuse: A Child Welfare Problem

Perhaps the first publicly identified case of child abuse was that of a badly abused foster child named Mary Ellen who was discovered by church workers in New York City in 1874. When the church workers tried to get aid for Mary Ellen, they found that the only available agency was the Society for the Prevention of Cruelty to Animals. Thus, they founded the first chapter of a similar society for children (Ross, 1977). For nearly the next century the child welfare community was virtually the only institution available to identify and treat cases of battered children.

The Kempe et al. paper (1962) introduced the problem of child abuse to the medical community and was instrumental in establishing mandatory reporting laws in all fifty states. Such laws vary, but the modal strategy is that the key agencies charged with the responsibility of initiating contact with reported abusive families and providing services are protective service agencies (Nelson et al., 1980). While the police are frequently included as part of an overall reporting and service plan in state child-abuse laws, the criminal justice system is clearly placed on the periphery of the system of social control and social services (Rosenthal, 1979). Even in the most notorious cases, where children are horribly maimed or killed, the police are most often cast in marginal roles. This frequently leads to conflict between public protective service agencies that view abuse from a child welfare perspective and police and district attorneys who react to particularly gruesome cases of child abuse by seeking prosecution and formal legal sanctions.

While some child abusers are officially charged with crimes (ranging from child abuse to assault or murder), and many are convicted, most instances of officially reported child abuse are confined to the child welfare system, with the involvement of the criminal justice system limited to the granting of temporary restraining orders or family or probate court proceedings bearing on the custody status of the child.

Wife Abuse: The Struggle for Recognition

The battered wife, who remained behind closed doors for a decade after the "discovery" of child abuse, found no official social service agency available to turn to for help, protection, or prevention. No "Society for the Prevention of Cruelty to Wives" was formed; no adult Mary Ellen galvanized public or professional attention to the plight of battered women. The problem battered women faced was to obtain official recognition of their situation and criminal justice redress or protection.

The criminal justice system, beginning with the role and actions of the police, tended to view the problem of battered women from various perspectives—denial, acceptance, lack of awareness, and helplessness. One view of the police and the criminal justice system is that they positively sanction violence against women by failing to treat such behaviors as criminal assault. The previously mentioned laws which "allowed" for some violence toward women were matched by informal procedures used by police, such as "stitch rules," which provided that a husband could not be arrested for assaulting his wife unless she had a wound that required a certain number of sutures (Field and Field, 1973). Prosecutors were castigated for not taking women's claims seriously and failing actively to pursue prosecution of assaultive husbands (Truninger, 1971).

On the other hand, the police and public prosecutors point to the actions of battered wives as "handcuffing" the effectiveness of the criminal justice system. Police frequently point to the women who attack and even kill police officers who intervene in domestic violence incidents (Parnas, 1967). Other police officers point to the numerous instances of women who fail to file charges against their husbands or who return to their husbands time after time (Parnas, 1967). Some prosecutors also point to numerous examples of women who fail to follow through in pressing charges against assaultive husbands or who drop charges at a trial and announce that "husbands are supposed to hit their wives, aren't they?" (Parnas, 1967).

The ten years since the identification of wife abuse as a social problem have seen a major effort on the part of organized groups advocating for battered women to obtain what they see as equal protection from the police. Three class-action suits best illustrate this struggle for a criminal perspective on wife-battering. In December 1976, wives in New York City filed a class-action suit *(Bruno v Maguire)* against the New York Police Department, probation officers, and family court employees for failing to prosecute abusive husbands. The police settled the case out of court in 1977. In 1974, a class-action suit was filed against the Cleveland district attorneys for denying battered women equal protection under the law by not following through on prosecution of abusive husbands. That suit was settled by a consent decree ordering the prosecutors to change their practices. In Oakland, the police department was accused of illegal conduct in its pattern and practice of discouraging arrests in cases of domestic violence. Similar proceedings followed these three cases, all with the goal of "criminalizing" violence against women (see *Response,* 1979, for complete details on the above legal proceedings).

The discussion of the police and prosecutor reactions to incidents of wife abuse is not without substantial rhetoric (Berk and Loseke, 1980). Clearly, the actions of the police are not nearly as single-mindedly discriminatory as some would have it (Berk and Loseke, 1980), nor are all battered women as masochistic and stubborn as painted by the police (Fields, 1978). Nevertheless, one thing remains clear: Husband-to-wife violence is neither uniformly nor completely recognized as an instance of criminal violence.

Husband Abuse: All Rhetoric and No Data?

In 1978 Steinmetz published an article designed to demonstrate that husbands as well as wives were the victims of violence in the home. Steinmetz (1978a) reviewed numerous investigations of family violence and found that, contrary to some feminist and scholarly rhetoric (see, for example, Dobash and Dobash, 1979), women were not the *only* victims of family violence. Steinmetz went on to claim that it was husband and *not* wife abuse that was the most underreported form of family violence. Steinmetz was immediately challenged and attacked by feminists and scholars alike for misreading, misinterpreting, and misrepresenting her findings (see Pleck et al., 1978).

The debate over the Steinmetz article played itself out in national news magazines (such as *Time*), talk shows (such as *The Today Show* and the *David Susskind Show*), and even in the syndicated column of Ann Landers (for a detailed discussion of the public debate, see Jones, 1980). Regrettably, the debate received no further discussion or airing in scholarly arenas, and the actual data on violence toward men took a back seat to the rhetoric. What the actual extent of the battering of husbands is remains muddied, if not unknown. Any criminal justice concern for battered husbands was lost amidst the vociferous claims by those concerned with battered women that the issue of battered men was a red herring (Jones, 1980).

Other Forms of Family Violence: Little Notice.

Discussion of violence toward children has been subsumed under the heading of child abuse; domestic violence has become a concept that actually refers only to violence toward wives (for example, the Office of Domestic Violence in the federal Department of Health and Human Services dealt only with violence toward wives); and despite the effort of some scholars (for example, Straus et al., 1980) to define the problem as one of *family* violence, the other forms of violence in the home are largely unrecognized by the public, the scientific community, and the criminal justice system. Violence between siblings is perhaps the best example of a form of family violence that gets no criminal justice attention, with the obvious exception of criminal homicides. Abuse of the elderly was recently discovered, if not by social scientists, at least by the media. Twelve states have passed "adult protective service" laws which attempt to increase the identification and servicing of elderly victims of family abuse (Mancini, 1980). Other forms of violence toward parents are largely unnoticed by social service or criminal justice systems.

Summary

In short, while the issue of family violence has captured considerable attention in the past decade, the problem either remains unrecognized or is responded to largely as a child or human welfare problem, as opposed to a criminal violence problem.

Social Scientific Perspectives

The scholarly approach to family violence has mirrored the legal and criminal justice approach—that is, violence in the home is considered a private, family matter that concerns criminologists only when someone is killed.

The early research and writing on child abuse, wife abuse, and family violence was clearly dominated by psychological, social service, and medical perspectives. The psychopathological model was the dominant theoretical framework guiding early studies of the extent, causes, and solutions to the abuse of women and children (Gelles, 1973, 1980b; Spinetta and Rigler, 1972). Prior to 1971, virtually all the scholarly literature on child abuse was authored by social workers, physicians, or psychiatrists (Gelles, 1973). Only two scholarly articles on wife abuse were authored prior to 1971, and both were by psychiatrists and their associates (Gelles, 1980b). The rare criminal justice work on family violence was done by those concerned with homicide (Wolfgang, 1958; Palmer, 1962; Pokorny, 1965; Guttmacher, 1960) or officially reported criminal assault (Pittman and Handy, 1964).

Since 1971 there has been a virtual explosion of literature on family violence, but here too the dominant perspectives have been those of psychology, medicine, social work, or family sociology. Within the discipline of sociology, the main thrust of work on family violence has been carried out by family sociologists such as Straus (1971, 1974a, 1974b, 1976, 1977a, 1977b, 1979a), Steinmetz (1971, 1974a, 1974b, 1977a, 1977b, 1977c, 1978a) and this author. Precious little research has been done by criminologists who apply criminal definitions and a criminal perspective to the problem of family violence.

Even the terms chosen by social scientists who investigate child abuse, wife abuse, and family violence reveal the lack of a criminal violence perspective. While scholars have spent pages detailing their definitions of abuse and violence (see Gelles, 1975a; Gelles and Straus, 1979), there has been no attempt to apply a criminal violence perspective by opting for the term "family assault" or "wife battery" in place of "family violence" or "wife abuse."

The record is clear in the definitions of violence, the research approaches to the problem, and the theoretical perspectives applied to and derived from the study of family violence that violence in the home still is essentially viewed as more of a family as opposed to a criminal problem.

FROM PRIVATE ISSUE TO PUBLIC PROBLEM

The prevailing public and social scientific attitude toward family violence through the mid-1970s was that family violence was rare and, when it did occur, was the product of mental illness or a psychological disorder. By the end of the 1970s, there had been a major revision of this line of thinking as there was wholesale increase in attention to, and published reports on, various aspects of violence in the home.

Straus (1974a) attempted to explain the shift from family violence as a private issue to a high-priority public social issue by positing that the emergence of family violence as an important research topic was the result of three cultural and social forces. First, social scientists and the public alike became increasingly sensitive to violence—including a war in Southeast Asia, assassinations, civil disturbances, and increasing homicide rates—in the 1960s. Second, the emergence of the women's movement played a part—especially by uncovering and highlighting the problems of battered women. One of the first major books on the topic of wife-battering was authored by Del Martin (1976), who organized and chaired the National Organization for Women task force on wife-battering. The third factor postulated by Straus was the decline of the consensus model of society employed by social scientists, and the ensuing challenge by those advancing a conflict or social action model.

Perhaps a fourth factor should be added. Someone had to demonstrate that research on family violence could be conducted. Researchers commencing projects in the early 1970s were constantly told that reliable and valid research on domestic violence could not be carried out. Investigators were reminded that they would literally have to ask, "Have you stopped beating your wife?" Early studies, such as those by O'Brien (1971), Levinger (1966), Straus (1971), and Steinmetz (1971), demonstrated that research could be done (using nonclinical samples) and outlined appropriate methods and sampling strategies for conducting research on domestic violence.

THE EXTENT OF FAMILY VIOLENCE[1]

As stated earlier, although violence between family members was largely hidden behind the closed doors of the home, resulting in a general lack of awareness of the seriousness and extent of domestic violence, there were various scattered data suggesting that the family was far more violent than either the public or professionals realized.

Physical Punishment

One of the more widespread and better documented forms of family violence is also the form that is most controversial to label "violent." General social surveys indicate that physical punishment is used by 84 to 97 percent of all parents at some time in their children's lives (Blumberg, 1964; Bronfenbrenner, 1958; Erlanger, 1974; Stark and McEvoy, 1970). While these studies do not define spankings as violent, and while they lack detailed analysis on such aspects as age-specific rates, they do illustrate that it is parent-to-child hitting that is perhaps the most widely practiced and socially accepted form of family violence.

Violence toward children does not cease when the children are old enough to walk, talk, and reason with. Four different studies of college and university students found that half of the parents of the students threatened or used physical punishment on their children while the students were seniors in high school (Straus, 1971; Steinmetz, 1971; Mulligan, 1977). The most recent of these studies reported that 8 percent of the students questioned reported that they had been "physically injured" by their parents during the last year they lived at home before entering college (Mulligan, 1977).

Child Abuse

Various techniques have been used in attempts to achieve an accurate estimate of child abuse in the United States. In 1967, Gil (1970) conducted a nationwide inventory of reported cases of child abuse (before, however, all 50 states had enacted mandatory reporting laws). He found 6,000 confirmed cases of child abuse. Gil also reported on an opinion survey which asked a representative sample of 1,520 individuals if they had knowledge of families where incidents of child abuse had occurred. Forty-five, or 3 percent of the sample, reported knowledge of 48 different incidents. Extrapolating this number to a national population of 110 million adults, Gil estimated that between 2.53 and 4.07 million children were abused the year prior to his study, or between 13.3 and 21.4 incidents per 1,000 persons in the United States. Gil's data were analyzed by Light (1974) to correct for possible instances where the same abuse incidents were known by more than one person. Light's refined estimate of child abuse was 500,000 abused children in the United States during the survey year.

Numerous other investigators have tried to estimate how many children are physically abused each year. Nagi (1975) surveyed community agencies which had contact with abused children. He estimated 167,000 cases of child abuse are reported each year, while an additional 91,000 cases go unreported. De-Francis (U.S. Senate, 1973) estimated that there are 30,000 to 40,000 truly abused children each year. Fontana (1973) placed the figure as high as 1.5 million children.

As we stated earlier, it is difficult to find consistent and precise definitions of child abuse in the literature. Moreover, as Nagi (1975) found, many cases of abuse go unrecognized and unreported. Thus, official reports of child abuse only hint at the true incidence.

Data on the number of children who are killed by their parents are equally varied and suspect. *Pediatric News* (1975) suggested that a child is killed each day (the yearly total would then be 365), while testimony before the U.S. Senate placed the figure at closer to 5,000 (1973). It is likely that numerous incidents of child murder are erroneously recorded as accidents, just as many instances of child abuse are recorded as accidents (Newberger et al., 1977).

Homicide

Homicide (with the exception of the murder of children noted above) is the one aspect of intrafamily violence on which there are reasonably reliable data (Steinmetz and Straus, 1974). Perhaps this is because this is a crime, and it leaves physical evidence which cannot be ignored in the same way that other incidents of family violence can be overlooked (Steinmetz and Straus, 1974). Researchers generally report that intrafamilial homicide accounts for between 20 and 40 percent of all homicides (Curtis, 1974).

Assault

Data on assault are more difficult to locate and interpret given the tradition of police departments to record domestic violence under the heading of domestic calls or domestic disturbances. In one study, aggravated assaults between husbands and wives made up 11 percent of all reported assaults (Pittman and

Handy, 1964), while another report indicated that husband-wife assaults constituted 52 percent of assaults in Detroit (Boudouris, 1971).

Applicants for Divorce

Studies of couples applying for divorce also provided some early data on the extent of husband-wife violence. Levinger (1966) found 22 percent of the middle-class and 40 percent of the working-class applicants for divorce whom he interviewed discussed "physical violence" as a major complaint. O'Brien (1971) reported that 17 percent of the couples he interviewed spontaneously mentioned violent behavior in their marriages.

Other Research on Family Violence

A survey conducted for the U.S. National Commission on the Causes and Prevention of Violence found one in four men and one out of six women stated that they approved of a husband hitting his wife under certain conditions (Stark and McEvoy, 1970). Other investigations on nonrepresentative samples reported rates of actual violence. Fifty-four percent of 80 individuals interviewed by Gelles (1974) mentioned at least one incident of husband-wife violence in their marriages. Steinmetz (1971) and Straus (1974a; 1974c) reported that 16 percent of the students they surveyed knew of one incident of violence between their parents during the last year the students lived in the home. Steinmetz's (1977c) survey of a probability sample of couples in New Castle, Delaware, revealed that 12 percent of those surveyed reported hitting a spouse with a hard object, while 22 percent reported that one partner had hit the other with his or her hand at least once in the marriage. Overall, 60 percent of the couples reported at least one violent episode in the marriage.

A National Survey of Family Violence

While each of the above-mentioned studies offers a clue to the actual level of intrafamily violence, and while the sum of the research suggests that the American family is a violent institution, the studies collectively and individually suffer from numerous methodological problems. Definitional problems, small or nonrepresentative samples, and reliance on official data all limit the generalizability, reliability, and validity of the findings. Worse, some publications offer estimates of the extent of one or all types of family violence based on no data whatsoever!

One study that was based on a nationally representative sample of families and that used a standard nominal and operational definition of violence was conducted by Straus et al. (1980). The nominal definition of violence was: "An act carried out with the intention, or perceived intention of physically hurting another person." This definition includes spankings and shoving as well as other forms of behavior that do not typically lead to injury. These investigators based their estimates of violence and abuse on self-reports of a nationally representative sample of 2,143 individual family members who responded to Straus's (1979b) Conflict Tactics Scale measure of violence.

Parent-to-Child Violence/Child Abuse

The national survey yielded an incidence rate of 3.8 percent of American children 3 to 17 years of age who were victims of severe or abusive violence each year (see Table 4.1). Projected to the 46 million children 3 to 17 who lived with both parents during the year of the survey, this meant that between 1.5 and 2 million children were abused by their parents (Gelles, 1978; Straus et al., 1980).

Marital Violence and Spouse Abuse

Focusing on violence between marital partners, the investigators report that 16 percent of those surveyed reported some kind of physical violence between spouses during the year of the survey, while 28 percent of those interviewed reported marital violence at some point in the marriage (Straus, 1978; Straus et al., 1980).

In terms of acts of violence that could be considered wife-beating, the national study revealed that 3.8 percent of American women were victims of abusive violence during the twelve months prior to the interview (see Table 4.2).

The same survey found that 4.6 percent of the wives admitted or were reported by their husbands as having engaged in violence which was included in

TABLE 4.1   Types of Parent-to-Child Violence (N = 1,146)

	Occurrence in Past Year (percentages)				
Incident	*Once*	*Twice*	*More Than Twice*	*Total*	*Occurrence Ever*
Threw something	1.3	1.8	2.3	5.4	9.6
Pushed/grabbed/shoved	4.3	9.0	18.5	31.8	46.4
Slapped or spanked	5.2	9.4	43.6	58.2	71.0
Kicked/bit/hit with fist	0.7	0.8	1.7	3.2	7.7
Hit with something	1.0	2.6	9.8	13.4	20.0
Beat up	0.4	0.3	0.6	1.3	4.2
Threatened with knife/gun	0.1	0.0	0.0	0.1	2.8
Used knife/gun	0.1	0.0	0.0	0.1	2.9

SOURCE: Richard J. Gelles, "Violence Towards Children in the United States," *American Journal of Orthopsychiatry,* 1978, 48 (October), p. 586. Reprinted, with permission, from the AMERICAN JOURNAL OF ORTHOPSYCHIATRY: copyright 1978 by the American Orthopsychiatric Association, Inc.
NOTE: On some items, there were a few responses omitted, but figures for all incidents represent at least 1,140 families.

TABLE 4.2   Comparison of Husband and Wife Violence Rates (in percentages)

| | Incidence Rate | | Frequency* | | | |
| | | | Mean | | Median | |
	H	W	H	W	H	W
Wife-Beating and Husband-Beating (N to R)	3.8	4.6	8.0	8.9	2.4	3.0
Overall Violence Index (K to R)	12.1	11.6	8.8	10.1	2.5	3.0
K. Threw something at spouse	2.8	5.2	5.5	4.5	2.2	2.0
L. Pushed, grabbed, shoved spouse	10.7	8.3	4.2	4.6	2.0	2.1
M. Slapped spouse	5.1	4.6	4.2	3.5	1.6	1.9
N. Kicked, bit, or hit with fist	2.4	3.1	4.8	4.6	1.9	2.3
O. Hit or tried to hit with something	2.2	3.0	4.5	7.4	2.0	3.8
P. Beat up spouse	1.1	0.6	5.5	3.9	1.7	1.4
Q. Threatened with knife or gun	0.4	0.6	4.6	3.1	1.8	2.0
R. Used a knife or gun	0.3	0.2	5.3	1.8	1.5	1.5

SOURCE: From Murray A. Straus, "Wife Beating: How Common and Why?" *Victimology,* 1978, 2(3/4), p. 446. Reprinted with permission.
*For those who engaged in each act (i.e., omits those with scores of zero).

the researchers' Husband Abuse Index. As stated earlier, this piece of data, as reported by Steinmetz (1978a) in her article on "battered husbands," set off a major controversy in the study of family violence in the 1970s. Steinmetz was accused by her critics (see Pleck et al., 1978) of having misstated and misrepresented the data. While there were significant political overtones to the debate and discussion, it became apparent that the presentation of only the incidence data did not fully represent the different experiences and consequences of violence undergone by men as opposed to women.

Violence Between Siblings

It is rare that someone considers a fistfight between siblings as violence. Stark and McEvoy (1970) found that 70 percent of a nationally representative sample of adults thought that it was important for a boy to have a few fistfights when growing up. The acceptance of hitting between siblings is underscored by a Bell System television commercial which, while extolling the virtues of how long distance telephone calls can bring families together, included the following line: "When we were little we fought like cats and dogs, just like normal kids, but I wouldn't let anyone hit him but me."

Given this attitude, it is not surprising that violence between siblings is *the most common form of intrafamilial violence.* Of the 733 children who lived with siblings in the national sample, four out of five were involved in at least one violent act in the survey year. Twenty percent of the respondents reported that one child "beat up" a sibling in the previous twelve months. Kicking, biting, or punching between siblings occurred at least once in 53 percent of the homes. Three children in 1,000 used a gun or a knife on a sibling in the previous

12 months. Extrapolating this figure to the 36 million children aged 3 to 17 years old who live with a sibling, 109,000 American children used a gun or a knife against a sib in the survey year.

Child-to-Parent Violence

Another form of family violence rarely mentioned in public discussions of family violence, and virtually ignored by researchers (with the recent exceptions of Steinmetz, 1978c, and Harbin and Madden, 1979), is children's use of violence against their parents. Subjects in the national survey were asked to report on whether their children had ever used violence against them. Sixteen percent of the parents reported they had been struck at least once during the previous twelve months. Nearly one in ten parents (9.7 percent) reported that their children had used a form of violence which we classified as "abusive" at least once in the survey year. These figures, however, tend to exaggerate the extent of parent abuse, since much of the so-called abusive violence (such as kicking, biting, punching) was carried out by children 3 or 4 years old. Clearly, while these acts could possibly hurt the adult, as carried out by preschoolers they probably would not result in injury; thus, by the definition used in the study, they could not be considered abusive. A better illustration of the extent of abusive violence directed toward parents are the data on abusive violence used by teenagers. More than 3 teenagers (aged 15 to 17 years of age) in 100 (3.5 percent) were reported as kicking, biting, punching, hitting with an object, beating up, threatening, or using a gun or a knife against a parent in the survey year. Nearly as many (2.9 percent) of those children between the ages of 10 and 17 used one of these forms of violence at least once.

Summary

While the national survey met the objective of basing an estimate of the incidence of family violence on a representative sample, there were methodological difficulties with the survey. Most obvious, the data were based on self-reports and it is probable that they underrepresent the true level of family violence. Second, no data on violence toward children under 3 years of age were provided, and there were no data on parental violence in single-person families (see Straus et al., 1980, for a complete explanation of the methodology). But even with the methodological problems, the study fulfilled the objective of exploding the myth that family violence is infrequent and rare in the society.

National Crime Survey Report

A second source of data on the extent and patterns of domestic violence is the National Crime Survey. The National Crime Survey estimates the amount of crime, whether reported or unreported to the police, committed against persons aged 12 and over and against households.

The publication, "Intimate Victims: A Study of Violence Among Friends and Relatives" (U.S. Department of Justice, 1980), reported on events occurring between 1973 and 1976 as derived from semiannual interviews with approximately 136,000 occupants of a representative sample of some 60,000 housing units in the United States. The key findings of the National Crime Survey were:

(1) There were about 3.8 million incidents of violence among intimates in the four-year period of the survey. Nearly a third (1.2 million) were committed by offenders related to the victims.

(2) More than half (55 percent) of incidents of intimate violence went unreported to the police.

(3) An analysis of the single-offender incidents revealed 1,055,000 incidents between relatives. Of this number, 616,000 (58 percent) were between spouses or ex-spouses; 57,000 victims (5 percent) were parents; 38,000 victims (4 percent) were the offender's own children; 76,000 victims (7 percent) were attacked by siblings; and the remaining 268,000 victims (27 percent) were other relatives. Thus, the most common form of violence between relatives was interspousal.

(4) Of the single-offender incidents, 80.9 percent of the spousal victims reported injuries, the most common being bruises, black eyes, cuts, scratches, or swellings. Of the parent victims, 89 percent reported injuries; 79.6 percent of the children reported injuries; 77.3 percent of the siblings reported injuries; and 70.4 percent of the other relatives reported injuries.

(5) More than half of the spouse victims (56.8 percent), child victims (58.8 percent), sibling victims (53.6 percent), and other relative victims (56.2 percent) reported their victimization to the police. Less than 50 percent of the parent victims (47.3 percent) reported their situation to the police. Of all the victims of intimate violence, relatives were most likely to make police reports.

The National Crime Survey offers an interesting source of data on violence among family members over 12 years of age. The report is limited in that no insight into violence toward children under 12 years of age can be gleaned, nor do we have data on sibling or parental violence for children under 12. Nevertheless, the report does offer new insights into the pervasiveness of family violence and offers data on patterns of violence that traditionally have been ignored (sibling violence and violence by children toward parents).

Violence Between Unmarried Intimates

The earliest studies of family violence often explained the high incidence of intrafamily violence by reference to the phrase "the marriage license is a hitting license" (Straus, 1974b, 1976; Gelles, 1974). This phrase implies that (1) there is something special about the institution or organization of family and marriage that leads to the high risk of violence, and (2) married intimates are more violent toward one another than unmarried intimates.

Later research found that intimate violence neither is confined to legally married couples nor is necessarily more common among those who are married compared to cohabitating couples.

Makepeace (1981) analyzed questionnaires completed by 202 students enrolled in introductory sociology classes at a midwestern university. More than one-fifth (21.2 percent) reported direct involvement in one incident of violence with a person whom they were dating. Students reported direct experience with choking (7.4 percent), assault with a weapon (7.9 percent), and punching (23.3 percent), as well as less severe forms of violence.

Yllo and Straus (1978) examined data from the national family violence survey (Straus et al., 1980) and found that cohabitating couples reported more violence than married couples. However, cohabitators who were over 30, had been together for more than 10 years, had high incomes, and were divorced had very low rates of violence.

FACTORS ASSOCIATED WITH FAMILY VIOLENCE

Early research and writing on family violence was dominated by the psychopathological model (Gelles, 1973; Spinetta and Rigler, 1972). Child-abuse researchers discounted social factors as playing any causal role in violence toward children (see, for example, Steele and Pollock, 1968, 1974). Rather, the explanation was thought to lie in personality or character disorders of individual battering parents (Steele and Pollock, 1968; Galdston, 1965; Zalba, 1971). The exception to this point of view was Gil's (1970) multidimensional model of child abuse, which placed heavy emphasis on factors such as inequality and poverty. The rare reports on wife abuse portrayed both the battering husband and his victim as suffering from personality disorders (Schultz, 1960; Snell et al., 1964).

The similarity of theoretical focus in early studies of family violence was probably a product of the similar methods of procedure employed by investigators. Nearly all published work on child abuse and family violence was based on clinical samples (such as hospitalized children and patients of psychiatrists or social workers) or officially reported cases of child abuse. Early studies of family violence typically failed to employ control or comparison groups, based conclusions on post-hoc explanation, and were based on small, nonrepresentative samples (Spinetta and Rigler, 1972).

Another methodological problem concerned ways of operationally defining child abuse which tend to overlook the fact that there is bias in the labeling process (Gelles, 1975a). Newberger et al. (1977) report that lower-class and minority children seen with injuries in a private hospital are more likely than middle- and upper-class children to be labeled as abused. Turbett and O'Toole (1980), using an experimental design, found that physicians are more likely to label minority children or lower-class children abused (a mock case was presented to the physicians, with the injury remaining constant and the race or class of the child varied). Giovannoni and Becerra (1979) found that attitudes to and definitions of child abuse varied by professional group. In all, operationally defining child abuse as those children publicly labeled abused produces the major problem of confounding the factors causally associated with abuse, with factors related to susceptibility or vulnerability to having an injury diagnosed as abuse.

Those studying wife abuse frequently develop similar operational definitions. A number of studies of battered women operationally defined victims of wife abuse as women who publicly admitted they were battered. This could range from responding to an advertisement placed in a popular periodical asking for battered women to complete a questionnaire (as was done by Prescott and Letko, 1977) to interviewing women in a shelter for battered women (as was done by Walker, 1979, and Dobash and Dobash, 1979). Another technique was to identify families through police records or social service agency files (Gelles, 1974). Again, since women who answer an advertisement, flee to a shelter, or become known to public and private agencies are but a nonrepresentative portion of the total number of abused wives, such techniques of operationally defining abuse produced systematic bias in the study results—ranging from lack of generalizability to confounding of variables.

While the methodological shortcomings of early research on family violence have not been completely overcome or solved, the conceptual models used to examine family violence expanded in later research. Research on intraindividual correlates with family violence was augmented with investigations which studied the social factors thought to be related to violence.

The remainder of this section reviews the state of knowledge about factors related to family violence. Key empirical studies as well as reviews of the literature are drawn upon to review those factors that have been found to be related to family violence.

Gender and Violence

Research on child abuse frequently reports that mothers are at least as abusive toward their children, if not more so, than are fathers (Bennie and Sclare, 1969; Steele and Pollock, 1974; Gil, 1970; Parke and Collmer, 1975; Straus et al., 1980). The simple explanation for mothers' violence is that they spend more time with their children than do fathers. The actual explanation of mothers' slightly greater use of violence is probably more complex. First, the mother role is invested with the greatest degree of responsibility for child rearing. Second, because mothers are viewed as more responsible, and child rearing is such a central aspect of the female family role, children are more likely to interfere with mothers' plans and self-concepts than with fathers' activities or sense of self. Mothers, then, are the parents with the highest degree of role commitment to parenting, the greatest role investment, and thus, probably experience the most stress and frustration in raising children.

As we stated earlier, there is considerable debate over the comparative rates of husband-to-wife violence and wife-to-husband violence. Dobash and Dobash (1979) state that women are the disproportionate victims of family violence. Steinmetz (1978a) presents data which show women are far from passive victims of violence in the home. Many women do attack their husbands and kill their husbands, albeit most often in self-defense (Pleck et al., 1978).

In terms of sibling violence, boys were found to be slightly more violent than girls (83 percent compared to 74 percent) in the national survey of family violence (Straus et al., 1980). More interestingly, all male sibships were found to have the highest rates of sibling violence (67 percent), followed by mixed-sex sibships (52 percent), with all female sibships being the least violent—40 percent (Straus et al., 1980).

The data on the relationship between gender and family violence are of interest because violence in the home, especially violence toward children, is the exception to the rule in studies of criminal violence that find males to be the predominant offenders and victims of violence outside of the home.

The Cycle of Violence

One of the consistent conclusions of domestic-violence research is that individuals who have experienced violent and abusive childhoods are more likely to grow up to become child and spouse abusers than individuals who experienced little or no violence in their childhood years (Spinetta and Rigler, 1971; Parke and Collmer, 1975; Kempe et al., 1962; Straus, 1979a; Steinmetz, 1977c; Gayford, 1975; Owens and Straus, 1975; Byrd, 1979; Gelles, 1974; Flynn, 1975). Steinmetz (1977c) reports that even less severe forms of violence are passed on from generation to generation.

Data from the national survey of family violence also lend support to the hypothesis that "violence begets violence" (Straus, 1979a; Straus et al., 1980). Subjects in the national survey were asked about their own parents' use of physical punishment when the subjects were 13 years old. Those who said their mothers had used physical punishment twice or more a year reported, as parents, a child abuse rate of 18.5. This rate is 57 percent greater than the rate (11.8) for parents in the survey who had experienced less physical punishment at age 13. Physical punishment by fathers made less of a difference. Subjects whose fathers punished them more than twice a year had a child-abuse rate of 16.7 percent compared to 13.2 percent for those whose fathers struck them less than twice a year.

Observing parents hit each other was also found to be related to violence as an adult. Being a son of a father who hit his wife is associated with a 39 percent higher rate of child abuse as opposed to being a son of a father who did not hit his wife (13.3 compared to 9.7). Daughters who remembered their fathers hitting their mothers had a rate of abuse of 19.7, compared to 17.4 for women who remembered no hitting between mother and father.

Last, experiencing violence as a teenager was related to marital violence reported by subjects. Husbands who were categorized as being reared in the most violent homes had a rate of wife abuse 600 times greater than husbands reared in the least violent homes.

Socioeconomic Status

Early research on child and wife abuse claimed that social factors were not related to acts of domestic abuse. Yet, the same articles that made these claims offered empirical evidence that abuse was more prevalent among those with low socioeconomic status (Gelles, 1973). Later research supported the hypothesis that domestic violence is more prevalent in low-socioeconomic-status families (Byrd, 1979; Gelles, 1974; Levinger, 1966; Gayford, 1975; Maden and Wrench, 1977; Elmer, 1967; Gil, 1970; Parke and Collmer, 1975; Straus et al., 1980). This conclusion, however, does not mean that domestic violence is confined to lower-class households. Investigators reporting the differential distribution of violence are frequently careful to point out that child and spouse abuse can be found in families across the spectrum of socioeconomic status (Steinmetz, 1978b).

Race

Examinations of the relationship between race and family violence have yielded mixed results. Data from official reports of child abuse indicate child abuse is greater among blacks than whites (Johnson, 1974; Thompson et al., 1971; Gil, 1970). Other studies have reported that blacks do not have a significantly higher rate of child abuse and violence than whites (Billingsley, 1969; Young, 1964; Elmer, 1967). Byrd's review of research on interspousal violence concluded that race was not related to intersexual assault in the home (1979— citing Gelles, 1974; Martin, 1976; Ball, 1977; Parker and Schumacher, 1977; and Gaquin, 1977-1978).

Data from the national survey of family violence (Straus et al., 1980) indicate no difference in the rates of abusive violence toward children among black and white families (15 percent in black families, 14 percent in white families). Cazenave and Straus (1978), in a more detailed examination of the national survey data, concluded that the aid and support, especially child care, provided by black extended family kin seem to reduce the risk of abusive violence directed toward children. A caution in interpreting these data and explanations must be added. The national family violence survey included *only intact families* in the sample. Thus, single-parent families were not included in the study. The rates of abusive violence in all black families may be higher than the rates in white households.

The recently completed *National Study of the Incidence and Severity of Child Abuse and Neglect* (Westat, Inc., 1980) found that black children were *underrepresented* in all child-abuse categories. Even when income was controlled for, the rate of abuse was lower in black than in white families (except for the highest income group).

The national family violence survey found that rates of abusive violence among couples, toward wives, and toward husbands was higher in black than in white families. Black couples reported a rate of abusive violence more than double the rate for whites (11 percent as opposed to 5 percent). Black males were more than three times more abusive toward their wives than white males (11 percent as opposed to 3 percent). Finally, black females' rates of abusive violence were exactly twice the rate for white wives (8 percent as opposed to 4 percent).

While the picture of the relationship between race and family violence is far from clear, it does appear that, in terms of marital violence, the differences between blacks and whites parallel differences found in studies of criminal violence. The two most recent national surveys of violence toward children and reported child abuse are exceptions to the trend of higher rates of criminal violence among blacks.

Stress

A third consistent finding of most domestic-violence research is that family violence rates are directly related to social stress in families (Gil, 1970; Maden and Wrench, 1977; Parke and Collmer, 1975; Straus et al., 1980). In addition to reporting that violence is related to general measures of stress, investigators report associations between various forms of family violence and specific stressful situations and conditions, such as *unemployment or part-time employment of males* (Gil, 1970; Parke and Collmer, 1975; Prescott and Letko, 1977; Straus, Gelles, and Steinmetz, 1980); *financial problems* (Prescott and Letko, 1977); *pregnancy,* in the case of wife abuse (Gelles, 1975b; Eisenberg and Micklow, 1977); and *single-parent family,* in the case of child abuse (Maden and Wrench, 1977).

Social Isolation

A fourth major finding in the study of both child and spouse abuse is that social isolation raises the risk that there will be severe violence directed at children or between spouses (Gil, 1970; Maden and Wrench, 1977; Parke and Collmer, 1975; Gelles, 1974; Ball, 1977; Borland, 1976).

In addition to the finding that these four general social factors are related to violence both toward children and between spouses, there have been studies directed at identifying specific factors related to child *or* spouse abuse.

In the case of violence toward children, some of the factors are larger-than-average family size (Light, 1974; Gil, 1970; Maden and Wrench, 1977; Parke and Collmer, 1975; Elmer, 1967; Straus et al., 1980); low birth weight of the child (Parke and Collmer, 1975); prematurity of the child (Elmer, 1967; Maden and Wrench, 1977; Parke and Collmer, 1975; Steele and Pollock, 1974); and lack of attachment between mother and child, sometimes as a result of low birth weight or prematurity (Klaus and Kennell, 1976). In addition, females are found to be slightly more likely to abuse their children (Maden and Wrench, 1977), and males are slightly more likely to be the victims of child abuse (Gil, 1970; Maden and Wrench, 1977). Last, researchers have proposed that children who are handicapped, retarded, developmentally delayed, or perceived by their parents as "different" are at greater risk of being abused (Friedrich and Boriskin, 1976; Gil, 1970; Steinmetz, 1978b).

Students of wife abuse have reported higher rates of abuse when husband and wife report low job satisfaction of the husband (Prescott and Letko, 1977), when the husband has no religious affiliation (Prescott and Letko, 1977), and when there are alcohol problems (Byrd, 1979; Gelles, 1974; Gayford, 1975; Eisenberg and Micklow, 1977).

Finally, investigators have pointed out that there is an interrelationship between spouse abuse and child abuse (Rounsaville and Weissman, 1977-1978; Straus et al., 1980).

Caveats for Understanding
Social Factors and Family Violence

While there appears to be consistent support for the existence and persistence of the associations between family violence and the four major factors and many of the minor factors, it is important to point out some caveats in accepting these findings uncritically.

For example, in the case of the proposed cross-generational pattern of violence, Potts and Herzberger (1979) explain that the hypothesis relating abuse as a child with adult abusive behavior is overstated. Potts and Herzberger argue that while some authors state that there is near-unanimity among researchers that abusing parents were themselves abused or neglected physically or emotionally (Spinetta and Rigler, 1972), the evidence on which this claim is based must be examined more critically. First, Potts and Herzberger note that some publications that are widely cited as supporting the cycle-of-violence hypothesis actually present no empirical data (see, for example, Curtis, 1963, as cited in Parke and Collmer, 1975, and Spinetta and Rigler, 1972). Where data exist, they typically are based on small case studies. Other papers present data, but the study designs included no comparison group(s), so that no actual evidence of a statistical association exists. Finally, Potts and Herzberger note that where reasonably reliable data are presented (for example, Straus, 1979a), the actual magnitude of the association is modest compared to the claims made by many researchers for the importance of violent childhood socialization in explaining later adult abusive acts.

Potts and Herzberger (1979) identify problems that are applicable to other areas of study in family violence research. One general problem is what Houghton (1979) calls the Woozle Effect (based on a Winnie-the-Pooh story, Milne, 1926). The Woozle Effect begins when one investigator reports a finding, such as Gelles's (1974) report that 54 percent of his sample of families reported one instance of conjugal violence in their marriages. The investigator may provide qualifications to the finding; in Gelles's case it was that the sample was small, nongeneralizable, and the sampling technique was designed to draw cases from police and social service agency files that would ensure that a large portion of the sample would have engaged in spousal violence. In the Woozle Effect, a second investigator will then cite the first study's data, but without the qualifications (such as done by Straus, 1974b). Others will then cite both reports and the qualified data gain the status of generalizable "truth." In the case of the Gelles statistic, by the time Langley and Levy cited the figure in 1977, it had become so widely cited that Langley and Levy used it to extrapolate an incidence estimate for all married women and concluded that 28 million women were abused each year!

A final problem, indirectly noted by Potts and Herzberger (1979), is that evidence will accumulate for an association without any measures of the magnitude of that association. Within a short amount of time, the fact that many researchers find an association between a factor and family violence will come to be interpreted as meaning that this factor is *strongly* associated with family violence. While most investigators find socioeconomic status, stress, isolation, and history of violence statistically related to family violence, the associations have in large part, both for each individual factor and for the factors combined, been relatively modest.

THEORIES OF INTRAFAMILY VIOLENCE

Family violence has been approached from three general theoretical levels of analysis: (1) the intraindividual level of analysis, or the psychiatric model; (2) the social-psychological level of analysis; and (3) the sociological or sociocultural level of analysis (Burgess and Conger, 1978; Justice and Justice, 1976; Gelles and Straus, 1979; Steinmetz, 1978b; Parke and Collmer, 1975).

The Psychiatric Model. The psychiatric model focuses on the offender's personality characteristics as the chief determinants of violence and abuse. The psychiatric model includes theoretical approaches that link mental illness, alcohol and drug abuse, and other intraindividual phenomena to acts of family violence.

The Social-Psychological Model. The second approach assumes that violence and abuse can be best understood by a careful examination of the external environmental factors that impact on the family. In addition, this model considers which everyday family interactions are precursors to violence. Theoretical approaches that examine stress, the transmission of violence from one generation to another, and family interaction patterns fit into the social-psychological model. Such general theories as learning theory, frustration-aggression theory, exchange theory, and attribution theory approach violence from the social-psychological level of analysis (Gelles and Straus, 1979).

The Sociocultural Model. The sociocultural, or sociological, model provides a macro-level analysis of family violence. Violence is considered in light of socially structured inequality and cultural attitudes and norms about violence and family relations. Structural-functional theory and subculture-of-violence theory are two of the better-known theoretical approaches that come under the sociocultural level of analysis.

Within the three general theoretical levels of analysis, a number of specific theories of violence have been applied to violence in the family. Gelles and Straus (1979) inventoried fifteen specific theories of violence and discussed how they could be applied to domestic assault. The distinctive contribution of each of the fifteen theories is summarized in Table 4.3.

Two of the fifteen theories were developed to explain specifically the phenomenon of family violence. In addition to these two, there have been at least three additional theories developed in the course of the last decade of intensive research on family violence. The following section briefly reviews these five theories.

Five Theories of Family Violence

Resource Theory

Goode's Resource Theory of Intrafamily Violence (1971) was the first theoretical approach applied explicitly to family violence. Goode states that all social systems "rest to some degree on force or its threat." Goode explains that within a social system, the greater the resources a person can command, the more force he or she can muster. However, the more resources a person can command, the less that person will *actually deploy* violence. Thus, violence is

(Continued on p. 228)

TABLE 4.3 Summary of the Distinctive Contributions of Selected Theories of Violence

Theory	Contribution
Psychopathology[a]	The fact that only a very small proportion of mentally ill persons are violent forces a search for the social factors that lead this minority to be violent.
Alcohol and drugs[a]	Has the same theoretical status as psychopathology, i.e., little evidence of any direct link to violence. What one does under the influence of alcohol and other drugs must be explained by reference to social-psychological and sociocultural factors. However, alcohol use is of great practical importance because of the frequency with which it is associated with violence in our society.
Frustration-aggression	Also occupies a theoretical position similar to that of psychopathology because the theory, as generally conceived, does not explain the process by which frustration is linked to aggression, except by positing an innate aggressive drive in response to frustration. However, when viewed as a special case of social learning theory, it explains why the tendency to respond to frustration by aggression is so common. It helps explain family violence because the family is the focus of high personal involvement and of high frustration.
Social learning	Asserts that human aggression and violence are learned conduct and specifies the learning process, especially direct experience and observing the behavior of others. Explains both the variation between persons and the variation between situations in the tendency to respond aggressively by reference to prior experience, reinforcement patterns, and cognitive processes.
Self-attitude	Asserts that in a society, culture, or group that values violence, persons of low self-esteem may seek to bolster their image in the eyes of others and themselves by carrying out violent acts. Explains the propensity to violence of those for whom society makes it difficult to achieve an adequate level of self-esteem.
"Clockwork Orange"	Asserts that there is an optimum level of stress or tension and that if the life circumstances do not provide this level, aggression and violence will occur as a means of moving toward the optimum level. Explains the "senseless" aggression and violence that can occur in highly integrated, smoothly functioning groups, such as an apparently model family.
Symbolic interaction	Specifies the process by which a self-image and identity of a person as "violent" are formed, and the process by which violent acts acquire individual and socially shared meaning. Explains the origin and maintenance of the structure of meaning that is necessary for all human social behavior, including violence.

—continued on the following page

225

TABLE 4.3 Continued

Theory	Contribution
Exchange	Asserts that interaction in marriage is governed by partners seeking to maximize rewards and minimize costs in their exchange relations; that actors expect rewards to be proportional to investments ("distributive justice"); and that costs and rewards are judged in the light of alternatives. Explains the growth of resentment, anger, and hostility when the principle of distributive justice is violated.
Attribution	Specifies the process used by actors to impute the dispositional state (motivations) of others. Explains how the structure of family relations is such that there is a high probability of malevolent intent being attributed to the actions of other family members, thereby setting in motion an escalating cycle of resentment and aggression.
Functional	Asserts that violence can be important for maintaining the adaptability of the family to changing circumstances and hence important to its survival. Explains why violence persists in human association, including the family.
Culture of violence	Asserts that social values and norms provide meaning and direction to violent acts and thus facilitate or bring about violence in situations specified by these norms and values. Explains why some sectors of society or different societies are more violent than others; essentially when they have cultural rules that legitimize or require violence.
Structural	Asserts that social groups differ in respect to their typical levels of stress, deprivation, and frustration and in the resources at their disposal to deal with these stresses. Explains why different sectors of society or different families are more violent than others: because they combine high stress with low resources. [b]

General systems	Describes the cybernetic and morphogenic processes that characterize the use of violence in family interaction. Explains the way in which violence is managed and stabilized.
Conflict	Asserts that fundamental causal factors leading to violence are the different "interests" of family members. Explains why there is conflict and violence in one of the most integrated and solitary of human groups.
Resource	Asserts that violence is one of the resources that individuals or collectivities can use to maintain or advance their interests. By pointing to the range of other resources available to a person or group, explains the circumstances under which violence is used: essentially when these other resources are not effective.

SOURCE: From Richard J. Gelles and Murray A. Straus, "Determinants of Violence in the Family: Toward a Theoretical Integration," in W.R. Burr, R. Hill, F.I. Nye, and I.L. Reiss (Eds.), *Contemporary Theories about the Family* (New York: Free Press), pp. 568-569. Copyright© 1979 by The Free Press, a Division of Macmillan Publishing Co., Inc. Reprinted with permission.

[a] The statements in this table about psychopathology and alcohol as causes of violence need further explication. In this space the best we can do is illustrate our reasoning. In respect to alcohol use as a cause of violence, we hold that the behavior of intoxicated persons reflects social definitions of what one does when drunk or high. In American society, actions of drunk or high individuals are typically viewed as behavior that the individual cannot control; thus drunk or high individuals are given a "time out" from normal social norms, and their behavior is viewed accordingly (Lang et al., 1975; Schachter and Singer, 1962; Washburn, 1961). Moreover, these definitions and normative statements vary from society to society and from sector to sector, as do the rates of alcohol and drug use. One must therefore have recourse to sociocultural factors to understand both the frequency and the nature of alcohol and drug use and the behavior associated with such use, and to social-psychological theories (especially social learning and symbolic interaction theories) to understand the aggressive and violent behavior of individuals under the influence of such drugs.

Our view of psychopathology as a cause of violence is directly parallel. Specifically, there is nothing known to be inherent in mental illness which leads the afflicted person to behave in an aggressive or violent way, except insofar as a person who is violent is labeled mentally ill. Rather, the behavior of mentally ill persons varies from society to society, from sector to sector of society, and according to the particular life circumstances of the afflicted person (Scheff, 1963).

[b] Also explains the emergence and maintenance of a culture of violence: When the structural conditions lead to violence as a characteristic mode of coping with the circumstances of a group, violence becomes codified in the form of values that justify and norms that simplify carrying out the violent acts. See Owens and Straus (1975).

used as a last resort when all other resources are insufficient or lacking. Applying this set of assumptions to the family, Goode explains that a husband who wants to be the dominant family member but has little education, job prestige, or income and lacks interpersonal skills may be likely to resort to violence to be the dominant person. Empirical data from O'Brien (1971) and Gelles (1974) support this theory.

General Systems Theory

The second theory developed to explain intrafamily violence was Straus's General Systems Theory (1973). Straus attempts to account for violence in the home by viewing the family as a purposive, goal-seeking, adaptive social system. Violence is viewed as a system product, or output, rather than an individual pathology. Straus specified "positive feedback" in the system, which can create an upward spiral of violence, and "negative feedback," which can maintain, dampen, or reduce the level of violence.

An Ecological Perspective

Garbarino (1977) proposed an "ecological model" to explain the complex nature of child maltreatment. The ecological, or human development approach, focuses on the progressive, mutual adaptation of organism and environment. Second, it focuses on the interactive and overlapping set of systems in which human development occurs. Third, the model considers "social habitability"— the question of environmental quality. Last, the model assesses the political, economic, and demographic factors that shape the quality of life for children and families. Garbarino identified cultural support for the use of physical force against children, and the inadequacy and inadequate use of family support systems as two necessary conditions for child maltreatment. In short, maltreatment is believed to arise out of a mismatch of parent to child and family to neighborhood and community.

An Evolutionary Perspective

Burgess (1979) proposed an evolutionary perspective for understanding child abuse. Burgess attempts to go beyond intraindividual or social-psychological levels of analysis to provide a model that can explain the current phenomenon of abuse as well as the socially patterned occurrence of abuse over time and across cultural groups. Using the concept of "parental investment," Burgess explains that in situations such as lack of bonding and parental uncertainty, the risk of child abuse would be increased (as has been found by investigators who report higher levels of abuse in families where the victims were stepchildren; Burgess and Conger, 1978). Burgess also proposes that an inadequate parenting resource base would decrease the probability of parental investment and thus raise the risk of abuse. Lack of parental resources would then explain the inverse relationship proposed between abuse and social class and the proposed positive relationship between family size and abuse. Last, Burgess (1979) points to problems with children that decrease parental investment and increase the risk of abuse—such as developmental problems, retardation, and Down's syndrome.

Patriarchy and Wife Abuse

Dobash and Dobash (1979) see the abuse of women as a unique phenomenon that has been obscured and overshadowed by what they refer to as the "narrow" focus on domestic violence. The Dobashes attempt to make the case that throughout history, violence has been systematically directed at women. Their central thesis is that economic and social processes operate directly and indirectly to support a patriarchal social order and family structure. Their central theoretical argument is that patriarchy leads to the subordination of women and contributes to a historical pattern of systematic violence directed against wives.

The Dobashes' theory, while perhaps the most macro-level approach to wife abuse, has the major drawback of being a theory that is essentially a single-factor (patriarchy) explanation of violence toward women.

LOOKING AHEAD

Zigler (1976), in reviewing the state of the art of child-abuse research and practice in 1974, equated the cumulative knowledge about the nature of child abuse to the 1940s knowledge base on the causes of mental illness. In some ways, Zigler may have been overly pessimistic, but in other ways he was perhaps overestimating the state of the art.

The development of knowledge about the nature of and causes of domestic criminal violence has been hampered by definitional problems, methodological inadequacies and errors, and failures in logic on the part of many investigators. We still have difficulty in precisely defining child abuse, wife abuse, and family violence. Controversy still surrounds estimates and research concerning the incidence and prevalence of domestic violence. Our knowledge about the causes of family violence is largely limited to research that is able to establish associations between psychological or sociological variables and family violence. The magnitude of the relationships, even those that are consistently found, are most often quite modest, although the magnitude is frequently inflated by reports on family violence that are more journalistic than social-scientific.

The theoretical work on family violence has been even more modest and primitive than the research on either incidence or associations of factors. The pattern of early research, that is, proposing theoretical models based on post-hoc examinations of data, still prevails. Few investigators attempt to establish a theoretical model and then test the model or propositions derived from the model. The work of Garbarino (1977) and Burgess (1979) speak to the kind of theoretical work needed.

While investigators have demonstrated that certain social factors are related to family violence and abuse, many of the associations found could be symmetrical. In other words, stress could lead to abuse or abuse could create family stress. A major gap in research in family violence is that there have been no longitudinal studies that can be used to reduce the number of plausible rival hypotheses concerning time order and causal direction.

Methodological Triangulation. There is a need for increased diversity of measurement instruments and data collection techniques to be used in the study of family violence. By and large, most research in the 1970s employed survey research designs and gathered data through questionnaires and interviews. Steinmetz's (1977c) use of daily diaries to record conflict and violence is a notable exception to this trend. Straus's (1979b) Conflict Tactics Scales, one of the only standardized measures of violence available, has been used and adapted in numerous investigations. It would be tragic if the field of family violence research changed from one "easy" research design (clinical case study of known abuse victims) to another easily available methodology (surveys using the CTS).

Cross-Cultural Research. Another shortcoming of current research on domestic violence is that it is largely confined to samples in the United States. Some research has been conducted in Great Britain (for example, Dobash and Dobash, 1979), and some in Canada, but the majority of all published work has been based on research carried out in the United States. There is a need to cast the net more widely and examine whether or not domestic violence occurs with less, equal, or greater frequency in other countries and in other societies. Much emphasis has been placed on the sociocultural explanation that there is considerable domestic violence in the United States because of the value our culture places on violence as a problem solver and a means of self-expression. We very much need research on domestic violence in other countries where the same norms and values are not present (such as Sweden) or other societies where the family is organized in a different fashion (for instance, hunting and gathering societies).

NOTE

1. Space precludes providing a complete and exhaustive reference list of articles and papers documenting each relationship. We have chosen to cite key studies and major review articles to document each relationship. The review articles (Maden and Wrench, 1977; Parke and Collmer, 1975; Byrd, 1979; Steinmetz, 1978b) should be consulted for the exhaustive documentation.

REFERENCES

Bakan, D. *Slaughter of the innocents: A study of the battered child phenomenon.* Boston: Beacon Press, 1971.

Ball, M. Issues of violence in family casework. *Social Casework,* 1977, 58(January), 3-12.

Bard, M. Family intervention police teams as a community mental health resource. *Journal of Criminal Law, Criminology, and Police Science,* 1969, 60(2), 247-250.

Bennie, A. B., and Sclare, A. B. The battered child syndrome. *American Journal of Psychiatry,* 1969, 125(January), 975-979.

Berk, S., and Loseke, D. "Handling" family violence: The situated determinants of police arrest in domestic disturbances. *Law and Society Review,* 1980, 15(2): 317-346.

Billingsley, A. Family functioning in the low income black community. *Casework,* 1969, 50, 563-572.

Blumberg, M. When parents hit out. *Twentieth Century,* 1964, 173(Winter), 39-44.

Borland, M. (Ed.). *Violence in the family.* Atlantic Highlands, NJ: Humanities Press, 1976.

Boudouris, J. Homicide and the family. *Journal of Marriage and the Family,* 1971, 33(November), 667-682.

Bronfenbrenner, U. Socialization and social class through time and space. In E. Maccoby, T. Newcomb, and E. Hartley (Eds.), *Readings in social psychology.* New York: Holt, Rinehart & Winston, 1958, 400-425.

Bruno v Maguire. New York Supreme Court, City of New York, Index No. 21946/76, consent decree.

Burgess, J. M., et al. Family size and family violence. Paper presented at the biannual meetings of the Southeastern Conference on Human Development, Atlanta, 1978.

Burgess, R. L. Family violence: Some implications from evolutionary biology. Paper presented at the annual meetings of the American Society of Criminology, Philadelphia, 1979.

Burgess, R. L., and Conger, R. D. Family interaction in abusive, neglectful, and normal families. *Child Development,* 1978, 49(December), 1163-1173.

Byrd, D. E. Intersexual assault: A review of empirical findings. Paper presented at the annual meetings of the Eastern Sociological Society, New York, 1979.

Calvert, R. Criminal and civil liability in husband-wife assaults. In S. Steinmetz and M. Straus (Eds.), *Violence in the family.* New York: Harper & Row, 1974, 88-90.

Cazenave, N. A., and Straus, M. A. The effect of social network embeddedness on black family violence attitudes and behavior: A search for potent support systems. Paper presented at the National Council on Family Relations Meetings, Philadelphia, October 19-22, 1978.

Curtis, G. C. Violence breeds violence—perhaps. *American Journal of Psychiatry,* 1963, 120, 386-387.

Curtis, L. *Criminal violence: National patterns and behavior.* Lexington, MA: D. C. Heath, 1974.

Davidson, T. *Conjugal crime: Understanding and changing the wifebeating pattern.* New York: Hawthorn Books, 1978.

DeMause, L. (Ed.). *The History of Childhood.* New York: Psychohistory Press, 1974.

DeMause, L. Our forebearers made childhood a nightmare. *Psychology Today,* 1975, 8(April), 85-87.

Dexter, L. A note on selective inattention in social science. *Social Problems,* 1958, 6(Fall), 176-182.

Dobash, R. E., and Dobash, R. *Violence against wives.* New York: Free Press, 1979.

Eisenberg, S. E., and Micklow, P. L. The assaulted wife: "Catch 22" revisited. *Women's Rights Law Reporter,* 1977, 3/4 (Spring/Summer), 138-161.

Elmer, E. *Children in jeopardy: A study of abused minors and their families.* Pittsburgh: University of Pittsburgh Press, 1967.

Erlanger, H. Social class and corporal punishment in childrearing: A reassessment. *American Sociological Review,* 1974, 39(February), 68-85.

Field, M., and Field, H. Marital violence and the criminal process: Neither justice nor peace. *Social Service Review,* 1973, 47(2), 221-240.

Fields, M. Wife beating: Facts and figures. *Victimology,* 1978, 2(3/4), 643-647.

Flynn, J. P. Spouse assault: Its dimensions and characteristics in Kalamazoo County, Michigan. Unpublished Field Studies in Research and Practice, School of Social Work, Western Michigan University, Kalamazoo, Michigan, 1975.

Fontana, V. *Somewhere a child is crying: Maltreatment—causes and prevention.* New York: Macmillan, 1973.

Friedrich, W. N., and Boriskin, J. A. The role of the child in abuse: A review of literature. *American Journal of Orthopsychiatry,* 1976, 46(4), 580-590.

Galdston, R. Observations of children who have been physically abused by their parents. *American Journal of Psychiatry,* 1965, 122(4), 440-443.

Gaquin, D. A. Spouse abuse: Data from the National Crime Survey. *Victimology,* 1977-1978, 2(3/4), 632-643.

Garbarino, J. The human ecology of child maltreatment. *Journal of Marriage and the Family,* 1977, 39(4), 721-735.

Gayford, J. J. Wife battering: A preliminary survey of 100 cases. *British Medical Journal,* 1975, 1(January), 194-197.

Gelles, R. J. Child abuse as psychopathology: A sociological critique and reformulation. *American Journal of Orthopsychiatry,* 1973, 43(July), 611-621.

Gelles, R. J. *The violent home.* Beverly Hills, CA: Sage Publications, 1974.

Gelles, R. J. The social construction of child abuse. *American Journal of Orthopsychiatry,* 1975, 43(4), 611-621. (a)

Gelles, R. J. Violence and pregnancy: A note on the extent of the problem and needed services. *Family Coordinator,* 1975, 24(January), 81-86. (b)

Gelles, R. J. Violence towards children in the United States. *American Journal of Orthopsychiatry,* 1978, 48(October), 580-592.

Gelles, R. J. A profile of violence towards children in the United States. In G. Gerbner, C. J. Ross, and E. Zigler (Eds.), *Child abuse: An agenda for action.* New York: Oxford University Press, 1980, 82-105. (a)

Gelles, R. J. Violence in the family: A review of research in the seventies. *Journal of Marriage and the Family,* 1980, 42(November), 873-885. (b)

Gelles, R. J., and Straus, M. A. Determinants of violence in the family: Toward a theoretical integration. In W. R. Burr, R. Hill, F. I. Nye, and I. L. Reiss (Eds.), *Contemporary theories about the family.* New York: Free Press, 1979, 549-581.

Gil, D. *Violence against children: Physical child abuse in the United States.* Cambridge: Harvard University Press, 1970.

Giovannoni, J. M., and Becerra, R. M. *Defining child abuse.* New York: Free Press, 1979.

Goode, W. J. Force and violence in the family. *Journal of Marriage and the Family,* 1971, 33(November), 624-636.

Guttmacher, M. *The mind of the murderer.* New York: Farrar, Straus, & Cudahy, 1960.

Harbin, H. T., and Madden, D. J. Battered parents—A new syndrome. *American Journal of Psychiatry,* 1979, 136(October), 1288-1291.

Houghton, B. Review of research on women abuse. Paper presented at the annual meetings of the American Society of Criminology, Philadelphia, 1979.

Johnson, C. L. Child abuse in the Southeast: An analysis of 1172 reported cases. Athens, GA: University of Georgia, Athens Welfare Research, 1974.

Jones, A. *Women who kill.* New York: Holt, Rinehart, & Winston, 1980.

Justice, B. and Justice, R. *The abusing family.* New York: Human Sciences Press, 1976.

Kempe, C. H., Silverman, F. N., Steele, B. F., Droegemueller, W., and Silver, H. K. The battered child syndrome. *Journal of the American Medical Association,* 1962, 181, 107-112.

Klaus, M. H., and Kennel, J. H. Maternal-infant bonding. St. Louis: C. V. Mosby, 1976.

Lang, A. R., et al. Effects of alcohol on aggression in male social drinkers. *Journal of Abnormal Psychology,* 1975, 84(October), 508-518.

Langley, R., and Levy, R. C. *Wife beating: The silent crisis.* New York: Dutton, 1977.

Levinger, G. Sources of marital dissatisfaction among applicants for divorce. *American Journal of Orthopsychiatry,* 1966, 26(October), 803-897.

Light, R. J. Abused and neglected children in America: A study of alternative policies. *Harvard Educational Review,* 1974, 43(November), 556-598.

London, J. Images of violence against women. *Victimology,* 1978, 2(3/4), 510-524.

Maden, M. F., and Wrench, D. F. Significant findings in child abuse research. *Victimology,* 1977, 2, 196-224.

Makepeace, J. M. Courtship violence among college students. *Family Relations,* 1981, 30(January), 97-102.

Mancini, M. Adult abuse laws. *American Journal of Nursing,* 1980, 80(April), 739-740.

Martin, D. *Battered Wives.* San Francisco: Glide Publications, 1976.

Milne, A. A. *Winnie-the-Pooh.* New York: Dell, 1926.

Mulligan, M. A. An investigation of factors associated with violent modes of conflict resolution in the family. Unpublished M.A. Thesis, University of Rhode Island, 1977.

Nagi, R. Child abuse and neglect programs: A national overview. *Children Today,* 1975, 4(May/June), 13-17.

Nelson, G. K., Dainauski, J., and Kilmer, L. Child abuse reporting laws: Action and uncertainty. *Child Welfare,* 1980, 59(2), 203-212.

Newberger, E. H., Reed, R. B., Daniel, J. H., Hyde, J. N., Jr., and Kotelchuck, M. Pediatric social illness: Toward an etiologic classification. *Pediatrics,* 1977, 60, 178-185.

O'Brien, J. E. Violence in divorce prone families. *Journal of Marriage and the Family,* 1971, 33(November), 692-698.

Owens, D., and Straus, M. A. Childhood violence and adult approval of violence. *Aggressive Behavior,* 1975, 1(2), 193-211.

Palmer, S. *The psychology of murder.* New York: Thomas Y. Crowell, 1962.

Parke, R. D., and Collmer, C. W. Child abuse: An interdisciplinary analysis. In M. Hetherington (Ed.), *Review of child development research* (Vol. 5). Chicago: University of Chicago Press, 1975, 1-102.

Parker, B., and Schumacher, D. N. The battered wife syndrome and violence in the nuclear family of origin: A controlled pilot study. *American Journal of Public Health,* 1977, 67(August), 760-761.

Parnas, R. The police response to domestic disturbance. *Wisconsin Law Review,* 1967, 914(Fall), 914-960.

Pediatric News. One child dies daily from abuse: Parent probably was abuser. 1975, 9(April), 3.

Pittman, D. J., and Handy, W. Patterns in criminal aggravated assault. *Journal of Criminal Law, Criminology and Police Science,* 1964, 55(4), 462-470.

Pokorny, A. D. Human violence: A comparison of homicide, aggravated assault, suicide, and attempted suicide. *Journal of Criminal Law, Criminology, and Police Science,* 1965, 56(December), 488-497.

Potts, D., and Herzberger, S. Child abuse: A cross generational pattern of child rearing? Paper presented at the annual meetings of the Midwest Psychological Association, Chicago, 1979.

Pleck, E., Pleck, J., Grossman, M., and Bart, P. The battered data syndrome: A comment on Steinmetz's article. *Victimology,* 1978, 2(3/4), 680-683.

Prescott, S., and Letko, C. Battered women: A social psychological perspective. In M. Roy (Ed.), *Battered women.* New York: Van Nostrand Reinhold, 1977, 72-96.

Radbill, S. A history of child abuse and infanticide. In R. Helfer and C. Kempe (Eds.), *The battered child* (2nd Ed.). Chicago: University of Chicago Press, 1974, 3-24.

Response. Battered women press police for equal protection. *Response,* 1979, 2(6), 3.

Rosenthal, M. P. Physical abuse of children by parents: The criminalization decision. *American Journal of Criminal Law,* 1979, 7(2), 141-169.

Ross, C. J. Society's children: The care of indigent youngsters in New York City, 1875-1903. Unpublished doctoral dissertation, Yale University, 1977.

Rounsaville, B. J., and Weissman, M. A. Battered women: A medical problem requiring detection. *International Journal of Psychiatry in Medicine,* 1977-1978, 8(2), 191-202.

Schachter, S., and Singer, J. E. Cognitive, social, and physiological determinants of emotional states. *Psychological Review,* 1962, 69(5), 379-399.

Scheff, T. J. The role of the mentally ill and the dynamics of mental disorder: A research framework. *Sociometry,* 1963, 26(December), 436-453.

Schultz, L. G. The wife assaulter. *Journal of Social Therapy,* 1960, 6(2), 103-111.

Shorter, E. *The making of the modern family.* New York: Basic Books, 1975.

Snell, J. E., Rosenwald, R. J., and Robey, A. The wifebeater's wife: A study of family interaction. *Archives of General Psychiatry,* 1964, 11(August), 107-113.

Spinetta, J. J., and Rigler, D. The child abusing parent: A psychological review. *Psychological Bulletin,* 1972, 77(April), 296-304.

Star, B. Patterns of family violence. *Social Casework,* 1980, 61(June), 339-346.

Stark, R., and McEvoy, J. Middle class violence. *Psychology Today,* 1970, 4(November), 52-65.

Steele, B. F., and Pollock, C. A psychiatric study of parents who abuse infants and small children. In R. E. Helfer and C. H. Kempe (Eds.), *The battered child.* Chicago: University of Chicago Press, 1968, 103-147.

Steele, B. F., and Pollock, C. A psychiatric study of parents who abuse infants and small children. In R. E. Helfer and C. H. Kempe (Eds.), *The battered child* (2nd Ed.). Chicago: University of Chicago Press, 1974, 89-134.

Steinmetz, S. K. Occupation and physical punishment: A response to Straus. *Journal of Marriage and the Family,* 1971, 33(November), 664-666.

Steinmetz, S. K. Occupational environment in relation to physical punishment and dogmatism. In S. Steinmetz and M. Straus (Eds.), *Violence in the family.* New York: Harper & Row, 1974, 166-172. (a)

Steinmetz, S. K. The sexual context of social research. *American Sociologist,* 1974, 9(3), 111-116. (b)

Steinmetz, S. K. The use of force for resolving family conflict: The training ground for abuse. *Family Coordinator,* 1977, 26(January), 19-26. (a)

Steinmetz, S. K. Wife-beating, husband-beating—A comparison of the use of physical violence between spouses to resolve marital fights. In M. Roy (Ed.), *Battered women.* New York: Van Nostrand Reinhold, 1977, 63-96. (b)

Steinmetz, S. K. *The cycle of violence: Assertive, aggressive, and abusive family interaction.* New York: Praeger, 1977. (c)

Steinmetz, S. K. The battered husband syndrome. *Victimology,* 1978, 2(3/4), 499-509. (a)

Steinmetz, S. K. Violence between family members. *Marriage and Family Review,* 1978, 1(3), 1-16. (b)

Steinmetz, S. K. Battered parents. *Society,* 1978, 15(5), 54-55. (c)

Steinmetz, S. K., and Straus, M. *Violence in the family.* New York: Harper & Row, 1974.

Straus, M. A. Some social antecedents of physical punishment: A linkage theory interpretation. *Journal of Marriage and the Family,* 1971, 33(November), 658-663.

Straus, M. A. A general systems theory approach to a theory of violence between family members. *Social Science Information,* 1973, 12(June), 105-125.

Straus, M. A. Forward. In R. J. Gelles, *The violent home: A study of physical aggression between husbands and wives.* Beverly Hills, CA: Sage Publications, 1974, 13-17. (a)

Straus, M. A. Leveling, civility, and violence in the family. *Journal of Marriage and the Family,* 1974, 36(February), 13-30. (b)

Straus, M. A. Sexual inequality, cultural norms, and wife beating. *Victimology,* 1976, 1, 54-76.

Straus, M. A. A sociological perspective on the prevention and treatment of wifebeating. In M. Roy (Ed.), *Battered women.* New York: Van Nostrand Reinhold, 1977, 194-238. (a)

Straus, M. A. Societal morphogenesis and intrafamily violence in cross-cultural perspective. *Annals of the New York Academy of Science,* 1977, 285, 717-730. (b)

Straus, M. A. Wife beating: How common and why? *Victimology,* 1978, 2(3/4), pp. 443-458.

Straus, M. A. Family patterns and child abuse in a nationally representative American sample. *Child Abuse and Neglect: The International Journal,* 1979, 3(1), 213-225. (a)

Straus, M. A. Measuring intrafamily conflict and violence: The conflict tactics (CT) scales. *Journal of Marriage and the Family,* 1979, 41(February), 75-88. (b)

Straus, M. A., Gelles, R. J., and Steinmetz, S. K. *Behind closed doors: Violence in the American family.* New York: Doubleday/Anchor, 1980.

Taylor, L., and Newberger, E. H. Child abuse in the International Year of the Child. *New England Journal of Medicine,* 1979, 301(November 29), 1205-1212.

Thompson, E. M., Paget, N. W., Morris Mesch, D. W., and Putnam, T. I. *Child abuse: A community challenge.* East Aurora, NY: Henry Stewart, 1971.

Truninger, E. Marital violence: The legal solutions. *Hastings Law Review,* 1971, 23(November), 259-276.

Turbett, J. P., and O'Toole, R. Physician's recognition of child abuse. Paper presented at the annual meetings of the American Sociological Association, New York, 1980.

U.S. Department of Justice. *Intimate victims: A study of violence among friends and relatives.* Washington, DC: Government Printing Office, 1980.

U.S. Senate. *Hearing before the Subcommittee on Children and Youth of the Committee on Labor and Public Welfare.* U.S. Senate, 93rd Congress, First Session (on S. 1191, Child Abuse Prevention Act). Washington, DC: Government Printing Office, 1973.

Walker, L. E. *The battered woman.* New York: Harper & Row, 1979.

Washburn, C. *Primitive drinking: A study of the uses and functions of alcohol in preliterate societies.* New Haven: College and University Press, 1961.

Westat, Inc. *Recognition and reporting of child maltreatment: Findings from the National Study of the Incidence and Severity of Child Abuse and Neglect.* Rockville, MD: Westat, Inc., 1980.

Wolfgang, M. E. *Patterns in criminal homicide.* New York: John Wiley, 1958.

Yllo, K., and Straus, M. A. Interpersonal violence among married and cohabiting couples. Paper presented at the annual meetings of the National Council on Family Relations, Philadelphia, 1978.

Young, L. *Wednesday's child: A study of child abuse and neglect.* New York: McGraw-Hill, 1964.

Zalba, S. Battered children. *Transaction,* 1971, 8(July/August), 58-61.

Zigler, E. Controlling child abuse in America: An effort doomed to failure. Paper presented at the First National Conference on Child Abuse and Neglect, Atlanta, January, 1976.

5

The Role of Firearms in Violent Crime
An Interpretive Review of the Literature

Philip J. Cook

The role of guns (and other types of weapons) in violent crime is a fit and important subject for scientific inquiry. No etiological theory of violent crime is complete without due consideration of the technology of violent crime. This would be true even in the absence of the public concern with gun-control policy.

Each of the major violent crimes—criminal homicide, aggravated assault, robbery, and rape—is committed with a variety of weapon types. Guns are used in a minority of violent crimes but are of special concern because they are used in almost two-thirds of the murders and because, unlike most other weapons commonly used in violent crimes (hands, kitchen knives, baseball bats), it is conceivable to reduce the availability of guns without imposing unacceptable costs on the public. The principal factual question in the gun-control debate is whether reducing gun availability will reduce the amount and/or seriousness of violent crime. Can potential violent criminals be deterred from obtaining guns, carrying guns, using guns in crime? If so, will this reduction in gun use make any difference, or will criminals simply substitute other weapons to equal effect? The answers to these questions are crucial to policy evaluation. Our ability to answer these questions—to make accurate predictions about the effects of legal interventions in this area—is one measure of our scientific understanding of the role of weapons in violent crime.

In this review, I develop a number of predictions concerning the effects of changes in gun availability on the rates and incidence of violent crimes. These

Author's Note: This revision reflects helpful suggestions received from a number of people, especially Michael Tonry, Mark Moore, Franklin Zimring, and Steve Mastrofski. The first draft was completed in November 1980.

predictions are motivated by an analysis of the patterns of weapon use in violent crime. To the extent that these predictions have been tested, the results of these tests are reviewed and critiqued. My principal conclusions are the following: (1) The role of firearms in violent crime is a fertile area for scientific inquiry, still largely unexplored. (2) A number of interesting predictions can be derived from the observation that guns are most likely to be used in homicide and robbery against relatively invulnerable victims. (3) Recently enacted legislation in the area of gun control provides a potential source of quasi-experimental evidence on the role of guns in violent crimes. This source of evidence is being exploited to some extent by social scientists, but their evaluations would benefit from a more fine-grained analysis of the expected effects of such legal intervention. (4) There is persuasive evidence that several gun-related legal interventions have been effective in reducing violent crime. (5) As always, more research is needed. I offer suggestions throughout this review concerning fruitful directions for research in this area.

RECENT TRENDS IN GUN AVAILABILITY

There were approximately 682 thousand violent crimes committed with firearms in 1977, including 11.3 thousand criminal homicides, 367 thousand assaults (ranging from criminal threats with a gun to attempted murder), 15 thousand rapes, and 289 thousand robberies (Cook, 1981b). This high volume of gun-related crime is a reflection of two unarguable facts: First, the rates at which people attacked and threatened each other with any and all types of weapons reached unprecedented levels during the 1970s; second, a large and probably increasing fraction of the U.S. public has ready access to firearms. Gun-control advocates focus on the second point, asserting that a reduction in the widespread availability of guns would ameliorate the violent crime problem—if guns become scarcer, so will murders. This and related claims about the relationship between firearms and violent crime are evaluated in subsequent sections. In this preliminary section, I attempt to define the key notion of "gun availability" and summarize what data there are on recent levels and trends.

Defining "Gun Availability"

What is meant by the term "gun availability"? The term is used widely in the gun-control literature, but with few attempts at a precise definition. One dimension of availability is the cost of acquisition—the price and perhaps also the amount of effort and legal risks entailed in acquiring a gun. We could conceivably combine these elements of the cost of acquisition into a single index; Moore (1977) has labeled such an index the "effective price."[1] The average effective price of a given type of gun differs across jurisdictions, depending on the stringency of local regulation of the gun market. The effective price also differs among individuals within a jurisdiction according to their legally relevant characteristics (that is, those characteristics that determine whether they are entitled to buy a gun legally) and their contacts with potential sellers. Unfortunately, data are rarely available for measuring effective prices for particular jurisdictions or groups of individuals.

A second operational definition for gun availability is "density of gun ownership." Among groups where gun ownership is widespread (such as farmers), it is likely that people involved in serious altercations will have ready access to guns—at least as close as their own homes. A third possible definition is the fraction of people who go armed—who are in the habit of carrying firearms in their vehicles or on their persons and hence have immediate access even when away from home. Most of the available data pertain to the second definition.

Recent Trends and Patterns
in Gun Ownership

National polls have in a number of instances asked questions about weapons ownership. Responses to these polls provide the best available information on the trends in number and distribution of handguns and longguns. Wright et al. (1981) have succeeded in demonstrating that estimates of the stock of guns based on these two sources of information (surveys, and manufacture and import data) yield similar estimates of the total stock of guns under certain reasonable assumptions: 100-400 million firearms, of which 30-40 million are handguns.

One rather surprising finding from the polls is that the fraction of U.S. households owning a gun has remained roughly constant for two decades. Gallup polls in 1959, 1965, 1966, and 1972, and the NORC general social surveys in 1973, 1974, 1976, and 1977, found that about half of U.S. households own at least one gun. This statistic differs a bit from poll to poll but shows no discernible trend over this twenty-year period. Reported *handgun*-ownership rates increased slightly (from 12.6 percent in 1959 to 15.4 percent in 1972) in the Gallup polls; the NORC general social surveys find a higher, untrended rate of about 20 percent between 1973 and 1977.[2] Two large national surveys conducted in 1978 by DMI and Cambridge Reports, Inc., found virtually identical handgun-ownership rates of 23 percent (DMI) and 24 percent (Cambridge Reports).[3] Reasonable conclusions from these polls are: (1) About half of U.S. households own a gun, and this fraction has not changed much since 1959. (2) About half of the gun-owning households currently own a handgun, and this fraction appears to have increased considerably since 1959. (3) The increase in the total stock of guns has been absorbed without an increase in the fraction of households that own guns by (a) an increase in the average number of guns per gun-owning household, and (b) an increase in the number of households (Wright et al., 1981).[4]

One implication of the survey-based estimates of the private gun inventory is that there are more than three guns for every gun-owning household. Table 5.1 summarizes the results of the DMI survey in 1978 on number of guns owned by the 47 percent of all households that reported ownership of at least one gun. These data permit a rough estimate on the degree of ownership concentration. A conservative estimate is that the top one-third of handgun-owning households (about 7.5 percent of all households) own over 60 percent of all handguns; the top one-third of all longgun-owning households (about 14 percent of all households) own over 60 percent of all longguns.[5]

Another inference from the statistics in Table 5.1 is that about three-quarters of the households that own handguns also own longguns. It seems likely, then, that much of the recent growth in handgun ownership has involved households that already own a rifle or shotgun.

In each of the years 1975 through 1979, the annual sum of handgun imports and domestic manufacture has been between 2.0 and 2.3 million units (Blose and Cook, 1980: 34). The total volume of import and manufacture for the last decade has exceeded the total volume for the preceding six decades combined (Wright et al., 1981), and there is ample reason to believe that the current volume is supporting a continuing buildup in the private inventory of handguns. However, the increase in the private inventory in any one year is substantially less than the number of units manufactured and imported. As shown in Figure 5.1, approximately 2,224 thousand handguns were manufactured or imported in 1975. Of these, less than 1,750 thousand were sold to private (household and business) domestic buyers. Furthermore, these new additions to the private inventory were compensated by the loss of over 150 thousand handguns to the police (that is, handguns confiscated by the police and not returned) and a probably larger (but unknown) number that were lost because of normal attrition. There may also be a significant number of illegal (hence uncounted) exports associated with the international trade in illegal drugs, in which hand-

TABLE 5.1   Number of Guns Owned by Gun-Owning Households, 1978 (percentages)

Number	Handguns	Rifles and Shotguns
None	46	14
One	30	29
Two	8	21
3-4	4	16
5-9	1	5
10+	1	2
Yes only	8	9
Refused	4	4

SOURCE: From James D. Wright, "Public Opinion and Gun Control: A Comparison of Results from Two Recent National Surveys," University of Massachusetts, Amherst, 1979. Compiled from data appearing in "Attitudes of the American Electorate Toward Gun Control, 1978," Decision Making Information, Inc., Santa Ana, California. Reprinted by permission.

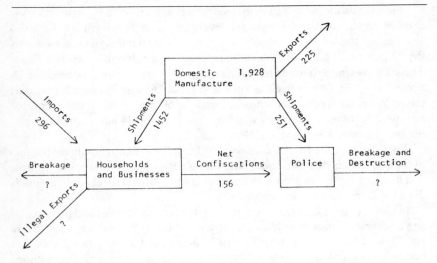

NOTES: Import and export statistics are for calendar year 1975. The manufacture statistic is an average of fiscal 1975 and 1976 (Blose and Cook, 1980: 34). Shipments to police are from the Census of Manufactures, "Preliminary Report on Small Arms," reported in Wright et al. (1981: 4-24). This statistic is for 1972 and includes only center-fire pistols and revolvers. The net confiscations statistic is estimated from data collected in a U.S. Department of Commerce, National Bureau of Standards study of police confiscations of disposal of firearms in 1971 (reported in Wright et al., 1981: 10-41; and Weber-Burdin et al., 1981: 4-29). Shipments from manufacturers to the private sector and calculated on the assumption that domestically manufactured handguns that are not shipped to police or exported are sold to households and businesses.

FIGURE 5.1   Handgun Flows ca. 1975 (all numbers in thousands)

guns are sometimes the medium of exchange. My conclusion is that we lack the data necessary to develop good estimates of year-to-year changes in the private inventory of handguns.

The incidence of firearms ownership is not uniform across society. Wright and Marston (1975) found that the fraction of households owning a gun increased with income, decreased with city size, and was higher in the South than elsewhere. The same patterns obtain when the analysis is limited to handguns only. Cook (1979) analyzed regional patterns of ownership for residents of large cities, using NORC polls taken in the mid-1970s; I found a range for handgun ownership from 5 percent for residents of large cities in New England and the mid-Atlantic up to 34 percent for residents of the mountain-region cities (Denver, Tucson, and Phoenix). The southern-region cities were relatively high—around 24 percent—and the Pacific and North Central cities low—around 13 percent. Similar regional patterns were also obtained for longgun ownership by urban residents in these regions: Only 10 percent of urban households in Boston and the mid-Atlantic cities owned any type of firearms, compared with about half of urban households in the mountain cities.

This brief review suggests that gun "availability," in the sense of the extent of ownership, has not been increasing over the last twenty years. Handgun ownership has become more widespread over this period, however. The private inventory of firearms is about 140 million, but this inventory is highly concentrated in the relatively small fraction of households that own three or more guns. Finally, gun "availability" differs widely across regions and by city size.

The Effective Price of a Handgun

The density of gun ownership is one dimension of gun availability, since gun owners obviously have more ready access to guns than do other people. The term "gun availability" is also frequently used in a second sense, namely, the cost and difficulty, or "effective price," of acquiring a gun. I begin my analysis of effective price with an assessment of trends in the money price of handguns. Discussions of regulations governing handgun commerce and the difficulty of circumventing these regulations follow.

Recent Trends in Handgun Prices

The Consumer Price Index only began including an item on firearms in 1977. The Producer Price Index (formerly known as the Wholesale Price Index) is more helpful. Table 5.2 presents the annual index for producer prices of "small arms and ammunition" from 1960 to 1980. A subcategory for revolvers was published beginning in 1972, and this index is also included in the table. As shown by the last two columns of the table, producer prices of small arms have kept pace with the Consumer Price Index; compared with the average price of other commodities, the prices of small arms were only slightly lower in 1980 than in 1960.

Table 5.3 gives the actual prices for eight popular handgun models in each of four years spanning this period. Nominal prices differ widely among models in any one year, but prices of each of the models have inflated by factors of between two and three during the years in question.

My tentative conclusion is that handgun "availability," in the sense of the price level, measured in constant dollars, has not changed substantially in the last twenty years. I have no statistics on trends in the prices of used guns, but it would be surprising if the used-price trend were not similar to that of new guns; used guns and new guns are substitutes for one another from the consumer's viewpoint.

Regulations on Handgun Commerce

Restrictions on handgun transfers have become more stringent in some states and cities since the mid-1960s. The overall effective price of a handgun may have increased in these jurisdictions as a result.

The federal Gun Control Act of 1968 imposed a national ban on mail-order

TABLE 5.2   Price Trends for Small Arms

Year	Price Index, Small Arms and Ammunition (1967 × 100)	Price Index, Revolvers (1967 × 100)	Consumer Price Index (1967 × 100)	$\frac{Small\ Arms\ Index}{CPI} \times 100$
1960	89.7		88.7	101.1
1961	93.1		89.6	103.9
1962	93.5		90.6	103.2
1963	93.7		91.7	102.2
1964	94.6		92.9	101.8
1965	97.4		94.5	103.1
1966	98.7		97.2	101.5
1967	100.0		100.0	100.0
1968	104.6		104.2	100.4
1969	108.1		109.8	98.5
1970	115.2		116.3	99.1
1971	119.4		121.3	98.4
1972	121.3	130.7	125.3	96.8
1973	123.5	133.3	133.1	92.8
1974	133.8	144.6	147.7	90.6
1975	149.3	159.6	161.2	92.6
1976	157.2	170.2	170.5	92.2
1977	169.5	184.1	181.5	93.4
1978	183.7	201.5	195.4	94.0
1979	200.5	216.3	217.4	92.2
1980	229.5	258.0	246.8	93.0

SOURCE: U.S. Bureau of Labor Statistics, *Producer Price Index*, various issues for the first two columns. The Consumer Price Index is taken from the *Economic Report of the President*, January 1981.

purchases of firearms except by federally licensed dealers, and it restricted interstate commerce in other ways as well. The intended effect of these regulations was to insulate the states from each other, so that the stringent regulations on firearms commerce adopted in some states would not be undercut by the greater availability of guns in other states.

A number of states have adopted significant restrictions on commerce in firearms, especially handguns. About half the states, comprising two-thirds of the U.S. population, currently require that handgun buyers obtain a permit or license (or at least send an application to the police) before taking possession of the gun (Cook and Blose, 1981). In most of these states, the objective of the permit or application system is to exclude felons and other undesirables from obtaining handguns, without infringing substantially on the majority's ability to purchase and possess. These state systems differ with respect to the fee, the waiting period, the involvement of state (as opposed to local) agencies, the thoroughness of the criminal record check, and so forth. Perhaps more important in practice are differences among states with respect to law enforcement

TABLE 5.3   Retail Prices for Handguns, 1964-1980

Model	1964	1970	1975	1980
1. Smith and Wesson				
Model 10	$ 65	$ 84.5	$ 102	$ 125
Model 15	74	89	125	149.5
Model 29	140	165	228	331.5
2. Colt				
Official Police*	79	110	133	216
Detective Special	76.5	93.5	127.5	225
Python	125	175	230	417
3. Ruger				
Standard	37.5	47.5	51.5	92
Black Hawk Revolver	87.5	98.5	109	180

SOURCE: *Shooters Bible,* Stoeger Inc., South Hackensack, New Jersey, various issues. These numbers were provided by William F. Riley, Program Planning Division, Bureau of Alcohol, Tobacco, and Firearms.
*In 1980, this gun was called the "trooper."

efforts aimed at plugging the inevitable "leaks" between the entitled and proscribed sectors: thefts, black-market sales, illegal sales by licensed dealers, and so forth. A transfer system that appears stringent on paper may be quite lax in practice, if law enforcement officials view enforcement activities in this area as being of low priority.

All but a few state transfer control systems are "permissive," in the sense that most people are legally entitled to be issued a permit and obtain a handgun. In a few jurisdictions, however—New York, Boston, Washington, D.C.—it is very difficult to obtain a handgun legally. Washington, D.C., is the most restrictive jurisdiction in this respect; there, only law enforcement officers and security guards are legally entitled to obtain a handgun under current law (Jones, 1981).

The effect of a permissive transfer control system is to increase the effective price of a legally purchased handgun by requiring a permit fee, and/or a waiting period, and by requiring applicants to do some paperwork and submit to a criminal record check. A number of states and cities adopted or strengthened requirements of this sort during the 1970s. A transfer control system may discourage some people from purchasing handguns and motivate others to evade the transfer regulations by purchasing from nondealers. (Transfer requirements usually apply to purchases from nondealers but are very difficult to enforce for such transactions.) While it is certainly possible to evade transfer requirements and the costs thereof, purchase from a nondealer may be costly in other ways—nondealer sources are typically less reliable and less accessible than dealers.

Evading Handgun Transfer Regulations

The majority of gun-owning households made their most recent purchases from licensed dealers, according to the survey results shown in Table 5.4. Of gun-owning respondents in the DMI national survey, 58 percent report sources

TABLE 5.4   Sources of Guns Owned by Households (percentages)

	U.S., 1978 Source of Most Recently Acquired Firearm[b]	California, 1976 Source of Most Recently Acquired Firearm[c]
Retail dealer[a]	54	53
Pawnshop	2	5
Gun show	2	n.a.
Gift or inheritance[d]	19	12
Private sale or trade	13	18
Other	5	7
Refused, don't know	4	6

a Includes gun shop, sporting goods store, department or discount store, and hardware store.
b Taken from question 60 of the Decision Making Information national survey, 1978
c Taken from the Field Institute California survey, 1976.
d The Field poll's category was simply "gift."

that are required to have a federal dealer's license (that is, the first three rows). The same percentage of California respondents reported obtaining their most recent handguns from such sources. Another important source in both surveys was "gifts," which presumably are mainly transfers within families. It is not reported where the giver obtained the gun in these cases, but retail dealers probably supply the majority of them. A reasonable guess from these data is that a quarter of the gun-owning households in the United States made their most recent acquisitions from sources other than retail dealers. The corresponding statistic for California handgun buyers is probably one-third or more.

These statistics are of some use, but they are not precisely what we want if the objective is to estimate the relative importance of different categories of sellers in gun commerce. In both surveys, respondents are asked only about their most recent acquisitions. For some respondents, the most recent acquisition may be a pistol they received as a birthday present in their youth; for other respondents, the most recent acquisition may be the tenth gun they have purchased in the preceding year. Clearly, the people who are currently active in the gun market should be weighted more heavily than the others in estimating the relative importance of sources for all guns traded in a given twelve-month period. These survey results do not permit such an estimate. We can safely conclude, however, that a significant percentage of guns that change hands each year are sold by nondealers. This finding is important because nondealers are legally exempt from federal regulations. State laws that regulate sales by nondealers are intrinsically difficult to enforce.

The crucial question is how guns that are used in crime are obtained. The Bureau of Alcohol, Tobacco, and Firearms' "Operation Identification" investigated one aspect of this question.[6] From their analysis of guns confiscated by the police in sixteen cities, they concluded that "in the study area, with a few exceptions, the percentage of out-of-state purchases is directly proportional to the strength of the local firearm regulations" (1976: 13). Of the police-confiscated guns that BATF was able to trace, 96 percent of New York City's sample were first sold at retail in another state. The corresponding figures for Detroit and Boston were 92 percent and 65 percent, respectively. The presumption is that most of these guns were imported illegally to evade relatively stringent state and local ordinances. Of course, it is quite possible that most guns *not* confiscated by the police in these cities had also been imported; even normally law-abiding citizens may turn to out-of-state sources if local ordinances are sufficiently stringent and taxing.

The most direct method for determining how criminals obtain their guns is to ask them. D. E. S. Burr (1977) interviewed a sample of Florida prisoners who had been imprisoned for assault, robbery, or burglary. He obtained information on 176 handguns, of which only one-quarter had been purchased from dealers. Twenty-three percent had been stolen and the rest acquired more or less legally from private parties. These results were in marked contrast to the distribution of handgun sources in Burr's Florida statewide survey of households—this distribution is similar to that for California discussed above. It should be noted that outside of Dade County, Florida does not require that handgun buyers submit to a police check or obtain a permit or license. Why did Burr's prison respondents avoid retail dealers when they were in the market for a handgun? One likely explanation is that they could obtain guns more cheaply on the street or by stealing them than from a retail dealer. It would be interesting to ask this same group how they obtained their watches, television sets, and so forth; I suspect that this group obtains most durable commodities by theft or from fences or acquaintances.

If we accept Burr's conclusion about the sources of guns to criminals, then the dimension of gun availability that is salient is the ease of stealing a gun or obtaining one on the black market or from a friend. In this sense, we would expect the effective price of guns to criminals to be closely related to the density of gun ownership. For example, the fraction of burglaries that result in the theft of guns will increase with the fraction of households that own guns (see Moore, 1981); as a result, we would expect the black market in guns to be more active in cities with high gun-ownership rates. Criminals will also find it easier to buy or borrow a gun from an acquaintance in cities with high gun-ownership rates, simply because criminals will tend to know more people who own guns in such cities. Thus, the effective price of a handgun will depend inter alia on the density of handgun ownership in a city.

The Propensity to Go Armed

My first two definitions of "gun availability"—gun-ownership density and "effective price"—are closely related in the sense that ownership density influences the effective price to criminals and others who tend to avoid retail dealers. My third definition focuses on the propensity to go armed in public places. This dimension of availability is also presumably related to gun owner-ship, but may also be influenced by the vigor with which anti-carrying laws are enforced and by other factors (such as the public's perceived need for protection against violent attack in public places).

State and local legislation tend to make a sharp distinction between keeping a gun in one's home or business and carrying a gun—particularly a concealed gun—in public. All but a very few states either ban concealed weapons entirely or require a special license for carrying concealed weapons. Many states also place special restrictions on carrying guns in cars. These laws reflect the public's justifiable concern about violent crime in the streets.

A recent national survey found that 7 percent of respondents carried a handgun outside of their homes for protection (Wright, 1979). The police can attempt to discourage this practice through proactive efforts to confiscate concealed weapons and/or arrest concealed-weapons offenders. Police practice differs widely among cities in this regard (Moore, 1980). The courts also play an important role in deterring the practice of going armed. There is some evidence, for example, that the severe penalties for carrying a gun without a license imposed by the Massachusetts Bartley-Fox Amendment had a substantial deterrent effect (Pierce and Bowers, 1981).

Conclusion

The three definitions of gun availability discussed above are conceptually distinct, and the distinctions help organize our thinking about gun-control measures and empirical patterns in the criminal use of guns. In the general discussion of weapons and violent crime developed in the next two sections, however, I find it convenient and appropriate to use the term "gun availability" without specifying a particular definition. The distinctions are revived in the subsequent sections that deal with empirical tests of the relationships between gun availability and violent crime.

THE ROLE OF WEAPONS
IN VIOLENT CRIME:
THEORETICAL FRAMEWORK

The most important question considered in research on the criminal use of weapons is how the availability of dangerous weapons, especially firearms, influences the incidence and seriousness of violent crime. The observed patterns of weapon use in violent crime suggest a number of testable hypotheses concerning the potential effects of changes in gun availability. These hypotheses are motivated and stated in the sections on patterns of gun use in robbery, murder, and assault and the role of weapon type in determining the outcome of violent attacks. The theoretical framework that guides this discussion is summarized here, without reference to sources or supporting evidence. This bare statement of the main ideas serves as a readers' guide to the more cluttered presentation of subsequent sections.

In addition to gun availability, there are three basic elements to the theoretical framework, as depicted in Figure 5.2: (1) The perpetrator's intent, or choice of task (such as which target to rob); (2) the type of weapon he or she uses in the crime; and (3) the outcome (Was the victim wounded, killed, or unharmed? Was the robbery successful?). There is some interrelationship between the type of weapon used in a violent crime and the criminal's intent or choice of task; the causal process can go either way. The actual outcome of the crime is of course influenced by both the perpetrator's intent and the choice of weapon, as shown in the figure. The fourth element of the theoretical framework, gun availability, influences weapon type and also has an effect on the quality of opportunities confronting the violent criminal.

The Relationship Between Task and Weapon Type

A gun has a number of characteristics that make it superior to other readily available weapons for use in violent crime: Even in the hands of a weak and unskilled assailant, a gun can be used to kill. The killing can be accomplished from a distance without much risk of effective counterattack by the victim, and the killing can be completed quickly, without sustained effort, and in a relatively "impersonal" fashion. Furthermore, because everyone knows that a gun has these attributes, the mere display of a gun communicates a highly effective threat. In most circumstances, a gun maximizes the probability of success for a would-be robber or murderer.

The value of a gun as a tool in violent crime is closely related to the vulnerability of the victim. A victim who is unarmed, alone, small, frail, or impaired by alcohol or drugs is highly vulnerable. Against a vulnerable victim, the probability of perpetrating a successful robbery or murder is only slightly

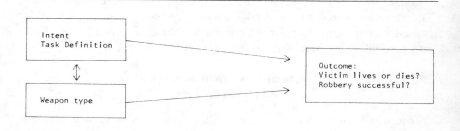

FIGURE 5.2   Elements of a Theoretical Framework

affected by the type of weapon employed. But a gun is essential for the purpose of murdering a police officer or robbing a bank. The value of a gun in a crime will influence the probability that a gun will be the weapon actually used in that crime. Hence we have the *vulnerability pattern:* The fraction of robberies involving guns is inversely related to the vulnerability of the victim. The same pattern is characteristic of murder.

A variety of possible explanations can be given for the vulnerability pattern. Two explanations of special interest are these: (1) "The tool determines the task." A robber's choice of target will be influenced by the type of weapon immediately available to him. In robbery or other confrontations, the impulse to kill is more likely to be acted on if an adequate weapon is available. (2) "The task determines the tool." In robberies and murders that involve some planning and preparation, the perpetrator will have a chance to equip himself with an adequate weapon. What the perpetrator considers "adequate" will depend on the vulnerability of the victim.

There is no need to choose between these two explanations—both no doubt have some validity.

A gun is usually the most effective weapon for launching a deadly attack or generating a convincing threat of deadly attack. But in most violent confrontations, the assailant's intent is not to kill (or threaten death), but rather to hurt or gain control over the victim. Casual observation suggests that schoolyard scuffles, routine family fights, even barroom brawls are typically completely lacking in homicidal intent and would not even be considered "crimes" by the participants or (in practice) the police and courts. In violent confrontations of this sort, the protagonists are unlikely to resort to deadly weapons, even when they are readily available. Husband and wife may exchange punches or throw dishes any number of times, always refraining from reaching for the carving knife or shotgun. These common sense observations suggest that the assailants' choice of weapon is a good indicator of his intent in assault offenses. The correlation between intent and weapon deadliness is by no means perfect, since weapon availability is an important intervening variable. Nevertheless, the assailant's intent is a major determinant of his or her choice of weapon. The assailant who clearly intends that the victim survive will not fire a gun at him. The assailant who is determined to kill the victim probably will use a gun, if one is available. Weapon choice in the intermediate case, in which the assailant's intent is ambiguous, may be governed by immediate availability.

Outcome as a Function of Intent and Weapon Type

The details of this causal process differ somewhat between assault and murder, on the one hand, and robbery, on the other. These two crime categories are hence treated separately here.

Assault and Murder

Whether the victim survives a serious assault with a deadly weapon depends in part on his ability to defend himself—the victim's vulnerability relative to the nature of the attack. But in a large proportion of assaults with deadly weapons, the assailant ceases the attack by choice, rather than because of effective victim resistance. We can infer in unsustained attacks of this sort that the assailant's intent is to injure or incapacitate the victim—that there is no deliberate, unambiguous intent to kill. Whether the victim does, in fact, die in such cases is largely a matter of chance—whether the first blow happens to strike a vital organ. Ambiguously motivated gun attacks are more dangerous than ambiguously motivated attacks with other weapons. This is the *objective dangerousness pattern:* Gun attacks have a higher probability of killing the victim than knife attacks in otherwise similar circumstances, and the difference is especially large when the intent of the assailant's attack is ambiguous.

Robbery Violence

In crimes in which the perpetrator's intent is to complete a robbery successfully, using force only as necessary to forestall or overcome victim resistance, the likelihood of physical attack or victim injury will be inversely related to the lethality of the robber's weapon—victims are less likely to attempt resistance to a gun than to other weapons. I have labeled this inverse relationship the *instrumental violence pattern* in robbery.

While the instrumental violence pattern is evident in robbery statistics, it is nonetheless true that some robbers engage in unnecessary violence. They injure or kill victims who are cooperating with the robber's demands. This *excess violence pattern* accounts for a large fraction of serious injuries and deaths for each of the weapon categories in robbery. The robber's intent in these cases is evidently to complete the robbery successfully *and,* as a separate matter, to injure or kill the victim.

The objective dangerousness pattern characterizes robbery as well as assault: The type of weapon employed has an important independent effect on the probability of victim death. This assertion appears valid, despite evidence that half or more of robbery murders are deliberate. The decision to kill is often made during the course of the robbery, rather than being planned in advance. Perhaps the relative ease of executing a victim with a gun encourages this decision.

The Effects of Gun Availability

Jurisdictions differ widely with respect to the percentage of households that own a gun, the cost and hassle entailed in obtaining a gun, and the legal risks in carrying a gun or using one in a crime (or in self-defense). Within each jurisdiction, some subsets of the population tend to have more ready access to guns than others. What effects do these differences in gun "availability" have on violent crime patterns? Gun availability may influence both the *capabilities* of potential offenders, and the quality of the various criminal *opportunities* that they confront. I deal with the capability issue first.

Suppose that a jurisdiction is successful in reducing gun availability to robbers and violence-prone individuals (or in increasing the cost of using guns in crime). I postulate two effects: a pure *weapon substitution* effect, and a *selective deterrence* effect.

Weapon Substitution. Pure weapon substitution occurs when the criminal simply substitutes a knife or club for the gun he would have preferred to use, without modifying his basic decision of what target to rob or whether to attack someone he wants to hurt or kill. By the objective dangerousness postulate, this type of substitution will reduce the murder rate. By the instrumental violence postulate, substitution will increase the victim injury rate in robbery.

Selective Deterrence. In addition to weapon substitution, we expect a reduction in gun availability to deter some types of violent crime, as suggested by the vulnerability postulate. The commercial robbery rate should be reduced, since the probability of failure of a nongun robbery against a commercial target is high (hence the high fraction of gun use in commercial robbery.) Since there may be some displacement to noncommercial targets, it is not clear whether the noncommercial robbery rate will fall or increase.

A reduction in gun availability should reduce the murder rate. The vulnerability postulate suggests that the murder victimization rate will fall the most (proportionately) for the least vulnerable victims. Controlling for the vulnerability of the victim, the murder offense rate should fall the most for the weakest potential killers (women, youths, elderly people). These predictions are predicated on the assumption that the reduction in gun availability is uniform across relevant subgroups of the population.

These predictions, which follow from an analysis of the offenders' capabilities, may have to be modified somewhat if the intervention that deprives offenders of guns also reduces gun availability to potential victims. If there is a general reduction in gun availability, then potential victims will be less likely to be armed with guns and hence more vulnerable to robbery or assault. In effect, a general reduction in gun availability changes the quality of opportunities available to criminals. One effect may be to increase the rate of (nongun) assault; individuals will be more likely to give vent to violent impulses if they are confident that their intended victim lacks a gun. There may also be some effect on robbery patterns, although not enough is known about self-defense in robbery to make specific predictions. In any event, it should be clear that some legal interventions (such as sentencing enhancements for criminals who use guns) will have little effect on general availability of guns, and others (such as an increase in the federal tax on handguns) will be very broad. Predictions should, of course, be tailored to the precise nature of the intervention.

The list of predictions discussed above is not complete, but perhaps it is sufficient to suggest that this line of inquiry is fertile and potentially important. The discussion of the following sections (on gun-use patterns and the role of weapon type in violent attacks) provides empirical evidence for some of the assertions made above, and motivates a number of specific hypotheses relating to the effects of gun availability on the incidence and seriousness of violent crime. The hypotheses are denoted H1, H2, and so on for ready reference. These hypotheses are testable and are intended to serve as a partial agenda for future research. Tests that have been applied to them are reviewed in the subsequent sections on gun availability and gun-control ordinances.

PATTERNS OF GUN USE IN ROBBERY, MURDER, AND ASSAULT

Firearms were used in 63 percent of the murders, 41 percent of the robberies, and 22 percent of the aggravated assaults reported to the police in 1978 (Uniform Crime Reports). These percentages have varied over time and differ across jurisdictions, for reasons that will be explored in subsequent sections. This section focuses on the pattern of gun use across the different circumstances in which these crimes occur. What characteristics of the assailant, the victim, and the immediate environment of the criminal act influence the likelihood that a gun is employed? Since this question has been more prominent in the literature on robbery than on murder, I begin with an analysis of gun use in robbery.

Robbery

Robbery[7] is defined as theft or attempted theft by means of force or the threat of violence. The robber's essential task is to overcome through intimidation or force the victim's natural tendency to resist parting with his valuables. A variety of techniques for accomplishing this task are used in robbery, including actual attack (as in "muggings" and "yokings") and the threatening display of a weapon such as gun, knife, or club. Whatever the means employed, the objective is to gain the victim's compliance quickly or render him helpless, thereby preventing the victim from escaping, summoning help, or struggling. The amount of what could be called "power" (capability of generating lethal force) the robber needs to achieve a high probability of reaching these objectives depends on the characteristics of the robbery target (victim) and, in particular, on the vulnerability of the target. The most vulnerable targets are people who are young, elderly, otherwise physically weak or disabled (for example, by alcohol), or alone and without ready means of escape. The least vulnerable targets are commercial places, especially where there are several customers and clerks and possibly even armed guards—a bank being one extreme example. A gun is the most effective tool for enhancing the robber's power. Unlike other common weapons, a gun gives a robber the capacity to threaten deadly harm from a distance, thus allowing him to maintain a buffer zone between himself and the victim and to control several victims simultaneously. A gun serves to preempt any rational victim's inclination to flee or resist.[8] Skogan (1978) documented the effectiveness of a gun in forestalling victim resistance in his analysis of a national sample of victim-reported robberies:[9] Only 8 percent of gun robbery victims resisted physically in noncommercial robberies, compared with about 15 percent of victims in noncommercial robberies involving other weapons.[10] Other types of resistance (arguing, screaming, fleeing) were also less common in gun robbery than robbery involving other weapons.

It seems reasonable to assume that, from the robber's viewpoint, the value of employing a gun tends to be inversely related to the vulnerability of the target. A gun will cause a greater increase in the likelihood of success against well-defended targets than against more vulnerable targets. A strong-arm technique will be adequate against an elderly woman walking alone on the street—a gun would be redundant with such a victim—but a gun is virtually a requirement for a successful bank robbery. Skogan (1978) provides evidence supporting this claim: He finds little relationship between robbery success rates and weapon type for personal robbery but a very strong relationship for commercial robbery. He reports that success rates in commercial robbery were 94 percent with a gun, 65 percent with a knife, and 48 percent with other weapons.

In economic terms, we can characterize robbery as a production process (Cook, 1979: 752-753) with weapons, robbers, and a target as "inputs." The "output" of the production process can be defined as the probability of success. This probability increases with the number and skill of the robbers, the vulnerability of the target, and the lethality of the weapons. For given robber and target characteristics, the "marginal product" of a gun can be defined as the increase in probability of success if the robber or robbers substitute a gun for, say, a knife. The evidence presented above suggests that the marginal product of a gun is small against vulnerable targets and relatively large against well-defended targets. We can go one step further and define the "value of a gun's marginal product" as its marginal product (increase in success probability) multiplied by the amount of loot if the robbery is successful. Since, for obvious reasons, targets with greater potential loot tend to be better defended against robbery,[11] the *value* of the gun's marginal product is even more strongly related to target vulnerability than is its marginal product. The conclusion can be put in the form of a proposition:

> The economic value of a gun in robbery tends to be greatest against commercial targets and other well defended targets, and least against highly vulnerable targets.

It makes good economic sense, then, for gun use in robbery to be closely related to target vulnerability. Cook (1980a) demonstrates that this is indeed the case, on the basis of tabulating results of more than 12,000 robbery reports taken from victim survey data gathered in 26 large cities. These results are reproduced in Table 5.5.

From the table (part A) we see that 55 percent of gun robberies committed by adults, but only 13 percent of other adult armed robberies, involve commercial targets. Those relatively few gun robberies that were committed against people on the street are concentrated on relatively invulnerable targets—groups of two or more victims, or prime age males—while street robbery with other weapons was most likely to involve women, children, and elderly victims. Skogan (1978) provides further detail for commercial robberies, reporting that the likelihood that a gun is present in such robberies is only 44 percent for commercial places that have only one employee but 68 percent for commercial places with two or more employees.[12]

What is the causal process that produces these patterns in gun robbery? There are two plausible explanations, both compatible with the evidence presented above: (1) Robbers who aspire to well-defended, lucrative targets equip themselves with a gun in order to increase their chance of success; or (2) robbers who happen to have a gun are more tempted to rob lucrative, well-defended targets than robbers who lack this tool. In short, the question is whether the

TABLE 5.5   (A) Distribution of All Robberies Across Locations (percentages)

	Gun	Knife or Other Weapon	Unarmed
Commercial	55.1	13.3	19.1
Residence	6.4	10.4	8.5
Street, vehicle, etc.	38.5	76.3	72.4
Total	100.0	100.0	100.0

(B) Distribution of Street Robberies by Victim Characteristics (percentages)

	Gun	Knife or Other Weapon	Unarmed
Male victim aged 16-54	59.8	53.8	41.1
Two or more victims	10.5	5.8	3.7
All others (young, elderly, and/or female victim)	29.7	40.4	55.2
Total	100.0	100.0	100.0

SOURCE: Adapted from Cook (1980a: 43). The distributions are calculated from National Crime Panel victimization survey data of 26 cities.
NOTE: All incidents involved at least one male robber age 18 or over. Entries in the table reflect survey sampling weights.

weapon is chosen to suit the task, or rather that the available weapon helps define the task. There is doubtless some truth in both explanations.

The first explanation suggests that the observed relationship between gun use and target choice is the result of differences between the kinds of people that rob lucrative targets and those who commit relatively petty street robberies—a difference reminiscent of Conklin's (1972) distinction between "professionals" and "opportunists." Victim survey evidence does suggest that gun robbers as a group have more of the earmarks of professionalism than other armed robbers: Beside the fact that they make bigger "scores," gun robbers are older, less likely to rob acquaintances, and less likely to work in large groups of three or more (Cook, 1976; Skogan, 1978). Cook and Nagin (1979: 25) demonstrated that the factors that determine a robber's choice of weapon have some tendency to persist: A cohort of adult men arrested for gun robbery in the District of Columbia showed a greater propensity to use guns in subsequent robberies than the corresponding cohort of nongun robbery arrestees.[13]

It seems reasonable to hypothesize, then, that robbers who engage in planning and who seek out big scores will take pains to equip themselves with the appropriate weapon—usually some type of firearm. The extent to which other, less professional robbers use guns, and hence the kinds of targets they choose, may be more sensitive to the extent to which such people have access to guns and are in the habit of carrying them, for whatever reason. Increased availability of guns may then result in some target switching by this group—substitution of more lucrative, better-defended targets for more vulnerable targets. Increased gun availability may also result in weapon substitution for a given type of target, implying an increase in the fraction of street robberies committed with a gun; that is; guns will be put to less valuable uses as they become "cheaper." These hypotheses can be stated more precisely as follows:

> An increase in gun availability in a city will have the following effects: (H1) increase the fraction of noncommercial robberies committed with a gun, and (H2) increase the fraction of robberies committed against commercial and other well-defended targets.

Murder

The qualities of a gun that make it the most effective robbery weapon, particularly against well-defended targets, are also of value to a killer. A decision to kill is easier and safer to implement with a gun than with other commonly available weapons—there is less danger of effective victim resistance during the attack, and the killing can be accomplished more quickly and impersonally, with less sustained effort than is usually required with a knife or blunt object. As in the case of robbery, a gun has greatest value against relatively invulnerable victims, and the vulnerability of the victim appears to be an important factor in determining the probability that a gun is used as the murder weapon.

The least vulnerable victims are those who are guarded or armed. All presidential assassinations in U.S. history were committed with handguns or rifles. Almost all law enforcement officers who have been murdered in recent years were shot: In 1978, 91 of 93 murdered officers were killed by guns.

Physical size and strength are also components of vulnerability. In 1977, 68.5 percent male homicide victims were shot, compared with only 51.0 percent of female homicide victims (U.S. Bureau of the Census, 1978). The age pattern, shown in Figure 5.3, is strikingly regular: About 70 percent of victims aged 20-44 are shot, but this fraction drops off rapidly for younger and older— that is, more vulnerable—victims.

Vulnerability is, of course, a relative matter. We would expect that the lethality of the murder weapons would be directly related to the *difference* in physical strength between the victim and killer, other things equal. To investigate this hypothesis, I used the FBI data coded from the supplemental homicide reports submitted for 1976 and 1977 by police departments in 50 large cities. These data include two demographic characteristics of the victim and (where known) the offender, as well as the murder weapon, immediate circumstances, and apparent motive of the crime. Tables 5.6 and 5.7 display some results that tend to confirm the relative vulnerability hypothesis. First, from Table 5.6 we see that women tend to use more lethal weapons than men to kill their spouses: 97 percent of the women, but only 78 percent of the men, used a gun or knife. The gun fractions alone are 67 percent and 62 percent—admittedly not a large difference, but one that is in the predicted direction. This result is especially notable since women typically have less experience than men in handling guns and are less likely to think of any guns kept in the home as their personal property. Table 5.6 also shows that women who kill their "boyfriends" are more likely to use a gun than men who kill their "girlfriends."

Table 5.7 focuses on killings resulting from arguments and brawls in which both the killer and the victim were males. The gun fraction increases with the age of the killer and is inversely related to the age of the victim: The highest gun

TABLE 5.6   Weapon Choice in Homicides Involving Spouses and
Intimates (percentages)

| Weapon | Identity of Victim | | | |
	Husband	Wife	Boyfriend	Girlfriend
Gun	67.1	61.6	58.4	53.5
Knife	29.8	16.3	38.0	19.1
Blunt object	1.6	4.9	1.4	5.3
Other	1.4	17.2	2.3	22.0
N	553	547	216	209

SOURCE: FBI Supplemental Homicide Reports, 50 cities, 1976 and 1977 combined.
NOTE: "Husband" and "wife" classifications include commonlaw relationships. Arson cases are omitted.

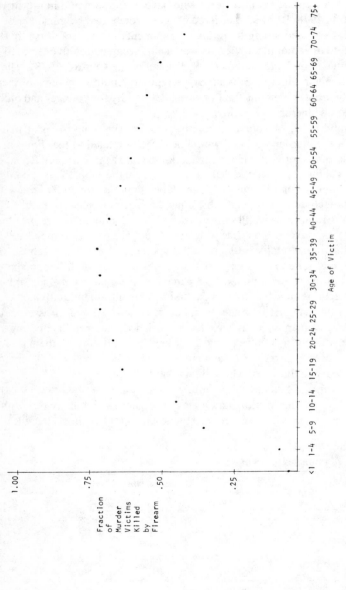

SOURCE: Uniform Crime Reports, 1978.

FIGURE 5.3   Fraction of Murder Victims Killed by Firearms, 1978, by Age of Victim

TABLE 5.7   Gun Use in Murders and Nonnegligent Homicides Resulting from Arguments or Brawls, Male Victim and Male Offender

Victim Age	Offender Age		
	18-39	*40-59*	*60+*
18-39	68.0%	79.6%	87.2%
N	(1,906)	(368)	(47)
40-59	54.5%	64.1%	66.7%
N	(398)	(245)	(57)
60+	48.3%	49.2%	63.3%
N	(58)	(61)	(30)

SOURCE: FBI Supplemental Homicide Reports, 50 cities, 1976 and 1977 combined.
NOTE: The sample size (i.e., the denominator of the fraction) is given in parentheses in each cell. Cases in which the age of the killer is not known are excluded.

fraction (87 percent) involves elderly killers and youthful victims; the lowest gun fraction (48 percent) involves youthful killers and elderly victims. Since age is highly correlated with strength and robustness, these results offer strong support for the relative vulnerability hypothesis.

Why are less vulnerable murder victims more likely to be shot than relatively vulnerable victims? A natural interpretation of this result is that intended victims who are physically strong or armed in some fashion are better able to defend themselves against homicidal assault than more vulnerable victims— unless the assailant uses a gun, the great equalizer. The "vulnerability pattern" can then be explained as resulting from some combination of three mechanisms: (1) Homicidal attacks are more likely to fail against strong victims than weak ones, and the difference in the likelihood of failure is greater for nongun attacks than attacks with a gun. (2) The likelihood that an individual will act on a homicidal impulse depends in part on the perceived probability of success. The intended victim's ability to defend himself or herself acts as a deterrent to would-be killers, but this deterrent is much weaker if the killer has a gun. (3) In the case of a planned murder, the killer will have the opportunity to equip himself with a tool that is adequate to the task. Against well-defended victims, the tool chosen will almost certainly be a gun, if one can be obtained without too much difficulty.

Each of these mechanisms is compatible with the prediction that a reduction in gun availability will cause a reduction in murder, a reduction that will be concentrated on killings that involve a victim who is physically stronger than the killer. A number of specific hypotheses are suggested by this observation, including the following: A reduction in gun availability will (H3) reduce the male/female victimization ratio in murders of spouses and other intimates; (H4) reduce the fraction of murder victims who are youthful males; and (H5) reduce the fraction of murders who are elderly. A number of similar hypotheses can be generated from the same perspective.

Assault

For a large percentage of violent crimes, it is in the assailant's interest to take care to *avoid* killing the victim. Robbery murder, for example, is a capital crime in many jurisdictions—even if the killing was an "accident" or a spontaneous reaction to victim resistance. Conklin (1972: 111) interviewed several robbery convicts who used an unloaded gun for fear that otherwise they might end up shooting their victims. In other violent confrontations, such as fights between family members, this same concern may deter the combatants from reaching for a gun—even when there is one readily available. A loaded gun is not an appropriate weapon when the assailant's intent is to hurt, but not kill, the victim. Phillips (1973) reasoned on the basis of such considerations that weapon choice in aggravated assault will be influenced by the probability and severity of punishment for criminal homicides; controlling for gun availability, the fraction of assaults committed with a gun should be inversely related to the perceived severity of sanctions. The results of his regression analysis of state-level data are compatible with this prediction.[14]

THE ROLE OF WEAPON TYPE IN DETERMINING THE OUTCOME OF VIOLENT ATTACKS

The main lessons from the previous section are common sense. Guns are more lethal than other readily available weapons. Killing with a gun requires less skill, strength, energy, and time than killing with a knife or club. A gun attack is harder to escape or otherwise defend oneself against than attacks with other weapons. For these reasons, guns are the most effective weapons in robbery and murder and are especially valuable (from the assailant's viewpoint) against victims who are relatively invulnerable. It is not surprising, then, that the likelihood that a gun will be used to commit robbery and murder is systematically related to the vulnerability of the victim. The task is chosen to suit the tool, or the tool is chosen to suit the task. Either way, the "vulnerability pattern" is the result.

These observations are reasonable and fit the data, but they do not tell the whole story, especially for murder. A large proportion of serious attacks are ambiguously motivated—the "task" is not clearly defined in the mind of the assailant. The outcome of such attacks appears to be largely a matter of chance. The probability that the victim will die as a result of such attacks (in my interpretation) reflects conscious choices made by violent criminals; the "objective dangerousness" pattern, on the other hand, is a probabilistic phenomenon.

I begin the discussion of objective dangerousness with a discussion of aggravated assault and murder. The use of violence in robbery needs a separate treatment, which is presented subsequently.

Intent and the Probability of Death
in Serious Attacks

The fraction of serious gun assaults that result in the victim's death is much higher than that of assaults with other weapons. Block (1977: 33), for example, found that of all aggravated assaults resulting in injury to the victim (and reported to the Chicago police), 14 percent of the gun cases, but only 4 percent of the knife cases, resulted in the victim's death.

One explanation for this result is that an assailant who intends to kill his victim is more likely to equip himself with a gun than an assailant who merely intends to hurt his victim. While this explanation may be valid for those murders in which there is some planning and preparation,[15] it is not a plausible explanation for the large proportion of deadly attacks that occur as the immediate result of an altercation or other provocation.

Zimring (1968, 1972) has demonstrated that a large proportion of murders are similar to serious assaults in that the attacks are unsustained—the assailant does not administer the coup de grâce, the blow that would ensure the death of his victim. Indeed, the victim was shot only once in about two-thirds of the gun murders in Zimring's Chicago samples. These cases differ very little from serious assaults: For every death resulting from a single wound in the head or chest, Zimring found 1.8 victims with the same type of wound who did not die[16]—victims who were clearly not saved by any differences in the gunman's intent, but rather just good luck with respect to the precise location of the wound.

Evidently, some proportion of gun murders are not the result of a clear intent to kill; given that the majority of murders are the immediate result of altercations, often involving alcohol and rarely much thought, it seems unlikely that many killers have *any* clearly formulated "intent" at the time of their attack. The assailant's mental state is characterized by an impulse—to punish, avenge an insult, stop a verbal or physical attack—backed by more or less cathexis. The immediate availability of a gun makes these circumstances more dangerous than would a less lethal weapon, because an unsustained attack with a gun—a single shot—is more likely to kill.

Zimring buttressed the conclusions from his first study, which compared knife and gun attacks, with a later (1972) study comparing large and small caliber gun attacks. Even after controlling for the number and location of wounds, he found that .38 caliber attacks were more than twice as likely to kill as .22 caliber attacks. It appears, then, that weapon dangerousness has a substantial independent impact on the death rate from serious assaults.

Zimring's seminal work in this area supports several important propositions, including two testable hypotheses:

(1) [H6] A restrictive gun-control policy that had the effect of causing knives and clubs to be substituted for guns would reduce the death rate in serious assault.[17]

(2) [H7] A gun-control policy focused on handguns may increase the death rate from gun assault, if shotguns and rifles were substituted for handguns as a result.[18]

(3) In setting prosecution and sentencing priorities for aggravated assault cases, gun assaults should be viewed as more serious than assaults with other weapons, ceteris paribus, since there was a higher probability of the victim's dying in the gun assaults. This is Zimring's "objective dangerousness" doctrine.[19]

Block (1977: 32) extended Zimring's work on instrumentality by comparing death rates in aggravated assault and robbery cases. He concludes that "the relative fatality of different weapons in violent crime may be a technological invariant. . . . The probability of death given injury and a particular weapon remains relatively constant and unrelated to the type of crime committed." The notion that the number of deaths per 100 criminal attacks is a "technical" constant, largely determined by the lethality of the weapon, is not supportable, however. Zimring demonstrated that the type of weapon was *one* important determinant of the outcome of serious attacks, but did not claim it was the only determinant. Presumably the weapon-specific death rates in such attacks will differ across jurisdictions and vary over time, depending on the mix of circumstances, the quality of medical care, and so forth. Swersey (1980) presents an interesting case in point.

Swersey reports that the number of assaultive (as opposed to felony) gun homicides in Harlem increased from 19 in 1968 to 70 in 1973, and then fell back to 46 in 1974. Much of the change between 1968 and 1973 was due to an increase in intentional killings resulting from disputes involving narcotics activities. The importance of changes in the intent of violent perpetrators during this period is indicated by the fact that the death rate in gun attacks *doubled* between 1968 and 1973, and then fell back in 1974. He shows that these changes reflect changes in murder—changes in intent to kill, rather than changes in the availability and quality of weapons and their spontaneous use. This conclusion is supported by observations on the circumstances and apparent motives of the murders.[20] Swersey concludes that more than 80 percent of the rise and fall in Harlem homicides was due to changes in the number of deliberate murders. He finds a similar pattern for the rest of New York City.

Swersey's findings do not undermine Zimring's position. Zimring did not deny that some killings were unambiguously motivated, or that the importance of intent in murder was subject to change over time, or that it might be more important in Harlem than in Chicago. In any event, Swersey's results are useful in documenting these possibilities.

TABLE 5.8   Percentage of Gun Assaults Resulting in Death for Selected Cities

	1965	1970	1972	1975
Atlanta	15.8	22.4	15.1	7.4
Chicago	13.2	12.5	12.2	10.6
Cleveland	14.7	14.1	15.4	10.7
Detroit	8.4	17.4	18.4	13.6
New York	9.4	9.2	9.7	7.5
Philadelphia	15.2	13.4	11.9	10.0

SOURCE: FBI Supplemental Homicide Reports (unpublished data file) and unpublished FBI data on assaults.
NOTE: The numerator of each entry is the number of gun murders and nonnegligent manslaughters, excluding felony or suspected felony-type murders. The denominators are the sum of this murder count and the number of gun-aggravated assaults reported to the police.

Calculations from the FBI's supplemental homicide reports file confirm that death rates in gun assault often vary over time by enough to have a substantial effect on the overall homicide rate. Table 5.8 reports death rates from gun assault for selected cities. Atlanta and Detroit exhibit the most extreme fluctuations during the 1965-1975 period. The death rate drops in all of these cities between 1972 and 1975, which is interesting, given the widely noted reductions in the big-city homicide rates during this period.

My conclusions can be briefly stated. The likelihood of death from a serious assault is determined, inter alia, by the assailant's intent and the lethality of the weapon he uses. The type of weapon is especially important when the intent is ambiguous. The fraction of homicides that can be viewed as deliberate (unambiguously intended) varies over time and space but is probably fairly small as a rule. The fraction of gun assaults that result in the death of the victim is one indication of the relative prevalence of deliberate gun murders.

Weapon Dangerousness in Robbery

The principal role of a weapon in robbery is to aid the robber in coercing the victim (either by force or threat) to part with his valuables. If the threat is sufficiently convincing, physical force is not necessary. For this reason, it is hardly surprising that the use of force is closely related to the weapon type in robbery, being very common in unarmed robbery and relatively rare in gun robbery. Table 5.9 documents this pattern for both commercial and noncommercial robberies committed by adult males. As shown in this table, gun robberies are less likely than other armed robberies to involve physical violence, and furthermore are less likely to injure the victim.[21] These patterns are compatible with the notion that violence plays an instrumental role in robbery—that it is employed when the robber believes it is needed to overcome or forestall victim resistance, and that this need is less likely to arise when the robber uses a gun than otherwise.

TABLE 5.9   Likelihood of Physical Attack and Injury in Robbery

	Gun[a]	Knife	Other Weapon	Unarmed
Noncommercial Robbery[b]				
Victim attacked	22.1%	39.4%	60.4%	73.5%
Victim required medical treatment[c]	7.2%	10.9%	15.5%	11.1%
Victim hospitalized overnight	2.0%	2.6%	2.7%	1.6%
N	892	841	1,060	1,259
Commercial Robbery				
Victim required medical treatment	4.8%	10.8%	17.9%	5.1%
Victim hospitalized overnight	1.5%	3.5%	6.0%	0.4%
N	2,307	288	117	570

SOURCE: National Crime Panel victimization surveys of 26 cities. This table is excerpted from Cook (1980a), Table 2.
NOTE: All incidents included in this table involved at least one male robber age 18 or over. Entries in the table do not reflect the survey sampling weights (which differed widely among the 26 cities).
a Many robberies involve more than one type of weapon. Incidents of that sort were classified according to the most lethal weapon used.
b Robberies occurring on the street, in a vehicle, or near the victim's home.
c Only about one-third of the injured gun robbery victims were actually shot. Two-thirds of the injured knife robbery victims were stabbed.

There is evidence, however, that this "instrumental violence" pattern can account for only a fraction of the injuries and deaths that result from robbery (Cook, 1980a). Three observations are relevant in this respect: First, over two-thirds of victims injured in noncommercial gun robberies do not resist in any way—even after the attack (1980a: 36); similarly, 20 out of 30 victims killed in gun robberies in Dade County between 1974 and 1976 did not resist the robber (1980a: 29). Second, the likelihood that the victim will be injured in an armed robbery is much higher if the robbery is committed by a gang of three or more than otherwise; since victims are *less* likely to offer resistance to a group of three or four robbers than to a lone robber, this result is clearly incompatible with the instrumental violence hypothesis. And third, judging from rearrest statistics for a large cohort of adult robbery arrestees in Washington, D.C., it appears that robbers who injure their victims tend to be more violence-prone than other robbers (Cook and Nagin, 1979: 39).[22] These findings are different aspects of an "excess violence" pattern: Much of the violence in robbery is not necessary, in the sense of being an instrumental response to anticipated or actual resistance by the victim. Rather, it is motivated by objectives or impulses that have little to do with ensuring successful completion of the theft. In particular, the high incidence of violence in street robberies committed by large groups (which typically have a low "take") are best viewed as a form of recreation, and the gratuitous violence against the victim may be just part of the fun.

Given these findings, it is useful to attempt a distinction between "robbery with intent to injure" or kill, and robbery without such intent (in which violence would be used only to overcome victim resistance). The latter form of robbery dominates the statistics: Most victims are not in fact injured, and the likelihood of injury is less with guns than with other weapons. However, the more violent strain of robbery, involving an intent to injure, apparently accounts for a high percentage of the serious injuries and deaths that do occur in the robbery context. Furthermore, the incidence of excess violence in robbery is subject to change over time, as Zimring (1977) demonstrated in his study of robbery murder in Detroit. He found a sharp discontinuity in 1972 in the fraction of victims killed in armed robbery: After ten years of stable weapon-specific death rates, this fraction doubled between 1971 and 1973 for gun robberies and increased even more during this period for other armed robberies.

Are gun robberies more dangerous than other armed robberies, in the sense of being more likely to result in the victim's death? Victims are killed in a higher fraction of gun as opposed to other kinds of robberies: Based on victim survey and homicide data in eight cities, I calculated that there are 9.0 victim fatalities for every 1,000 gun robberies, compared with 1.7 victim fatalities per 1,000 nongun armed robberies (Cook, 1980a: 39). Furthermore, it appears that the type of weapon plays an independent role in determining the likelihood of robbery murder; in a cross-section analysis of 50 cities, I found that the fraction of robberies resulting in the victim's death is closely related to the fraction of robberies that involve firearms (Cook, 1979: 775).[23] Thus, the objective dangerousness pattern applies to robbery as well as assault, for reasons that remain a bit obscure.

Why does the presence of a (loaded, authentic) gun in robbery increase the probability of the victim's death? My studies of robbery murder in Atlanta (Cook and Nagin, 1979) and Dade County (Cook, 1980a) indicated that in at least half of the cases the killing was deliberate: For example, a victim was tied and then executed or shot several times from close range. But insofar as intent could be ascertained from police reports, it appears that these intentional killings were not premeditated, but rather decided on during the course of the robbery. Perhaps the explanation for why these spontaneous decisions are more likely to occur when the robber is holding a gun is related to Wolfgang's (1958: 79) suggestion: "The offender's physical repugnance to engaging in direct physical assault by cutting or stabbing his adversary may mean that in the absence of a firearm no homicide occurs."

Two propositions can be inferred from the discussion above:

(1) [H8] A reduction in gun availability will increase the robbery injury rate (Skogan, 1978) but reduce the robbery murder rate.
(2) Given the excess violence pattern in robbery, the robbery cases in which the victim is injured should be allocated special emphasis in establishing criminal prosecution and sentencing priorities (Cook, 1980). In a high proportion of these crimes, the attack that caused the injury was not instrumental to the robbery, but rather was a distinct act. A relatively severe judicial response to such cases might act as a deterrent to excess violence in robbery.

Coercion and Assault

Does the instrumental violence pattern in robbery have any parallel in assault? I suspect the answer is yes, but know of no empirical evidence. Some (unknown) fraction of assault cases are similar to robbery in that the assailant's objective is to coerce the victim's compliance—the assailant wants the victim to stop attacking him (physically or verbally), or stop dancing with his girlfriend, or get off his favorite barstool, or turn down the stereo. Moreover, as in the case of robbery, the probability of a physical attack in such cases may be less if the assailant has a gun than otherwise, because the victim will be less inclined to ignore or resist a threat enforced by the display of a gun. (It may also be true that the assailant would be more hesitant to use a gun than another weapon to make good his threat). If this reasoning is correct, it supports the following:

[H9] A general increase in gun availability will reduce the number of assault-related injuries.

MEASURING GUN AVAILABILITY

The preceding discussion included detailed descriptive information on weapon use in violent crime and provided interpretive labels for certain patterns in the data. Nine hypotheses were suggested concerning the relationship between gun availability and violent crime. While these hypotheses are plausible and receive some support from the descriptive data, it is difficult to say how much confidence can be placed in them until they have been subjected to direct test. More generally, it would be useful to measure the quantitative importance of these hypothesized relationships to ascertain whether they are worth taking into account in policy design.

Without valid measures of one or more dimensions of availability, it is not possible to measure directly the effect of gun availability on violent crime. An indirect approach to this measurement problem is to evaluate the impact of specific gun-control ordinances on violent crime, on the assumption that gun availability is the intervening condition by which the ordinance's effects on crime are transmitted. This approach mitigates the need to measure availability directly, and evaluations of this sort are in any event interesting in their own right. Of course, if the ordinance in question has no discernible effect, it is not possible in the absence of a direct measure of gun availability to distinguish between two possible explanations: (1) The ordinance had no effect on availability, or (2) the ordinance reduced availability, but the change in availability had no effect on crime.[24]

The remainder of this section reviews various attempts to measure availability and use the resulting measures to study the effect of availability on crime. A review of policy impact evaluations is left to the following section's discussion of gun-control ordinances.

Gun Use in Homicide as an Availability Measure

Perhaps the most commonly used measure of gun availability is the fraction of criminal homicides committed with a gun. A number of authors have related this gun fraction to the homicide rate across jurisdictions or over time in a single jurisdiction. A positive correlation is interpreted as evidence that increased gun availability causes increases in the murder rate.

One of the first systematic studies of this sort was by Brearley (1932: 68-71), who found a correlation of .61 for a cross-section sample of states (1924-1926 averages). He interpreted this high correlation as evidence supporting a crackdown on the common practice of carrying concealed weapons. Brearley's high correlation, incidentally, is primarily the result of regional differences—the South was high in both gun ownership and homicide, and New England was very low in both respects.[25]

Several authors have used international comparisons to make a similar point. Etzioni and Kemp (1973) compared U.S. homicide rates with those of several other economically developed nations, and interpreted the vast difference between the United States and the other nations as evidence that the relatively strict gun-control measures in these comparison countries were highly effective in suppressing homicide rates (an amazing conclusion, given that the U.S. *nongun* homicide rate exceeds the total homicide rate for every one of these comparison countries). Curtis (1974: 103-113) performed the most comprehensive set of international comparisons. He demonstrated that for some clusters of countries, the correlation between homicide rates and proportion involving guns is *negative*. Almost any cluster that includes the United States will produce a positive correlation because the United States is so extreme on both variables.

Fisher (1976) reports a correlation between homicide rate and the gun fraction of .78 for Detroit, 1926-1968.[26] The intertemporal relationship between these variables for the United States as a whole is also close to linear, as shown in Figure 5.4 and Table 5.10. Note, for example, that the homicide rates are about the same in 1929 and 1970 (8.3-8.4) and the gun fraction in these years is also virtually identical (two-thirds). The trough in the murder trend that occurred in the 1950s is accompanied by an all-time low in the gun fraction (about one-half). The 1974 peak in the murder rate coincides with a peak in the gun fraction.[27] Clearly there is something going on here—but what is it? Were firearms less available in the 1950s than in the 1930s or 1970s? Was availability less in 1975 than in 1974? Or are there other reasonable interpretations of these results?

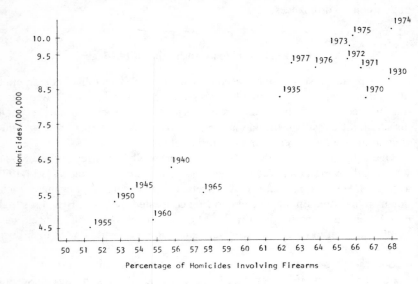

SOURCE: See Table 5.10.
NOTE: Points are labeled with the year to which they refer.

FIGURE 5.4   Relationship Between Homicide Rate and Gun Fraction in Homicide, 1930-1977

The fraction of murders involving guns is not just a supply (availability) phenomenon; it also may reflect "demand" in two senses. First, a change in the fraction of murders that are planned in advance should cause a corresponding change in the gun fraction. Second, a change in the relative distribution of murders among geographic areas, circumstances, or demographic categories is likely to change the observed gun fraction even if gun availability does not change. Such changes in the composition of murder do occur and tend to undermine the validity of the gun fraction as a proxy for gun availability. For example, Block (1977: Ch. 4) found that the vast increase in Chicago homicides, 1965-1974, was accompanied by equally impressive changes in the distributions of motives, ages of victims and offenders, prior relationships between victims and offenders, and so forth—all factors that may help account for the large increase in the gun fraction during this period in Chicago. Therefore it is questionable how much of this increase in the gun fraction is due to increased density of gun ownership.

Correlations between the homicide rate and the gun fraction do not serve as useful statistics for testing the hypothesis that an increase in gun availability will cause an increase in the homicide rate. The high positive correlation

TABLE 5.10   Relationship Between Homicide Rate and Gun Fraction in Homicide, 1930-1975

Year	Gun Fraction	Homicides/100,000
1930	67.7	8.8
1935	61.5	8.3
1940	55.9	6.3
1945	53.4	5.7
1950	52.6	5.3
1955	51.3	4.5
1960	54.7	4.7
1965	57.5	5.5
1970	66.6	8.3
1971	66.2	9.1
1972	65.6	9.4
1973	65.7	9.8
1974	67.9	10.2
1975	65.8	10.0
1976	63.8	9.1
1977	62.5	9.2

SOURCE: Data for 1930-1970 taken from U.S. Bureau of the Census, *Historical Statistics, Colonial Times to 1970*, p. 409. Remaining data are from the *Statistical Abstract of the U.S., 1978*.

between these variables over the last five decades in the United States is intriguing and warrants further investigation. But it does not shed much light on the causal role of weapons in murder. A persuasive empirical analysis of this role requires, inter alia, a validated proxy for gun availability and a technique for controlling for variables other than gun availability that influence the murder rate.

Other Availability Measures

A variety of proxy measures for gun availability have been suggested in the literature. Most of these proxies were intended to reflect gun availability in the sense of density of gun ownership. For some purposes, it may be useful to refine this definition by distinguishing between density in the sense of the number of guns per capita, and density in the sense of the fraction of households that possess at least one gun. There is also an important distinction between handguns and longguns; most of the guns used in crime are handguns, even though they constitute only a fraction (less than one-third) of the guns in private hands; for this reason most researchers view handgun availability as more germane to the violent-crime problem than overall gun availability.

Manufacture, Import, and Sales Data

Newton and Zimring (1969) assembled an historical series on gun manufacture and import and used this series as a basis for estimating the current private stocks of handguns and longguns. This approach can provide only a rough approximation of the stock, and the rate at which this stock is changing over time, for several reasons: Imports are not measured accurately;[28] there are few data available on exports;[29] and, most important, the rate at which old guns are removed from the private stock (that is, scrapped or lost) is not known (see the discussion of trends in gun availability at the beginning of this chapter). Newton and Zimring's approach to estimating the stock was to sum new manufactures and known imports since 1899. This approach assumes that other additions and subtractions to the stock cancel out: that subtractions, the sum of exports and attrition due to breakage, are equal to additions, the sum of unmeasured imports, military weapons entering private circulation, and so forth.

Phillips et al. (1976) used the Newton-Zimring measure of the U.S. handgun stock for the years 1951-1968 in their time-series study of U.S. homicide rates. They divided the stock in each year by the "population of the FBI's sample of cities" (1976: 468), and labeled the result an "index of the causal factors affecting willful homicide" (1976: 468). From their discussion, it appears that the authors intended this variable both as a measure of gun availability per se and as a proxy for other variables important to the etiology of homicide. The only other variable in their homicide equation is the "clearance ratio" for homicide. The equation is estimated using two-stage least squares, with the rather unreasonable result that "a 10% reduction in handgun density could lead to a 27.4% reduction in the homicide offense rate" (1976: 474).

While manufacture and import data give some indication of how the total U.S. stock of guns is changing over time, these data are of no use for comparing jurisdictions or analyzing trends in availability for a city or state. One alternative for jurisdictions that have a handgun permit system is to use the rate at which permits are issued as a proxy for changes in handgun density. To date, only one published study has made use of such data to test hypotheses relating gun availability and violent crime.[30] Fisher (1976) used a measure of "firearm availability" in Detroit that was essentially a weighted average of handgun licenses issued and handguns registered per year.[31] Note that this is not a measure of the total stock of handguns or even a direct measure of the rate at which the handgun stock is changing (since he does not subtract removals from the handgun stock from his measure of new acquisitions). However, his measure is no doubt highly correlated with the rate of change of the handgun stock.

Fisher performs a regression analysis of the effect of his firearm availability measure and two other factors on homicide rates in Detroit, using a very short time series (1963-1971). His availability measure is statistically significant.

Sample Surveys

While poll results help quantify and give some structure to recent trends in gun density, poll-based estimates are not available for enough years to support intertemporal correlational studies of its relationship to violent crime. Furthermore, national polls cannot be used to estimate the geographical structure of gun ownership, other than urban/rural or regional comparisons. Murray (1975) uses poll-based estimates of handgun ownership rates for the four census regions as a measure of handgun availability. His 1970 state cross-section regression analyses of homicide, robbery, and assault use this measure as one of the independent variables; in constructing this variable, Murray assigned each state the handgun ownership fraction of the region to which it belongs. His de facto assumption that all the states in a region have approximately the same density of handgun ownership is rather far from the truth. For example, the western region includes both the Pacific states and the mountain states; the former tend to be low and the latter very high in density of handgun ownership (see Cook, 1979). The crudity of Murray's measure of handgun availability may account for his finding that this variable has no discernible effect on violent-crime rates.

Newton and Zimring (1969) used estimates of regional handgun-ownership rates derived from their Harris poll in a more straightforward manner. They note that the fraction of homicides and assaults committed with a gun are highest in the South and lowest in New England; this pattern corresponds to the interregional pattern of handgun-ownership rates, as predicted by the hypothesis that gun availability influences the choice of weapon in violent crime.

Firearm Accidents and Hunting Licenses

Estimates of the density of gun ownership based on polls or manufacturing data have the virtue of being direct measures of gun availability, but are not useful in correlational studies of the relationship between gun availability and violent crime due to the paucity of distinct observations. To remedy this problem, a number of proxy measures have been employed in correlational studies.

As noted earlier, Phillips (1973) used the fatal firearms accident rate for each state as a measure of gun availability. He makes no effort to demonstrate the validity of this measure, and its validity is certainly questionable. A gun becomes involved in a fatal accident through misuse. People who cause such accidents are disproportionately involved in other accidents, violent crime, and heavy drinking (Newton and Zimring, 1969: 29). The interstate distribution of accidental firearms fatalities may therefore reflect the incidence of violence proneness and alcohol abuse, as well as firearms ownership, across states.

The number of hunting licenses issued per capita has more obvious problems as a proxy for gun ownership—especially for handguns, which are rarely acquired for use in hunting. Krug's (1967) use of this measure has been criticized by Zimring (1968).

Measures Based on Weapon-Choice Statistics

Several measures of gun availability are variants on the measure discussed in the section on intent and probability of death: the fraction of homicides involving firearms. Brill (1977) defines his "choice availability" measure as the fraction of all criminal homicides, robberies, and aggravated assaults in a city that involves guns. Cook's (1979) gun availability index is the average of the gun fraction in suicide and the gun fraction in assaultive homicide (nonfelony homicide) in a city.

How can such indexes be justified? To be specific, what is the logical relationship between, say, the gun fraction in suicide and the fraction of households that own a gun? Under certain assumptions, we can view suicides as a representative sample of households on the dimension of gun ownership: (1) A person who decides to commit suicide uses a gun if he or she is a member of a household that owns a gun, and otherwise employs some alternative means. (2) People who decide to commit suicide are just as likely to own a gun as the others in their jurisdiction. (3) The likelihood that a suicide attempt with a gun is successful is the same as for attempts by other means. Under these assumptions, the gun fraction in suicide would serve as a direct estimate of the fraction of all households that own a gun. These assumptions are not supportable, however. But even if the suicide gun fraction is not an unbiased estimate of the gun-ownership fraction, these fractions may still be highly correlated with each other—in which case the suicide gun fraction will serve as a valid proxy or index for gun availability. A high correlation may obtain under much weaker assumptions than the three given above: Basically, what is required is a systematic positive relationship between gun availability and weapon choice in suicide.

Brill makes no effort to validate his choice availability measure, and it is not clear that his measure is an improvement on simply using the gun fraction in homicide. His measure can be viewed as a weighted average of the gun fractions in homicide, robbery, and aggravated assault, where the weights are given by the relative frequencies of these crimes in a city. This weighting scheme undermines the validity of his measure for two reasons. First, Brill's index will be influenced by crime-reporting practices in a city: Cities differ widely with respect to the fraction of robberies and assaults reported to police, and these differences may have a weapon-specific component. Second, Brill's index will be influenced by the true underlying mix of assaultive violence and robbery in a city. For example, the gun fraction in homicide is typically much higher than the gun fraction in robbery. Even though the relative frequencies of homicide and robbery in a city have little to do with gun availability, Brill's index weights these two crimes in proportion to these relative frequencies. Atlanta, with relatively few robberies per homicide, will for that reason have a higher index than New York or Boston, which have relatively many robberies per homicide.

Brill (1977: 21) compared his choice availability measure with robbery and criminal homicide rates for ten cities. He concluded on the basis of a rank-order comparison that homicide is closely related to gun availability, but robbery is not.

Cook (1979) calculated the gun fractions for suicide and assaultive homicide for each of 50 large cities, combining 1973 and 1974 data for each. The distribution of suicides and murderers differ from each other rather dramatically in terms of race, age, socioeconomic status, and so on, and of course the immediate circumstances in which these acts occur are very different. Nevertheless, the gun fractions for suicide and assaultive homicide are highly correlated across these 50 cities (.82), suggesting that environmental determinants of weapon choice for both types of violent acts are similar. I assumed that the underlying environmental determinant was gun availability, and constructed an index of gun availability by averaging these two fractions in each city. The validity of this index was tested by the following technique: The fifty cities were divided into eight regional subsets and an "urban regional index" constructed by combining the indexes for each city. This urban regional index was then compared with the fraction of urban households in each region that reported owning a gun in one of the recent NORC general social surveys (three surveys were combined to achieve sufficiently large sample sizes).[32] My index proved completely compatible with the survey results.

This index was then used as a measure of gun availability in a regression analysis of robbery rates.[33] Controlling for other variables important in explaining intercity differences in robbery, the principal results were as follows: (1) A 10 percent reduction in the number of handguns in a city is associated with about a 5 percent reduction in the gun robbery rate. (2) The overall robbery rate is not discernibly influenced by gun availability in a city. (3) A 10 percent reduction in the number of handguns in a city is associated with about a 4 percent reduction in the number of robbery murders. Thus, gun density influences weapon choice in robbery but not the overall robbery rate. Weapon choice is important because it influences the likelihood that a robbery victim will be killed.

Other Definitions of Gun Availability

The indexes of gun availability discussed above are most naturally interpreted as measuring the density of gun (or handgun) ownership. An alternative definition of gun availability, focusing on the effective price of a gun, is also of interest. Of course, effective price and density are somewhat related, through both demand and supply effects: A high price will reduce the rate of acquisitions (quantity demanded); on the other hand, a high density of guns will tend to reduce the effective price of guns by supporting active secondhand and black markets.

However, the distinction between gun density and effective price is important for some purposes. For example, when a state or city institutes a new restriction on handgun transfers, the short-term effect on effective price will presumably be much larger than its effect on the existing stock of guns. Such a restriction will influence crime only in the short run if the effective price of handguns has an effect on violent crime independent of gun density.

The relevant price is that typically paid by active criminals and others who are highly prone to use their guns in crime. As explained at the beginning of this chapter, "crime guns" are usually not purchased from licensed dealers but rather from fences or personal contacts.[34] Prices paid by undercover agents in a city are a potential source of relevant information, but this information is sparse and difficult to obtain.

One indirect measure of effective price in a state is the fraction of crime-related guns purchased out of state. Zimring (1976) proposed an alternative measure of effective price.[35] He used Project Identification data to analyze the age distribution of handguns confiscated by police and found that recently manufactured guns are disproportionately represented in this distribution. There are a variety of possible explanations for this effect. One plausible explanation is that the frequency with which a gun is used is greatest immediately after acquisition and declines thereafter.[36] Since about half of all handgun transactions involve new guns (Blose and Cook, 1980), new guns will be used more actively than older ones. Since guns are rarely confiscated except while in use—being carried away from home, or used in crime—the "new gun" pattern will be evident in samples of confiscated guns. If a local ordinance is adopted that is designed to increase the effective price of new guns, then the age distribution of guns in use should shift accordingly. Hence, measures such as the average age of confiscated handguns or the fraction of such guns first sold within two years prior to confiscation may serve as indicators of effective price.

None of these indicators can be calculated from data that are routinely collected and reported by law enforcement agencies. However, it may be worthwhile to collect such data for the purpose of evaluating the effect of an important gun-control ordinance at the time of its implementation.

Reflections on
Gun Availability Studies

Gun availability is a somewhat elusive concept. The difficulty in finding an operational definition that can be implemented from published data may have helped deter a potential boom in correlational studies relating gun availability to various measures.

However, those who are inclined to pursue this line of research on violent crime do have several reasonably good measures to choose from. Not surprisingly, I believe, my index has the greatest claim to validity for cross-section work. Time-series analyses can best be conducted utilizing data on handgun permits, in jurisdictions that have required such permits for a number of years.

The strongest finding that has emerged from the studies reviewed in this section is that the fractions of homicides, suicides, and robberies that involve guns are highly correlated with each other across jurisdictions, and that these gun fractions reflect density of gun ownership. In short, the likelihood that a gun will be the weapon of choice in committing a violent act is closely related to the density of gun ownership. The more interesting question—whether gun availability influences the overall rates of homicide, robbery, and so on—has not received a definitive answer, though the answer appears to be no for robbery and yes for robbery murders.

The generic problems with correlational studies are well known and should serve to chill enthusiasm for this approach a bit (Cook, 1980b). In particular, consider the difficulty in interpreting the results of cross-section studies relating density of gun ownership to, say, the criminal homicide rate. There is a reasonably stable historical pattern of both gun ownership and homicide across regions in the United States (for example, the South is high on both variables, while the Northeast is low). These patterns may reflect underlying cultural differences that influence both variables. To partial out the causal effect of gun ownership on homicide requires that cultural differences be "controlled for" in the specification of the regression equation. But that is difficult to accomplish in convincing fashion, to say the least.

Persuasive time-series analysis also requires that other variables be controlled for in assessing the independent effect of gun availability on violent crime. Given our high level of ignorance concerning the etiology of violent crime, there is considerable uncertainty about the appropriate specification of the regression equation. Furthermore, in using time-series observations, the possibility of reverse causation must be considered—it is entirely possible that an increase in violent crime causes an increase in the rate of gun acquisition in a jurisdiction. This causal interaction between guns and crime can in principle be modeled and possibly estimated, but it has not been done yet.

An alternative approach to assessing the effect of gun availability on violent crime is to evaluate the effects of legal interventions designed to reduce availability. This approach promises to eventually provide more definitive tests of my hypotheses (and others) than the correlational studies reviewed above.

EVALUATING GUN-CONTROL ORDINANCES

The enactment of a major piece of federal or state gun-control legislation, or the implementation of a strenuous enforcement effort for existing legislation, can be viewed as "natural experiments" to test the effects of gun availability on violent crime. A comparison of jurisdictions that differ with respect to stringency of firearms regulation can also yield evidence on this issue. These approaches seem promising but have for the most part been neglected by researchers.

Guns are subject to a variety of regulations; these regulations differ widely among states, and the effects of these regulations are mediated inter alia by the

effort devoted to their enforcement. This complex picture is further complicated by the fact that many cities have enacted their own gun ordinances, more
stringent than those in effect in their respective states. Research evaluating the
effects of these ordinances has taken one of two approaches. Some studies
employ a cross-section regression analysis approach in which one or more of
the independent variables is an index of state regulatory stringency. A second
approach focuses on the impact of the implementation of a new ordinance or
enforcement policy in a single jurisdiction.

Cross-Section Studies

Three cross-section studies evaluating the effectiveness of gun-control ordinances have been published (Geisel et al., 1969; Magaddino, n.d.; Murray,
1975). Each of these studies (summarized in Table 5.11) uses cross-section data
on the 50 states and reports regression analyses relating various measures of
violence rates to a number of independent variables—including one or more
indicators of the stringency of state gun-control legislation.

The first challenge in this type of study is to develop a numerical characterization of state gun-control ordinances. For ordinances that are targeted on gun
availability (such as purchase permit requirements), the ideal measure would be
an accurate indicator of the average effective price of handguns in a state. For
restrictions on carrying, the criterion is not obvious; certainly one candidate
here would be measures of the likelihood and severity of punishment for carrying a concealed gun. In any event, it is clear that appropriate indicators should
be sensitive not only to the presence or absence of a particular type of regulation, but also to the quality of the enforcement effort. In the case of gun-control
ordinances that can be expected to achieve their full effect only after some delay
(for example, restrictions on purchase), it is important to choose an indicator
that distinguishes between newly enacted laws and those that have been on the
books for a number of years. The indicator variables actually used in these three
studies, however, do not come close to approximating these criteria: A state's
score on each of these studies' measures depends only on how many and which
type of regulations it has on the books, and is not sensitive to duration or quality
of enforcement. To illustrate the deficiency of these measures, it is enough to
point out that none of them would distinguish between the carrying law in
Massachusetts (where convicted violators are subject to a mandatory prison
term of one year) and otherwise similar carrying laws in other states that lack
the mandatory provision and are typically treated as minor cases by the courts.[37]

Of the three studies, Murray's (1975) has received the most attention, in
congressional hearings and elsewhere. Jones (1980) has pointed out several
problems with Murray's data (including a serious misclassification of gun-control ordinances in one state). Murray's stepwise regression procedure is also
unsatisfactory, since it in effect minimizes the chance of finding a statistically

TABLE 5.11 State Cross-Section Regression Analyses of Gun-Control Effectiveness

Author	Dependent Variables	Indicators for Gun Controls	Other Variables	Basic Findings for Gun-Control Indicators (significant at alpha = .10)
Geisel, Roll, and Wettick (1969)	Rates, for 1960 and 1965, of the following: firearm and total homicide, firearm and total suicide, accidental firearm deaths Rates, for 1965 only: firearm and total assault, robbery	Single index consisting of the sum of scores on each of 8 dimensions. Scoring system based on "best fit" criterion.	Income Education Demographic variables Police employees Licensed hunters	Gun-control stringency index has negative effect on the following: firearms homicides, firearms and total suicides, accidental firearm deaths
Magaddino (n.d.)	1970 rates of homicide, aggravated assault, and robbery	Separate dummy variables for each of 17 dimensions of gun-control legislation.	Income Education Demographic variables Police employees Percentage of crimes cleared by arrest Average prison time served	No clear-cut results

—continued on the following page

TABLE 5.11 Continued

Author	Dependent Variables	Indicators for Gun Controls	Other Variables	Basic Findings for Gun-Control Indicators (significant at alpha = .10)
Murray (1975)	1970 rates of homicide, assault, robbery, suicide, firearms accidents.	Separate indicator variables for 7 dimensions of gun-control legislation (most are dummy variables)	Income Education Demographic variables Log of total state population Poverty Unemployment Occupational distribution (Note: Choice of variables differs among crime types)	Gun-control indicators, when added last in stepwise procedure, do not make a significant addition to total variance explained.

significant result for the gun-control indicators. Geisel et al. (1969), who *do* find that some measures of violent crime are responsive to their gun-control index, also suffer from technical problems; in particular, their procedure for choosing a scoring system for gun-control measures is virtually guaranteed to produce an exaggerated estimate of the precision of their estimates.[38]

Perhaps the most fundamental problem with this type of correlational study is that the causal process which generates crime rates and a structure of gun-control regulations is not clear. Gun regulations are not distributed randomly among states—they are adopted or rejected as part of a political process that may well be influenced by both violent-crime rates and the public attitudes toward guns. Regions characterized by high gun-ownership rates (like the mountain states) have weak or nonexistent regulations, presumably because the public's respect for the "right" to bear arms is more intense in these states than elsewhere. But if the stringency of state regulations tends to be influenced by and highly correlated with public attitudes toward guns and gun-ownership rates, then it is not clear how to interpret the results of the type of study reviewed here. Is it the regulations per se that influence violent-crime rates? Or is it that the cultural differences between states determine *both* the stringency of state regulation *and* the propensity of residents to acquire guns and use them when the occasion arises? The intrinsic difficulty in sorting out this causal process from cross-section data suggests that this cross-section regression approach will never produce persuasive results.[39]

The prognosis for evaluations of the impact of a new regulation in a jurisdiction is more hopeful.

Evaluating the Impact of New Regulations

Three major statutes have been subjected to evaluation: The federal Gun Control Act, the Bartley-Fox Amendment (Massachusetts), and the Firearms Control Act (District of Columbia).[40] These three statutes represent three distinct strategies for reducing gun availability and hence violent crime involving guns. My discussion includes a number of suggestions relevant to evaluating the effects of each type of intervention.

The Gun Control Act of 1968

As noted above, a major purpose of the GCA was to ban mail-order sales of guns to private individuals, and otherwise interdict the interstate traffic in firearms. Zimring (1975: 176) observes that "if the Gun Control Act and its enforcement has led to a reduction in interstate firearms traffic, this reduction should be evident in New York City and Boston, the principal cities in the two most restrictive handgun-licensing states in the United States, because out-of-state handguns are a higher proportion of total handguns in these cities than in other metropolitan areas." Zimring finds that the trends in such variables as handgun homicides, firearm assaults, and the percentage of total homicides involving handguns provide no support for the hypothesis that the GCA reduced gun availability in New York and Boston. All these variables trend upward during 1966-1973, and these trends are not discernibly different from corresponding trends in Philadelphia, or the total of 57 large cities. Based on these findings and evidence from ATF tracing studies, Zimring concludes that the Gun Control Act had failed to diminish handgun migration.

One explanation for this apparent failure is the lack of enforcement effort on the part of the Bureau of Alcohol, Tobacco, and Firearms—the federal agency responsible for interdicting illegal interstate movements of firearms. This explanation received partial support from Operation DC, in which the ATF enforcement staff in the District of Columbia was increased from 7 to between 35 and 50 special agents for the first six months of 1970. The gun murder rate dropped significantly during this period and rebounded thereafter, while the nongun murder rate remained roughly constant. The result is highly supportive of the claim that gun availability is sensitive to law enforcement efforts and, further, that gun availability influences the gun murder rate and the overall murder rate. However, this picture is clouded somewhat by the fact that the gun assault pattern shows no corresponding pattern during the period Operation DC was in effect. Possibly the main effect of this operation was on deliberate, planned killings—though Zimring presents no evidence on this issue.

The Bartley-Fox Amendment

The Bartley-Fox Amendment has received more scholarly scrutiny than any other single piece of gun-related legislation. Unlike most "natural experiments," the lessons of this intervention will not be lost for want of scholarly attention.

The Bartley-Fox Amendment, which took effect on April 1, 1975, established a minimum sentence of one year for an initial violation of Massachusetts's legal requirements for carrying a gun away from home or office. The amendment did not eliminate the possibility of charge bargaining in the prosecution of such cases, but did effectively tie the hands of the sentencing judge. This mandatory sentence provision received tremendous publicity at the time the amendment was implemented. The immediate impact was clear-cut: Thousands of gun owners applied for licenses to carry (required to carry a handgun legally), and most gun owners obtained a Firearms Identification Card (required of all gun owners, and sufficient for carrying a longgun legally). Indeed, 100,000 FID cards were issued in the month of April 1975—more than had been issued in all of 1973 and 1974 combined (Beha, 1977).

Beha's early analysis of the effect of this amendment found that the police and courts were making a conscientious effort to implement the spirit of the new law. It had little effect on the court processing of robberies and murders, but it did increase the likelihood of prison time for defendants accused of assault with a firearm. Most important, cases in which illegal carrying was the most serious charge had an increased chance of resulting in a prison term. Beha found some indication (from interviews with law enforcement officers and a few criminals in Boston) that the propensity of the "streetwise" to go armed had been reduced somewhat by the threat of the law.

Pierce and Bowers (1979) assessed the impact of Bartley-Fox (B-F) on violent crime through 1977. They constructed annual time series on a number of violent-crime measures for Massachusetts, Boston, and several comparison groups. Reductions in gun-related crime that occurred around the implementation of Bartley-Fox (April 1, 1975) are interpreted as evidence that this law had a deterrent effect—an interpretation that is validated by comparison of Massachusetts crime patterns with those of other jurisdictions. Pierce and Bowers believe their evidence is generally supportive of the proposition that this law had a major effect on violent crime. In what follows, I use the data included in their paper to assess this claim. My analysis is limited to Boston.

The first problem which must be faced by anyone attempting to evaluate the impact of B-F is that the long-term upward trend in a number of violent-crime statistics was reversed in the mid-1970s—not only in Boston, but in large cities throughout the nation. The following variables peaked in large cities in 1974 (the year before B-F): the homicide rate, the assault-precipitated gun homicide rate, the overall gun homicide rate, the fraction of homicides committed with a gun, and the fraction of armed assaults committed with a gun. Other related variables peaked in 1975, including the felony gun homicide rate, the gun robbery rate, the overall armed robbery rate, and the rate of gun assaults. All of these variables declined in subsequent years. Obviously B-F did not have a nationwide effect; it is simply coincidence that the implementation of this amendment coincided with a reversal in the national violent-crime trends of the preceding decade. In any event, the case for B-F must be evaluated within this national context, with emphasis on the precise timing or the magnitude of the changes observed in Boston, as compared with other cities.

Bartley-Fox received a tremendous amount of publicity around the time of its implementation, and the huge increase in applications for FID cards and licenses to carry indicates that gun owners were aware of its provisions by April 1975. There is no reason to believe that its effect would be delayed or gradual; indeed, it is quite plausible that its greatest impact would occur during the first few months and attenuate thereafter as it fell from public attention. For this reason, I focus on the change in Boston crime rates that occurred in 1975, as compared with earlier years. Short-term changes are also most informative in the sense of being less subject to the influence of changes in other etiological factors.

Table 5.12 is an extract from the voluminous data provided by Pierce and Bowers (1979). If B-F was effective in discouraging violence-prone people from going armed, we would expect a reduction in the fractions of armed assaults, armed robberies, and homicides committed with a gun. These declines did occur, and in each case exceeded the corresponding decline in other cities of similar size to Boston. Furthermore, the per-capita rate of gun assault, robbery, and homicide declined in Boston between 1974 and 1975, and again these declines were larger than in the comparison group. The relative increases in nongun armed assault and robbery are predictable "displacement" effects, as criminals substitute other weapons for guns. All of these results are compatible with the proposition that B-F had a considerable deterrent effect. But other results shown in the table cast some doubt on this proposition. First, the rate of gun homicide in Boston started falling *before* the implementation of B-F, declining 14 percent between 1973 and 1974 (a time when this rate was still increasing in other cities). The gun fraction in Boston homicides also peaked in 1973, and fell substantially between 1973 and 1974. The changes in these variables between 1974 and 1975 may be interpreted as merely a continuation of this new "trend," rather than as a result of B-F. Second, the 1974-1975 decline in the fractions of gun assaults and gun robberies that result in the victim's death are problematical. There is no reason to think that B-F would cause a reduction in the "kill rate" in a gun crime; indeed, we might expect the kill rate to increase in gun assault, if B-F has a greater effect on ambiguously intended gun assaults than on deliberate murders. Unfortunately, Pierce and Bowers offer no data for other cities on these variables. As shown in Table 5.4, however, a number of large cities did experience a decline in the kill rate during this period.

The statistical technique employed by Pierce and Bowers in this evaluation is a pretest-posttest design with a control group (Campbell and Stanley, 1966). The persuasiveness of findings generated by this technique depends on the following condition: The control group is not affected by the intervention, but otherwise the change in the criterion variables in the control group is governed by the same factors that influence the experimental group, and with similar effect. In other words, the criterion variable for the experimental group must be highly correlated with the control group prior to and following the intervention. Unfortunately, Pierce and Bowers do not justify their choice of control groups by reporting such correlations; rather, their choice is justified by the reasonable claim that Massachusetts's neighboring jurisdictions will have similar crime patterns (or, in the case of Boston, that cities of similar size will have similar crime patterns) in the absence of a major intervention.

An alternative approach to evaluating Bartley-Fox is suggested by Deutsch and Alt (1977). They use a stochastic modeling technique, applied to monthly time-series data on armed robbery, homicide, and gun assault in Boston (Janu-

TABLE 5.12   Violent Crime Trends in Boston and Other Large Cities, 1973-1975

	1973	1974	1975	B-F Change
1. Gun assault rate/100,000				
Boston	89	101	88	−15%
Other cities, .5-1.0 million	106	112	114	
2. Nongun armed assault rate/100,000				
Boston	251	290	380	+28%
Other cities, .5-1.0 million	172	179	185	
3. Gun percentage in armed assault				
Boston	26.2	25.9	18.8	−26%
Other cities, .5-1.0 million	38.1	38.5	38.1	
4. Gun robbery rate/100,000				
Boston		363	357	−9%
Other cities, .5-1.0 million		250	268	
5. Nongun armed robbery rate/100,000				
Boston		320	423	+27%
Other cities, .5-1.0 million		81	85	
6. Gun percentage in armed robbery				
Boston		53.2	45.8	−11%
Other cities, .5-1.0 million		75.5	75.9	
Boston street robbery		34.6	29.3	
Boston commercial robbery		83.8	80.8	
7. Number of gun homicides				
Boston	81	70	55	−15%
Other cities, .25-1.00 million	2,882	3,140	2,933	
8. Nongun homicides				
Boston	54	64	64	−9%
Other cities, .25-1.00 million	1,391	1,379	1,507	
9. Gun percentage in homicide				
Boston	60.0	52.2	46.2	−7%
Other cities, .25-1.00 million	67.4	69.5	66.1	
10. Percentage of gun assaults resulting in death				
Boston	18.8	13.2	13.0	
11. Percentage of gun robberies resulting in death				
Boston		0.88	0.54	

SOURCE: Various tables in Pierce and Bowers (1979).
NOTE: "B-F Change" is the algebraic difference between the percentage change in Boston and the percentage change in other cities for the variable in question. This measure is one possible measure of the effect of Bartley-Fox. See discussion in text.

ary 1966 to October 1975). The basic assumption underlying this technique is that Boston's crime data are generated by a stable dynamic process, characterized by estimable trends, seasonal effects, and random error. The parameters of this process can be estimated from historical data, and the resulting equation used, in effect, to predict what crime rates would have been in the absence of the intervention (Bartley-Fox). If actual postintervention rates are significantly different from predicted rates, the difference is attributed to the effect of the intervention. Deutsch and Alt (1977) find significant reductions in armed robbery and gun assault, but not homicide, during the first six months following implementation of Bartley-Fox. In a follow-up study of the same three violent-crime measures, utilizing 30 months of postintervention data, Deutsch (1980) finds large reductions in all three series, allegedly resulting from the law.

The problem with Deutsch's approach, especially for long-term follow-ups, is that there is no reason to believe that crime rates are generated by a stable dynamic process, interrupted only by highly visible interventions such as Bartley-Fox. As noted above, a number of large cities other than Boston experienced declines in various measures of violent crime around the time Bartley-Fox was implemented. This coincidence casts doubt on Deutsch's interpretation of his results.

The Bartley-Fox Amendment represents one generic approach to taking the guns out of violent confrontations—deterring people from going armed when away from home by increasing the threatened penalty for this crime. Other examples of policies with the same basic objective are a more proactive policing effort against concealed weapons, or a ban on small handguns.[41] Such policies have no effect on gun availability, defined as the density of gun ownership, or the effective price of acquiring a gun. In some respects, then, we would expect this type of policy to have an impact different from that of policies to increase effective price. Consider the following predictions for any policy to get the guns off the streets:

—The deterrence effect will be concentrated on violent crimes committed away from the perpetrator's home. Anticarrying policies will have little effect on family fights. The ratio of nonfamily to family assaults and murders should therefore fall as a result of the implementation of such a policy.

—The deterrence effect will be concentrated on violent crimes committed without advanced planning. People traveling directly from their home to the scene of the crime with the specific intent of committing robbery or murder will have only a brief exposure to an arrest on an illegal carrying violation, and a strong incentive to go armed. The effect of an anticarrying policy should therefore be to reduce the ratio of impulsive to planned assaults and robberies. Police do not classify reported crimes by whether they are planned or impulsive, but police crime statistics give some indications of the relative mix. For example, it seems reasonable to suppose that commercial robberies are more likely to be planned than street robberies, and that murders involving sober victims are more likely to be planned than murders of drunks.

These detailed predictions are useful because they yield statistical comparisons that are particularly sensitive to the intervention that is being evaluated. For example, the sharp reduction in gun assaults following Bartley-Fox suggests that this intervention was effective; this inference would be greatly strengthened if it could be demonstrated that the reduction was concentrated on assaults occurring away from the assailant's home. In effect, the at-home gun assault rate serves as a control group in evaluating the effect of B-F on other types of assault.

The Firearms Control Act of 1975

In February 1977, the District of Columbia implemented the strictest gun-control ordinance in the nation. The effect of the provisions of this ordinance is to ban the acquisition or transfer of a handgun by any District resident (with the exception of law enforcement officers and a few others). The only residents who can legally possess a handgun are those who acquired and registered them before the ordinance went into effect. To acquire handguns in the District, residents must steal them or make illegal purchases in the black market or in neighboring states.

Unlike Bartley-Fox, we would expect the crime-related effects of the Firearms Control Act to increase over time, and to be quite small for the first few months or even years. This lack of a temporally concentrated impact increases the difficulty of evaluating this ordinance. The first evaluation that was attempted (U.S. Conference of Mayors, 1980) compared average crime rates for a three-year period subsequent to implementation (1977-1979) with corresponding rates for 1974-1976. Rates of gun robbery, assault, and homicide were all lower in the postimplementation period. Jones (1981) has extended this analysis in several respects. His criterion variables are percentages of robberies and aggravated assaults committed with a gun. He compared the intertemporal changes in these percentages between the two periods (1974-1976 and 1977-1979) in Washington with nine other cities that were similar in terms of size and certain other respects. For robbery, the percentage gun use declines more (in absolute terms) in Washington than in all but two of the comparison cities; for aggravated assault, only Seattle out of the nine comparison cities had a greater decline in percentage gun use. Jones also compared the distribution of circumstances of handgun homicides in Washington in 1974 with 1978. He found that murders involving family and acquaintances declined relative to felony-type murders. There was no such decline in Baltimore, which was his only control city in this case.

These tests of the law's effectiveness are not overwhelmingly persuasive. If data were available on the black market in handguns, it would be possible to work with variables that are probably more responsive to this type of intervention. We would expect an increase in the theft of firearms and in the price of firearms charged by fences and other black-market dealers. If the interdiction on handgun commerce is effective, then the average age of guns confiscated by police should gradually increase. Fewer people will risk confiscation by carrying guns on the street (due to the increase in value of guns), which may be reflected in the confiscation rate.

Given that the interdiction effort is successful, the increased scarcity of firearms should have the greatest initial impact on youthful offenders who did not acquire a gun prior to the implementation of the ordinance and who are less able to afford the increased effective price of guns than adults. Other effects of the law (such as the predictions contained in the nine hypotheses presented earlier) should become stronger over the first few years of the law, with variations thereafter due to variations in enforcement efforts by police and BATF agents.

NOTES ON A RESEARCH AGENDA

It is my impression that social scientists tend to ignore each other's suggestions for future research, unless they are funded and come in the form of a request for proposals. Rather than suggest specific research projects, my objective in this review has been to demonstrate that the technology of violent crime is an interesting and important topic, a topic that is eminently researchable and yet has been largely neglected by social scientists qua scientists. The choice of weapon by the assailant in a violent criminal encounter is not just an incidental aspect of this encounter, but rather may be every bit as important in shaping the encounter and determining the outcome as the underlying motivation and state of mind of the assailant, the relationship between assailant and victim, the location of the attack, and so forth. More generally, the extent to which firearms are available to violent criminals may have a profound influence on the nature and seriousness of violent crime. I submit the following list of propositions as a credible summary of the likely effects of gun availability on violent crime:

—Gun availability does not have much effect on the rates of robbery and aggravated assault, but does have a direct effect on the fractions of such crimes that involve guns.
—Since gun attacks are intrinsically more deadly than attacks with other weapons, gun availability is directly related to the homicide rate.
—Increased gun availability promotes a relative increase in robberies and homicidal attacks on relatively invulnerable targets.

There is some evidence available supporting these propositions, which I have reviewed above. More work is needed.

If funding were available for research in this general area, I would recommend that highest priority be given to two types of projects:

(1) fine-grained evaluations of the impact of legal interventions; and

(2) interviews with violent criminals to answer questions such as these:

—Where and how do criminals obtain guns? How do state and local ordinances affect the distribution of sources of guns?

—Do violent criminals who use other weapons have ready access to guns? If so, why do they not use them? In particular, why are less than half of all robberies committed with guns?

—Why are handguns used in such a high percentage of gun-related crime, given that longguns are more widely available and generally more effective?

—What is the mix of motives that result in the decision of many criminals to carry a gun?

This is enough of a "shopping list," given the current austerity of funding for criminal justice research.

I have not emphasized the policy-relevance of research in this area, in part because I thought it was important to emphasize that the role of weapons in violent crime should be of as much interest to criminologists as to policy analysts and polemicists. Ultimately, however, the policy applications cannot be ignored. It is not too far-fetched to hope that the accumulation of knowledge in this area will encourage the adoption of wiser and more effective policies.

NOTES

1. "The 'effective price' includes everything that makes a particular use of a gun by a particular individual, in a particular circumstance, difficult, inconvenient, or risky" (Moore, 1977).

2. These results were provided by James Wright, in private correspondence.

3. See Wright (1979) for a discussion of these two polls.

4. Wright et al. (1981) give evidence that some substantial portion of the increase in the handgun sales was the result of increased demand by local police departments.

5. I assume that household respondents who admit owning a gun of the specified sort but refuse to say how many are distributed similarly to other households. I also assume that the average number of guns in the open-ended category is 12. Both of these assumptions are highly conservative, in the sense that they probably lead to an underestimate of the degree of concentration in ownership.

6. Brill (1977: Ch. 2) has pointed out that about one-third of the handguns traced in Project Identification were not involved in any crime, and most of the remainder were confiscated because they were being carried illegally. Few were known to have been used in serious street crimes. The results of Project Identification should be interpreted accordingly.

7. The perspective of this section was first developed in Conklin's (1972) seminal work on robbery in Boston. Cook (1976) dubbed it "strategic choice analysis," and was the first to employ

large victimization survey data sets in documenting weapon use patterns of this sort. Other important contributions are cited in subsequent notes.

8. Conklin (1972: 110-111) analyzes the gun's usefulness in terms of the ability it provides the robber to (1) maintain a buffer zone, (2) intimidate the victim, (3) make good the threat if necessary, and (4) ensure escape.

9. Skogan used the robbery incident reports collected from the National Crime Panel which occurred during calendar 1973. This and subsequent citations to Skogan's work refer to an unpublished manuscript that was subsequently published in abbreviated form (as Skogan, 1978). It should be noted that any analysis of victim survey data relies on the victim's impression of the nature of the weapon that was employed in the robbery. In some cases the "gun" may be a toy, or simulated; Feeney and Weir (1974: 33) report that of 58 "gun" robbers interviewed in Oakland, 3 claimed to have used toys and 4 to have simulated the possession of a gun.

10. Block (1977) found from studying robbery police reports in Chicago that victims who resisted with physical force typically did so in response to the robber's use of force (68 percent). Other types of resistance typically preceded the robber's use of force (70 percent).

11. It is obvious that commercial targets tend to be more lucrative than noncommercial targets, and that a group of two or more victims will be more lucrative on the average than a single victim. Feeney and Weir (1974: 24) report the not-so-obvious result that robberies of male victims resulted in a much higher median take ($50) than did robberies of female victims (less than $20).

12. Calculated from the statistics reported in Table 5.3 of Skogan's article.

13. Based on 541 adult male gun robbery arrestees and 761 nongun robbery arrestees. This cohort, which was arrested in 1973, was tracked through 1976 through PROMIS. The robbery rearrest rate for the gun cohort was .43, of which 58 percent were gun robberies. The robbery rearrest rate for the nongun cohort was .45, of which 40 percent were gun robberies. The two cohorts had the same rearrest rate for burglary (.13), but the nongun cohort was much more likely to be rearrested for assaultive crimes (.22, as opposed to .13 for the gun cohort). See Cook and Nagin (1979: Table 9).

14. One flaw in Phillips's analysis is that he omitted from his regression specification the sanction severity for aggravated assault. Deterrence theory would suggest that it is not the absolute severity of sanctions for criminal homicide that is salient to the choice of weapon, but rather the *difference* between sanction severity in assault and murder.

15. Wolfgang (1958: 80-81) concludes from his study of homicide in Philadelphia: "The murderer who carefully plans his felonious, willful, and malicious assault is more likely to employ a weapon that performs his intended task quickly and efficiently. In such a situation a pistol or revolver probably will be used. During a drunken brawl, or in the white heat of passion, an offender uses whatever weapon is available."

16. Computed from Zimring (1972: 104, Table 7).

17. Zimring (1969) titled his original article, "Is Gun Control Likely to Reduce Violent Killings?" His work was a response to a view espoused by Wolfgang (1958: 83): "It is the contention of this observer that few homicides due to shootings could be avoided merely if a firearm were not immediately present, and that the offender would select some other weapon to achieve the same destructive goal"—a viewpoint expressed more succinctly by the bumper strip: "Guns don't kill people; people kill people."

Seitz (1972) attempts to test Wolfgang's substitution hypothesis directly by calculating the correlation coefficient between total homicide rates and firearms homicide rates across states. For 1967, this correlation coefficient is .98. Seitz claims that the substitution hypothesis predicts that this correlation should be about zero. The problem with Seitz's inference, of course, is that he makes no attempt to control for the underlying etiological factors that largely determine both the gun and the nongun homicide rates in a state—indeed, these are highly positively correlated with each other.

18. This implication has been pointed out by Kleck (1980).

19. "In the generality of cases, how likely is it that conduct such as that engaged in by the offender will lead to death?" (Zimring, 1972: 114).

20. Swersey also notes several other indications of an increasing fraction of deliberate murders in the homicide statistics for New York City as a whole. During the 1970s, the clearance rate declined for homicide, as did the fraction of homicides occurring on the weekend and the fraction involving family members.

21. Other sources on this pattern include Conklin (1972), Cook (1976), and Skogan (1978).

22. The subset of the robbery arrest cohort that had injured their victims were less likely to be rearrested for robbery than the remainder of the cohort—but this subset was much more likely to be rearrested for assault and murder.

23. The regression equation is as follows:

$$\frac{\text{Robbery Murders}}{1,000 \text{ Robberies}} = \underset{(1.16)}{1.52} + \underset{(2.38)}{5.68} \frac{\text{Gun Robberies}}{\text{Robberies}}$$

A closely related result uses the per-capita (rather than the "per-robbery") murder rate:

$$\text{Robbery Murders}/100,000 = \underset{(.232)}{-.284} + \underset{(.089)}{.907} \text{ Gun Robberies}/1,000$$
$$+ \underset{(.072)}{.136} \text{ Nongun Robberies}/1,000$$

(Numbers in parentheses are the standard errors of the ordinary least squares regression coefficients.) The data for 50 cities are 1975-1976 averages.

The second equation has an R^2 of .82, suggesting that robbery murder is very closely linked with robbery. Inclusion of the assaultive murder rate in this equation as an independent variable does not affect the other coefficients much, and the coefficient on the murder variable is not statistically significant. I conclude that robbery murder is more robbery than murder.

24. The methodological issues here are precisely analogous to those that arise in the study of deterrence. In the deterrence context, the analogue of gun availability is the perceived risk and severity of punishment. Empirical studies of the deterrence effect either use an observable proxy for this perception or evaluate directly the impact of a deterrence-related policy change on crime rates. See Cook (1980b) for a more complete discussion of this issue.

25. Within regions there is no discernible relationship between homicide rate and the gun fraction.

26. Fisher suggests that there may be an analogue here to Verkko's Law. Verkko (1967) proposed, on the basis of rather scanty evidence, that the homicide rate is positively correlated with the fraction of homicide victims who are males—that the female homicide victimization rate is relatively constant over time and across jurisdictions, and that changes in homicide rates disproportionately involve males.

27. Block and Block (1980) make some similar observations for historical homicide patterns in Chicago.

28. Zimring (1975) finds that two government agencies—the Bureau of Alcohol, Tobacco, and Firearms, and the Census Bureau—give wildly disparate estimates of imports of handguns for some years. Furthermore, Newton and Zimring (1969) note that many imports may go unrecorded by either agency.

29. Blose and Cook (1980) find that handgun import and export rates are close to equal, at least for the last five years.

30. Clotfelter (1981) and Bordua and Lizotte (1979) use permit data to study the demand for handguns.

31. Fisher starts with a list of eight variables he believes relevant to explaining homicide trends in Detroit. This list includes handgun licenses and registrations. He reduces this list to three principal components, of which one loads primarily on these two measures of firearm availability.

Seitz (1972: 606) also used a factor analysis procedure to construct his "index of the accessibility of firearms for criminal and extra-legal purposes." His procedure is less easily justified than Fisher's. Seitz analyzed a matrix consisting of a state cross-section on per-capita rates of each of the FBI index crimes (except murder) and accidents, suicides, and homicides involving firearms. One of the factors that emerged from this hodgepodge of variables loaded on aggravated assaults, firearm accidents, and firearm homicides. He chose this as his "firearms accessibility" index, without any attempt at validation. Since aggravated assault and firearm homicide rates have much more to do with the overall propensity to violence in a state than with gun availability, this index is not of much interest.

32. Survey-based estimates of this sort are not strictly valid, since the sampling frame is not constructed to produce representative samples in these regional city clusters.

33. This index has also been used by Moore (1980) and Sherman (personal communication). Sherman finds a high correlation between this measure of gun availability and the number of police killed in a city.

34. Moore (1981) has the most complete discussion on sources of guns to criminals.

35. Zimring's (1976) definition of handgun availability is "the relative ease or difficulty with which a nonowner of a handgun may acquire a gun at a particular time."

36. This explanation is mine, not Zimring's.

37. On court processing of weapons cases in Michigan, see the *Michigan Law Review* (1976); for the District of Columbia, see Cook and Nagin (1979).

38. They experiment with 30 different weighting schemes, ultimately choosing the one that yields the highest $\bar{R}^2$ for the most dependent variables.

39. For an illuminating discussion of similar concerns about cross-section evaluations of capital punishment, see Ehrlich (1977).

40. The Jamaican Gun Court Act has also been evaluated (Gendreau and Surridge, 1978). Unfortunately, the implementation of this act was accompanied by other changes in law enforcement (including the imposition of a curfew and increased police activity), and it is difficult to partial out the effect of the act.

41. These alternatives lack one feature of Bartley-Fox. Aggravated gun assault defendants can in some cases be charged with a Bartley-Fox violation in connection with their crime, and are more likely to receive an active prison term as a result. B-F may therefore have a direct deterrent effect on the use of guns in assault, as well as an indirect effect by discouraging the practice of going armed.

REFERENCES

Beha, J. A., III. "And nobody can get you out": The impact of a mandatory prison sentence for the illegal carrying of a firearm on the use of firearms and the administration of criminal justice in Boston (Parts I and II). *Boston University Law Review*, 1977, 57.

Block, C. and Block, R. *Patterns of change in Chicago homicide: The twenties, the sixties, and the seventies.* Chicago: Illinois Law Enforcement Commission, 1980.

Block, R. *Violent Crime*. Lexington, MA: D. C. Heath.

Blose, J. and Cook, P. J. Regulating handgun transfers: Current state and federal procedures, and an assessment of the feasibility and cost of the proposed procedures in the Handgun Crime Control Act of 1979. Unpublished manuscript, Duke University, Durham, North Carolina, 1980.

Bordua, D. J., and Lizotte, A. J. Patterns of legal firearms ownership: A cultural and situational analysis of Illinois counties. *Law & Policy Quarterly*, 1979, 1(2), 147-175.

Brearely, H. C. *Homicide in the U.S.* Chapel Hill: University of North Carolina, 1932.

Brill, S. *Firearm abuse: A research and policy report.* Washington, DC: Police Foundation, 1977.

Bruce-Briggs, B. The Great American Gun War. *Public Interest,* 1976, 45 (Fall), 1-26.

Bureau of Alcohol, Tobacco, and Firearms. *Project Identification: A study of handguns used in crime* (ATF P 3310.1, May). Washington, DC: Government Printing Office, 1976.

Burr, D. E. S. Handgun regulation (final report). Tallahassee, FL: Bureau of Criminal Justice Planning and Assistance, 1977.

Campbell, D. and Stanley, J. C. *Experimental and quasi-experimental designs for research.* Chicago: Rand McNally, 1966.

Clotfelter, C. T. Crime, disorders, and the demand for handguns: An empirical analysis. *Law and Policy Quarterly,* 1981, 3(4), 425-441.

Conklin, J. E. *Robbery and the criminal justice system.* Philadelphia: Lippincott, 1972.

Cook, P. J. A strategic choice analysis of robbery. In W. Skogan (Ed.), *Sample surveys of the victims of crimes.* Cambridge, MA: Ballinger, 1976.

Cook, P. J. The effect of gun availability on robbery and robbery murder: A cross section study of fifty cities. In R. H. Haveman and B. B. Zellner (Eds.), *Policy studies review annual* (Vol. 3). Beverly Hills, CA: Sage Publications, 1979.

Cook, P. J. Reducing injury and death rates in robbery. *Policy Analysis,* 1980, 6(1), 21-45. (a)

Cook, P. J. Research in criminal deterrence: Laying the groundwork for the second decade. In N. Morris and M. Tonry (Eds.), *Crime and justice: An annual review of research.* Chicago: University of Chicago Press, 1980. (b)

Cook, P. J. The effect of gun availability on violent crime patterns. *The Annals of the American Academy of Political and Social Science,* 1981 (May). (a)

Cook, P. J. Guns and crime: The perils of long division. *Journal of Policy Analysis and Management,* 1981. (b)

Cook, P. J., and Blose, J. State programs for screening handgun buyers. *The Annals of the American Academy of Political and Social Science,* 1981 (May).

Cook, P. J., and Nagin, D. *Does the weapon matter?* Washington, DC: Institute for Law and Social Research, 1979.

Curtis, L. A. *Criminal violence.* Lexington, MA: D. C. Heath, 1974.

Deutsch, S. J. Intervention modeling: Analysis of changes in crime rates. In *Frontiers in Quantitative Criminology.* New York: Academic Press, 1980.

Deutsch, S. J., and Alt, F. B. The effect of Massachusetts' gun control law on gun-related crimes in the city of Boston. *Evaluation Quarterly,* 1977, 1(4), 543-568.

Ehrlich, I. Capital punishment and deterrence: Some further thoughts and additional evidence. *Journal of Political Economy,* 1977, 85(4), 741-788.

Etzioni, A., and Kemp, R. A technology whose removal "works": Gun control. In *Technological shortcuts to social change.* New York: Russell Sage Foundation, 1973, 103-151.

Feeney, F., and Weir, A. *The prevention and control of robbery: A summary.* Davis, CA: University of California, Center on Administration of Criminal Justice, 1974.

Fisher, J. Homicide in Detroit: The role of firearms. *Criminology,* 1976, 14(3), 387-400.

Geisel, M. S., Roll, R., and Wettick, R. S., Jr. The effectiveness of state and local regulation of handguns: A statistical analysis. *Duke Law Journal,* 1969, 647-676.

Gendreau, P., and Surridge, C. T. Controlling gun crimes: The Jamaican experience. *International Journal of Criminology and Penology,* 1978, 6(1), 43-60.

Heumann, M., and Loftin, C. Mandatory sentencing and the abolition of plea bargaining: The Michigan Felony Firearm Statute. *Law & Society Review,* 1979, 13, 393-430.

Hindelang, M. J., Gottfredson, M. R., and Garofalo, J. *Victims of personal crime: An empirical foundation for a theory of personal victimization.* Cambridge, MA: Ballinger, 1978.

Hoffman, F. L. *The homicide problem.* Newark, NJ: Prudential Press, 1925.

Jones, E. D., III. Handguns, gun control laws, and firearm violence: A comment. Washington, DC: U.S. Dept. of Justice, Office for Improvements in the Administration of Justice, 1980. (Mimeo)

Jones, E. D., III. The District of Columbia's "Firearms Control Regulations Act of 1975": The toughest handgun control law in the United States—Or is it? *The Annals of the American Academy of Political and Social Science,* 1981 (May).

Kleck, G. The assumptions of gun control. Unpublished, Florida State University, Tallahassee, 1980.

Krug, A. S. *The true facts on firearm legislation—Three statistical studies.* National Shooting Sports Foundation, 1967. (Cited in Zimring, 1968.)

Loftin, C. "One with a gun gets you two": Mandatory sentencing and firearms offenses in Detroit. Ann Arbor: Center for Research on Social Organization, University of Michigan, 1980.

Loftin, C. and McDowall, D. "One with a gun gets you two": Mandatory sentencing and firearms violence in Detroit. *The Annals of the American Academy of Political and Social Science,* 1981 (May).

Lundsgaarde, H. P. *Murder in space city.* New York: Oxford University Press, 1977.

Magaddino, J. P. Towards an economic evaluation of state gun control laws. Long Beach: California State University, n.d.

Michigan Law Review. Some observations on the disposition of CCW cases in Detroit. *Michigan Law Review,* 1976, 74(3), 614-643.

Moore, M. Managing the effective price of handguns: A conceptual basis for the design of gun control Policies. Cambridge: Kennedy School of Government, Harvard University, 1977.

Moore, M. The supply of handguns: An analysis of the potential and current importance of alternative sources of handguns to criminal offenders. Cambridge: Kennedy School of Government, Harvard University, 1979.

Moore, M. The police and weapons offenses. *The Annals of the American Academy of Political and Social Science,* 1980 (November), 22-32.

Moore, M. Keeping handguns from criminal offenders. *The Annals of the American Academy of Political and Social Science,* 1981 (May).

Murray, D. R. Handguns, gun control laws, and firearm violence. *Social Problems,* 1975, 23(1), 81-93.

Newton, G. D., Jr., and Zimring, F. E. *Firearms & violence in American life.* Washington, DC: Government Printing Office, 1969.

Phillips, L. Crime control: The case for deterrence. In S. Rottenberg (Ed.), *The economics of crime and punishment.* Washington, DC: American Enterprise Institute, 1973.

Phillips, L., Votey, H. L., Jr., and Howell, J. Handguns and homicide: Minimizing losses and the costs of control. *Journal of Legal Studies,* 1976, 5(2), 463-478.

Pierce, G. L., and Bowers, W. J. The impact of the Bartley-Fox gun law on crime in Massachusetts. Evanston, IL: Northwestern University, Center for Applied Social Research, 1979.

Pierce, G. L., and Bowers, W. J. The Bartley-Fox gun law's short-term impact on crime in Boston. *The Annals of the American Academy of Political and Social Science,* 1981 (May).

Rushforth, N. B., Ford, A. B., Hirsh, C. S., Rushforth, N. M., and Adelson, L. Violent death in a metropolitan county: Changing patterns in homicide (1958-74). *New England Journal of Medicine,* 1977, 297(10), 531-538.

Seitz, S. T. Firearms, homicides, and gun control effectiveness. *Law and Society Review,* 1972 (May), 595-611.

Silberman, C. E. *Criminal violence, criminal justice.* New York: Random House, 1978.

Skogan, W. G. Weapon use in robbery: Patterns and policy implications. Evanston, IL: Northwestern University, Center for Urban Affairs, 1978.

Swersey, A. J. A greater intent to kill: The changing pattern of homicide in Harlem and New York City. New Haven, CT: Yale School of Organization and Management, 1980.

U.S. Bureau of the Census. *Statistical Abstract, 1978.* Washington, DC: Government Printing Office, 1978.

U.S. Conference of Mayors. The analysis of the Firearms Control Act of 1975: Handgun control in the District of Columbia. Washington, D.C., 1980. (Mimeo)

Verkko, V. Static and dynamic "laws" of sex and homicide. In M. E. Wolfgang (Ed.), *Studies in homicide*. New York: Harper & Row, 1967.

Weber-Burdin, E., Rossi, P. H., Wright, J. D., and Daly, K. *Weapons policies: A survey of police department practices and related issues*. Amherst: University of Massachusetts, Social and Demographic Research Institute, 1981.

Wolfgang, M. E. *Patterns in criminal homicide*. Philadelphia: University of Pennsylvania Press, 1958.

Wright, J. D. Public opinion and gun control: A comparison of results from two recent national surveys. Amherst: University of Massachusetts, 1979.

Wright, J. D., and Marston, L. L. The ownership of the means of destruction: Weapons in the United States. *Social Problems*, 1975, 23(1).

Wright, J. D., Rossi, P. H., Daly, K., and Weber-Burdin, E. *Weapons, crime, and violence in America: A literature review and research agenda*. Amherst: University of Massachusetts, Social and Demographic Research Institute, 1981.

Zimring, F. Is gun control likely to reduce violent killings? *University of Chicago Law Review*, 1967, 5,35, 721-737.

Zimring, F. Games with guns and statistics. *Wisconsin Law Review*, 1968, 1113-1126.

Zimring, F. The medium is the message: Firearm calibre as a determinant of death from assault. *Journal of Legal Studies*, 1972, 1(1), 97-124.

Zimring, F. Firearms and federal law: The Gun Control Act of 1968. *Journal of Legal Studies*, 1975, 4(1), 133-198.

Zimring, F. Street crime and new guns: Some implications for firearms control. *Journal of Criminal Justice*, 1976, 4, 95-107.

Zimring, F. Determinants of the death rate from robbery: A Detroit time study. *Journal of Legal Studies*, 1977, 6(2), 317-332.

APPENDIX

Summary of John Monahan's Comments on Philip Cook's Chapter

1. The discussion settled upon the appropriate level of specificity in its hypotheses. More general and they would have lacked applicability; more specific and they would have bogged down in detail.

2. The discussion focused on the perpetrators of violent crime (reasonably so). Mention might be made of violence committed with guns by persons who mistakenly believe they are to be the *victims* of violent crime: for example, people shooting "intruders" who turn out to be spouses or others who mean no harm.

3. I presented for discussion the recent arguments against gun control, which analogize the criminalization of gun possession with the criminalization of alcohol or marijuana possession. In all three cases, many people possess the objects in issue and do not perceive themselves as "criminal" for so doing. The argument is that if gun possession is criminalized, it will have the same alleged consequences as in the case of alcohol or marijuana possession:

   (a) Many otherwise law-abiding people will be labeled "criminals." Their reaction will be to lower their respect for the law.

   (b) An underground will develop to supply the demand for illegal guns (bootlegging).

   (c) Enforcement of gun laws will necessarily be arbitrary and selective.

   (d) Some increase in the victimization will occur, since some people, but for the law, would have possessed a gun and been able to ward off attack by "true" criminals.

6

Situational Approaches to Understanding and Predicting Individual Violent Behavior

John Monahan
Deidre Klassen

"Situational" or "environmental" approaches to the study of violent behavior have been highly touted in recent years. This is partly by default. Individual-level analyses have produced disappointing results for both the anticipation of violence and the modification of violent dispositions when they become manifest. Situational approaches, since they have been tried less often, have had less of an opportunity to fail. Yet there is a growing body of theory that suggests that situational approaches—in interaction with individual-level strategies—may have a genuine contribution to make in the analysis, if not the control, of violent behavior. In those circumstances where one could *identify* salient aspects of situations more easily than one can identify salient aspects of individuals, the situational approach could result in improved *predictions* of violent behavior. In those circumstances where one could *change* salient aspects of situations more easily than one could change salient aspects of individuals, the situational approach could result in the improved *prevention* of violent behavior. It is the enticement of these dual benefits that motivates the search for situational determinants of violence.

In this chapter, we will spend considerable effort in reviewing attempts by psychologists and others to define and conceptualize what is meant by the term "situation," giving particular attention to accounts that may be fruitful for the purposes of the individual prediction of violence. We will then review the research findings on situational correlates of violence. Finally, we will discuss the nature of the contribution that situational approaches may make to the prediction of violent behavior.

THE NATURE OF SITUATIONS

There appear to be four central issues in the conceptualization of environments from a psychological perspective that must be addressed before classifying situations relevant to violent behavior. They are (1) the definition of a situation or environment, (2) the size of the environmental unit to be employed, (3) the perceived versus the actual situation, and (4) the interactive nature of persons and situations. Two of these issues, the definition of a situation or environment and the interaction of persons and environments are conceptual in nature. The other two issues, the size of the environmental unit to be employed and the use of perceived versus actual measures, tend to be more operational research questions. In addition to a discussion of these four issues, this section includes a review and discussion of previously existing work on the dimensions and classifications of environments.

It should be noted that the words "environment" and "situation" are for the most part used here interchangeably. "Environments" are probably generally perceived as broader than "situations." However, since our purpose is to concentrate on variables outside the person and since some range exists in the size of environment that may be predictive of violence, we have considered it appropriate not to draw precise distinctions in the use of these terms.

Definition of Situations

A review of the literature on situations and environments indicates that, surprisingly, few explicit definitions of situations or environments are provided. (Pervin, 1978; Ekehammer, 1974). Similarly, researchers in the area of person versus situational determinants of behavior and person by situation interactions do not address the question of the boundary of the person and situation but seem to assume that the distinction is understood. The boundary line used here appears to be the person's skin: Within the skin is the "person," outside the skin is the "environment." Only Rausch (1977) seems to have explicitly discussed this question of drawing the line between person and situation. He concludes that the distinction is more vague than generally believed, pointing out, for example, that a dream is part of a person yet becomes an internal stimulus to which we respond. Even the term "internal stimuli" implies an ambiguity between person and situation. Both are within the skin. Another example of this ambiguity is that an alcoholic drink in a person's hand is part of the "situation," yet after it is consumed it is a "personal" factor.

In common parlance, however, we tend to distinguish personal factors as having more to do with the psychological "self" than with everything that goes on within our skins. For example, a flu virus that exists within the skin is generally thought of as external to the self and is something we "fight" rather than being a part of us.

Another difficulty in distinguishing person and situation has to do with the variable of time. Situations might be viewed as existing in the present only in that our memories and interpretations of past situations become incorporated into our selves. The effects of past situations are found in current psychological "traits." This raises the question of at what point in time past situations become part of the person. To describe situations as existing only in the immediate present would seem too limiting and would provide only micro-level analyses of situational factors.

In spite of these difficulties of distinguishing persons from situations, it seems useful to have a working definition of situations before undertaking a study of situations. Perhaps the best general definition of a situation is that given by Pervin (1978: 79-80): "an organism's engagement with an array of objects and actions which covers a time span. A situation is defined by *who* is involved including the possibility that the individual is alone, *where* the action is taking place and the nature of the action or activities occurring."

Size of the Environment Unit

In any study of environment's effects, a major decision to be made concerns the level of analysis to be employed. Environmental units can range from the micro to the macro level. Pervin (1978), for example, describes three levels of environmental units: stimuli, situations, and environments.

Magnusson (1980) has presented a more detailed description of units that consists of four broad categories. The categories are arranged in such a way that the concepts and definitions become broader and less specific along two dimensions; from *molecular* to *molar* units and from the *physical* to the *perceived* properties of situations. The first category is the "actual" situation, which is defined in physical and biological terms as that part of the total environment that is available for perception for a specified period of time. This actual situation is composed of two subunits: situational stimuli and situational events. Situational stimuli are units that function as signals in themselves—for example, a sound or a snake. Situational events are specific parts of a total situation, such as parts of a conversation. The second category is the perceived situation, defined as an actual situation as it is construed and represented in the mind of an individual. Within the perceived situation are two subunits; within-situation factors and general or overall situation factors. Within-situation factors are defined as the continuous flow of situational stimuli and situational events as interpreted by an individual. General situation factors consist of the perceived and interpreted characteristics of total situations that function as frames of reference and steer a person's selection and interpretation of specific stimuli and events. The situation type is the third category. It is conceived of as the general class of a particular kind of actual or perceived situation without reference to time or place—for example, a supermarket. The fourth and largest category is the life situation, which refers to those parts of the total world that an individual perceives and interprets as having reference to himself or herself.

Perceived versus Objective Situations

A distinction that is frequently made in reviews of literature on situations is whether the situation is defined in objective terms, as it "actually" is, or whether it is defined in terms of the perceptions of subjects. Bowers (1973) advocates a situation-perception definition and states that a situation must be specified in terms of the particular organism experiencing it. In general, this is the position taken by the interaction researchers. Magnusson and Endler (1977) state that one of the basic assumptions of the person-by-situation interaction model is that it is the psychological meaning of the situation that is important in describing the situation. As Kiritz and Moos (1974) point out, social stimuli do not act directly on individuals. Rather, it is the perception of the social environment that affects persons directly and in turn affects personality and behavior.

According to Magnusson and Endler (1977), an important assumption regarding the perception of situations is that there are individual differences in perception. This assumption has received empirical support. There is evidence that individuals perceive identical situations differently and that they exhibit different perceptual styles (Golding, 1977). Novaco's (1979) model of anger arousal which is discussed in a subsequent section for its relevance to violence prediction emphasizes the effect or perception on affect.

Other authors have argued for measures of the "actual" situation (Rotter, 1955; Sells, 1963; Wohlwill, 1973). Wohlwill, for example, states that "the environment is not in the head" and that our interest should be in behavior and environment in a mutually interacting system.

Interactive Nature of Situations

In conceptualizing the situation as a determinant of behavior, psychologists have in the not-too-distant past behaved as if the situation were a state of affairs imposed upon the individual. This is probably due to the fact that most research came out of the laboratory, where experimenters created situations and imposed them on subjects. As Bowers (1977) points out, this is in marked contrast to clinical studies, which have emphasized the individual's role in creating his or her own situations.

The current view of situations recognizes that persons and situations are not independent. According to Magnusson and Endler (1977), the behavior of persons and settings are inextricably interwoven into an ongoing process. Nuttin (1977) has stated that personality and environment should not be considered as two autonomously preexisting units interacting with each other at a given moment in time, but that they exist as two interdependent poles of a unitary behavioral process. As Rausch (1977) has stated, for psychology, situations exist only with respect to persons. The opposite perspective is also true. We cannot conceive of persons in the absence of situations.

Stokols (1978), in his review of environmental psychology, has identified the transactional nature of human-environment relations as one of the major themes in that field. In a transactional view, any attempt to conceptualize environment-behavior relationships must account not only for the effects of the environment on people, but also for the impact of people upon their environments.

As seen above, both Magnusson and Endler (1977) and Stokols (1978) emphasize the interactive or transactional nature of situations and environments. What are the implications of this view for conducting research? One possible conclusion is that only dynamic models would be appropriate. Unfortunately, virtually all existing methodologies are static. Rausch (1977) and Fiske (1977), in accepting this definition of situations, have approached the problem by taking a more molecular approach. The unit of analysis here is individual acts within situations which are short, temporal sequences involving interchanges between two or more persons. For example, an argument between a married couple would be broken down into components of action, such as speaking turns. It may also be possible to acknowledge this view of persons and environments while taking a more moral approach. In the work of Pervin (1977), molar person-situation interactions are used as the unit of analysis.

Dimensions and Classifications of Environments

Fredericksen (1972), in his review of taxonomies of situations, states that it is important to distinguish taxonomies of attributes of situations (dimensions) and taxonomies of situations themselves (classifications). The major way in which these differ is in the methods of developing the taxonomies. Factor analysis of variables describing situations would produce taxonomies of attributes of situations, that is, of the dimensions along which the situation could be described. Cluster analysis would be an appropriate technique for developing taxonomies of situations themselves in which the result would be groupings or categorizations of the situations. Either approach can provide useful information. Whether one or the other approach should be taken depends on the purposes to which the taxonomy will be applied.

Studies of dimensions of situations are highly diverse. Some are based on a priori conceptualizations and others on data analysis. Most come from laboratory studies in which the "situations" consist of written descriptions of situations presented to subjects; others come from open-ended questions to subjects about situations they have encountered; and some come from field research in natural settings. These studies also vary in terms of the definitional issues discussed above. Perhaps the way in which they differ most, however, is in regard to the kinds of dimensions and classifications obtained.

There is much agreement in the literature that the dimensions of environments have been inadequately studied (Sells, 1963; Frederickson, 1972; Pervin, 1978). In an apparent attempt to cover all potentially relevant aspects of situations, Sells (1963) has presented an outline intended as a preliminary step toward the development of dimensions of the stimulus situation. This outline contains several hundred items ranging from physical features of the natural environment, such as meteorological variables, to organizational variables related to institutions.

In reviewing the research on human environments, Moos (1973) has categorized six major methods by which characteristics of environments have been found to be related to indices of human functioning. These are (1) ecological dimensions, which include both geographical-meteorological and architectural-physical design variables; (2) behavior settings; (3) dimensions of organizational structure; (4) dimensions identifying the collective personal and/or behavioral characteristics of the milieu inhabitants; (5) dimensions related to psychosocial characteristics and organizational climates; and (6) variables related to the functional or reinforcement analyses of environments.

Concentrating on the psychosocial environment leads to somewhat more manageable lists of dimensions. One of the earlier suggestions of relevant dimensions was by Sherif and Sherif (1956). They presented four types of factors, presumed to be interrelated, which should be considered in describing a social situation. These are: (1) factors related to individuals (number, homogeneity of background, age, sex, relationships among individuals, and so on); (2) factors related to the task; (3) factors related to the site and facilities; and (4) the relationship and relevance of the previous three factors for the individuals participating.

Barker's (1968) development of ecological psychology represents a unique contribution to the study of environments. In this research, observational techniques are used to classify the components of complex, naturally occurring environments, such as total communities. The unit of analysis is the behavior setting that includes both physical and behavior properties existing in relationship to one another. Unlike other research in environments, the boundaries of the units have been clearly specified. This approach emphasizes the "objective" environment. It views behavior settings as controlling the behavior of the inhabitants. According to Pervin (1978), the concept of behavior settings is similar to the concept of situations. Little work has been done in developing taxonomies of behavior settings. Barker has done some classification in regard to genotypes, such as business, education, nutrition, and personal grooming, but this has been done a priori.

One exception to this is a study by Price and Blashfield (1975). They used data collected by Barker consisting of a set of 455 behavior settings comprising all those occurring in a small midwestern town. The results indicated that the primary dimensions along which behavior settings were grouped were variables relating to the age and sex of members and targets of the setting. While this is an interesting exercise and tells us much about the social stratification existing in public settings in small towns, the taxonomy developed appears to be of little use for other purposes.

According to Moos (1973), the behavior setting is probably the best conceptualized and the most studied basic unit in the area of environmental research. However, there has been relatively little work using this methodology other than by Barker and his students. An exception to this is work done by O'Connor and Klassen and their colleagues (Klassen, 1977; O'Connor et al., 1979; O'Connor and Daniels, 1979). In this research, behavior settings are used as units of analysis describing a person's interactions with his or her environment. Persons were interviewed to determine all behavior settings entered by him or her during a specified time period. Within each setting, the respondents were asked to report the amount of time spent in the setting, the zone of penetration, presence of other occupants, and satisfaction with the setting. Settings were categorized according to type, as work, education, recreation, social, commercial, legal/governmental, private/intimate, family, health, or transit. Since these studies relied on interview data, the delineation of settings was no doubt not as precise as that obtained by Barker and his colleagues with observational techniques; however, the authors believed that good approximations were achieved.

A major body of research in the area of environments has been produced by Moos and his associates. Scales have been developed to measure the social climate of treatment environments (Moos, 1973), correctional environments (Moos, 1968), educational environments (Gerst and Moos, 1972), work environments, small group environments, and family environments (Moos et al., 1974). These scales are developed by having participants in these environments respond to a series of items about the characteristic behavior of persons in the setting. Across these very different types of settings, three types of common dimensions have emerged. These are: (1) relationship dimensions. (2) personal development dimensions, and (3) system maintenance and system change dimensions (Insel and Moos, 1974). Relationship dimensions concern the nature and intensity of personal relationships within the environment. Personal development dimensions refer to the opportunity in the environment for personal growth and the development of self-esteem. System maintenance and system change dimensions include subjects' expectations concerning the extent to which the environment is orderly and clear, maintains control, and is responsive to change.

The work of Mehrabian and Russell (1974) centers on the use of human emotional responses to environments. On the basis of their data, they suggest that there are three basic emotional responses: pleasure, arousal, and dominance. Environments are rated on each of these dimensions and then classified according to their degree of similarity. Though this research is based on settings that are, for the most part, descriptions of the physical environment, the authors suggest that these basic dimensions are also applicable to social settings.

Pervin (1977) has argued that in order to have ecological generalizability, we need to sample broadly across situations, and that persons should be studied in situations that are as nearly representative of their daily living as possible. This latter point has to do with the relevance of situations to individuals. In order to meet these criteria, Pervin used a free-response method and asked subjects to list the situations in their current lives. The subjects then described each situation, how they felt in each situation, and their behavior in each situation. Each situation was then rated on each description provided by the subjects. The results were factor analyzed to produce a taxonomy of situations in an individual's life.

Stokols (1979) has presented a model for the analysis of human stress that is based on the sociophysical context in which events occur. Central to Stokols's model is the concept of "environment behavior congruence," which is the extent to which the environment accommodates the needs and goals of its users. Environmental congruence consists of two components: environmental controllability and environmental salience. The controllability of a setting is defined as the degree to which it can be modified or maintained in accordance with an individual's personal preference and well-being. This is actually a composite of several need dimensions, each of which may be either facilitated or constrained by the environment. Environmental salience concerns the extent to which settings are associated with psychologically important needs and goals.

In the studies described above, there is little convergence. The exception to this has to do with affect as a dimension of situations. As described previously, Mehrabian and Russell (1974) used affective responses to describe situations. The use of affect was decided upon a priori. However, results from two empirical studies support affect as an important dimension in the classification of situations. Magnusson (1971) used multidimensional scaling techniques to examine perceived dimensions of situations. Positive or negative affect was a major dimension along which settings were differentiated. In Pervin's (1977) work, described earlier, affect also emerged as a major dimension of situations. Not only were situations described in terms of affects, but also situations were organized in terms of the similarity of affects aroused in them.

The diversity of findings presented here should not be interpreted as discouraging further attempts to develop taxonomies of situations. We should not expect there to be one set of dimensions and categories. As Magnusson (1980: 44) has stated,

It need hardly be said that one cannot expect a single, definite solution. There is not one given set of categories or dimensions that is appropriate for effectively resolving all the psychological problems that require knowledge about situations. Not all categorical or dimensional solutions are appropriate for every problem; but each problem may have its adequate solution. Then the essential basis for analyses of situations and situational conditions is the set of psychological problems that we formulate. Depending on the problem, the appropriate situation characteristics to investigate, the appropriate kind of data—quantitative or qualitative—and the appropriate method of data analysis, all vary.

Thus a study of situations as they relate to violence would involve deciding upon a definition of what is "situational," a determination of the size of the environmental unit, whether to use perceived versus actual measures, whether or not to incorporate the interaction of persons and situations, and isolation of the relevant situational and environmental dimensions. It would of course be possible to include in a single study multiple levels of environmental units and both perceived and actual measures. For purposes of prediction at the individual level, it would seem most fruitful to concentrate on middle-level units of the environment, such as the individual's home setting. Even though it is possible that general economic indicators may predict increased rates of violence, we would not expect the state of the economy to be a good predictor for individuals. At the other end of the scale, very molecular units are not likely to be predictable. If it is possible to incorporate perceived measures, it seems that this should be done in order to maximize predictive accuracy. For individual predictors, it appears critical to include person-by-situation interactions . Specific methods for using a person-by-situation interaction approach are described in detail in the next sections.

MAJOR SITUATIONAL CORRELATES
OF VIOLENT BEHAVIOR

Despite its early stage of development and the attendant lack of conceptual clarity outlined above, much may be learned from the study of environments in terms of understanding violence. The following are what appear to be the best candidates for situational or environmental correlates of violent behavior that could be of use at the level of the individual. The first three can be conceptualized either as environmental "support systems" used by an individual for coping with life stress (President's Commission on Mental Health, 1978) or as the sources of the life stress itself.

Family Environment

One of the best predictors of whether released mental patients will survive in the community without being rehospitalized is the degree of support provided by their families (Fairweather et al., 1974). As Stone (1975: 13) stated, "a principal social function of the law-mental health system is to provide technical care for those individuals who are temporarily or permanently extruded from society's principal caretaking unit, the family. The wisdom and morality of this extrusion and the quality of this technical care are the bedrock problems of the law-mental health system."

In the case of violent behavior, the family context is crucial, since family members are so frequently the victims of violent behavior (Monahan, 1977). Skodol and Karasu (1978) found that in 77 percent of emergency commitment cases in which the patients admitted to actively considering violence, the victims were family members. The frequency of violence in police family-crisis interventions has been well documented (Bard, 1969; Driscoll et al., 1973). There is also evidence that the occurrence of such interventions may predict subsequent violence. In an unpublished study submitted to the Police Foundation by the Northeast Patrol Division Task Force, cited by Wolfgang (1978), 90 percent of family homicide victims and suspects had had previous disturbance calls to their addresses.

The family environment may be critical because of its role in supporting or discouraging violent behavior on the part of the family member whose behavior is being predicted. The probability of a person being violent may be greater if he or she resides in a family that encourages robbery as a career and where violence by other family members is a frequent occurrence, than if he or she has support and models for nonviolent modes of interaction and needs satisfaction. Though their prior records may be the same, the probability of recidivism of a released offender living with grandparents on a farm may be substantially less than that of another offender living with alcoholic friends in an inner city.

A fundamental property of physical environments is the amount of space available. Stokols (1976) has suggested that crowding is more important in primary than in secondary environments, that is, environments in which much time is spent and important needs and goals are pursued. Thus, living environments would seem to be the most likely candidates for observing the effects of crowding on aggression and violence. Megargee (1977) found such an effect in a correctional institution. The total amount of personal space and an index of population density were significantly correlated with the number and rate of violations for disruptive behavior. However, crowding in an institutional environment in which residents have little control over the environment may be different from the family environment. Studies of the effects of crowding in family environments have produced mixed results. In one of the best controlled studies of crowding and family relations (Booth and Edwards, 1976), crowding was found to have little effect. However those effects that were found occurred in the measures of conflict and aggression: Congestion in the household had a small positive influence on the incidence of sibling quarrels and the incidence of parents striking their children. Psychiatric impairment in parents intensified the effects of crowding on these measures as well as on measures of arguments between spouses.

Residential mobility of the family has been found to be related to family violence. In a representative national sample of more than 2,000 couples, Straus et al. (1980) found that having lived in a neighborhood less than two years was correlated with violence toward both spouse and children for fathers and violence toward spouse for mothers. Residential mobility has also been found to be related to delinquency (Wolfgang et al., 1972).

Children may be important as potential sources of stress and family conflict. The Straus et al. survey (1980) found that the number of children in the home was related to violence against both spouse and children in all but the higher family income brackets. In a study of abused wives, Gelles (1975) found that one-quarter of all attacks occurred when the wife was pregnant. Conflicts over children were more highly correlated with violence toward spouse than any other area of marital conflict in the Straus et al. study.

The relationship between husband and wife has been examined for correlates of marital violence. O'Brien (1971) found that violence of husbands toward wives was more frequent when the husband was in a state of status deficiency relative to the wife. Similarly, Allen and Straus (1980) found that when the wife's resources (both sociodemographic and interpersonal) exceeded those of the husband, the husband was more likely to have used physical force against the wife. Straus (1980) has suggested that sexual inequality and traditional beliefs about male prerogatives create a situation in which violence toward the wife is more acceptable and therefore more likely to occur. This is supported by results from Allen and Straus (1980) regarding the power of working-class husbands and from Straus et al. (1980), who find that shared decision-making between husbands and wives was preventative of violence toward spouse for both husbands and wives. In addition, families in which the husband was dominant in decision-making had higher incidences of spouse abuse than did families in which the wife was dominant. Economic dependence of the wife on the husband was also related to violence toward wives.

Some studies of criminal recidivism have focused on the supportive role of families. Davies (1969), in a study of young male probationers, found that men having a cohesive family network and compatible parents were less likely to be reconvicted and that the relationship between fathers and sons was particularly important. Waller (1974) examined rearrest rates for a sample of men released from prison and found that recidivism was higher for parolees who were unmarried and that living with wife and children was preventative of rearrest for both parolees and those released unconditionally.

In sum, many aspects of the family environment have been related to violent behavior. Crowding appears to have a slight effect but is probably more important in interaction with other variables. Residential mobility, pregnancy, and number of children in the family (particularly unwanted children or too many children for the family's financial resources) are sources of family stress found to be related to violence. The assumption of traditional male roles in marriages was seen to be important in marital violence and may be related to other types of violent behavior. The presence of supportive others in the family is likely to predict nonviolence. The quality of family relationships probably reflects both stress and support and is a likely correlate of violence.

Peer Environment

There is an enormous sociological literature on peer-group influences on behavior, particularly adolescent behavior. Likewise, numerous psychological studies attest to the effects of one's friends as behavior models (Bandura, 1969). There is, in addition, ample folk wisdom about the effects of "getting in with the wrong crowd" on criminal activity. Gang violence is probably the paradigmatic case of peer-induced harm. To the extent that a person's violent behavior in the past has occurred in a particular social context (rather than "as a loner," for example), it may be important to ascertain whether the same peers who encouraged previous violence are likely to provide similar encouragement in the future. Support for this notion comes from Davies (1969), who found that associating with delinquents was associated with reconviction for young male probationers. Thus, the person returning to the same friends who participated in the last robbery may have a greater likelihood of future violent crimes than the person who has broken contact with a criminally oriented group of friends.

Peers are also important because of their roles as victims. In a study of Philadelphia homicides, Wolfgang (1958) found that the largest category of relationship between victim and offender was that of relatively close friendships. Of all homicides, 28 percent were in this category, surpassing even the category of family relationships, which comprised 25 percent of the cases.

Friends as well as family members can be important sources of social support and as such may function to reduce the probability of violence. Davies (1969) also found that having some friends as opposed to being a loner was preventative of reconviction. Garbarino (1977), in reviewing the literature on child abuse, concluded that social isolation of the family is an important correlate of child abuse. This social isolation may consist of the absence of close, intimate friends or more structured ties to the community at large. For example, Straus et al. (1980) found that fathers who neither belonged to nor attended organized groups were more likely to be violent toward their children than were fathers who did participate in these types of groups. The findings about the relationship of residential mobility to violence discussed in the previous section on the family environment may also reflect friendships and ties to the community in that new residents are less likely to have established such peer relationships.

The preceding literature suggests multiple ways in which the peer environment may be important in violence. The criminal behavior of friends and the acceptance of violence as an appropriate or even encouraged behavior may be significant in many kinds of violence. Since friends are frequently victims of violence as well as potential sources of social support, it seems critical to do a more systematic analysis of peer environments and violence, one that would examine under what conditions friends become victims and under what conditions they play a preventative role. The quality of peer relationships and the number of relationships, frequency of contacts, types of activities with friends, characteristic places frequented with friends, and duration of friendships would bear further investigation. More formal, structured peer activities in the form of participation in organized groups are also peer environments and are likely to be negatively related to certain kinds of violence. A social network approach might be a useful tool for the study of peer environments and violence.

Job Environment

There is a growing body of research on the effect of employment upon criminal behavior, although the research generally does not separate violent from nonviolent crime (Monahan and Monahan, 1977). At monthly intervals, Glaser (1964) interviewed a sample of 135 parolees released from federal institutions in 1959 and 1960. In comparing the jobholding activity of the men who completed parole with that of men returned to prison, he found that the eventual successes acquired their first jobs sooner and, during the initial period of parole, earned a higher monthly income than did the eventual recidivists.

Cook (1975), studying 327 male felons released from Massachusetts prisons in 1959, found that 65 percent of those who held a "satisfactory" job (defined as a job that lasted 1 month or more) during the first 3 months of parole were eventually successful in completing an 18-month parole period, compared with a 36 percent success rate among those who did not have a satisfactory job during the first 3 months. Of parolees holding a satisfactory job during the second 3 months of parole, 75 percent were eventual successes, compared with 40 percent of those who did not hold a satisfactory job. Of those having a satisfactory job at the end of their first year on parole, 89 percent completed the parole period without revocation, while only 50 percent of those not satisfactorily employed successfully completed their terms of parole.

Cook (1975) also found that steady jobholding was related to parole success, while frequent job changing increased the likelihood that a parolee would recidivate. The probability of recidivism during the second 3 months on parole increased directly with the number of jobs held during the first 3 months, from 11 percent recidivism when one job was held to 43 percent when five jobs were held.

Sviridoff and Thompson (1979), in a retrospective study of the linkage of unemployment and crime, found that approximately half of a sample of men released from prison reported committing illegal activities only when unemployed.

While such data do not prove a causal relationship between employment and crime (since some third factor may cause both the reduction in recidivism *and* whether one is employed), it would appear that holding a job that is both satisfying and supportive reduces the probability of recidivism for at least some criminal offenders.

Evidence specifically linking violence (as opposed to crime in general) to unemployment comes from Straus et al. (1980). In this study, unemployment and only part-time employment of the husband correlated with the incidence of violence toward both spouse and children as well as the severity of violence in the home.

Satisfaction in the work environment may be related to violence. O'Brien (1971) found that husbands who were seriously dissatisfied with their jobs were more likely to be wife abusers than were men who were not seriously dissatisfied. However, Davies (1969) found that job satisfaction and probationers' attitudes toward their bosses and work colleagues were not related to criminal recidivism.

Other job-related variables likely to be important correlates of violence are income and financial stresses. Wife abuse was found to be more frequent in homes where income was a serious source of conflict between husbands and wives (O'Brien, 1971). The findings of Straus et al. (1980) are similar, in that they showed husbands being very worried about economic security was related to both wife-beating and husband-beating, and wives being very worried about financial security was related to wife-beating. The latter study also found that low income correlated with family violence and that income interacted with the number of children in the family, indicating that actual as well as perceived financial strains are likely to predict violence.

Various aspects of work have been found to be related to crime and violence. This is particularly true for unemployment. Job changing or the duration of jobs held seem to correlate with criminal recidivism. The duration of unemployment, though not included in the studies cited here, would seem to be a likely correlate of violence, in that unemployment of only a few durations may have relatively few effects, but unemployment ranging over many months is likely to be more problematic to the individual for many reasons. Satisfaction with the type of work and satisfaction with work colleagues may have some relationship to violence, though the evidence is not clear. Other uninvestigated aspects of the work environment that might be suggested as potential predictors are the amount of control over tasks, other workers, and the physical environment of the job. The actual income received from the job and its adequacy to meet one's financial needs have been shown to bear some relationship to violence. It seems important to consider the individual's perception of financial stresses as well as more objective measures. For example, whether the salary is considered fair for the type of work or whether one believes that others in similar jobs are better paid, as well as the perceived adequacy of the income to meet one's current and near-future financial obligations, are suggested topics of future investigation.

It is important to note that most of the studies cited regarding family, peer, and work environments show correlative rather than causal relationships, since there is very little data of the latter kind available. Nevertheless, correlative data can be useful for prediction and certainly allow for the identification of variables that should be investigated for possible causal relationships.

Availability of Victims

Violence, as Toch (1969) has emphasized, may be thought of as an interactional concept. It takes two for a murder to occur. Clearly, some persons are relatively indiscriminate in the victims they choose. Megargee (1976: 8) quotes a steel worker interviewed by Studs Terkel in *Working:* "All day long I wanted to tell my foreman to go fuck himself, but I can't. So I find a guy in a tavern. To tell him that. And he tells me too. . . . He's punching me and I'm punching him, because we actually want to punch somebody else" (Terkel, 1974: xxxiii). Consistent with the frustration-aggression hypothesis and theories of displacement, it is likely that both parties to this dispute would have found other "victims" had they not chanced upon each other.

There may be other types of individuals who are quite specific in their choice of victim and will not be violent other than to a given victim or class of victims. Spouse murderers, for example, have a very low recidivism rate, since they have removed their source of irritation. Incest offenders may desist when their children grow up. The now famous *Tarasoff* case (1976) is a clear example of victim-specific violence (Roth and Meisel, 1977; Wexler, 1979). A client revealed in therapy his intention to kill a woman who had rejected his romantic interests. The client then committed no violent acts for two months while the woman was on vacation. Shortly after she returned home, he murdered her. As Shah (1978: 180) has noted:

Decision-makers may wish to know whether the dangerous acts are more likely to occur against some *particular persons* (e.g., a spouse or girl friend, the individ-

ual's own children, or a neighbor with whom long-standing conflicts have occurred) and/or against some *broader group* of people (e.g., minor boys or girls in
the case of a pedophile, adult women in the case of certain exhibitionists or
rapists, etc.); and/or a *more dispersed segment of the community* (e.g., the likely
victims of "purse-snatchings" and other street robberies, potential victims of
recidivistic drunken drivers, etc.).

Availability of Weapons

Finally, the availability of weapons increases the likelihood that they will be
used. Equally important, weapons may influence not only the occurrence but
the *severity* and *lethality* of violent behavior (Newton and Zimring, 1970;
Zimring, 1977). The difference between assault and murder frequently re-
volves around whether the offender had a knife or only a fist at his or her
disposal. The difference between murder and attempted murder likewise is
often determined by whether the offender has access to a gun or knife.

Just as the possession of the "means" to commit suicide is a frequently used
predictor of suicide (Beck et al., 1974), so the person who reveals possession of
a household arsenal may be more likely to harm another than the individual
without such means of destruction.

Whether or not the presence of weapons actually instigates aggression is not
clear. In laboratory studies, Berkowitz and LePage (1967) found that the presence of a gun in the experimental situation increased the number of shocks
given to confederates. However, there have been several failures to replicate
this effect. Page and Scheidt (1971) conducted a series of experiments that led
them to conclude that the results obtained by Berkowitz and LePage were due to
demand awareness in the experimental situation. Buss et al. (1972) also failed
to replicate the effect and concluded that there was no evidence that the presence, firing, or long-term use of guns enhances subsequent aggression.

Availability of Alcohol

Based on an extensive literature review, Collins et al. (1980) concluded that
there is considerable evidence that the consumption of beverage alcohol is
associated with the occurrence of some serious crime, particularly assaultive
crime. In addition, they reported that alcohol use was found to be associated
with domestic violence, that drinking behavior and assaultive behavior both
have their highest incidence in young adult males, and that it is likely that other
situational factors interact with alcohol use in predicting violent behavior.

Baron (1977), in reviewing the literature on laboratory studies of the relationship between alcohol and aggression, found that small doses of alcohol
appear to inhibit later aggression, while larger doses seem to facilitate its
occurrence. The studies cited here also support the interaction of alcohol and
other situational variables in producing aggression.

There is a great deal of literature on criminology relating the high frequency of violent behavior in and near bars and taverns (for example, Wolfgang, 1958). At least for those persons whose previous violent behavior has been associated with a state of intoxication, the easy availability of alcohol and the presence of a support group that encourages its excessive use (drinking buddies) may constitute a high-risk context for the occurrence of violent behavior.

Other Situational Factors

There are other situational factors that have been found to be related to aggression, crime, and violence, such as heat and noise (Baron, 1977) and architectural design (Newman, 1972). However, these factors seem less useful as predictors of violence for individuals and will not be discussed in detail.

ASSESSING INTERACTIONS BETWEEN PERSONS AND THEIR ENVIRONMENTS

It is surely true, as discussed above, that the very definition of "situation" is interdependent with an individual's personality (Bem and Allen, 1974). A situation that one person perceives as a threat to his or her social status may be perceived by another as nonthreatening or even status enhancing. People often *choose* the situation they are in (for example, going to a bar that one knows has a high frequency of fights), and situations often draw certain kinds of people to themselves (pawnshops, for instance, sometimes draw people with stolen property). How, then, are we to describe a "situation" or a "context" for the purpose of prediction? One major proposal was recently made.

Bem and Funder (1978) demonstrated that situations can be described in terms of how different types of people are expected to behave in them. The probability that a particular person will behave in a given way in a certain situation is a function of the similarity between his or her characteristics and the characteristics of the people (called "templates" by Bem and Funder) that typically frequent the situation. For example, assume that for a given community program for offenders, records reveal that the people in the program who have assaulted other participants tended to be characterized as "highly resentful of authority," "refusing group activities," and "addicted to heroin." If one wished to predict whether *this* potential referral to the program would be assaultive, one would want to see how closely he or she matched these three characteristics. If the characteristics of the potential referral did, indeed, match the characteristics of the kinds of people who have been found to be violent in that environment in the past, the probability of favorable outcome would be decreased. If the characteristics of the potential referral were very different from those of the people who had been violent in that environment, a more favorable prediction could be made.

Note how this "situation-centered" perspective differs from the "variable-centered" perspective just discussed. Rather than ask what characteristics of situations in *general* relate to violent behavior, Bem and Funder (1978) ask how this *particular situation* influences different types of people to act. One situation may elicit violence in a certain kind of person and helping behavior in another. The question in predicting the behavior of a *particular person* in that environment, then, becomes whether he or she has more of the characteristics of the violent or of the helping person. A second environment may elicit violence from a completely different type of person.

Describing situations in terms of how given types of people are expected to behave in them may have much utility for preventing violence by modifying environmental characteristics. But for the purpose of predicting the behavior of an individual across a variety of environments in the community, there may be a better approach. "Rather than describing a situation in terms of how a set of hypothetical ideal persons behave within it, we should now describe a person in terms of how he or she behaves in a set of hypothetical ideal situations" (Bem and Funder, 1978). For example, one could give an individual a set of items describing properties of situations (such as "is unstructured," "is characterized by the presence of an authority figure") and ask the person to state the degree to which these properties typify the situations in which he or she behaves violently. (There is a formal technique, the Q-Sort [Block, 1961], in which statements are sorted into nine categories, from the least characteristic to the most characteristic of what is being measured. It might have utility for the purpose being discussed here [Bem and Funder, 1978]).

Alternatively, if the individual was unable or unwilling to do the rating, a clinician familiar with the case or the file could do it. One way to decide whether a given item describes the kind of environment in which the individual can be expected to be violent is to rate the kinds of environments in which the person has been violent in the past. Thus, if the individual had four previous assaults, and two of them were against males and two against females, one would rate an item "victims tend to be females" as neither characteristic nor uncharacteristic of the environments in which violence has occurred. If all four victims were females, the item would be rated highly characteristic, and if all four were males, the item would be rated highly uncharacteristic.

After one has obtained a profile of the kinds of situations in which the individual is expected to be (or, better yet, has in the past been) violent, it remains to categorize the environments in which he or she will probably be functioning during the period for which one is predicting. Often, much of this environment will be unknown, but many characteristics may be available. For example, if one highly salient aspect of the environments in which a person committed previous assaults was that his wife was present in them as the victim, but the wife has since divorced him and moved to a different city, it might be possible to affix a substantially lower probability of violence than if the wife were still at home. While many other aspects of the individual's environment may be unknown, the presence or absence of the wife may be available information.

The approach put forward by Bem and Funder (1978) to categorize people in terms of the environments that elicit given behaviors from them has potential not only for improving the prediction of violent behavior, but also for generating differential predictions that may be useful in placement or treatment decisions. If a person tends to be violent in environments characterized by factors A, B, and C, and one is faced with the choice of recommending that he or she be placed in one environment that is characterized by A, B, and D or in another setting that is characterized by factors A, D, and E, one might wish to recommend the latter, since only one of its three principal characteristics is similar to those that trigger violence in the individual, while two of the three characteristics of the former setting are similar.

The Bem and Funder (1978) model, therefore, poses three questions:

(1) What characteristics describe the situations in which the person reacts violently?
(2) What characteristics describe the situations the person will confront in the future?
(3) How similar are the situations the person will confront in the future to those that have elicited violence in the past?

Another possible approach is to assess persons as embedded in their environments, so that the person-situation interaction is the unit of analysis. Klassen (1981) compared the family, peer, and work environments of three groups of men: (1) men who had recently been committed to an emergency mental health unit as dangerous to others as a result of threats toward or attacks against other persons, (2) men who were committed to the same facility but were not dangerous to others, and (3) a control group obtained from a medical outpatient clinic. The subjects were matched on age, race, and socioeconomic status. Interviews were conducted assessing the structure, quality, and salience of the subjects' family, peer, and work environments during the past three months. The results showed that the violent mental patients differed from the other groups in some aspects of each of these environments, though there were also many similarities. Briefly, the violent patients had the smallest proportion living with spouse or having a regular ongoing relationship with a woman. Violent patients' peer environments were characterized by patterns of interactions with friends that involved fewer activities and fewer places gone to with friends, even though the number of friendships was not different. They also spent fewer hours in recreational activities. Both patient groups had experienced longer durations of unemployment than the controls, but the violent patients rated the importance of having regular, full-time employment higher than did the other two groups. Discriminant analysis using variables from all three environments correctly classified the subjects' group memberships in more than 80 percent of the cases, indicating that these measures, when taken together, strongly differentiated the groups.

Though the above study is limited by its cross-sectional design, it would be possible to incorporate this type of approach in a study of individuals over time. This could be done in either a retrospective or a longitudinal design. The data would consist of measures of family, peer, and work environments of persons who had committed violent acts at different points in time—ideally both prior to violent episodes as well as during periods of nonviolence. This type of design would allow for findings regarding general predictors as well as more idiosyncratic predictors of violence for individuals.

SITUATIONAL APPROACHES TO THE PREDICTION OF VIOLENCE

One concept that may provide an organizing principle for many of the issues in situational violence prediction is that of stress. Stress can be understood as a state of imbalance between the demands of the social and physical environment and the capabilities of an individual to cope with these demands (McGrath, 1970; Mechanic, 1968). The higher the ratio of demands to resources, the more stress is experienced. Stress is thus to be thought of in terms of transactions between persons and their environments over time (Lazarus and Launier, forthcoming). The voluminous literature on stress and its regulation has been masterfully systematized by Novaco (1979). Novaco presents a model of anger arousal as one form of reacting to stress, and his model, with some modification, may provide a vehicle for explicating many (but not all) of the factors involved an individual's responding to a "provoking" situation in a violent manner (see also Levinson and Ramsay, 1979). It is presented in Figure 6.1.

Stressful or aversive situations such as frustrations, annoyances, insults, and assaults by another are seen in this model as filtered through certain cognitive processes in the individual who is the subject of assessment. Novaco conceptualizes these cognitive processes as of two types: appraisals and expectations.

Appraisals refer to the manner in which an individual interprets an event as a provocation and therefore experiences it as aversive. Perceived intentionality is perhaps the clearest example of an antagonistic appraisal (for example, "You didn't just bump into me, you meant to hit me"). How a person cognitively appraises an event may have a great influence on whether he or she ultimately responds to it in a violent manner. Some persons may be prone to interpret seemingly innocuous interactions as intentional slights. The chips on their shoulders may be precariously balanced.

Expectations are seen as cognitive processes that may influence the occur-

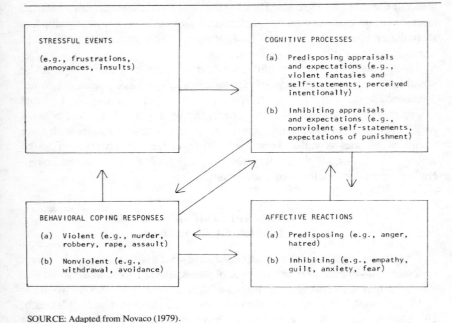

SOURCE: Adapted from Novaco (1979).

FIGURE 6.1   A Model of Some of the Factors to Be Assessed in the Prediction of
Violent Behavior

rence of violence in several ways. If one expects a desired outcome (such as a
raise in pay or an expression of gratitude for a favor done) and it fails to occur,
emotional arousal may ensue, and, depending upon the context, it may be
perceived as anger. If one appraises an event as a provocation, the occurrence of
violence may still depend upon whether one expects violence to be instrumental
in righting the perceived wrong or whether one can expect violence to be met
with a counterforce. One may, for example, regard having sand kicked in one's
face as a deliberate affront and yet, upon learning that the agent of provocation
is built like a football linebacker, have such low expectations for successful
retaliation that violence is no longer under consideration. Alternatively, should
the provocateur resemble Woody Allen, one's expectation that violence will
prevail may rise accordingly.

Both expectations and appraisals may be reflected in the "private speech" or
self-statements a person uses regarding violent behavior (for example, "Any-
body who insults my wife gets hit"). Violent delusions and fantasies may be
thought of as extreme forms of such private conversations, and statements of
intention that are directly verbalized (threats of violence) may be particularly
significant. For our purposes, appraisals and expectations may both be catego-

rized as cognitive factors that "predispose" toward or "inhibit" violent behavior. These cognitive processes, in turn, may either give rise to certain affective or emotional reactions or directly propel a behavioral response. One need not be emotionally aroused to commit a violent act (witness the stereotypic hit man of *Godfather* fame). If, as is more typical, affective reactions are intervening, they may be viewed as of either a predisposing or an inhibiting type. Affective reactions predisposing a person toward violence would include the emotions of anger and hatred. While anger is not necessary for the occurrence of violent behavior, its arousal is a significant antecedent to aggression (Rule and Nesdale, 1976). Fortunately, excellent work on the clinical assessment of anger is currently available (Novaco, 1975, 1976, 1978, 1979). Affective reactions inhibiting violence (or, to put it more positively, predisposing toward peacefulness) include what have been called the "moral emotions" of empathy for the source of a frustration and guilt about injuring another, as well as anxiety reactions about engaging in violence or about the victim's possible retaliation. The lack of capacity for such affect has been viewed as the hallmark of the "sociopath" (Dinitz, 1978).

These affective reactions are then behaviorally expressed in terms of a coping response which, for our purposes, may be dichotomized as violent or nonviolent. The type of response chosen may go on to influence further stressful events, as would be the case when a divorce would eliminate interaction with a frustrating spouse or murder would precipitate the stresses of imprisonment. Whether or not a given coping response attenuates or exacerbates life stresses would have relevance to whether a given level of violence potential could be expected to increase or decrease. As Toch (1969) emphasized, violence may be thought of as interactional in nature. If one person's coping response (such as insulting a person perceived as a threat) leads the other to escalate his or her provocations, violence may eventually ensue.

Several of the relationships expressed in Figure 6.1 are bidirectional (as indicated by the arrows). This is meant to indicate that affective reactions can influence cognitive processes ("I feel so upset that I must be really angry") and that behavioral responses can affect both cognitions ("I hit him; therefore I must want to hurt him") and emotions ("I avoided her; therefore I must be angry at her").

The Novaco model of anger, as adapted here, is not exhaustive of the factors that influence violence. Demographic and historical factors, for example, are not addressed. But as a depiction of the cognitive and affective factors involved in how situations are perceived and lead to violent behavior, the adapted Novaco model seems to capture well the essence of much of what is involved.

The kinds of stressors in which we are interested are those likely to be met with violent coping responses. While the kinds of stressors (such as frustrations, annoyances, insults, injuries) likely to result in violence are dependent upon the ways in which the individual cognitively and affectively processes them, and in fact may be thought of as fundamentally idiosyncratic in nature, some commonalities may exist among the kinds of situational demands likely to lead to violence. Based on the earlier analysis of the situational correlates of violent behavior, at least three broad areas of concern suggest themselves:

(1) *Family Stressors.* The frustrations and annoyances attendant to husband-wife and parent-child relationships, as many have noted, appear particularly susceptible to violent resolution. An assessment of the individual's current living situation and the quality of social interactions involved would appear to be a priority endeavor.

(2) *Peer-Group Stressors.* Analogous to the family as a source of stress, the relationships of the individual to persons he or she considers, or until recently has considered, friends may be germane. In addition to disruption of friendship patterns being an instigator of stress, the role of peers as models for violent behavior (Bandura, 1973, 1969) and as sources of social support for violent or nonviolent lifestyles (President's Commission on Mental Health, 1978) suggests that peer relations should be carefully investigated.

(3) *Employment Stressors.* While often overlooked, the stress associated with unemployment or with aversive employment situations may have a significant effect upon criminal behavior. These stressors may take the form of a recent firing, disputes with superiors or co-workers, or dissatisfaction with the nature of the work performed or the level of compensation paid for it.

As described above, the situational prediction model suggested by Bem and Funder (1978) would lead to the assessment of (1) the characteristics of the situations in which the person tends to react violently, and (2) the characteristics of the situations in which the person is likely to be functioning in the future. The third step (3) would then be to estimate the degree of similarity between these two kinds of situations. The more the similarity, the higher the probability of violent behavior occurring. This approach is conducive to offering differential predictions, such as that the person has X probability of violence in situations typified by A, B, and C, and Y probability in situations typified by D, E, and F. Such predictions may prove useful in deciding among various forms of placement.

Another way of making the same point may be to reconstruct the pattern of violent behavior in the individual's past and to ascertain whether it is likely to repeat itself. Did the person become violent in the past when he or she was ending a relationship, or in a "manic" state, or when unemployed for several months, or when under the influence of alcohol or other drugs? If reliably so, is he or she now or in the near future likely to be ending a relationship, or in a "manic" state, or unemployed for several months, or under the influence of alcohol or other drugs? Note that one is here individualizing the situational and personality bases for prediction. It is not that all people or even most people react violently in the given situations, but rather that this particular person, when confronted in the past with this particular constellation of events, has evidenced a pattern of violent behavior. Likewise for dispositional states: It is not that psychological disorder is associated with violence, but rather that this particular person, when experiencing this particular disorder, has tended to react violently in the past. While individualizing predictions in this manner may be a researcher's nightmare, it may also constitute an occasion on which the value of clinical judgment is maximized.

Viewing this approach as analogous to a person-by-situation interaction model indicates that few situations would have strong main affects in producing violent behavior. There are very few situations that would evoke violence in all or even most people. Immediate danger of harm to oneself or loved ones might be an example of such situations. For the most part, the search will be for situations that have weak main effects but strong interaction affects with person variables. Thus, there will be certain person types who will be violent in situations that usually do not evoke violence in other persons.

In addition to the above approach to situations, one may wish to single out for special attention the likely victims of a person's violent behavior. As an initial step, the demographic composition of the past-victim pool (for example, women, the elderly) should be ascertained and, to the extent possible, an account constructed of the cognitive and affective factors motivating the individual to choose them rather than others as victims. For example, the past-victim pool may have been limited to males who cast aspersions upon the individual's sense of masculinity, to a particular person such as a spouse or child, or to the indiscriminate choice of the next person encountered (Shah, 1978).

One would then wish to know how likely the environments in which the person will function in the future are to contain persons of similar characteristics. In situations in which a large class of persons forms the potential victim pool (such as women, in the case of a rapist), there will surely be many persons at risk for potential victimization. But where only one or a small group of persons is the target of potential violence, the unavailability of those persons may preclude violent behavior. Thus, a father guilty of forced incest may desist from violence when his daughter is older. Removal of the potential victim (say, the spouse or adolescent child) from the family through separating residences may decrease the frequency of interaction and, hence, the probability of violence.

SUMMARY

In this chapter, we have proposed some approaches to studying the relationships of situations and violent behavior based on the current literature. Four issues were identified that are important in conceptualizing situations. These are the definition of a situation, the size of the environmental unit, the perceived versus the actual situation, and the interactive nature of persons and situations. Existing works on the classifications and dimensions of environments were reviewed. The major situational correlates of violent behavior were discussed and the family, peer, and work environments were suggested to be the most promising areas for violence prediction. Situational approaches to studying violent behavior were proposed, with emphasis on how one model for studying person-situation interactions (Bem and Funder, 1978) could be implemented for violence prediction. There seems to be ample material in the literature that could stimulate research incorporating situational variables in violence prediction.

REFERENCES

Allen, C. M., and Straus, M. A. Resources, power and husband-wife violence. In M. A. Straus and G. T. Hotaling (Eds.), *The social causes of husband-wife violence*. Minneapolis: University of Minnesota Press, 1980.

Bandura, A. *Principles of behavior modification*. New York: Holt, Rinehart & Winston, 1969.

Bandura, A. *Aggression: A social learning analysis*. Englewood Cliffs, NJ: Prentice-Hall, 1973.

Bard, M. Family intervention police teams as a community mental health resource. *Journal of Criminal Law, Criminology and Police Science,* 1969, 60, 247-250.

Barker, R. *Ecological psychology*. Stanford, CA: Stanford University Press, 1968.

Baron, R. A. *Human aggression*. New York: Plenum Press, 1977.

Beck, A., Resnick, H., and Littieri, D. *The prediction of suicide*, Bowie, MD: Charles, 1974.

Bem, D., and Allen, A. On predicting some of the people some of the time: The search for cross-situational consistencies in behavior. *Psychological Review,* 1974, 81, 506-520.

Bem, D., and Funder, D. Predicting more of the people more of the time: Assessing the personality of situations. *Psychological Review,* 1978, 85, 485-501.

Berkowitz, L., and LePage, A. Weapons as aggression-eliciting stimuli. *Journal of Personality and Social Psychology,* 1967, 7, 202-207.

Block, J. *The Q-Sort method in personality assessment and psychiatric research*. Springfield, IL: Charles C Thomas, 1961.

Booth, A., and Edwards, J. N. Crowding and family relations. *American Sociological Review,* 1976, 41, 308-321.

Bowers, K. S. Situations in psychology: An analysis and a critique. *Psychological Review,* 1973, 80, 307-336.

Bowers, K. S. There's more to Iago than meets the eye: A clinical account of personal consistency. In D. Magnusson and N. S. Endler (Eds.), *Personality at the crossroads*. Hillsdale, NJ: Lawrence Erlbaum Associates, 1977.

Buss, A., Booker, A., and Buss, E. Firing a weapon and aggression. *Journal of Personality and Social Psychology,* 1972, 22, 296-303.

Collins, J. J., Guess, L. L., Williams, J. R., and Hamilton, C. J. *A research agenda to address the relationship between alcohol consumption and assaultive criminal behavior*. Submitted to the Center for the Study of Crime Correlates and Criminal Behavior, National Institute of Justice, 1980.

Cook, P. The correctional carrot: Better jobs for parolees. *Policy Analysis,* 1975, 1, 11-54.

Davies, M. *Probationers in their social environment*. London: Her Majesty's Stationery Office, 1969.

Dinitz, S. Chronically antisocial offenders. In J. Conrad and S. Dinitz, *In fear of each other: Studies of dangerousness in America*. Lexington, MA: D.C. Heath, 1978, 21-42.

Driscoll, J., Meyer, R., and Schanie, C. Training police in family crisis intervention. *Journal of Applied Behavioral Science*, 1973, 9, 62-82.

Ekehammer, B. Interactionism in personality from a historical perspective. *Psychological Bulletin*, 1974, 81, 1026-1048.

Fairweather, G., Sanders, D., and Tornatzky, L. *Creating change in mental health organizations*. New York: Pergamon, 1974.

Fiske, D. W. Personologies, abstractions, and interactions. In D. Magnusson and N. S. Endler (Eds.), *Personality at the crossroads*. Hillsdale, NJ: John Wiley, 1977.

Fredericksen, N. Toward a taxonomy of situations. *American Psychologist*, 1972, 27, 114-123.

Garbarino, J. The human ecology of child maltreatment. *Journal of Marriage and the Family*, 1977, 39, 721-735.

Gelles, R. J. Violence and pregnancy: a note on the extent of the problem and needed services. *Family Coordinator*, 1975, 24, 81-86.

Gerst, M., and Moos, R. The social ecology of university student residences. *Journal of Educational Psychology*, 1972, 63, 513-522.

Glaser, D. *The effectiveness of a prison and parole system*. Indianapolis: Bobbs-Merrill, 1964.

Golding, S. L. The problem of construal styles in the analysis of person-situation interactions. In D. Magnusson and N. S. Endler (Eds.), *Personality at the crossroads*. Hillsdale, NJ: John Wiley, 1977.

Insel, P. M., and Moos, R. Psychological environments. *American Psychologist*, 1974, 29, 179-188.

Kiritz, S., and Moos, R. Physiological effects of the social environment. In P. M. Insel and R. Moos (Eds.), *Health and the social environment*. Lexington, MA: D. C. Heath, 1974.

Klassen, D. Person, setting and outcome in drug abuse treatment. *Psychiatric Annals*, 1977, 7, 80-104.

Klassen, D. Family, peer and work environment correlates of violent behavior. Unpublished doctoral dissertation, University of California, Irvine, 1981.

Lazarus, R., and Launier, R. Stress-related transactions between persons and environment. In L. Pervin and M. Lewis (Eds.), *Internal and external determinants of behavior*. New York: Plenum, forthcoming.

Levinson, R., and Ramsay, G. Dangerousness, stress, and mental health evaluations. *Journal of Health and Social Behavior*, 1979, 20, 178-187.

Magnusson, D. An analysis of situation dimensions. *Perceptual and Motor Skills*, 1971, 31, 851-867.

Magnusson, D. Wanted: A psychology of situations. In D. Magnuson (Ed.), *Toward a psychology of situations: An interactional perspective*. Hillsdale, NJ: Lawrence Erlbaum Associates, 1980.

Magnusson, D., and Endler, N. S. Interactional psychology: Present status and future prospects. In D. Magnusson and N. S. Endler (Eds.), *Personality at the crossroads*, Hillsdale, NJ: Lawrence Erlbaum Associates, 1977.

McGrath, J. *Social and psychological factors in stress*. New York: Holt, Rinehart & Winston, 1970.

Mechanic, D. *Medical sociology: A selective view*. New York: Free Press, 1968.

Megargee, E. I. The prediction of dangerous behavior. *Criminal Justice and Behavior*, 1976, 3, 3-21.

Megargee, E.I. The association of population density, reduced space, and uncomfortable temperatures with misconduct in a prison community. *American Journal of Community Psychology*, 1977, 5, 289-298.

Mehrabian, A., and Russell, J. A. *An approach to environmental psychology*. Cambridge: MIT Press, 1974.

Moos, R. The assessment of social climates of correctional institutions. *Journal of Research in Crime and Delinquency,* 1968, 5, 178-188.

Moos, R. Conceptualizations of human environments. *American Psychologist,* 1973, 28, 652-665.

Moos, R., Insel, P. M., and Humphrey, B. *Preliminary manual for family environment scale, work environment scale, and group environment scale.* Palo Alto, CA: Consulting Psychologists Press, 1974.

Monahan, J. Empirical analyses of civil commitment: Critique and context. *Law and Society Review,* 1977, 11, 619-628.

Monahan, J. *The clinical prediction of violent behavior.* Washington, DC: Government Printing Office, 1981.

Monahan, J., and Monahan, L. Prediction research and the role of psychologists in correctional institutions. *San Diego Law Review,* 1977, 14, 1028-1038.

Newman, O. *Defensible space.* New York: Macmillan, 1972.

Newton, G., and Zimring, F. *Firearms and violence in American life: Staff report to the National Commission on the Causes and Prevention of Violence.* Washington, DC: Government Printing Office, 1970.

Novaco, R. *Anger control: The development and evaluation of an experimental treatment.* Lexington, MA: D. C. Heath, 1975.

Novaco, R. The function and regulation of the arousal of anger. *American Journal of Psychiatry,* 1976, 133, 1124-1128.

Novaco, R. Anger and coping with stress. In J. Foreyt and D. Rathjen (Eds.), *Cognitive behavior therapy: Theory, research and practice.* New York: Plenum, 1978.

Novaco, R. The cognitive regulation of anger and stress. In P. Kendall and S. Hollon (Eds.), *Cognitive-behavioral interventions: Theory, research, and procedures.* New York: Academic Press, 1979, 241-285.

Nuttin, J. R. A conceptual frame of personality-world interaction: A relational theory. In D. Magnusson and N. S. Endler (Eds.), *Personality at the crossroads.* Hillsdale, NJ: Lawrence Erlbaum Associates, 1977.

O'Brien, J. E. Violence in divorce prone families. *Journal of Marriage and the Family,* 1971, 33, 692-698.

O'Connor, W. A., and Daniels, S. *Psychological ecosystems: A multi-level model.* Paper presented at the annual meeting of the American Psychological Association, September 1979.

O'Connor, W. A., Klassen, D., and O'Connor, K. S. Evaluating human service programs: Psychosocial methods. In P. Ahmed and G. Coelho (Eds.), *Toward a new definition of health.* New York: Plenum Press, 1979.

Page, M. M., and Scheidt, R. J. The elusive weapons effect: Demand awareness, evaluation apprehension, and slightly sophisticated subjects. *Journal of Personality and Social Psychology,* 1971, 20, 304-318.

Pervin, L. A. The representative design of person-situation research. In D. Magnusson and N. J. Endler (Eds.), *Personality at the crossroads.* Hillsdale, NJ: John Wiley, 1977.

Pervin, L. A. Definitions, measurements, and classifications of stimuli, situations, and environments. *Human Ecology,* 1978, 6, 71-105.

President's Commission on Mental Health. Report to the President. Washington, DC: Government Printing Office, 1978.

Price, R. H., and Blashfield, R. K. Explorations in the taxonomy of behavior settings. *American Journal of Community Psychology,* 1975, 3, 335-351.

Rausch, H. L. Paradox, levels, and junctures in person-situation systems. In D. Magnusson and N. S. Endler (Eds.), *Personality at the crossroads,* Hillsdale, NJ: John Wiley, 1977.

Roth, L., and Meisel, A. Dangerousness, confidentiality and the duty to warn. *American Journal of Psychiatry,* 1977, 134, 508-511.

Rotter, J. B. The role of the psychological situation in determining the direction of human behavior.

In M. R. Jones (Ed.), *Nebraska Symposium on Motivation*. Lincoln: University of Nebraska Press, 1955.

Rule, B., and Nesdale, A. Emotional arousal and aggressive behavior. *Psychological Bulletin,* 1976, 83, 851-863.

Sells, S. B. Dimensions of stimulus situations which account for behavior variance. In S. B. Sells (Ed.), *Stimulus determinants of behavior*. New York: Ronald Press, 1963.

Shah, S. Dangerousness and mental illness. Some conceptual, prediction and policy dilemmas. In C. Frederick (Ed.), *Dangerous behavior: A problem in law and mental health* (NIMH; DHEW Publication [ADM] 78-563). Washington, DC: Government Printing Office, 1978, 153-191.

Sherif, M., and Sherif, C. W. *An outline of social psychology*. New York: Harper & Row, 1956.

Skodol, A., and Karasu, T. Emergency psychiatry and the assaultive patient. *American Journal of Psychiatry,* 1978, 135, 202-205.

Stokols, D. The experience of crowding in primary and secondary environments. *Environment and Behavior,* 1976, 8, 49-86.

Stokols, D. Environmental psychology. *Annual Review of Psychology,* 1978, 29, 253-295.

Stokols, D. A congruence analysis of human stress. In I. G. Sarason and C. D. Spielberger (Eds.), *Stress and anxiety* (Vol. 6). Washington, DC: Hemisphere Press, 1979.

Stone, A. *Mental health and the law: A system in transition* (NIMH; DHEW Publication [ADM] 76-176). Washington, DC: Government Printing Office, 1975.

Straus, M. A. Sexual inequality and wife beating. In M. A. Straus and G. T. Hotaling (Eds.), *The social causes of husband-wife violence*. Minneapolis: University of Minnesota Press, 1980.

Straus, M. A., Gelles, R. J., and Steinmetz, S. K. *Behind closed doors*. Garden City, NY: Anchor, 1980.

Sviridoff, M., and Thompson, J. W. *Linkages between employment and crime: A qualitative study of Rikers releases*. New York: Vera Institute of Justice, 1979.

Tarasoff v. Regents of the University of California, Sup. 131 Cal. Rptr. 14, 1976.

Terkel, S. *Working*. New York: Pantheon, 1974.

Toch, H. *Violent men*. Chicago: Aldine, 1969.

Waller, I. *Men released from prison*. Toronto: University of Toronto Press, 1974.

Wexler, D. Patients, therapists, and third parties: The victimological virtues of Tarasoff. *International Journal of Law and Psychiatry,* 1979, 2, 1-28.

Wolfgang, M. E. *Patterns in criminal homicide*. Philadelphia: University of Pennsylvania Press, 1958.

Wolfgang, M. E. Violence in the family. In I. L. Kutash, S. B. Kutash, and L. B. Schlesinger (Eds.), *Perspectives on murder and aggression*. San Francisco: Jossey-Bass, 1978.

Wolfgang, M. E., Figlio, R. M., and Sellin, T. *Delinquency in a birth cohort*. Chicago: University of Chicago Press, 1972.

Wohlwill, J. F. The environment is not in the head. In W. F. Preiser (Ed.), *Environment design research*. Stroudsburg, PA: Dowden, Hutchinson, & Ross, 1973.

Zimring, F. Determinants of the death rate from robbery: A Detroit time study. *Journal of Legal Studies,* 1977, 6, 317-332.

7

The Violent Offender in the Criminal Justice System

Peter W. Greenwood

Among all forms of criminal activity, there is little doubt that violent crimes are the most threatening to the public's sense of security. The mugging of an old woman on her way home from the store, the rape of a coed in an unlighted parking lot, the robbery of a liquor store by several armed bandits—these are the crimes that citizens fear most when they talk about crime in the streets. These are the crimes that cause inner-city residents to stay locked in their homes or to move to the suburbs when they can afford to do so.

Within the criminal justice system, violent crimes receive the most attention. Reports of violent crimes in progress receive first priority in dispatching patrol cars. Reported violent crimes are more systematically investigated than any other type. Violent offenders are more rigorously prosecuted and more likely to be imprisoned than offenders charged with other types of crimes.

Whenever there is an unexpected rise in violent crime, the political and public reaction is predictable. More police and tougher sentences are called for. The judiciary is castigated for its lenient sentencing.

Is the criminal justice system too easy on violent criminals? Would more police and prosecutors make a difference? Would the public be safer if prison terms were longer? These are the fundamental questions that must be addressed when we look at how the criminal justice system deals with violent crime.

There are no easy answers to any of these questions. The most common forms of violent crime—rape, robbery, and assault—are more notable for their differences than for their similarities. The characteristics of victims and places where crime occurs differ widely. The motivation and characteristics of their perpetrators are also dissimilar.

Author's Note: This chapter originally appeared as #P-6638 of the Rand Paper Series, June 1981.

Given the great concern with violent crime and the amount of effort expended by the criminal justice system in dealing with it, it is somewhat surprising to observe that there has been very little systematic research concerning how the activities of the criminal justice system affect violent crime or violent offenders. Most research of this nature does not distinguish violent crime from other types of offenses. Since the few studies that do contain detailed information on the processing of violent offenders by the system have been done at different sites, using different methodologies, they provide only a rough sense about what the linkages are between policy options and system outcomes. The objective of this chapter is to review what these studies have shown about how the system works and to point out where our knowledge is deficient.

In discussing the treatment of violent offenders, I will limit myself to offenders who are charged with homicide, forcible rape, robbery, or assault—the four categories of violent crime included in the FBI's Uniform Crime Index. These also happen to be the offense categories usually distinguished in research on prosecution or sentencing. This distinction is somewhat arbitrary. We could just as well restrict our attention to only those crimes in which violence actually occurred, eliminating a high proportion of robberies; or we could expand the definition to include those offenses that have the possibility of leading to violence, such as burglary or illegal weapons possession. Since many recidivists exhibit a pattern of both property and violent offenses, it would also not be unreasonable to categorize as violent any offender with a previous conviction for a violent crime.

This chapter begins by briefly reviewing the evidence concerning how criminal justice activities can affect crime—through deterrence, rehabilitation, and incapacitation. It then looks at how specific types of offenders are treated within the system. In the final section, it examines more closely the issues involved in determining appropriate sentence lengths.

THE CRIMINAL JUSTICE SYSTEM'S EFFECT ON VIOLENT CRIME

There are three general ways in which the criminal justice system can attempt to reduce violent crime. They involve the concepts of deterrence, rehabilitation, and incapacitation. Deterrence refers to the inhibiting effect that sanctions may have on potential offenders who would commit crime if it were not for the risk of being caught and punished. Deterrence theory holds that increasing the probability of arrest, conviction, or incarceration, or increasing sentence lengths, will decrease the willingness of potential offenders to commit crimes. Rehabilitation refers to the effect of any postconviction treatment in reducing an offender's propensity to engage in crime. Incapacitation refers to the fact that an offender is physically restrained from committing crimes against the general public while he or she is confined.

The Deterrent Effect of Sanctions

All theories of deterrence predict a negative association between aggregate crime rates and sanctions, with levels of sanctions measured either by severity or by risk. Most of the empirical research on deterrence has involved analysis of natural variations in crime rates and sanctions across sites. With few exceptions, these studies consistently find a negative association between crime rates and the risks of apprehension, conviction, or imprisonment.

The problem with these studies is that they all use the same questionable data sources—aggregate statistics on crime rates, arrest rates, and prison populations from the few years for which such data are available. Rather than thirty independent studies, the deterrence literature actually represents only two or three basic studies replicated many times over by different authors with minor variations in their statistical methodologies. A National Academy of Sciences panel (Blumstein et al., 1978) that recently reviewed these studies found that the evidence did not warrant an affirmative conclusion regarding the existence of deterrence because of an inability to eliminate other factors that could account for the observed relationship, even in the absence of deterrence. The most important factors cited by the panel were the possibility that crime rates might influence sanctions, as well as vice versa, and the possibility that errors in measuring crime rates might produce the observed relationship.

The negative associations between crime rates and sanctions found in these studies appear strongest for the probability of arrest and incarceration and weakest for the length of time served. This tentative finding is important for violent crimes, where the question is most frequently not whether a convicted offender should be incarcerated, but for how long.

In summation, it is quite possible that an increase in the risk of incarceration would result in a reduction in violent crime. However, until additional evidence on deterrence is forthcoming from more experimental or quasi-experimental studies, the existence and magnitude of any deterrence effect resulting from sanctions will remain in doubt.

Do Police Prevent Crimes?

One special form of the deterrence issue concerns whether increasing the number of police will reduce crime, aside from any effects on sanctions. Many people apparently believe that it will, and some studies have found this effect.

In 1966, New York City increased the level of police manning in one of its high-crime precincts by more than 40 percent. An evaluation that used carefully selected control precincts to compare with what happened in the experimental precinct found that outside robberies were reduced by 33 percent (Press, 1971) with the higher level of manning.

During the period 1965-1971, New York City also dramatically increased the number of uniformed patrolmen on its subway system in an effort to cut down on robberies. An analysis by Chaiken et al. (1974) found that the number of subway robberies did indeed drop as a result of the extra police presence.

Of course, one of the questions raised by this type of focused police presence is whether or not the robberies that were assumed to be prevented are simply displaced to another location. Both Press and Chaiken found significant displacement effects to nearby targets.

The most ambitious attempt to determine the impact of additional police presence on crime rates was the Kansas City Preventive Patrol Experiment. In 1972 the Police Foundation and the Kansas City Police Department initiated the experiment, which systematically varied the level of preventive patrol across different areas of the city. In some cases the amount of preventive patrol was doubled, while in others it was completely eliminated. After one year of operation, the evaluators of the experiment (Kelling et al., 1974) did not find that differences in the level of patrol had any effect on crime rates or on citizens' perceptions of safety. There was not even any displacement of crime from the highly patrolled areas to the underpatrolled areas.

Therefore, until there is additional contrary evidence, it is not clear that additional police presence, over and above that required to supply called-for services, will produce any reduction in crime.

Rehabilitation

Over the past few decades there have been numerous attempts at developing treatment programs aimed at reducing the criminal activity of released offenders. These attempts have included such diverse interventions as psychotherapy, behavior modification, vocational training, work release, and cosmetic plastic surgery.

However, another National Academy of Sciences panel (Sechrest et al., 1979), which reviewed the research findings from these efforts, concluded that we know very little about what works and what does not. The general problem with rehabilitation research has been that the evaluation methodology is usually inadequate. However, unlike the research on deterrence, there have been a number of carefully run experimental studies that attempted to measure the rehabilitation effect. The few sound studies that do exist have not found any significant effects of treatment on subsequent recidivism.

Therefore, as with deterrence, until there is some evidence that a particular form of treatment (sentence) will result in a subsequent reduction in crime, rehabilitation objectives do not provide any useful guide to establishing appropriate sentences.

Incapacitation

The most certain way that sanctions can affect rates is through incapacitation. As long as there is a reasonable presumption that some offenders will continue to commit crime if they are not confined, and confinement makes them no worse, then crime will be reduced in proportion to the time that offenders' street time is reduced. The magnitude of this incapacitation effect is sensitive to both the current level of sentencing and the rate at which offenders tend to commit crime. Empirical research is just beginning to produce reliable estimates of how individual offense rates are distributed.

APPREHENDING VIOLENT OFFENDERS

If the criminal justice system can have any effects on violent crime, its effects depend primarily on its success in identifying and apprehending violent offenders. Higher apprehension rates will produce larger deterrent and incapacitation effects. The more the system knows about an offender's violent crimes, the greater is its ability to predict his or her future dangerousness.

In 1979 the percentage of reported violent crimes that were cleared by arrest (U.S. Department of Justice, 1980) was as follows:

	Percentage
Murder	73
Aggravated assault	59
Forcible rape	48
Robbery	25

Of course, not all violent crimes are reported to the police, and "exceptional clearances" by the police will cause the reported clearance rates to overestimate the true risk faced by an offender. Self-reported offense and arrest frequencies provided by incarcerated offenders indicate that the probability of arrest for armed robbery is only about 12 percent (Peterson et al., 1980).

Although clearance rates for violent crime may vary considerably across departments, there is only limited information about what can be done to change them. There is a clear association between the likelihood of arrest and the number of police officers per capita, but not with the number of detectives or how they are organized (Greenwood et al., 1977). Research on the investigation process indicates why this is so. Most cases are solved by on-scene arrest or because a witness can identify the offender. It is an extremely rare occurrence when a partial identity or physical evidence leads to the apprehension of a suspect (Greenwood et al., 1977). Since most police departments have far more detectives than they need to interview victims and witnesses in those cases where the offender's identity is known, variations in the amount of excess manpower do not produce differences in arrest rates.

Since many violent crimes occur in places that are not open to police scrutiny, the apprehension of violent offenders is highly dependent on victim and witness identifications. One of the consequences of this dependence is that violent offenders who attack acquaintances are much more likely to be arrested than those who attack strangers. This phenomenon is illustrated in Table 7.1,

TABLE 7.1   Victimization and Arrests Involving Nonstrangers (percentages)

	Victimization[a]	*Adult Arrests*[b]
Rape	33	83
Robbery	18	36
Assault	41	69

[a] From U.S. Department of Justice, 1977.
[b] From Vera, 1977.

which compares the percentage of victimizations with adult arrests involving nonstrangers. Clearly, violent predators who confine their attacks to strangers can do much better than average in avoiding arrest.

James Q. Wilson and Barbara Boland (1979) have suggested that the effectiveness of patrol officers in making arrests for stranger-to-stranger street crimes may be affected by the aggressiveness with which they patrol. In a comparative study of police practices in 35 large American cities, they found that robbery arrest rates were positively related to the number of citations issued for moving traffic violations. They speculate that the same degree of patrol aggressiveness that would result in more traffic citations would also be reflected in a greater number of street stops or field interrogations, which in turn result in more spontaneous arrests.

WHAT HAPPENS AFTER AN ARREST FOR VIOLENT CRIME

All that the police need to make an arrest is probable cause to believe that a crime was committed and that the suspect was the one who did it. In order for the suspect to be convicted of a specific crime, there must be proof beyond a reasonable doubt. Between the arrest and conviction, each case goes through a number of procedural steps in which the strength of the evidence and the seriousness of the alleged behavior are evaluated. At any one of these steps the charges against the suspect can be dropped or modified.

Figure 7.1 traces the pattern of dispositions for a sample of 650 adult robbery arrests selected from four Southern California counties in 1973. The numbers at each node represent the probability that a case will reach that point. The numbers on each branch represent the conditional probability that a case that has reached the preceding node will receive that disposition.

Moving from left to right in the figure, the first disposition choice is made by the police—whether or not to seek a formal complaint from the prosecutor. In 23 percent of the robbery arrests, no complaint was sought. This situation occurs when the police investigation following an arrest fails to support the charges. In a robbery, this could occur when the victim cannot identify the suspect in a lineup, or the investigation discloses that the act in question

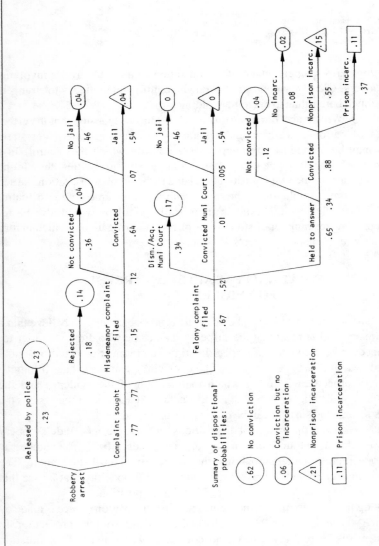

SOURCE: 1973 OBTS Arrest File (N = 650) and 1973 Superior Court File (N = 4,000).

FIGURE 7.1 Disposition of Robbery Arrests

involves a dispute over gambling debts, rather than a true robbery as originally alleged by the victim.

The next decision is made by the prosecutor—the specific charges to be alleged in the complaint. In most large prosecutors' offices, this function is performed by a small number of senior deputies who must evaluate the quality of the evidence and the seriousness of the defendant's behavior in deciding what they can prove in court. Returning to Figure 7.1, 18 percent of the robbery cases brought to the prosecutor by the police were rejected for insufficient evidence, 15 percent were filed as misdemeanors (such as simple assault or petty theft), and 67 percent were filed as felonies. At this stage, the prosecutor will also allege specific facts that may enhance the eventual sentence, such as the defendant's prior record, his or her use of a gun, or additional counts of robbery.

The next evaluation of the case occurs at a preliminary hearing in municipal court, where the prosecutor presents evidence before a judge. If the judge finds that the evidence is strong enough to support the felony charges alleged, the defendant is held to answer in the superior court. Figure 7.1 shows that 34 percent of these preliminary hearings resulted in dismissal or acquittal, 1 percent resulted in a reduction to misdemeanor charges, and 65 percent of the defendants were held to answer.

Of those held to answer, 88 percent were convicted on some charges, most by entering a plea of guilty. The remaining 12 percent were either dismissed or acquitted. Some of these dismissals occur after a successful motion by the defense to exclude some of the evidence because of improper police procedures.

Of those convicted, only 8 percent were not required to serve time, 37 percent were sent to state prison, and the remaining 55 percent were given either jail terms or committed to the California Youth Authority (CYA).

Figure 7.2 shows the pattern of dispositions for all adult violent felony arrests in California in 1979. The numbers on each of the branch networks are conditional percentages that show what happens to the cases that have survived until that stage in the system. For example, out of 1,813 homicide arrests, the police requested the prosecutor to file charges in 90 percent of the cases. The other 10 percent were released without any court processing. For all those arrests in which a complaint was requested, 90 percent resulted in some charges being filed by the prosecutor. Of those cases filed, 75 percent resulted in conviction on at least one charge, while 25 percent resulted in either dismissal or acquittal.

The percentage of filed cases that result in conviction is remarkably consistent across crimes, varying from a low of 72 percent for robbery and rape to a high of 75 percent for homicide. This consistency in conviction rates across crime types clearly reflects the effects of prior screening by the police and the prosecutor, aimed at weeding out the weaker cases. The lower attrition rate for

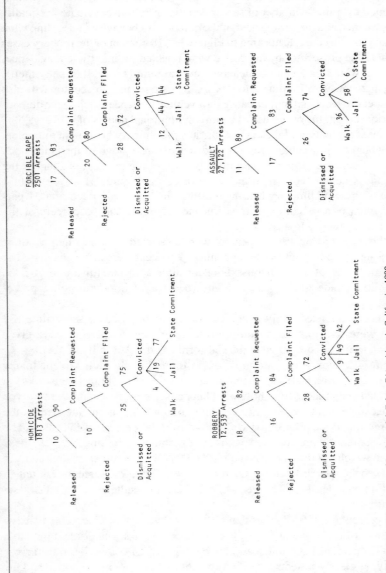

SOURCE: California Department of Justice, *Adult Felony Dispositions in California*, 1980.

FIGURE 7.2   Violent Felony Arrest Disposition Patterns for California, 1979

328

homicide cases suggests that the police have conducted a more thorough investigation prior to making an arrest.

Of those defendants who were arrested for homicide and eventually convicted on any charges, only 4 percent received sentences that do not involve any incarceration, 19 percent served up to one year in the county jail, and 77 percent are sentenced to state institutions. The percentage of convicted defendants who do not serve any time is also quite small for robbery and rape. Only in assaults, which can be quite minor or involve fights between acquaintances, do we see a substantial percentage who do not serve any time. Among the forcible rape defendants who are convicted and sentenced to state institutions, approximately 15 percent receive civil commitments as mentally disordered sex offenders to a special treatment facility.

Since many of those arrested on violent felony charges may eventually be convicted of less serious charges, a more accurate method of portraying the sentence severity of the court is to look at the sentences imposed on those actually convicted of violent offenses.

Table 7.2 displays this data for defendants convicted in California in 1979. For homicide and assault, the sentencing pattern is quite similar to that based on arrest charges, suggesting that there is little charge reduction taking place. This is not the case for robbery and rape, which show a much higher commitment rate to state institutions based on conviction charges.

Knowing how one jurisdiction disposes of its violent felony cases tells us little about what to expect in another. As is indicated by the data in Table 7.3, there is considerable cross-site variation in the frequency with which incarceration is imposed. There is no obvious organizational explanation for why defendants in Indianapolis are consistently sentenced more harshly than those in Los Angeles or Detroit. Nor is there a clear explanation for why robbery defendants in Detroit are sentenced more harshly than robbery defendants in Los Angeles, but assaulters and rapists are not.

The judges in one jurisdiction may be more likely than judges elsewhere to view a particular type of offense as less serious. The average offense within any particular crime category, such as robbery, may in fact be less serious in the degree of force involved or the degree of injury to victims. The prosecutor in one jurisdiction may be more willing to grant sentencing concessions in return

TABLE 7.2   California Sentences by Convicted Offense

Sentence	Homicide	Forcible Rape	Robbery	Assault
Probation	2.3	3.3	2.0	29.7
Jail	12.8	18.9	30.1	63.2
State institution	84.4	77.8	67.9	7.1

SOURCE: California Department of Justice, *Adult Felony Dispositions in California,* 1980.

TABLE 7.3   Variation in Incarceration Rate Across Cities (percentages of convicted defendants incarcerated)

Convicted Offense	Detroit	New Orleans	Los Angeles	Indianapolis
Rape	52		75	82
Robbery	73	91	66	91
Assault	26		50	62

SOURCE: Kathleen Brosi, *A Cross-City Comparison of Felony Case Processing*, 1979.

for a guilty plea by the defendant. A study that examined sentencing practices in the Los Angeles Superior Court (Greenwood et al., 1976) found that the percentage of convicted defendants who were sentenced to state prison varied by more than a factor of two across different branches of the court. This difference was attributed to a stricter plea-bargaining stance by the prosecutor in one branch, combined with tougher sentencing by the judges.

As another illustration of the effects that plea bargaining and sentencing practices can have on dispositions, consider the figures in Table 7.4, comparing the outcome of robbery cases between New York City and California. In California, robbery arrests are much more likely to result in a state prison term. As a result, defendants are more likely to request a jury trial and a lower percentage are convicted.

FACTORS EXPLAINING THE
DISPOSITION OF CASES

In the previous section we observed that only about half of the arrests for violent felonies result in conviction. Of those convicted, less than half are sentenced to state prison. In order to understand the adjudication process more fully, we must ask how these extremely divergent outcomes are distributed across different types of cases. Is the probability of conviction affected by the characteristics of the defendant? Are the more serious defendants sentenced to prison, or is sentencing affected more by the strength of the case and hence the prosecutor's plea-bargaining power?

Only a few published studies provide information on these issues for violent offenses, and none of them is completely satisfactory. The Vera Institute (1977) examined the outcomes for a sample of 1971 adult felony arrests in New York City, which included a sufficient number of robberies and assaults for statistical analysis. But Vera's analysis focused on only a few factors that might affect case dispositions. Williams (1978) and Williams and Lucianovic (1979) analyzed a sample of sexual assault and robbery cases prosecuted in the District of Columbia between 1971 and 1975, but their analyses did not attempt to explain sentence severity. Cook and Nagin (1979) also analyzed a sample of robbery

TABLE 7.4   Disposition of Robbery Arrests in California, 1979, and New York, 1970 (percentages)

	California	New York
Convicted	49	58
Incarcerated	45	38
Prison	21	12
Jury trials	4	2

cases prosecuted in the District of Columbia in an attempt to explain the effects of weapon use on case dispositions. Their analysis does attempt to predict sentence severity. Greenwood (1980) has analyzed California robbery arrest dispositions to determine the effects of prior record on sentence severity.

Who Gets Convicted?

We can hypothesize two different patterns of conviction rates, depending on the priorities of the prosecutor. If prosecution manpower is allocated equally among all cases, then we would expect no systematic variation in conviction rates among different types of cases. If, on the other hand, prosecution resources are concentrated on the more serious defendants, we might expect to find lower conviction rates among the less serious cases.

Vera found that a prior relationship between the victim and offender had a very strong effect on conviction rates in robbery and assault cases. For robbery arrests, the conviction rate in stranger cases (88 percent) was more than twice that in nonstranger cases (37 percent). This effect is not surprising. In nonstranger cases there is a much larger chance that the crime may involve a dispute between the two parties rather than an unprovoked attack. Also, when the victim and offender are acquainted there is more of a chance that victims will refuse to cooperate with the prosecutor, because they are afraid of further retribution or because of a reconciliation with the offender.

In the Williams studies of robbery and sexual assault, prior relationship did not have an effect on conviction rates. Since these studies involve only those cases filed by the prosecutor, it suggests that the prosecutor's screening policy is successful in weeding out those cases where the victim is no longer interested in prosecution.

The principal factors affecting conviction rates that are identified in the Williams studies have to do with the quality of evidence. Cases in which physical evidence or property are recovered and cases involving multiple witnesses are more likely to result in conviction than cases that do not. In another study, Forst et al. (1977) demonstrated that some policemen are more successful than others in securing physical evidence and multiple witnesses. This suggests that the frequency with which these items are obtained can be affected by training or other departmental policies.

In the one study in which offense seriousness did appear to play a role in determining conviction rates, Cook (1979) found that unarmed robbers were less likely to be convicted than armed robbers. This result might suggest that the charge of robbery is more difficult to prove where a weapon is not involved. Since unarmed robberies are more likely to involve young, unsophisticated offenders, it might be that the lower conviction rate reflects intentionally lenient treatment.

Explaining Sentence Severity

Sentence severity includes both the likelihood of incarceration and the length of time to be served. For violent offenses, length of time served is particularly important, because a large percentage of convicted offenders are incarcerated. None of the recent studies provides information on time served, and most look at only a few characteristics in attempting to explain the probability of incarceration. The five factors considered are prior record, victim-offender relationship, arming, victim injury, and age.

As we might expect, all of the studies (Vera Institute of Justice, 1979; Cook, 1979; Greenwood, 1980) find that prior record has an effect on the likelihood of incarceration. Greenwood found that for robbery arrests in California in 1973, only 5 percent of the defendants with minor records were sentenced to prison, as opposed to 22 percent of those who had been sentenced to prison before. The Vera Institute study showed that in robbery cases involving strangers, the probability of being sentenced to felony time was only 17 percent for those defendants with no prior arrests, as opposed to 42 percent for those with priors.

Both the Vera and the Cook studies also found that crimes between acquaintances were less likely to result in incarceration. None of the robberies between acquaintances in the Vera study resulted in a sentence to felony time.

Again, these results are not surprising. We would expect more mitigating circumstances in a crime between acquaintances as opposed to a crime between strangers. We would also expect the court to be less lenient in granting probation to a recidivist as compared to a first offender.

In the only study that looks at the issue of arming directly, Cook (1980) found that defendants who were armed with guns were more likely to receive prison commitments than those who were not. Arming with other weapons did not have any consistent effect on sentence severity.

More surprising, Cook found that the degree of injury to victims did not have any effect on sentence severity. One possible explanation of this anomaly might be that unarmed robbers are more likely to injure their victims than are robbers who are armed with a gun. But even within each specific weapon category, victim injury did not appear to affect sentence severity.

Given the finding that sentence severity increases with prior record, and the opportunity to accumulate a prior record increases with age, we might also expect sentence severity to increase with age. In fact, observed differences between age-specific arrest rates that peak at around age 18 and age-specific imprisonment rates that peak at around 30 have caused some critics of the system to assert that young adult offenders are treated too leniently.

A recent Rand study (Greenwood et al., 1980) examined sentence severity patterns by age across three jurisdictions and concluded the following:

(1) Sentencing breaks for young adult offenders vary considerably across jurisdictions. In Los Angeles County, young adults were not less likely to be incarcerated or committed to state institutions than older offenders. In Franklin County (Columbus), Ohio, young adults (18-19) were much less likely to be incarcerated during their first few years in the adult system. In New York City, young adults were also less likely to be incarcerated during their first years in the adult system. But since the maximum age jurisdiction of the juvenile court is 16 in New York, compared to 18 in Ohio, the youth breaks come at an early age. By age 18 in New York, age effects on sentence severity had disappeared.

(2) It appears that the degree to which young adult offenders are afforded differential leniency is affected by the maximum age jurisdiction of the juvenile court, the accessibility of juvenile court records to adult prosecutors and the availability of special institutions for young adults.

(3) The conviction rate and incarceration rate for older juveniles is similar to that of young adults who are convicted of similar crimes.

WOULD MORE PROSECUTORS MAKE A DIFFERENCE?

One of the explanations that is frequently offered for the low conviction rates and heavy reliance on plea bargaining usually found in criminal courts is the fact that the system is overloaded, the implication being that if prosecutors had more time to devote to each case, conviction rates and incarceration rates would be increased.

In 1975, the Law Enforcement Assistance Administration (LEAA) initiated a special discretionary grant program to do just that. The program was called Career Criminal Prosecution. It was based on the premise that since a small number of recidivists (career criminals) accounted for a disproportionate share of crime, a concentrated effort to get these recidivists convicted and locked away would lead to a reduction in street crime.

The premise of the program is not important. What is important is that a large number of prosecutors received special federal grants to seek increased conviction rates and longer terms for whomever they define as career criminals.

Many of the programs focused on robbers exclusively. Others included a mixture of street crimes. Each prosecutor used a different combination of prior record and current offense seriousness to determine whom his program would handle.

The Career Criminal Prosecution (CCP) programs that were developed involved a number of departures from routine practices. Typical features were as follows:

(1) A special unit was established within the prosecutor's office to handle career criminal cases.
(2) The CCP unit might become involved in a case earlier than normal in order to assist the police with arrest and investigation procedures.
(3) A special investigator might be attached to the CCP unit to help expedite case preparation.
(4) A single deputy prosecutor was assigned responsibility for each case from start to finish, rather than the normal assembly-line processing.
(5) Plea bargaining was highly circumscribed, if permitted at all.

One result of these procedures is that career criminal cases cost about three times as much to prosecute as do comparatively routine cases.

The system processing objectives of the career criminal program were to: (1) increase conviction rates, (2) increase the strength of convictions, (3) increase the severity of sentences, and (4) decrease processing time for career criminal cases. Evaluations of specific local programs have found conflicting results. The basic design for these evaluations involves comparing career criminal case dispositions with a sample of similar cases selected from a time period before the program was initiated. In order to control for changes in disposition patterns that are unrelated to the program, these evaluations also examine changes in the disposition of noncareer criminal cases over the same time period.

Chelimsky and Dohmann (1980) used this design to evaluate four of the programs initially funded by the LEAA. In none of the four did they find that CCP increased conviction rates. In two of the four they found an increase in the likelihood that CCP defendants would be convicted of the most serious charges. In none of the four was there any increase in percentage of convicted defendants incarcerated. In one site there was an increase in average sentence length. In only one site was there a reduction in processing time.

A later evaluation of twelve CCP programs in California (Office of Criminal Justice Planning, 1980) found considerably different results. That study found a small but significant increase in conviction rates, a large increase in the fraction of defendants convicted of the most serious charge, increases in incarceration and imprisonment rates, and an increase in average sentence length. How can these different findings be resolved, assuming that the evaluation accurately reflected real changes in case disposition patterns? Three explanations are possible.

First, the Mitre evaluation looked at the earliest CCP programs during their first year of operation. It is possible that the program became more successful over time as techniques were developed.

Second, the initial program sites covered by the Mitre evaluation were selected because they were thought to be progressive in their management approach. It might be that there was less room for improvement at these sites than at those covered by the later California evaluation.

Third, the most reasonable explanation for the differences in findings is that in California prosecutors may simply have more control over the disposition of cases than in other states. In the Mitre evaluation, the one site that consistently showed improvements on all measures, compared to the other sites, was in California.

Two characteristics of California's criminal justice system suggest that this may be true. In California, prosecutors control plea bargaining with very little interference from the bench. If they want to change a policy, they can. Also in California, sentence severity is directly related to the seriousness of the charges on which the defendant is convicted. The prosecutor can have a direct impact on sentence severity by charging and proving special enhancements, such as gun use, priors, or multiple counts.

In summary, the CCP evaluations suggest that in those sites where the prosecutors play a dominant role in determining the severity of sentencing, extra attention devoted to specific types of cases can increase the severity of dispositions.

WHAT HAPPENS IN PRISON?

In comparison to other offenders, defendants convicted of violent offenses are more likely to be sentenced to prison and to serve longer terms. What happens to these offenders as they serve their time? In what kinds of programs do they participate? How are they treated differently from other inmates?

These issues are examined in a recent study of prison inmates in three states—California, Texas, and Michigan (Petersilia et al., 1980). Information on a sample of prison inmates in each of these states was obtained from official records and through a survey questionnaire.

One of the findings of this study was that neither conviction offense nor prior record had any impact on participation rates in programs or on the rate of disciplinary infractions. In fact, both classification (as to security level) and programming were governed by prior and current institutional behavior rather than by criminal record.

The four most frequent types of treatment programs identified by the study were education, vocational training, alcohol treatment, and drug treatment. Inmates with a "high need" for treatment in any of these areas were identified as follows:

—*Education:* Less than a ninth-grade education or reading level below the ninth grade.

—*Vocational Training:* No employment or schooling during the two years preceding the current commitment.

—*Alcohol:* Self-report of serious drinking problem during the two years preceding the current commitment.

—*Drugs:* Self-reported daily use of hard drugs during the two years preceding the current commitment.

Figure 7.3 displays the percentage of inmates within each state who were identified as having a high need for each of the four program types. It also shows the percentage of high-need inmates who were participating in the relevant treatment programs.

The variation in treatment needs and participation levels across states is considerable. Probably the most striking finding from these data is the small percentage of offenders with serious drug problems who are being treated in California and Texas. This is particularly surprising, given the clear association between drug abuse and crime established in other studies.

The reason most frequently cited by high-need inmates for not participating in treatment is a belief that they do not need it. More than 60 percent of those with poor educational skills or alcohol problems cited this reason. About 25 percent do not participate because of security reasons or because of discouragement by the staff. Of those with drug problems, 33 percent do not participate because no drug treatment programs are available within their institutions.

From these data it appears that a substantial portion of the inmate population with severe educational, vocational, or drug-related problems are not being treated. Many do not believe they would benefit from assistance. A substantial proportion do not participate because the programs are not available to them.

About half of the inmates claimed to have a work assignment that required about 30 to 40 hours per week. Most of those without work assignments appeared not to want them. Only about 20 percent of those without work assignments reported that no jobs were available to them.

CAN LONGER SENTENCES REDUCE
VIOLENT CRIME?

The most predictable response to a sudden rise in the violent-crime rates is a demand for stiffer prison terms. "We have to teach them, and others like them, a lesson" (deterrence). "If we can get these fellows locked up, we can give the streets back to the citizens" (incapacitation).

The evidence on deterrence was reviewed in the first section of this chapter. Because of methodological issues in the studies that have been conducted thus far, it is not possible to establish either the existence or the magnitude of

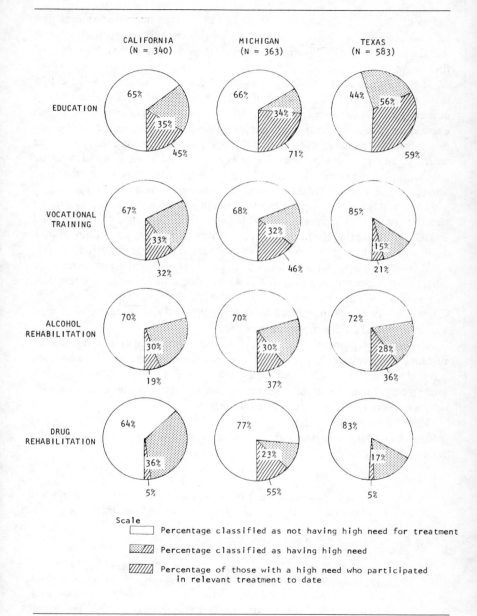

FIGURE 7.3   Correspondence Between High Need for Treatment and
Treatment Received

338   CRIMINAL JUSTICE SYSTEM

deterrent effects of sanctions on crime. To the degree that these studies find relationships that are consistent with the deterrence hypothesis, they suggest that the probability of incarceration is much more important than the length of time served.

The evidence on incapacitation is more positive. As long as there is a reasonable presumption that some offenders would have continued to commit crimes if left on the street, and they are not made any worse by their prison experience, there will be an incapacitation effect. The magnitude of that effect depends on such factors as the types of crime an offender commits, the rate at which he or she commits them, his or her chance of being arrested, and the length of his or her criminal career. These issues are just now being studied in an attempt to explore the dynamics of criminal careers. Even when these factors are known, it is a very complicated modeling process to estimate the effects of a specific change in sentencing policy. In particular, we do not now have good models for estimating the tradeoffs in crime reduction between a policy of long sentences for a few offenders versus shorter sentences for many offenders.

This issue of appropriate sentence lengths is probably the most important single issue in determining how to deal with violent crime. The natural response to a wave of violent crime is to raise penalties, particularly for recidivists. Who can argue with the proposal that offenders convicted for their second or third violent felony should be sentenced for life?

The counterargument is economic. The criminal justice system has limited resources for dealing with crime. Sending some offenders away for very long terms ties up resources that might be used more productively in other ways. Just within corrections, increasing terms for some means decreasing terms for others or reducing the percentage sent to prison.

There are several incapacitation studies that address the issue of violent crime specifically. One method of estimating incapacitation effects uses the following procedure:

(1) Select a sample of offenders who have been arrested (or convicted, if you do not trust arrest records) for the type of crime you want reduced through incapacitation.
(2) For members of the sample, code their complete conviction records, including dates, types of offense, and times served.
(3) In order to determine the additional incapacitation effects that would result from a harsher sentencing policy, look back at the preceding conviction and determine if the policy to be tested would have increased the sentence length. If the sentence would have been lengthened, would the defendant have been free at the time of his or her current offense? Assuming that arrestees are a random sample of offenders, the percentage of offenses in the sample that would have been prevented by longer terms at previous convictions is an estimate of the percentage by which that crime would be reduced.

Two studies have used this procedure. Van Dine et al. (1979) analyzed the 342 adult defendants who were charged with violent felonies and whose cases were completed in Franklin County (Columbus), Ohio, in 1973. Of these defendants, 53 percent had no prior felony convictions and only 18 percent had prior violent felony convictions. Under current sentencing policy, only about half of the convicted violent offenders were sentenced to state time.

The analysis showed that by imposing a mandatory five-year term on every adult convicted of a felony, adult violent crime would be reduced by 18 percent. If only those who were convicted of violent crimes were given the mandatory five-year term, for the violent convictions and any subsequent convictions, the reduction in adult violent crime would be only 6 percent.

Petersilia and Greenwood (1978) analyzed a sample of 625 adult felons who were convicted in the Denver, Colorado, District Court between 1968 and 1970. Of those defendants charged with violent crimes, only 39 percent had a prior adult felony conviction; 23 percent had no juvenile or adult record.

With this cohort the analysis showed that the imposition of a five-year mandatory term for every conviction would reduce adult violent crime by 31 percent. If the five-year mandatory term were restricted to only those convicted of violent felonies, the reduction in adult violent crime would be 6 percent.

These sentencing options are not cheap. The average sentence for those convicted of a violent felony is only 1.3 years (including those who serve no time at all). If every defendant who was convicted of a violent felony was given a five-year term, the prison population would increase by 150 percent—in order to produce a 6 percent reduction in adult violent crime.

This study also provides some evidence on the "long sentence for a few versus short sentences for many" argument. Two different sentencing policies would result in about the same increase in prison population—about 50 percent. The first involves a five-year mandatory term for every defendant convicted of violent crime with at least one prior. The other involves a one-year mandatory term for anyone convicted of a felony, regardless of priors. The first policy reduces the adult felony crime rate by only 3 percent. The latter reduces it by 11 percent and is clearly more efficient. This finding suggests that the maximum incapacitation effect for any given increase in prison population can be achieved by imposing modest terms on those who now serve no time.

An alternative means for estimating incapacitation effects was proposed in a paper by Shinnar and Shinnar (1975). Their analysis involves a simplified model of an individual's criminal career which allows one to estimate directly the amount of crime that is prevented by different sentencing policies. In this model all criminals are assumed to commit crimes at the same Poisson rate. They are subject to arrest and conviction with probability q and to imprisonment given conviction with probability J. The actual sentence served is exponentially distributed with mean S, and the length of criminal careers is exponentially distributed with mean T.

The expected number of crimes any one criminal would commit if he were never incarcerated is λT.[1] If, on the other hand, he is arrested, convicted, and sent to prison, his total number of crimes is reduced by the same percentage of time that his time free is reduced. The fraction of time that an offender will be free is

$$\eta = \frac{1}{1 + \lambda qJS}$$

If offenders commit violent crimes at the rate of four per year and have a 10 percent chance of being arrested and convicted for any one crime, then an average sentence of two years for every defendant convicted would result in a 44 percent reduction in crime. If offenders commit only two violent crimes per year, then the same sentencing policy would result in only a 29 percent reduction in crime.

In a parametric analysis of the Shinnar model, Cohen (1978) has shown that the relative crime reduction achieved by changes in sentencing policy is sensitive to both the value of λ and current sentence lengths. Under this model, the percentage increase in prison population (P) required to achieve a 1 percent reduction in crime is

$$P = \frac{1}{\lambda qJS}$$

Assuming $\lambda = 5$ and $q = 0.1$, if the average term served per conviction is already quite high, say two years, then P is fairly small—in this case, 1 percent. However, if the average term is currently low, say only 6 months, then P is much larger—4 percent, in this case.[2]

Although it may be useful for exploring some of the basic relationships between sanction policy and incapacitation effects, the Shinnar model is much too simplistic to be used for deriving actual sentencing policies. Offenders commit different types of crime that carry different types of penalties, and they commit them at different rates. Offense rates may change over the course of a career. Any sentencing policy that attempts to improve the incapacitation effects achieved within a given prison population limit must account for these differences.

As a means of collecting data to estimate the distribution of offense rates over the active offender population, Rand has conducted a self-reporting survey of 625 California prison inmates (Peterson et al., 1980). In addition to a number of personal and prior record items, the survey instrument asked respondents about the number of times they had committed specific criminal acts during the three years preceding their current commitments. The survey also asked about the percentage of their time that they were free.

The responses to this survey indicate that most active offenders engage in a variety of different crime types during any one period in their careers. For instance, among inmates convicted for robbery, 60 percent had also committed assaults, 52 percent had committed burglary, and 37 percent had sold drugs. Among inmates committed for burglary, 27 percent had committed armed robbery, 60 percent had committed assault, and 46 percent had sold drugs. Given this mixture of crime types, it is easy to see why it becomes difficult to characterize offenders as violent or property offenders on the basis of their records. Most offenders are both.

Another important characteristic of individual offense rates revealed by this survey is the fact that they are highly skewed to the low side. Among armed robbers, the mean armed robbery rate was 4.6 crimes per year. The median rate was 1.5 crimes per year. About 10 percent committed armed robberies at a rate higher than 30 crimes per year. This same pattern held up for every type of crime that was examined. If it can be shown that these differences in offense rates between offenders persist throughout long periods of the career, then this would argue for a policy that attempts to distinguish these high-rate offenders for longer terms.

The individual characteristics identified by the Rand survey analysis as associated with high rates were prior convictions (not prior prison terms), age at first arrest, seriousness of juvenile records, drug use, and age (inverse relationship).

Suppose that a jurisdiction decides that it will attempt to reduce violent crime through incapacitation by imposing harsher sentences. How should it proceed? There are basically two approaches:

Under a *generalized* incapacitation approach, the jurisdiction will attempt to increase sentence severity across the board or for special categories of offenders based on "just deserts" alone. It will not make any attempt to maximize the incapacitation effects of the resulting increase in prison population by concentrating on high-rate offenders. Policies that attempt to achieve this goal might include:

(1) eliminating the possibility of probation for anyone convicted of a violent felony;
(2) lengthening the base term or minimum eligible parole date for violent offenders; and
(3) adding additional time to the terms of violent defendants who have previous felony convictions.

An alternative approach to reducing crime could involve *selective* incapacitation. Under this approach, sentence lengths would be adjusted on the basis of actuarial experience to reflect future risk. The goal of selective incapacitation would be to maximize the amount of crime prevented within any fixed prison population constraint. The advantages of the selective incapacitation approach can be illustrated by the following example.

Suppose there is a jurisdiction where the probability of arrest and conviction for armed robbery is 0.05 and every convicted armed robber serves a term of three years. Furthermore, assume that the incarcerated armed robbers can be divided into two groups with average annual offense rates of 1.0 and 10.0, respectively, and that the prison population of 1,000 armed robbers contains equal members of these two groups. This is approximately the situation found in the Rand survey of California prison inmates (Peterson et al., 1980).

Using the Shinnar model to estimate the total number of armed robbers of each type, we find that there are 3,833 offenders with $\lambda = 1$, and 833 offenders with $\lambda = 10$: 500 of each group are incarcerated. Note that a much higher percentage of high-rate offenders are incarcerated at any one time simply by chance.

If no offenders were ever incarcerated, the annual number of armed robberies would be the total number of offenders in each group multiplied by their respective offense rates: $(3,833 \times 1) + (833 \times 10) = 12,163$. However, with the current sentencing policy of three years for every conviction, the annual number of armed robberies is 6,667—about half what it would be without incarceration.

If the jurisdiction attempted further to reduce the armed robbery rate by 20 percent through a general incapacitation approach, by increasing sentences for all armed robbers equally, sentence lengths would have to be increased to 5.2 years and the number of armed robbers incarcerated would increase by about 40 percent, to 1,393—791 low-rate offenders and 602 high-rate offenders.

Using a selective incapacitation approach, it would be possible to achieve the same 20 percent reduction in crime without any increase in the total incarcerated population. This could be achieved by decreasing the sentence length of all low-rate offenders to two years and increasing the sentence length of high-rate offenders to seven years. The total number of incarcerated armed robbers would remain at 1,000, but the composition would change to include 349 low-rate offenders and 651 high-rate offenders.

Selective incapacitation is based on the knowledge that criminals vary widely in their offense rates. Most commit crimes at very low rates, while only a few commit crimes at high rates. On the average, high-rate offenders can be distinguished from low-rate offenders on the basis of such characteristics as prior record—both juvenile and adult, age, drug use, and employment.

Selective incapacitation involves giving longer terms to some offenders on the basis of their predicted future criminality. It also involves shorter terms for a larger number of offenders. The prediction is based on the experience of other offenders with similar characteristics, not a clinical diagnosis of a particular offender's traits. In any such prediction there will be errors. Some offenders who are predicted to have high rates will not. But, on the average, more crimes will be prevented by increasing the terms of the predicted high-rate offenders than by any across-the-board approach.

In the hypothetical case of the armed robbers, selective incapacitation results in the high-rate offenders receiving terms that are 1.8 years longer than they would have received if sentences were increased for all offenders equally. But the selective sentencing also avoids a 40 percent increase in the prison population.

At the present time, incapacitation is the only sure method the system has for reducing violent crime. The amount of crime prevented by incapacitation can be increased by increasing the percentage of offenders who are sent to prison or increasing the length of their terms.

Research on criminal career patterns has established that individual offense rates are distributed so as to make selective incapacitation an attractive option. The critical issue to be determined now is how accurately the high-rate offenders can be identified. Although retrospective studies provide some evidence, this issue can only be resolved by a prospective study in which the postrelease offense rates of convicted offenders are estimated from information about their subsequent arrests.

SUMMARY

During periods of rising violent crime, there is public pressure for changes in the criminal justice system that many believe will increase public safety. It is generally assumed that more police and tougher sentencing will reduce crime.

According to the research literature, the impact of more police or tougher sentencing is problematic. In some instances, large increases in the number of police in specific locations have reduced crime, although displacing some of it elsewhere. But, in a careful experiment, changes in the level of preventive patrol did not lead to changes in crime.

Evaluations of treatment programs for offenders have not found any consistent rehabilitative effects, and cross-sectional deterrence studies are not able to show that harsher sanctions lead to reduced crime, due to methodological limitations inherent in the research designs. The only sure impact of harsher sentencing results from incapacitation; that is, offenses are prevented during the period that offenders are incarcerated.

As is the case with other types of felonies, only about half of those adults arrested for violent crimes are ever convicted. The two principal factors that appear related to the chances of conviction are whether the victim and offender were acquainted prior to the crime and the strength of the evidence. The characteristics of the offense or offender do not appear to matter.

Most of those convicted for violent felonies are incarcerated, but incarceration rates vary considerably across jurisdictions. Factors that appear to increase the likelihood of incarceration for any specific violent offense are the defendant's prior record, the fact that the victim and offender were strangers, the offender's use of a gun, and the offender's age. The degree of injury suffered by the victim does not appear to matter.

Special career criminal prosecution programs designed to increase the severity with which career criminals are treated do not appear to have increased conviction rates significantly. Later programs do appear to have increased sentence severity.

Once offenders are in prison, their treatment is affected more by their previous institutional behavior than by their current conviction offenses. Within prison there are a larger number of offenders with serious educational, vocational, drug, or alcohol problems who are not participating in treatment programs. Some of them are unwilling to participate, but for many the proper programs are not available.

Many jurisdictions now find themselves with a prison population nearing or exceeding capacity yet confronted with strong demands for tougher sentences to control crime. This situation makes them more receptive to research that can show how to utilize their scarce prison space more effectively.

Research on criminal career patterns has shown that the distribution of individual offense rates is highly skewed toward the low end, with many offenders committing crimes at fairly low rates and only a few who are very active. This distribution of offense rates suggests that a sentencing policy resulting in longer terms for the few high-rate offenders and shorter terms for the majority, who are low-rate offenders, could increase the magnitude of incapacitation effects achieved by a given prison population size. The key research issue yet to be resolved is the accuracy with which the system can discriminate between the high-rate and low-rate groups.

NOTES

1. This assumes that the crime rate is constant throughout the career and the intervals between crimes are independently and identically exponentially distributed with parameter $1/\lambda$.

2. The steady state prison population (P) under sentencing policy q, J, S, with N active offenders, is

$$P = \frac{N\lambda qJS}{1 + \lambda qJS}$$

REFERENCES

Blumstein, A., Cohen, J., and Nagin, D. (Eds.). *Deterrence and incapacitation: Estimating the effects of criminal sanctions on crime rates*. Washington, DC: National Academy of Sciences, 1978.

Brosi, K. B. *A cross-city comparison of felony case processing*. Washington, DC: INSLAW, April 1979.

California Department of Justice. *Adult felony arrest dispositions in California*. Sacramento, CA: Bureau of Criminal Statistics and Special Services, September 1980.

Chaiken, J. M., Lawless M., and Stevenson, K. A. *The impact of police activity on crime: Robberies on the New York City subway system* (R-1424-NYC). Santa Monica, CA: Rand Corporation, 1974.

Chelimsky, E., and Dohmann, J. *Career criminal program national evaluation summary report*. McLean, VA: MITRE Corporation, 1980.

Cohen, J. The incapacitation effect of imprisonment: A critical review of the literature. In A. Blumstein, J. Cohen, and D. Nagin (Eds.), *Deterrence and incapacitation: Estimating the effects of criminal sanctions on crime rates*. Washington, DC: National Academy of Sciences, 1978.

Cook, P., and Nagin, D. *Does the weapon matter?* (PROMIS Research Project Publication 8). Washington, DC: INSLAW, December 1979.

Forst, B., Lucianovic, J., and Sarah, J. C. *What happens after arrest?* Washington DC: INSLAW, 1977.

Greenwood, P. W. *Rand research on criminal careers: An update on progress to date* (N-1572). Santa Monica, CA: Rand Corporation, 1980.

Greenwood, P. W., Chaiken, J. M. and Petersilia, J. *The criminal investigation process*. Lexington, MA: D. C. Heath, 1977.

Greenwood, P. W., Petersilia, J., and Zimring, F. E. *Age, crime, and sanctions: The transition from juvenile to adult court* (R-2642). Santa Monica, CA: Rand Corporation, 1980.

Greenwood, P. W., Wildhorn, S., Poggio, E. C., Strumwasser, M. J., and DeLeon, P. *Prosecution of adult felony defendants*. Lexington, MA: D. C. Heath, 1976.

Judicial Council of California. *Sentencing Practices Quarterly*, 9/10, State of California, Quarters Ending September 30, 1979, and December 31, 1979.

Kelling, L., Pate, T., Dieckman, D., and Brown, C. E. *The Kansas City Preventive Patrol Experiment: A summary report*. Washington, DC: Police Foundation, 1974.

Office of Criminal Justice Planning. *California career criminal prosecution program: Second annual report to the legislature*. Sacramento, CA: Office of Criminal Justice Planning, 1980.

Petersilia, J., and Greenwood, P. W. Mandatory prison sentences: Their projected effects on crime and prison populations. *Journal of Criminal Law and Criminology*, 1978, 69(4), 604-615.

Petersilia, J., and Honig, P., with Hubay, C. *The prison experience of career criminals* (R-2511-DOJ). Santa Monica, CA: Rand Corporation, 1980.

Peterson, M. A., and Braiker, H. B., with Polich, S. M. *Doing crime: A survey of California prison inmates* (R-2200-DOJ). Santa Monica, CA: Rand Corporation, 1980.

Press, S. J. *Some effects of an increase in police manpower in the 20th precinct of New York City* (R-704-NYC). Santa Monica, CA: Rand Corporation, 1971.

Sechrest, L., White S. O., and Brown, E. D. *The rehabilitation of criminal offenders: Problems and prospects*. Washington, DC: National Academy of Sciences, 1979.

Shinnar, S., and Shinnar R. The effects of the criminal justice system on the control of crime: A quantitative approach. *Law and Society Review*, 1975, 9, 581-611.

U.S. Department of Justice. *Criminal victimization in the United States, 1975*. Washington, DC: U.S. Department of Justice, Law Enforcement Assistance Administration, December 1977.

U.S. Department of Justice. *Crime in the United States, 1979*. Washington, DC: Government Printing Office, 1980.

Van Dine, S., Conrad, J. P., and Dinitz, S. *Restraining the wicked*. Lexington, MA: D. C. Heath, 1979.

Vera Institute of Justice. *Felony arrests: Their prosecution and disposition in New York City's courts*. New York: Vera Institute of Justice, 1977.

Williams, K. M. *The prosecution of sexual assaults* (PROMIS Research Project Publication 7). Washington, DC: INSLAW, December 1978.

Williams, K. M., and Lucianovic, J. *Robbery and burglary* (PROMIS Research Project Publication 6). Washington, DC: INSLAW, March 1979.

Wilson, J. Q., and Boland, B. *The effect of the police on crime*. Washington, DC: U.S. Department of Justice, Law Enforcement Assistance Administration, 1979.

About the Editors and Authors

MARVIN E. WOLFGANG, professor of sociology and of law and director of the Center for Studies in Criminology and Criminal Law at the University of Pennsylvania, is also the president of the American Academy of Political and Social Science and a member of the American Philosophical Society and the American Academy of Arts and Sciences. Dr. Wolfgang has served on numerous boards and commissions, including the Panel on Social Indicators, the National Commission on the Causes and Prevention of Violence, and the National Commission on Obscenity and Pornography. His publications include *Patterns in Criminal Homicide, The Measurement of Delinquency, The Subculture of Violence, Crime and Race, Delinquency in a Birth Cohort, Criminology Index,* and *Evaluating Criminology.* His current projects include a follow-up study of *Delinquency in a Birth Cohort,* a longitudinal study of biosocial factors related to delinquency and crime, and the national survey of crime severity.

NEIL ALAN WEINER, research associate at the Center for Studies in Criminology and Criminal Law at the University of Pennsylvania, is project director of the Center for the Interdisciplinary Study of Criminal Violence. While at the Criminology Center, Dr. Weiner has supervised the preparation of the present volume, a set of bibliographies on selected topics in criminal violence, and a report to the United Nations that reviews the literature on violence from a cross-national perspective. His ongoing work includes research on criminal careers, on unemployment and crime, and on criminological theory. Dr. Weiner received both his M.A. (1972) in criminology and his Ph.D. (1978) in sociology at the University of Pennsylvania. Following completion of his doctoral work, Dr. Weiner spent two years in residence as a postdoctoral fellow at the Urban Systems Institute at Carnegie-Mellon University.

PHILIP J. COOK is associate professor of public policy studies and economics at Duke University and associate director of the Institute of Policy Sciences and

Public Affairs. He received his Ph.D. in economics from the University of California, Berkeley, in 1973. His main research interests are in the preventive effects of punishment, the regulation of unsafe and unhealthy behavior, and the role of weapons in violent crime. He served as the special editor of the May 1981 issue of *The Annals* of the American Academy of Political and Social Science ("Gun Control") and in 1979 co-authored *Does the Weapon Matter?*

DAVID P. FARRINGTON is a lecturer in criminology at Cambridge University. He received his Ph.D. in experimental psychology from Cambridge University in 1970, and has been on the staff of the Cambridge University Institute of Criminology since 1969, apart from periods spent with the Research Division of the Solicitor General's Department in Ottawa and as a visiting fellow at the National Institute of Justice in Washington, D.C. His major interests have centered on longitudinal research on crime and delinquency and field experiments on stealing, and he has also carried out research on juvenile diversion, prison overcrowding, sentencing, and a national (English) survey of self-reported offending by adults. He is on the organizing committees of the British Society of Criminology, the British Psychological Society Division of Criminological and Legal Psychology, and the Social Science Research Council Law and Psychology Seminar Group.

WILLIAM F. GABRIELLI, Jr., is a research associate at the Social Science Research Institute. He recently received his doctorate in Psychology from the University of Southern California. His general interests include quantitative psychological research, criminology, and alcohol research.

RICHARD J. GELLES is an associate professor and chair of the Department of Sociology and Anthropology at the University of Rhode Island. He has written widely on the subjects of wife abuse, child abuse, and family violence, including *The Violent Home* and *Family Violence*. He is co-author of *Behind Closed Doors: Violence in the American Family*. In addition to his writings on family violence, he is co-author of *Sociology: An Introduction* and *Social Problems*. He is currently the project director of the National Study of Spouse Abuse and continues to work as a research director for Louis Harris and Associates.

PETER W. GREENWOOD is a senior researcher at the Rand Corporation. He is a graduate of the U.S. Naval Academy and holds M.S. and Ph.D. degrees in industrial engineering from Stanford University. He is the author of numerous publications in the fields of criminal justice and education. His specific areas of expertise include policing, prosecution and sentencing, juvenile justice, and criminal careers. His current work focuses on the crime control effects of criminal justice policies. Dr. Greenwood has served on the faculties of the

California Institute of Technology and the Rand Graduate Institute. He is the founder of the Effectiveness Training Institute, an organization that conducts training workshops for senior executives and professionals.

DEIDRE KLASSEN is a psychologist and consultant residing in Kansas City, Missouri. Her current work deals with the assessment of state facilities for the developmentally disabled, and with the prediction of violent behavior on the part of individuals remanded to prisons or mental health facilities. Dr. Klassen has codirected studies of mental health assessment and of drug abuse treatment centers in the Kansas City area, as research associate at the Greater Kansas City Mental Health Foundation.

SARNOFF A. MEDNICK is professor of psychology and research professor at the University of Southern California, Social Science Research Institute. He graduated from Northwestern University in 1954 with a Ph.D. in psychology and earned his Dr. Med., from the University of Copenhagen, Faculty of Medicine, in 1976. He is investigating the biosocial influences on the etiology of criminal behavior. His work centers on prospective longitudinal studies of large cohorts. He is also involved in research on the etiology of schizophrenia in the context of a longitudinal prospective study.

EDWIN I. MEGARGEE received his B.A. in psychology *magna cum laude* from Amherst College in 1958 and his Ph.D. in clinical psychology from the University of California at Berkeley in 1964. He is professor of psychology at Florida State University, where he directs the predoctoral and postdoctoral training programs in the applications of psychology to crime delinquency and criminal justice and pursues research on psychological assessment and criminal behavior patterns. Author of five books and over a hundred other scholarly publications, Professor Megargee is past president of the American Association of Correctional Psychologists and past member of the boards of directors of the American Correctional Association and the International Differential Treatment Association. Currently he is a consultant to the U.S. Secret Service and the Federal Bureau of Prisons, a fellow of a number of professional organizations, and a member of the editorial boards of several professional journals.

JOHN MONAHAN is a psychologist and professor of law, psychology, and legal medicine at the University of Virginia School of Law. He is also associate director of the Institute of Law, Psychiatry and Public Policy at the University of Virginia School of Medicine. Dr. Monahan has been a fellow in law and psychology at the Harvard and Stanford law schools, and a member of the Panel on Legal Issues of the President's Commission on Mental Health and the Panel on Offender Rehabilitation of the National Academy of Sciences. He is the current president of the Division of Psychology and Law of the American

Psychological Association. Dr. Monahan has testified before congressional committees on matters of mental health and criminal justice policy and his work in this area has been cited in decisions of the U.S. Supreme Court, the California Supreme Court, and other judicial bodies. His most recent book is *Predicting Violent Behavior: An Assessment of Clinical Technique*.

VICKI POLLOCK is a Ph.D. candidate in clinical psychology at the University of Southern California. She graduated with honors from Washington University in St. Louis, where she received her A.B. degree in 1977. From 1977 to 1979, she studied human psychophysiology at the Missouri Institute of Psychiatry. During 1979 to 1981, Ms. Pollock directed a psychophysiology laboratory in Copenhagen in conjunction with a prospective research study on alcoholism.

JAN VOLAVKA was born in Prague, Czechoslovakia. He graduated from the Charles University Medical School in 1959, and earned his Ph.D. in medical sciences at the Academy of Sciences in Prague in 1964, specializing in clinical neurophysiology. He worked at the Psychiatric Research Institute in Prague from 1963 to 1966, was a fellow at the EEG Department of The London Hospital (London, England) in 1966-1967, and at the Max Planck Institute for Psychiatry (Munich, West Germany) in 1968-1969. He was Assistant and later Associate Professor of Psychiatry at New York Medical College, 1969-1976, and Professor of Psychiatry at the Missouri Institute of Psychiatry 1976-1979. He is now Professor of Psychiatry at New York University, located at Manhattan Psychiatric Center. Dr. Volavka has published more than 100 papers and book chapters on EEG, psychopharmacology, and psychopathology.